EMPLOYMEN

CW00591591

SECOND EDITION

By

Malcolm R. Mackay, W.S., MIPD
Solicitor

and

Shona M. W. Simon, M.A., (HONS), LL.B., MICG
Solicitor

EDINBURGH
W. GREEN/Sweet & Maxwell
2001

Published in 2001 by W. Green & Son Ltd
21 Alva Street
Edinburgh EH2 4PS

Typeset by J. P. Price, Chilcompton, Somerset
Printed and bound in Great Britain by
Athenaeum Press, Gateshead, Tyne and Wear

No natural forests were destroyed to make this product;
only farmed timber was used and replanted

A CIP catalogue record of this book is available from the British Library

ISBN 0 414 01402 2

PREFACE TO THE SECOND EDITION

In the relatively short time between the first and second editions of this work there have been a huge range of significant developments falling within the scope of employment law, extending beyond the substantive areas we covered previously. Many of these developments have their origin in European Community Law, which is continuing to have a dramatic effect, and in the growing recognition that the regulatory framework needs to encompass measures which ensure that the human rights and health and safety of "workers" are protected in an economy which is increasingly affected by the impact of information technology. IT not only provides jobs, it influences the way in which a whole range of occupations can now be performed and the administration of the working environment. These legal developments have led to the addition of a number of new chapters to this edition.

Our use of the word "workers", in this context, is deliberate—much of the new legislation which we examine confers rights not just upon employees, in the strict sense, but on a wider grouping of individuals who work for those willing to engage their services. This is a trend which needs to be borne in mind when advising in this area—"employment" law increasingly encompasses more than "employees".

Consequent upon these developments a whole raft of new claims can now be brought before an employment tribunal; year upon year since our first edition tribunal claims in Scotland have soared and the average length of cases has increased. We hope that this text, written as it is by two practitioners, will, in some small way, assist those involved in presenting or defending claims to do so efficiently and effectively.

Our heartfelt thanks go to our colleagues who assisted us with the preparation of this edition—to David Leckie, who wrote the chapter on Human Rights and to Jane Fraser and Alan Delaney who made very significant contributions to the chapters dealing with data protection, TUPE and regulation of working time and wages. We would also like to thank Ross Anderson, Louise Adamson and Sarah Coleman for their assistance with research and proof reading. Any errors or omissions, of course, are ours.

We would also particularly like to thank our families, including Shona's mother, Margaret, for their support and understanding which allowed us to produce this second edition—particularly since we told them we would never do it again when we finished the first edition!

MALCOLM MACKAY
SHONA SIMON

November, 2001

PREFACE TO THE FIRST EDITION

Despite the significant levels of unemployment experienced in our society in the latter part of the twentieth century the employment relationship remains, for millions of people at any given time, one of the most crucial relationships which they experience in their lifetime. That is reason enough for the law to intervene to regulate the relationship and to dictate what is reasonable conduct for the parties involved in it.

The last 25 years in particular has seen a dramatic burgeoning of statutory intervention in the employment field and an increase in judicial creativity (possibly encouraged by the influence of European Community law) when the rights and obligations arising out of the relationship have been subject to judicial scrutiny.

These developments, in turn, have led to a shift in the balance of power between employer and employee. While it would be wrong to assert that the employer is no longer the stronger party in the relationship employees now have a myriad of rights, including the right not to be unfairly dismissed and the right to equality of treatment in the work place, irrespective of sex, race or disability.

We are a long way from what was once adequately described as the "law of master and servant". Now we have "employment law" (and needless to say, employment lawyers!); a complex and dynamic field of study and practice. As practising employment lawyers it is this we hope to describe as concisely as possible, giving where appropriate practical suggestions to assist those involved or likely to be involved shortly in dealing with employment claims.

Our sincere thanks go to Ian Watson for his very substantial input into Chapter 12, "Negotiating and Funding Employment Claims". Shona would also particularly like to thank her Mother, Margaret and also Duncan and Susan without whose babysitting services we would never have reached this point.

MALCOLM MACKAY
and SHONA SIMON

July, 1997

For Charlotte, Charlie and Hugo
and
For Ellis, Matthew and Aaron

CONTENTS

CONTENTS

TABLE OF CASES

TABLE OF STATUTES

TABLE OF STATUTORY INSTRUMENTS

TABLE OF EUROPEAN LEGISLATION

Treaties and Conventions

Directives

CHAPTER 1

THE EMPLOYMENT RELATIONSHIP

The employment relationship is very common but it is much more 1.01
difficult than one might expect to identify when that relationship exists in
law. The position is undoubtedly complicated by the variable statutory
definitions given to the words "employment" and "employee". The use
of the concept "worker" in certain domestic statutes and within European Community law complicates the position further. For example, for
the purposes of the Employment Rights Act 1996[1]:

> (i) A "contract of employment" means a contract of service or
> apprenticeship.[2]
> (ii) "Employee" means an individual who has entered into or
> works under (or, where the employment has ceased, worked
> under) a contract of employment.[3]
> (iii) "Worker" means an individual who has entered into or
> works under (or, where the employment has ceased, worked
> under) a contract of employment or any other contract . . .
> whereby the individual undertakes to do or perform person-
> ally any work or services for another party to the contract
> whose status is not by virtue of the contract that of a client
> or customer or of any profession or business undertaking
> carried on by the individual.[4]

"Employment" in relation to an "employee" is defined by section 230(5)
of the ERA as "employment under a contract of employment" whereas
"employment" in relation to a worker is defined as "employment under
his contract".

The practical significance of all of this is exemplified by the fact that
protection against unfair dismissal is available to "employees"[5] while
protection against unauthorised deductions from wages is given to the
wider grouping of "workers".[6]

If one turns to the definition of "employment" for the purposes of the 1.02
Sex Discrimination Act 1975[7] and the Race Relations Act 1976[8] one
finds that it covers "employment under a contract of service or of

---

[1] Hereinafter "ERA".
[2] ERA, s.230(2).
[3] *ibid.,* s.230(1).
[4] *ibid.,* s.230(3).
[5] *ibid.,* s.94(1).
[6] *ibid.,* s.13(1).
[7] Hereinafter "SDA", see s.82(1).
[8] Hereinafter "RRA", see s.78(1).

apprenticeship or a contract to personally execute any work or labour
and related expressions shall be construed accordingly".[9] In practice this
means that an individual providing work to another could be at the same
time an "employee" for the purpose of protection against unlawful
discrimination and not an "employee" for the purpose of protection
against unfair dismissal.[10]

Given these varying definitions it is important if one is dealing with a
possible statutory claim to study the definition section in the relevant
statute to clarify whether the protection sought or claimed is available.

THE CONTRACT OF EMPLOYMENT—THE COMMON LAW POSITION

1.03 Despite the increasingly large role played by statute, the common law
remains extremely significant as a source of employment law. Indeed,
one of the most fundamental issues to arise in both theory and practice
is the need to identify whether an individual providing work is engaged
under a contract of service (note the importance of that phrase in the
foregoing statutory definitions of "employment") or a contract for
services (characteristic of self-employment). Statute is of little assistance
in answering this question and it is to common law principles that one
must turn. Similarly, when one has identified that a contract of service
(or, leaving aside the vagaries of statutory definitions, what is commonly
referred to as a "contract of employment") exists, the basic principles of
contract law concerning the interpretation and implication of contractual
terms take on great significance as does the common law concerning
breach of contract.

CONTRACT OF SERVICE OR CONTRACT FOR SERVICES?

1.04 To take an example close to home: solicitors carrying out work for a
client are not employed by that client. In other words, a contract of
service does not exist. Yet, work is done, payment is made (hopefully!)
and the solicitor acts upon the instructions of the client. What then is the
difference between a contract of service and a contract for services?

As Denning L.J. put it "it is often easy to recognise a contract of
service when you see it, but difficult to say wherein the difference lies".[11]
It is important to note that policy considerations may affect the
assessment of whether or not a contract of service is held to exist in
given circumstances. For example, different factors may weigh in the
assessment depending on the issues under consideration by the court; a
contract of service may be held to exist by a court examining whether an
"employer" should be held vicariously liable for the actings of his
"employee" which caused injury to a third party but the same conclusion
might not be reached where the issue is one relating to the status of the

---

[9] The definition found in the Disability Discrimination Act 1995 (hereinafter "DDA"), is
almost identical. See DDA, s.68.

[10] *Gillick v. 1. Roevin Management Services, 2. BP Chemicals Ltd* (Case No. S/4248/91,
decision registered February 24, 1994, unreported).

[11] *Stevenson, Jordan & Harrison Ltd v. McDonnell & Evans* [1952] 1 T.L.R. 101 at 111.

worker for taxation purposes. Nonetheless, over the years, a number of factors (often formulated by judges as "tests") have emerged as significant in assessing whether a contract of service exists, particularly for the purpose of assessing whether statutory and other employment protection rights should be available.

As the labour market has developed, offering an ever increasing range 1.05 of employment, with some workers requiring to be highly skilled and self reliant, the "test" in judicial vogue has changed and the factors taken into account in assessing whether a contract of service exists have increased in number. It is impossible to draw up an all inclusive list of features which will be useful in identifying whether a contract of service exists. On balance, the authorities suggest that whether or not a person is employed under a contract of service is a mixed question of fact and law. Much will certainly depend on the facts as found by the employment tribunal or other court of first instance, usually making it difficult to challenge an assessment on appeal.[12]

It is submitted that in the modern employment context, consideration 1.06 of the following matters will be important in assessing the nature of the contract between the parties although no one factor will be conclusive[13]:

(i) Personal service—a contract of service is founded upon an obligation to provide services personally to the "master". If a worker is entitled, as a matter of course, to send along a substitute to perform the duties in question that in itself will normally be enough to demonstrate that the contract is not a contract of service,[14] although a limited power of delegation in certain circumstances will not necessarily preclude the existence of a contract of service.[15] However, it does not follow from this that if there is an obligation to provide services personally a contract of service exists. Independent contractors providing services may also undertake to render personal service.

(ii) Degree of control—an employer will (at least in theory) have a high degree of control over the way in which an employee carries out his duties and when he undertakes them. Looking back to the foundations of employment law, the "master" has a degree of control over his "servant" which he does not have over an independent contractor. Currently, of course, the complex nature of the work carried out by many employees and the high level of skill required

---

[12] *Lee Ting Sang v. Chung Chi-Keung and Shun Shing Construction and Engineering Co. Ltd* [1990] I.R.L.R. 236, PC. Exceptionally,the issue of whether an applicant was employed under a contract of employment will be treated as a question of law to be determined solely by reference to documents only where it appears from their own terms and/or from what the parties said or did that the parties intended all the terms of the contract (apart from any implied by law) to be contained in the documents. *Carmichael v. National Power plc* [2000] I.R.L.R. 43, HL.

[13] *Market Investigations v. Minister of Social Security* [1969] 2 Q.B. 173—this case provides a very helpful analysis of the range of factors which may be relevant.

[14] *Ready Mixed Concrete (South East) Ltd v. Minister of Pensions and National Insurance* [1968] 2 Q.B. 497; *Express and Echo Publications Ltd v. Tanton* [1999] I.R.L.R. 367.

[15] *MacFarlane and another v. Glasgow City Council* [2001] I.R.L.R. 7, EAT.

for its performance make control by the employer less a practical reality than a theoretical possibility. In the first half of this century a great deal of weight was placed upon this single criterion. However, more recently, it has been held that "the most that can be said is that control will no doubt always have to be considered, although it can no longer be regarded as the sole decisive factor".[16]

(iii) Regular payment—payment of a regular wage or salary will point in the direction of a contract of service, as does payment of sick pay. Remuneration wholly in the form of a share of profits or payable on an irregular basis on completion of a task points towards some other form of arrangement.[17]

(iv) Capital investment and risk of loss—if a worker has invested capital in a business and bears a risk if losses are sustained this will point away from the relationship being that of a contract of service.

(v) Provision of tools and equipment—those engaged under a contract for services will often provide their own tools and equipment. Those working under a contract of service will normally be provided with the materials and equipment to do the job.

(vi) Arrangements for payment of tax and national insurance—while the arrangement made for payment of tax (*i.e.* whether Schedule D or Schedule E is used) and national insurance is a factor to be taken into account in assessing the nature of the relationship, it is by no means conclusive. It is perfectly possible for an individual to have paid tax on the basis that he is a self-employed contractor and for a court or tribunal to find a contract of service exists where other factors (such as the degree of control) point in that direction.[18]

(vii) The place of performance of the work—if an individual works at his own premises this will point in the direction of a contract for services but again this is by no means conclusive. It is, for example, perfectly possible for home workers to have a contract of service.

(viii) Termination of the relationship and discipline—a power of dismissal and the right to discipline will point in the direction of a contract of service.

(ix) The type of relationship which the parties believe they are engaged upon—the label attached by the parties to the relationship is a factor in the assessment exercise but no more than that. The nature of the legal relationship cannot be altered by mislabelling whether deliberate or inadvertent.[19] However, in a border line case an express declaration

---

[16] *Market Investigations Ltd v. Minister of Social Security* [1969] 2 Q.B. 173.

[17] *Hitchcock v. Post Office* [1980] I.C.R. 100, EAT.

[18] *Young & Woods v. West* [1980] I.R.L.R. 201, CA.

[19] *Ferguson v. John Dawson & Partners (Contractors) Ltd* [1976] I.R.L.R. 346, CA; *Young & Woods Ltd v. West* [1980] I.R.L.R. 201, CA—"The label which the parties choose to use to describe their relationship cannot alter or decide their true relationship".

by the parties as to the nature of the relationship may tip the balance in that direction.[20]

(x) Mutuality of obligation—the extent to which the "employer" is obliged to provide work where it is available and the worker to perform it is of significance in assessing whether a contract of service exists, particularly in the case of atypical workers such as those engaged on a casual basis or who work from home.

So far as the latter criterion is concerned, the approach in *O'Kelly v.* 1.07 *Trusthouse Forte plc*[21] is to be preferred to that in *Nethermere (St Neots) Ltd.*[22] The latter case suggested that even if there were no fixed hours of work, or any obligation on the employee to accept work offered, there was still an "umbrella" or "overall" contract of employment between the parties governing their relationship when work was in fact undertaken.[23] However if there is no obligation on the employee to accept work offered then "There would therefore be an absence of that irreducible minimum of mutual obligation necessary to create a contract of service".[24] Any agreement to provide work if and when it arises is, if anything, a contract *for* work, not a contract *of* work.[25]

A similar point can be made in relation to individuals who work for 1.08 employment agencies on a series of temporary contracts. In *McMeechan v. Secretary of State for Employment*[26] it was held that an individual, whose services were provided through an employment agency to third party clients on a temporary basis, was an employee of the employment agency, at least in respect of each assignment actually worked. In other words, a contract of service existed between the agency and the worker during each specific engagement. This was so, notwithstanding the fact that the written agreement between the parties stated the worker was providing his services "as a self-employed worker and not under a contract of service", he was not obliged to accept the offer of an assignment nor to work any particular number of hours in a week. The written conditions governing the relationship also made it clear that there could be periods between assignments when no work would be available and that the worker had no entitlement to paid holidays, sick pay nor any pension rights. However, a number of factors pointed in the direction of the existence of a contract of service including the fact that Mr McMeechan was to be paid a weekly wage at a specific hourly rate, subject to deductions for tax and national insurance, the agreement stated that if he did take an assignment he would be "required to fulfil the normal common law duties which an employee would owe to his employer so far as they are applicable", he could be dismissed by the

---

[20] *Massey v. Crown Life Insurance Co.* [1978] I.R.L.R. 31, CA.
[21] [1983] I.C.R. 728, CA.
[22] [1984] I.R.L.R. 240, CA.
[23] It is generally difficult to prove the existence of an "umbrella" contract—see *Clark v. Oxfordshire Health Authority* [1998] I.R.L.R. 125, CA on this point.
[24] *Carmichael v. National Power plc* [2000] I.R.L.R. 43 *per* Lord Irvine of Lairg LC at para. 18 (HL); *Johnson Underwood Ltd v. Montgomery* [2001] I.R.L.R. 269, CA.
[25] See Lord Donaldson MR in *O'Kelly op. cit.* at 763; Brodie, 1999 J.R. 247; Collins (2000) 29 I.L.J. 73.
[26] [1997] I.R.L.R. 353, CA.

agency for improper conduct and ordered by the agency to end an assignment with a client at any time. Furthermore, he also had access to a grievance procedure. Again, this case shows how dangerous it can be to act on the basis of labels and assumptions that atypical workers are something other than "employees".

THE USE OF TESTS TO DETERMINE THE NATURE OF A RELATIONSHIP BETWEEN THE PARTIES

1.09 The foregoing sets out a range of factors likely to be influential in the assessment of whether or not a contract of service exists. Over the years judges have also formulated various formal "tests" which they have used to carry out the assessment exercise. Unfortunately, no single test is conclusive in proving the existence of a contract of service but each encapsulates one or more significant ideas which are useful in considering the nature of the relationship between the parties.

(a) The Control Test

1.10 This is the earliest and most straightforward of the tests. It focuses simply on the issue of control. It has its origin in the master and servant relationship in the fullest sense. In essence, the greater the degree of control exerted by the master over not only what the worker does but how and when he does it, the greater the likelihood that a contract of service exists.[27]

In the early twentieth century a strict application of this test led to unsatisfactory results. For example, nurses were held not to be employees of a hospital when carrying out duties in the operating theatre due to the lack of control which the hospital authority had over the manner in which the work was performed.[28] This led to the test being modified over the years to take account of the fact that in our complex industrial society many employees are more highly skilled than their employers and perform work which the employer does not have the capacity to control in any practical sense. What remains important is the right to control rather than the practical ability to do so. However, this test is by no means conclusive; independent contractors can agree to enter into a relationship characterised by a significant degree of control on the part of the individual providing the work.[29]

(b) The Integration Test

1.11 This test was formulated by Denning L.J., partly in an attempt to avoid some of the problems experienced with the control test. In essence, this test is based upon the proposition that under a contract of service a worker is employed as part of the business with the work also being performed as an integral part of it. In contrast, under a contract

---

[27] *Performing Rights Society v. Mitchell & Booker (Palais de Danse) Ltd* [1924] 1 K.B. 762.
[28] *Hillyer v. Governors of St Bartholomew's Hospital* [1909] 2 K.B. 820.
[29] This was the case in *Ready Mixed Concrete (South East) Ltd v. Minister of Pensions and National Insurance* [1968] 2 Q.B. 497.

for services, the work done for the business is not integrated into it but only accessory to it.[30] In a later formulation Denning L.J. restated the test by asking whether the worker was "part and parcel of the employer's organisation".[31]

This test is often criticised for being too vague; there is no attempt to define what is meant by "integration" or "organisation". Nonetheless, it is submitted that it is a useful adjunct to the control test, particularly in relation to the assessment of highly skilled workers.

(c) The Economic Reality Test

This test assesses the status of the worker by asking exactly the opposite question from that addressed by the integration test. Is the worker truly independent of the organisation or, in the words of Cooke J.: " 'Is the person who has engaged himself to perform these services performing them as a person in business on his own account?' If the answer to that question is 'yes', then the contract is a contract for services. If the answer is 'no' then the contract is a contract of service".[32]

While no all-embracing list can be compiled of the considerations which are relevant in answering that question the type of factors to be taken into account include "whether the man performing the services provides his own equipment, whether he hires his own helpers, what degree of financial risk he takes, what degree of responsibility for investment in management he has, and whether and how far he has an opportunity of profiting from sound management in the performance of his task".[33]

It is submitted that this test is not of any greater assistance in dealing with borderline cases than the integration test.

(d) The Multiple Test

All three of the foregoing tests have proved to be inadequate in one way or another when it comes to deciding whether or not a worker is engaged under a contract of service.

The latest, and most helpful, test is known as the "multiple" test since it focuses on a number of key features in the relationship between the parties and brings together strands from the other tests. It asks for three questions to be addressed[34]:

(1) Did the worker undertake to provide his own work and skill in return for remuneration?
(2) Was there a sufficient degree of control to enable the worker fairly to be called a servant?
(3) Were there any other factors inconsistent with the existence of a contract of service?

1.12

1.13

---

[30] *Stevenson, Jordan & Harrison Ltd v. Macdonald & Evans* [1952] 1 T.L.R. 101, CA.
[31] *Bank voor Handel en Scheepvaart NV v. Slatford (No. 2)* [1953] 1 Q.B. 248.
[32] *Market Investigations Ltd v. Minister of Social Security* [1969] 2 Q.B. 173, *per* Cooke J. at 185 and 186.
[33] *ibid.*
[34] *Ready Mixed Concrete (South East) Ltd v. Minister of Pensions and National Insurance* [1968] 2 Q.B. 497.

These questions have been designed bearing in mind some of the criticisms which have been made of the other tests. However, even this test is not entirely satisfactory, leaving scope, for example, to debate about what amounts to a sufficient degree of control. Nonetheless, this is certainly the most sophisticated and useful of the tests developed to date.[35]

The best approach is to act on the basis that each of the tests may be of some assistance in the assessment exercise but that, in the final analysis, all relevant factors in a particular case must be weighed in the balance before deciding whether it is likely that a contract of service exists. This is the approach which an employment tribunal is likely to take.

OTHER WORKERS

1.14 The following workers have a relationship with the work provider which is neither a contract of service nor a contract for services:

(a) Apprentices

Contracts of apprenticeship are much less common now than in the past. Nevertheless, they do still exist. It should be noted that such contracts normally require to be constituted in writing[36] and the right to dismiss is more limited than under a contract of service.[37] However, contracts of apprenticeship are now included in most statutory definitions of employment.[38]

(b) Office holders

An office holder is not a servant. His duties and rights depend upon the office held rather than upon contract.[39] An office holder's statutory rights are more limited than those of an employee[40] while his common law rights may be greater.[41]

The most important examples of office holders are:

(i) Police constables

A police officer is regarded as an office holder rather than one who works under a contract of service. Police officers are excluded from most of the rights set out in the ERA[42] although they are deemed to be

---

[35] For a recent example of the multiple test in operation see *Johnson v. Montgomery* [2001] I.R.L.R. 269, CA.

[36] *Murray v. M'Gilchrist* (1863) 4 Irv. 461.

[37] *Wallace v. CA. Roofing Services Ltd* [1996] I.R.L.R. 435. This case is also interesting because it was held that an oral agreement between the parties amounted to a contract of apprenticeship. Accordingly, the contract was not terminable by reason of redundancy, being a contract for a fixed term.

[38] For example, ERA, s.230; *cf. Edmunds v. Lawson* [2000] I.R.L.R. 391, CA.

[39] *McMillan v. Guest* [1942] A.C. 561.

[40] For example, see ERA, s.159.

[41] *Ridge v. Baldwin (No. 1)* [1964] A.C. 40, HL.

[42] ERA, s.200.

employees for the purposes of the SDA,[43] the RRA,[44] and they are "workers" for the purpose of the Working Time Regulations.[45]

(ii) Clergymen

Clergymen are office holders in respect of their role in pastoral care of a congregation.[46] While there is no barrier in principle to a contract of employment regulating the duties of a minister of religion, there is a presumption that, where the duties are essentially spiritual, there is no intention to create legal relations under the civil law.[47]

(iii) Company directors

Company directors are office holders by virtue of their appointment as a director.[48] However, they can also enter into a service agreement with the company, which may be express or implied, thereby also becoming an employee of the company. *Secretary of State for Trade and Industry v. Bottrill*[49] discusses some of the factors which will be taken into account in deciding whether a company director is an employee of the company. That the director is also the majority or sole shareholder is not fatal to a finding of employment, though it will be a relevant consideration.[50]

(c) Crown servants

The nature of the relationship between Crown servants and the Crown is unclear. It is not even certain that a contract exists between the parties at all. What is clear is that if a contract does exist it is not a contract of service in the normal sense.[51] The special status of Crown employment is recognised by ERA, s.191 which extends most of the provisions of that legislation to those in Crown employment. Additionally, ERA, s.192 extends many of the provisions of the Act to the armed services, including the right not to be unfairly dismissed.[52]

CREATING THE EMPLOYMENT RELATIONSHIP

The employment relationship is a contract and the general principles of 1.15 contract law, such as those dealing with capacity to contract, are relevant to its formation and construction, albeit that some of them are not easily

---

[43] SDA, s.16.

[44] RRA, s.17.

[45] Reg. 41(1).

[46] *Diocese of Southwark v. Coker* [1998] I.C.R. 140, CA..

[47] *Percy v. Board of the National Mission of the Church of Scotland*, 2001 S.C. 757; 2001 S.L.T. 497.

[48] *McMillan v. Guest* [1942] A.C. 562.

[49] [1999] I.R.L.R. 326, CA.

[50] *Fleming v. Secretary of State for Trade and Industry* [1997] I.R.L.R. 682, IH, followed by the Court of Appeal in *Bottrill*; *Secretary of State for Trade and Industry v. Smith* [2000] I.R.L.R. 6, EAT; *Sellars Assurance Ltd v. Connelly* [2001] I.R.L.R. 222, CA.

[51] Compare *R v. Civil Service Appeal Board, ex p. Bruce* [1988] I.C.R. 649 and *R. v. Lord Chancellor's Department, ex p. Nangle* [1991] I.R.L.R. 343.

[52] See also ERA, s.193 for restrictions imposed on the rights of Crown employees as a result of requirements of national security.

adapted to coping with the complexity and developmental nature of the employment relationship. As in the general law of contract issues of public policy do arise when considering whether a contract term is enforceable[53] as does the law concerning illegal contracts (both that relating to illegality in inception and illegality in the manner of performance). Occasionally, contracts of employment are held to be unenforceable at the instance of one or other party due to the taint of illegality. The most common cause of illegality is a fraud on the Inland Revenue (for example, gross rather than net payments of some kind being made).[54]

1.16   It is not normally necessary for the employment contract to be reduced to writing.[55] In practice, many employees never receive a written contract or any other document evincing the terms of the contract throughout the course of their employment. Employees often say "I don't have a contract" but, of course, they do, although it may be oral in nature (making its terms difficult to prove at times), and supplemented by implied terms. There may be little or nothing in the way of negotiation between the parties. New employees may simply be told at a brief meeting that they are to start the next week with no more than a general indication perhaps of expected wages, hours of work and duties. These matters and others are clarified by the subsequent course of dealings between the parties.

This situation can be contrasted with that which may prevail, for example, in the case of a highly skilled employee of great value to the employer (and to competitors!) where there may be extensive negotiations leading to an agreement being set out at considerable length in a written contract. Often agreements of this type record particular restrictions which are to be placed upon such employees, which extend far beyond normal common law obligations.[56] Agreements of this type are not uncommon in the case of company directors who may enter into a Service Agreement with the company which will govern the individual's role as an employee of the company. Agreements of this type can involve extensive negotiations between parties with both sides being legally represented. At the end of the day a document will be drawn up which records the terms of the contract of service. The existence of such a Service Agreement and its terms can be crucial if the Director (or the company) subsequently needs to show that he was an employee of the company[57] although it is possible for a Service Agreement to be implied.[58]

---

[53] See in particular the law governing restrictive covenants in Chap. 2.

[54] See *Hyland v. J. H. Barker (North West)* [1985] I.R.L.R. 403 and *Salvesen v. Simons* [1994] I.R.L.R. 52 for examples of unenforceable contracts and contrast with *Annandale Engineering v. Sampson* [1994] I.R.L.R. 59. Claims under the SDA may be treated differently, since they are not viewed as founded on the contract itself but as statutory torts: *Hall v. Woolston Hall Leisure Ltd* [2000] I.R.L.R. 578, CA. *Hall* also emphasises that, even in a claim which is founded on the contract, knowledge of the illegality will not necessarily preclude reliance on the contract, although participation in the illegal arrangement will usually do so.

[55] The position in respect of a contract of apprenticeship has already been highlighted.

[56] See Chap. 2.

[57] *Albert J. Parsons & Sons Ltd v. Parsons* [1979] I.R.L.R. 117.

[58] *Folami v. Nigerline (U.K.)* [1978] I.C.R. 277, EAT.

It should also be borne in mind that although individual employees 1.17 may not be involved in lengthy negotiations with the employer it may be that the employment will be subject to the provisions of a local and/or national collective agreement, negotiated between a trade union and the employer, the terms of which may be incorporated into the individual contract of employment.[59]

However complex or simple the negotiation process and the resulting agreement between the parties, it must be understood that the employment relationship is founded upon one of the most fluid and dynamic contracts that one is ever likely to come across; whatever the terms of the original contract, and whatever its form, it is entirely possible that in any subsequent dispute the contract will be held to have been modified by the express or implied agreement of the parties. The terms of any written agreement may well fail to record the alterations which have taken place. Whether a contractual change has, in fact, occurred (rather than something less such as flexibility being shown in relation to the performance of the original contract terms which remain in place) is a matter of evidence.

SOURCES OF CONTRACTUAL TERMS

A contract of employment is made up of: (a) express terms; (b) 1.18 incorporated terms; (c) imposed terms; and (d) implied terms.

(a) Express terms

Quite simply, express terms are those expressly agreed between the 1.19 parties. While they are often written terms this is not necessarily so. Express terms may be the product of a simple oral agreement. For example, an employer states "I will pay you £x per week" and the employee accepts the job on that basis. It is possible for there to be an express term in the contract which sets out an agreement to incorporate provisions found in another document (for example, a collective agreement).[60] Express terms normally cannot be overridden by implied terms.[61] However, the case of *Johnstone v. Bloomsbury Health Authority*[62] is of particular note since the Court of Appeal held that an express term governing hours of work had to be exercised by the employer subject to the implied obligation upon the employer to take reasonable care of the employee's health. It should be noted that where a contract contains an express term which confers an apparently unfettered discretion on the employer, the exercise of that discretion is likely to be subject to the implied obligation not to undermine the trust and confidence between

---

[59] See later in this chapter.
[60] See Incorporated Terms, below.
[61] *Malik v. BCCI* [1998] A.C. 20; [1997] I.R.L.R. 462, HL; *Johnson v. Unisys Ltd* [2001] I.R.L.R. 279, HL.
[62] [1991] I.R.L.R. 118, CA.

the parties.[63] Indeed it is arguable that all aspects of an employer's prerogative will be subject to this implied obligation.[64]

(b) Incorporated terms

1.20   The parties may agree expressly or impliedly to incorporate terms into the contract from other sources, the most common being provisions from a collective agreement or a works rule book/employee handbook.

The legal position with regard to the incorporation of collective agreements is particularly complex and has given rise to much academic debate. Detailed commentary on the incorporation of collective agreements is beyond the scope of this text. Generally, however, it should be noted that it is possible to incorporate either specific provisions from a collective agreement by express reference to them or for a more general reference to be made to the agreement as a whole. Where a document is expressly incorporated by general words it is still necessary to consider, in conjunction with the words of incorporation, whether any particular part of that document is apt to be a term of the contract; if it is inapt, the correct construction may be that it is not a term of the contract.[65]

1.21   By way of example, a collective agreement was held to be incorporated into an individual's contract of employment in *Marley v. Forward Trust Group*.[66] Of particular interest in this case is the fact that the final clause in the collective agreement stated "This agreement is binding in honour only and it is not intended to give rise to any legal obligation". The EAT, adopting a similar line to the employment tribunal, held that the rights conferred on the individual employee under the agreement were taken away by the final clause which took the entire agreement out of the sphere of legal enforceability. However, the Court of Appeal held that the terms of an unenforceable collective agreement could be incorporated into an individual's contract of employment and if they were so incorporated they were enforceable by the employee since they had legal effect as terms of the contract between the employer and the employee.[67] It is also worth noting that it is not necessary for an employee to be a member of the relevant (or any) trade union for one or more of the provisions of a collective agreement to become incorporated into his contract of employment or for the employee to understand the

---

[63] In *United Bank v. Akhtar* [1989] I.R.L.R. 507, the EAT held that the employer must exercise his discretion concerning a mobility clause reasonably. In *Clark v. BET Plc* [1997] I.R.L.R. 348, QBD, it was held that there would be a breach of the implied term where the employer determined the increase in an employee's salary in an annual review at nil. See also *Chequepoint (UK) Ltd v. Radwan* [2001] Emp L.R. 98, CA, *cf. Clark v. Nomura International plc* [2000] I.R.L.R. 766, QBD where it was held that provided the discretion was not exercised perversely, a discretionary bonus could be determined at nil, the obligation being qualified to the extent that the employer must not *without reasonable and proper cause* undermine the relationship of trust and confidence

[64] *National Grid (Co.) plc v. Mayes* [2000] I.C.R. 173, CA; [2001] I.C.R. 544, HL.

[65] *Alexander v. Standard Telephones (and Cables Ltd) (No. 2)* [1991] I.R.L.R. 286, which also discusses the even more stringent conditions which require to be met for implied incorporation. *Alexander* was followed in *Wandsworth LBC v. D'Silva* [1998] I.R.L.R. 193; *Grant v. South West Trains Ltd* [1998] I.R.L.R. 188 and *Henry v. London General Transport Services Ltd* [2001] I.R.L.R. 132, EAT. See also *Hamilton v. Futura Floors* [1990] I.R.L.R. 478.

[66] [1986] I.R.L.R. 369, CA.

[67] See also *Robertson v. British Gas Corporation* [1983] I.R.L.R. 302.

impact which a collectively negotiated agreement may have on the contract of employment.[68] Similarly, where one or more of the provisions of a collective agreement have been incorporated into the individual's contract of employment the fact that the employer subsequently terminates the collective agreement will not affect the contractual term.[69]

Where the terms of a collective agreement are incorporated into the contract, it has been held in the Outer House that these terms can be negatively enforced by interdicting the employer from acting contrary to the terms of the agreement, there being no suggestion that the employer had lost trust and confidence in the employee.[70] So far as work rules are concerned these may be incorporated if it can be reasonably inferred that the parties intended them to have contractual effect.[71] It is certainly not the case that the provisions of a staff handbook or works rule book will necessarily have contractual effect. Indeed, it could be argued that the more extensive the provisions of any handbook or rule book the less likely that it will be inferred that the parties intended them to have contractual effect.[72] *Dryden v. Greater Glasgow Health Board*[73] provides a good example of the introduction of a works rule which was held not to have contractual effect (and therefore was unable to form the basis of a constructive dismissal complaint). In *Secretary of State for Scotland v Taylor*[74] it was held that an equal opportunities policy was incorporated into the contract, and was not a mere policy document.

(c) Imposed terms

Occasionally, contract terms will be imposed by statute. Of particular 1.22 significance in this regard is section 1(1) of the Equal Pay Act 1970[75] which states: "If the terms of a contract under which a woman is employed at an establishment in Great Britain do not include (directly or by reference to a collective agreement or otherwise) an equality clause they shall be deemed to include one".[76]

(d) Implied terms[77]

Two types of implied terms can be distinguished: (i) Those which will 1.23 be implied into a particular contract on the basis that it can be inferred that the parties intended these terms to be part of the bargain, although

---

[68] *Henry v. London General Transport* [2001] I.R.L.R. 132
[69] See *also British Leyland (U.K.) Ltd v. McQuilken* [1978] I.R.L.R. 245, EAT where it was decided that the collective agreement in this case was a long-term plan dealing with policy rather than the rights of employees and as such was not capable of incorporation within an individual contract of employment.
[70] *Anderson v. Pringle of Scotland Ltd* [1998] I.R.L.R. 64; *Peace v. City of Edinburgh Council* [1999] I.R.L.R. 417
[71] For an example of a clause in an employee handbook which was held to have contractual effect see *Dal v. Orr* [1980] I.R.L.R. 413, EAT.
[72] *Secretary of State for Employment v. Association Society of Locomotive Engineers and Firemen (No. 2)* [1972] 2 Q.B. 455, CA.
[73] [1992] I.R.L.R. 469, EAT.
[74] [2000] I.R.L.R. 502, HL.
[75] Hereinafter "EqPA".
[76] See Chap. 4 for detailed discussion of the EqPA and this deemed contractual term.
[77] See Mr Justice Lindsay (2001) 30 I.L.J. 1; *Liverpool City Council v. Irwin* [1977] A.C. 239.

they did not expressly say so.[78] (ii) Those implied by common law, which generally deal with the rights and obligations of both parties involved in any employment relationship.

(i) Particular implied terms

1.24   It is possible for contractual terms to be implied from the conduct of the parties in a particular case. It is also possible for a term to be implied on the basis that it is so obvious that the parties would say "of course" it is a term of the contract if asked the question by an "officious bystander".[79]

A court may also imply a term into a contract in the interests of "business efficacy", *i.e.* where it is necessary to make the contract work. This test is perhaps narrower in scope but closely related to the "officious bystander" test since one assumes that the parties to the relationship would say "of course" we intended this term to be part of the contract if it is indeed a necessary term to make the contract work.[80]

A term may also be implied into a particular contract if it is a term which is customary in a particular trade or industry. The custom must be proved and must be "reasonable, notorious and certain", *i.e.* fair, well known and precise.[81] It is rare, particularly nowadays, for customary terms to be implied.

Occasionally, a term will be implied into a contract which is derived from the custom and practice of the employer. Again, it is difficult to persuade a court to imply a term on this basis since such practices are normally introduced unilaterally by the employer. An example might be the practice of paying more than the statutory redundancy payment. In *Duke v. Reliance Systems*[82] an employer sought to argue that the company policy that women retire at the age of 60 had become an implied term in the contract. The EAT held that "a policy adopted by management unilaterally cannot become a term of the employee's contract on the ground that it is an established custom and practice unless it is at least shown that the policy has been drawn to the attention of the employees and has been followed without exception for a substantial period". In *Quinn v. Calder Industrial Materials Limited*[83] the court refused to accept that a practice of making enhanced redundancy payments had led to an implied contractual right to such payments.

(ii) Implied terms from common law

1.25   The terms implied into a contract of employment by the common law can usefully be considered within the context of an examination of the rights and duties which characterise the employment relationship. This is

---

[78] See *Christian Salvesen Food Services Ltd v. Ali* [1997] I.R.L.R. 17, CA for a consideration of the law governing the implication of contractual terms.

[79] See *Shirlaw v. Southern Foundries (1926) Ltd* [1939] 2 All E.R. 113 for the "officious bystander" test.

[80] See *Apaau v. Iceland Frozen Foods Plc (No. 1)* [1996] I.R.L.R. 119 for an example of a failed attempt to meet the requirements of the business efficacy test.

[81] *Devonald v. Rosser and Sons* [1906] 2 K.B. 728.

[82] [1982] I.R.L.R. 347, EAT.

[83] [1996] I.R.L.R. 126; followed in *McGowan v. Joint Receivers of Clyde Shaw Ltd,* 2000 S.C.L.R. 898. *Quaere* however the effect of the implied obligation of mutual trust and confidence in protecting legitimate expectations, see *Dunlop Tyres Ltd v. Blows* [2001] I.R.L.R. 629.

so because these rights and duties can, in fact, be viewed as terms of the contract implied by common law, although it is possible to contract out of some of them if the parties do so expressly. On this point, the dictum of Lord Steyn in *Malik v. Bank of Credit and Commerce International SA*[84] that "implied terms operate as default rules. The parties are free to exclude or modify them" is worthy of note. In recent years, some courts and tribunals have made creative use of implied terms (particularly the implied term governing trust and confidence). It is certainly not beyond the realms of possibility that additional implied terms may emerge. The following is a summary of the current position with regard to the duties of the employee and the employer.

Duties of The Employee

1. Duty to serve—one of the foundation stones of the employment 1.26 contract is the employee's duty to render personal service. This means that the employee must be ready and willing to work. Accordingly, employees who go on strike will usually be in breach of contract.[85]

2. Duty to obey reasonable orders/carry out reasonable instructions— what is reasonable will depend, among other things, on the nature of the job. A reasonable instruction to a firefighter may not be reasonable if made to a clerical officer. It is generally accepted that an employee is not obliged to carry out instructions outwith the scope of the contract[86] and he is perfectly entitled to refuse to obey an order requiring him to do something illegal.

However, employees are expected to adapt to new working methods within reason.[87] In case of any doubt, it should also be noted that breach of this duty will not necessarily justify dismissal at common law. Obviously, this is an area where the statutory law of unfair dismissal is highly relevant.[88]

3. Duty of fidelity—an employee has an obligation to serve honestly and faithfully. In particular he must: (a) not make secret profits and account to his employer for any profit which he does make.[89] Exceptionally, the court may award the discretionary remedy of restitutionary damages for breach of contract simpliciter[90]; (b) not compete with his employer or work for a rival during the course of his employment[91]; (c)

---

[84] [1997] I.R.L.R. 462, H.L.

[85] *Simmons v. Hoover Ltd* [1977] Q.B. 284, EAT, although see *Morgan v. Fry* [1968] 2 Q.B. 710, CA for an alternative view which may be relevant in limited circumstances.

[86] Although note the decision in *Farrant v. The Woodroffe School* [1998] I.R.L.R. 176, EAT, in which the EAT held that it was not necessarily unfair to dismiss an employee for refusing to obey an unlawful instruction. According to the EAT, the question of whether the instruction was lawful, as a matter of contract, will be a relevant but not decisive factor in considering the overall question of reasonableness raised in an unfair dismissal case.

[87] *Cresswell v. Board of Inland Revenue* [1984] I.C.R. 508.

[88] See Chap. 11.

[89] For a discussion of when an employee may be in breach of a fiduciary duty requiring an account of profits to be rendered see *Nottingham University v. Fishel* [2000] I.R.L.R. 471.

[90] *Attorney-General v. Blake* [2001] 1 AC 268; [2001] I.R.L.R. 36, HL.

[91] *Hivac Ltd v. Park Royal Scientific Instruments Ltd* [1946] All E.R. 350, CA.

disclose information which comes to him on behalf of his employer[92]; and (d) not disclose confidential information or trade secrets.[93]

4. An employee is under a duty to take reasonable care in the performance of his duties.[94]

5. An employee promises that he is reasonably competent to perform the job he is employed to do.[95]

6. An employee is under a duty to co-operate with the employer and not impede the employer's business.[96]

7. An employee is under a duty not to act in such a way as to destroy the mutual respect and trust which should exist between the parties to the contract.[97]

DUTIES OF EMPLOYER

1.27 The following obligations are imputed to the employer:

1. The duty to pay wages—generally the amount of wages to be paid will form an express term of the contract. However, in the event that it is not possible to identify an express or implied term as to the amount of wages to be paid the parties are entitled to rely upon the *quantum meruit* principle. It should be noted that while in most contracts the obligation will be to pay for service (*i.e.* the employee's willingness and availability to work) it is possible to have an agreement that the employee will receive wages only for work done. This would be the case for workers paid wholly on the basis of piece work.

If the former obligation applies, an employee may be entitled to rely upon a presumption at common law, in the absence of any express or implied term or other evidence to the contrary, that a worker is entitled to sick pay for temporary absence. The latter type of obligation will not give rise to such a presumption.[98] However, usually this is a matter dealt with expressly or by an implied term in the contract.[99]

2. The duty to take care of employees by providing a safe system of work, selecting proper staff and providing adequate materials. While the law of delict has much to say about the employer's duty of care to his employees it should not be forgotten that this duty is also a contractual one. Accordingly, a material breach of this duty can give rise to a constructive dismissal.[1]

---

[92] Specific provisions cover inventions and discoveries made in the course of employment: see Patents Act 1977, s.40.

[93] See *Faccenda Chicken Ltd v. Fowler* [1986] I.R.L.R. 69; [1987] Ch. 117, CA for a detailed discussion of the implied terms governing confidential information which apply during and after employment.

[94] *Lister v. Romford Ice and Cold Storage Co. Ltd* [1957] A.C. 555; *Janata Bank v. Ahmed* [1981] I.R.L.R. 457 (where the employee was liable for pure economic loss to the employer).

[95] *Harmer v. Cornelius* (1858) 5 C.B. (N.S.) 236.

[96] *Secretary of State for Employment v.* ASLEF (No. 2) [1972] 2 Q.B. 455.

[97] See para. 1.25 above.

[98] *Mears v. Safecar Security* [1982] I.R.L.R. 183, CA.

[99] See also the provisions of ERA, s.1 governing specification of particulars relating to sickness and sick pay which is dealt with later in this chapter.

[1] *British Aircraft Corporation v. Austin* [1978] I.R.L.R. 332, EAT; *Johnstone v. Bloomsbury Health Authority* [1991] I.R.L.R. 118.

3. The duty to indemnify the employee in respect of expenses incurred in carrying out his duties.

4. A duty to co-operate in maintaining the relationship of trust and confidence between employer and employee. The law on this implied duty is still developing rapidly (and creatively!).[2] Increasingly, courts appear willing to limit the scope of express powers under the contract by reference to the implied duty of mutual trust and confidence. While it would not be quite accurate to state that this duty requires the parties to behave reasonably towards each other, much of the case law does not fall that far short of supporting this proposition. However it is formulated it will not come as a surprise that many constructive dismissal cases[3] are based upon an alleged breach of this implied term.[4]

In many respects the development of this term reflects the evolution of the employment relationship in recent years into a contractual relationship which is more balanced so far as the obligations of the parties are concerned. This has been recognised judicially by the House of Lords: "Freedom of contract meant that the stronger party, usually the employer, was free to impose his terms upon the weaker. But over the last 30 years or so, the nature of the contract of employment has been transformed. It has been recognized that a person's employment is usually one of the most important things in his or her life. It gives not only a livelihood but an occupation, an identity and a sense of self-esteem. The law has changed to recognise social reality".[5] While the term imposes reciprocal obligations on employer and employee, its greatest impact is upon the employer[6] who shall not "without reasonable and proper cause, conduct itself in a manner calculated and likely to destroy or seriously damage the relationship of trust and confidence and trust between the employer and employee".[7] The term is of crucial importance in regulating the practical aspects of the employment relationship which are not the subject of specific statutory protection, such as protecting the legitimate expectation of an employee that he would receive an interest free bridging loan to cover relocation costs.[8] While it strikes at "bad" behavior on the part of the employer it may also impose positive obligations upon him, *e.g.* to advise his employees that they may have certain pension rights.[9] Moreover it survives the termination of the contract and is relevant to the dismissal of an employee.[10] There are however two limitations on the effect of the term.

---

[2] *Malik v. Bank of Credit and Commerce International SA* [1997] I.R.L.R. 462, HL.; *Johnson v Unysis* [2001] I.R.L.R. 279 and para. 1.25 above.

[3] For example, *Courtaulds Northern Textiles Ltd v. Andrew* [1979] I.R.L.R. 84, EAT.

[4] Accordingly, this matter will be examined in more detail in Chap. 11.

[5] *per* Lord Hoffman in *Johnson v. Unysis* [2001] I.R.L.R. 279 at para. 35.

[6] *Malik* at p. 46C.

[7] *Woods v. W. M. Car Services (Peterborough) Ltd* [1981] I.C.R. 666.

[8] *French v. Barclays Bank Plc* [1998] I.R.L.R. 646.

[9] *Scally v. Southern Health Board* [1992] 1 A.C. 294; *BG Plc v. O'Brien* [2001] I.R.L.R. 496, EAT. *cf. University of Nottingham v. Eyett (No. 1)* [1999] I.R.L.R. 87 and *Outram v. Academy Plastics Ltd* [2000] I.R.L.R. 499, CA.

[10] *Neary v. Dean of Westminister* [1999] I.R.L.R. 288 in which Lord Jauncey, sitting as a Special Commissioner, stated "that conduct amounting to gross misconduct justifying dismissal must so undermine the trust and confidence which is inherent in the particular contract of employment that the master should no longer be required to retain the servant in his employment" (para. 23).

Firstly, "terms which the courts imply into a contract must be consistent with the express terms. Implied terms may supplement the express terms of the contract but cannot contradict them".[11] The second point is that recourse cannot be made to the implied term where there would be no relevant claim under employment protection legislation because the employee does not qualify for protection or that any award of compensation for a successful claim under the legislation would be capped. The common law cannot subvert the intention of the legislature that only a limited class of employees should qualify for protection.[12]

5. A duty to provide a system for redress of grievances—this could be considered the latest discovery in implied terms! It has its origin in the case of *W. A. Goold (Pearmark) Limited v. McConnell*.[13] Here, the EAT supported the conclusion of an employment tribunal "that there was an implied term in the contract of employment that the employers would reasonably and promptly afford a reasonable opportunity to their employees to obtain redress of any grievance they may have". This implied term, it was reasoned, was supported by the fact that the statement of particulars to be issued under section 1 of the ERA requires specification of certain information concerning redress of grievances. It is worth noting, in particular, the focus on the concept of "reasonableness". It is submitted that, in fact, there was no need to add a "new" implied term into the contract in the circumstances of this particular case; the employer's behaviour could have been considered as a breach of the duty to maintain the trust and confidence which should exist between the parties to an employment relationship. Such an approach is evident in *Reed v. Bull Information Systems and Stedman*[14] in which the employer's failure to investigate the applicant's complaints of harassment was sufficient to justify a finding of breach of trust and confidence by the employer.

STATUTORY DUTY TO PROVIDE A STATEMENT OF EMPLOYMENT PARTICULARS

1.28 Given the fluidity of the employment contract it is perhaps fortunate that an employer is obliged to give an employee a written statement of particulars of employment within two months of the commencement of employment.[15] The statement can be given in instalments so long as there is compliance with the time-limit.[16]

A few classes of employment are excluded from this right[17] but the effect of this is very limited and it should be noted, in particular, that all part-time employees are entitled to such a statement.[18] Note also that a

---

[11] *per* Lord Hoffman in *Johnson v. Unysis* at para. 37.

[12] *Johnson v. Unisys*, para. 50 *et seq.*

[13] [1995] I.R.L.R. 516, EAT.

[14] [1999] I.R.L.R. 299, EAT.

[15] ERA, ss.1(1) and (2).

[16] *ibid.*, ss.1(2).

[17] See ERA, s.199 as amended. Note also s.198 which excludes employees whose contract of employment continues for less than one month.

[18] The exclusion of those who worked for less than eight hours per week was repealed with effect from February 6, 1995 as a consequence of the provisions of the Employment Protection (Part-time Employees) Regulations 1995 (S.I. 1995 No. 31).

statement must be given to an employee even if the employment ends before he has completed eight weeks service[19] and that employees who are to begin work outside the United Kingdom for a period of more than one month are entitled to a statement prior to their departure even if that date occurs before eight weeks service has been completed.[20]

The statement must contain particulars of: 1.29

   (i)   the names of the employer and the employee;

   (ii)   the date when the employment began;

   (iii)   the date on which the employee's period of continuous employment began[21];

   (iv)   the scale or rate of remuneration or the method of calculating remuneration;

   (iv)   the intervals at which remuneration is to be paid (for example weekly or monthly);

   (vi)   any terms and conditions relating to hours of work (including any terms and conditions relating to normal working hours);

   (vii)   any terms and conditions relating to holidays, including public holidays, and holiday pay (sufficient to enable the employee's entitlement to be calculated, including any entitlement to accrued holiday pay on the termination of employment);

   (viii)   the title of the job which the employee is employed to do or a brief description of the work for which he is employed;

   (ix)   either the place of work or, where the employee is required or permitted to work at various places, an indication of that and of the address of the employer;

   (x)   terms and conditions relating to incapacity for work due to sickness or injury, including any provision for sick pay;

   (xi)   provisions concerning pensions and pensions schemes;

   (xii)   the length of notice which the employee is obliged to give and entitled to receive to terminate the contract of employment;

   (xiii)   where the employment is not intended to be permanent, the period for which it is expected to continue or, if it is for a fixed term, the date when it is to end;

   (xiv)   any collective agreements which affect the terms and conditions of the employment including, where the employer is not a party, specification of the persons by whom they were made; and

   (xv)   where the employee is required to work outside the United Kingdom for a period of more than one month—(a) the period for which he is to work outside the United Kingdom; (b) the currency in which remuneration is to be paid while he is working outside the United Kingdom; (c) any additional

---

[19] ERA, s.2(6).

[20] ERA, s.2(5).

[21] *Quaere* whether, if the date when continuous employment began for redundancy purposes is different from the date when continuous employment began for other purposes, both dates should be specified. It may be best to err on the side of caution and specify both dates.

remuneration payable to him, and any benefits to be provided to or in respect of him, by reason of his being required to work outside the United Kingdom; and (d) any terms and conditions relating to his return to the United Kingdom.

In the event that there are no particulars relating to any of the above terms that fact should be stated.[22]

Particulars (i)–(ix) above must be included in a single document.[23] However, particulars relating to sickness and sick pay and to pensions and pension schemes can be set out in some other document which is reasonably accessible as long as the principal statement makes that fact clear.[24]

So far as particulars concerning notice of termination are concerned an employee can be referred to the law (*i.e.* where statutory notice periods apply) or to a collective agreement, which directly affects the terms and conditions of employment, so long as that is reasonably accessible to the employee.[25]

1.30 The statutory statement must also include a note specifying:

(a) any disciplinary rules applicable to the employee or referring the employee to the provisions of a reasonably accessible document which specifies such rules[26];

(b) a person to whom the employee can apply if dissatisfied with a disciplinary decision relating to him or if he has any other grievance and the manner in which any such application should be made[27];

(c) any further steps, with an explanation of them, which form part of the disciplinary or grievance procedures. In the alternative, the employee can be referred to another reasonably accessible document where such steps are explained; and[28]

(d) whether there is a contracting out certificate in force for retirement pension purposes.[29]

1.31 However, the obligation to supply a note covering these issues does not apply in relation to rules, disciplinary decisions or grievances relating to health and safety.[30] Similarly, the provisions of section 3(1) (with the exception of the need to specify a person to whom the employee can apply for the purpose of seeking redress of a grievance) do not apply if, on the date the employee's employment began the number of employees employed by the employer, added to any employed by an associated employer, was less than 20.[31]

---

[22] ERA, s.2(1).
[23] *ibid.*, s.2(4).
[24] *ibid.*, s.2(2). Section 6 specifies what will amount to reasonable accessibility.
[25] *ibid.*, s.2(3).
[26] *ibid.*, s.3(1)(a).
[27] *ibid.*, s.3(1)(b).
[28] *ibid.*, s.3(1)(c).
[29] *ibid.*, s.3(5).
[30] *ibid.*, s.3(2).
[31] *ibid.*, s.3(3) and (4). This exception is under review by the government; the possibility of its repeal is mooted in the consultation document "Routes to Resolution: Improving Dispute Resolution in Britain" published by the DTI on July 20, 2001

Particulars included in a section 1 statement

In the event that there is any change in the particulars which require 1.32 to be specified the employer is required to give the employee a written statement containing particulars of the change[32] within one month after the change[33] or, if the change results from the employee being required to work outside the United Kingdom for one month or more, by the date he leaves the United Kingdom to begin work if that is earlier.[34]

In respect of any change to particulars concerning sickness, sick pay, pensions, disciplinary rules or the further steps involved in progressing a grievance or appealing against a disciplinary decision after the initial notification of the grievance or appeal it is acceptable to provide the employee with a statement of change which refers him to the provisions of some other reasonably accessible document.[35] Similarly, any statement concerning changes to the provisions governing notice can refer the employee to the law or to a reasonably accessible collective agreement.[36]

In the event that the name of the employer is changed (without any change in the employer's identity) or the identity of the employer is changed without continuity being broken the new (or newly named) employer does not have to provide an entirely new statement but can simply treat the change as one falling within section 4.[37] However, if there is a change in the identity of the employer, without a break in continuous service, the statement of change must restate the date on which the employee's period of continuous employment began.[38]

The Section 1 Statement and the Contract of Employment

It is not uncommon for employers and employees to refer to the 1.33 statutory statement issued under section 1 of the ERA as the employee's "contract" but this is inaccurate. The statement is simply evidence (not necessarily conclusive) of the terms of the contract.[39] It is open to either party to show that the statutory statement does not, in fact, reflect the terms of the contract although it is submitted that it will be easier for the employee to do this than for the employer, given the latter is the party who has issued the statement.[40]

Enforcement of Provisions Governing Written Statements

If an employer fails to issue a statement (or a statement of change) or 1.34 a statement is issued which does not comply with what is required (in the sense that it is incomplete) the employee may refer the matter to an employment tribunal which can determine what particulars ought to

---

[32] ERA, s.4(1).
[33] *ibid.*, s.4(3)(a).
[34] *ibid.*, s.4(3)(b).
[35] *ibid.*, s.4(4).
[36] *ibid.*, s.4(5).
[37] *ibid.*, s.4(6) and (7).
[38] *ibid.*, s.4(8).
[39] *System Floors (U.K.) v. Daniel* [1981] I.R.L.R. 475, EAT; *Robertson v. British Gas Corporation* [1983] I.R.L.R. 302, CA.
[40] *Lovett v. Wigan MBC*, Court of Appeal, January 12, 2001, unreported.

have been included or referred to in the statement[41] and these particulars will then be deemed to have been given by the employer to the employee.[42] In addition, where a statement has been given under section 1 or section 4 and a question then arises as to the particulars which ought to have been included or referred to in the statement to comply with the legislative requirements either the employer or employee can refer the matter to a tribunal[43] (except if the question raised is whether the employment is contracted out for pension purposes).[44] This provision deals with the situation where a statement is issued but it is considered inaccurate in some respect. On determining a reference under section 11(2) a tribunal may affirm, amend or replace the particulars already issued by the employer and the employer is deemed to have given the corrected particulars to the employee.[45]

Although there have been some decisions to the contrary it is submitted that the authority given to employment tribunals by section 12 to determine the particulars which "ought to have been included" in the statement does not extend to allowing the tribunal to simply invent the terms of the contract (*i.e.* to make the agreement for the parties by deciding what should have been agreed). All the tribunal can do is to record accurately the particulars relating to any contractual term which it finds agreed either expressly or impliedly. If there is nothing to support the existence of an agreement in respect of a particular matter the statement should simply record that there are no particulars.[46]

Any reference to an employment tribunal, whether under section 11(1) or (2) should be made during the course of the employment or within three months of its termination,[47] although the tribunal has a discretion to extend this period if it considers that it was not reasonably practicable for the reference to be made within that time.[48]

STATUTORY EMPLOYMENT RIGHTS AND OBLIGATIONS

1.35 In addition to the rights and obligations deriving from express or implied contractual terms there is an entire framework of rights and obligations derived from statute, including the right not to be unfairly dismissed, the obligation not to discriminate against workers on the grounds of sex, race or disability and a whole complex web of rights and obligations connected with pregnancy and maternity, to name but a few.

Much of the remainder of this text is given over to setting out the statutory rights and obligations which underpin the employment relationship.

---

[41] ERA, s.11(1).
[42] *ibid.*, s.12(1).
[43] ERA, s.11(2).
[44] *ibid.*, s.11(3)(a).
[45] *ibid.*, s.12(2).
[46] *Eagland v. British Telecommunications plc* [1992] I.R.L.R. 323, CA.
[47] ERA, s.11(4)(a).
[48] *ibid.*, s.11(4)(b).

CHAPTER 2

PROTECTION OF THE EMPLOYER'S BUSINESS INTERESTS

IMPLIED AND EXPRESS TERMS IN THE CONTRACT OF EMPLOYMENT

In an increasingly competitive commercial world, employers are seeking 2.01
to protect themselves against leakage of trade secrets and confidential
information by their employees and against the improper use of such
information by former employees. Often, they will also wish to safeguard
themselves against unfair competition from employees and ex-employees
(for example, the enticement of customers). Normally, once these needs
are recognised, the employer will seek to include express terms in the
contract of employment to deal with these matters (for example, a
restrictive covenant). However, there is also a term implied into the
contract of employment which will be of considerable significance where
no express clauses exist.

THE IMPLIED DUTY

There is implied into the contract of employment an obligation of loyalty 2.02
or fidelity on the part of the employee although the limits have not been
clearly defined.[1] Of particular concern is the extent to which such an
implied obligation may survive the termination of the contract of
employment (see below). It should be noted that this term is closely
allied to the "mutual trust and confidence" term; frequently these are
discussed together and often a breach of one can be found to amount to
a breach of the other. In general, the duty of fidelity requires an
employee, during the period when his contract of employment subsists,
to use all reasonable means to advance his employer's business and to
refrain from activities that could injure that business.[2] While a breach of
this term will constitute misconduct and may be such as to justify
dismissal the employer must take care to ensure that the statutory test of

---

[1] *Chill Foods (Scotland) Ltd v. Cool Foods Ltd*, 1977 S.L.T. 38 — see comments of Lord
Maxwell at p.40 but doubted by Lord Osborne in *Joe Walker (Capital Business) Ltd v.
Stuart* 1999 GWD 3–128 in so far as Lord Maxwell suggested that *interim* interdict can be
pronounced even where no *prima facie* case is shown but there is a very strong argument
on the balance of convenience.

[2] *Graham v. R. S. Paton Ltd*, 1917 1 S.L.T. 66.

reasonableness is satisfied and in particular that dismissal lies within the band of reasonable responses. To a large degree, each case must be determined on its own facts but an employer might be justified in taking into account the nature of the business itself, the seniority of the employee, the extent to which the employee has access to confidential information, and the extent to which those activities could damage the business in assessing whether dismissal is appropriate. There is a fine line between having an intention to set up in competition with your employer and taking steps that breach the implied duty of fidelity and if the employee crosses that line then dismissal is likely to be fair.[3]

Seeking employment with a competitor

2.03   Seeking employment with a competitor or giving notice prior to going to work for one is not generally an admissible reason for dismissal, unless there are grounds to believe that the employee is doing so in order to abuse his access to confidential information.[4] In *Attrill v. EAI Limited*[5] the employee was a research physicist involved in highly confidential work. He was summarily dismissed when his employer found a letter on his desk from an employment agency arranging a job interview. The employment tribunal found that there was nothing in the letter to suggest that the employee intended to pass trade secrets to competitors. Thus, there was no breach of his implied duties and the dismissal was unfair.

Employers interests are paramount

2.04   In the event that conflict arises, an employee must place his employer's interests before his own. This is illustrated by one case[6] in which an employed solicitor was informed by a valued client of his employers that the client was dissatisfied with the treatment he received from the employer. The employee was offered and accepted an in-house position with the client to carry out the legal work currently being done by his employing firm. It was held that the implied duty of fidelity required the employee to tell the employer of the client's dissatisfaction rather than saying nothing and accepting the client's offer of employment.

Performing work for another during working hours

2.05   It is clear that the implied duty of fidelity imposes an obligation on employees to work loyally and faithfully for the employer during normal working hours. Thus, an employee who works for another or for himself during those hours will almost certainly be in breach of contract whatever the type of work involved. As the Court of Appeal has made clear[7] an employee is employed to look after his employer's interests, not his own. It will therefore be of little importance whether the work undertaken is in direct competition with the employer or not.

---

[3] *Adamson v. B. & L. Cleaning Services Ltd* [1995] I.R.L.R. 193.
[4] *Harris & Russell Ltd v. Slingsby* [1973] I.C.R. 454.
[5] COIT 2055/158.
[6] *Sanders v. Parry* [1967] 1 W.L.R. 753.
[7] *Wessex Dairies Ltd v. Smith* [1935] 2 K.B. 80.

Spare time working

Does the implied term prevent spare time working? Taking a job   2.06
outside normal working hours is not in itself a breach of the implied duty
of fidelity even where that job involves working for a competitor. The
general rule is that, in the absence of an express term to the contrary, an
employee is free to do what he likes in his spare time. However, any such
activities must not harm or interfere with the employer's legitimate
business interests. Generally, the kind of factors that will be taken into
account in determining whether the damage to the employer is so great
as to breach the employee's implied obligation of fidelity include the
nature of the spare time work, the position of the employee in the main
employer's organisation, his or her hours of work and the risk and extent
of potential commercial harm to the employer. One other point to bear
in mind, however, is that if an employee engages in part-time work—
whether for a competitor or not—and this leads to inefficient performance of his main job this may lead to a fair dismissal[8] on the ground of
capability. Employers who are concerned about spare time working
should be advised to include an express term in contracts of
employment.

Confidential information

With regard to employers' confidential information it has long been   2.07
established that the implied duty of fidelity prevents an employee
disclosing or exploiting confidential information belonging to the
employer to which he has access by virtue of his employment.[9] While it is
difficult to define the exact limits of this duty it is certainly far wider than
that imposed on former employees. The cases suggest that the employee
is required to protect all information conveyed to him in confidence by
his employer. In the leading case of *Faccenda Chicken Ltd v. Fowler*[10] the
Court of Appeal suggested that during the contract the employee is
required by his implied duty to protect his employer's trade secrets,
knowledge he obtains of the employer's customers and their requirements, knowledge of employer's pricing and tendering policies and
generally any other information imparted to him in confidence which
cannot be regarded as trivial. What will be "confidential" will vary from
case to case, depending on the circumstances. What is common
knowledge in one company may be treated as secret and confidential in
another.

In *Norbrook Laboratories Limited v. King and Sands*,[11] the employee,
who happened to be the company accountant, told striking employees
that the company had recently received a substantial grant and that a
large bonus had been paid to the company electrician. He also gave the
strikers information about various payments that had been made to
management. The court held that the employee had breached his

---

[8] *Currie v. Glasgow Central Stores Ltd* (1905) 12 S.L.T. 651.
[9] *Robb v. Green* [1895] 2 Q.B. 315, CA; *Bents Brewery Company Ltd v. Hogan* [1945] 2
All E.R. 570; *Chill Foods (Scotland) Ltd*, above.
[10] [1986] I.C.R. 297; followed in *Poeton Industries Ltd v. Horton* [2000] I.C.R. 1208, CA;
Intelsec Systems Ltd v. Grech Cini [2000] 1 W.L.R. 1190, HC.
[11] [1984] I.R.L.R. 200.

implied duty in disclosing information, which both parties clearly regarded as important information and which the company considered to be confidential and wished to keep hidden. This information was confidential notwithstanding the fact that it could have been ascertained by other means without too much trouble. It should be noted that the mere fact that information has become known to a third party or has been published in some way will not per se mean that a court will not grant an interdict to prevent further disclosure of confidential information.[12] The implied duty will also be broken by the employee memorising a list of his employer's customers for transmission to a third party.[13]

Public interest exception

2.08   The Public Interest Disclosure Act 1998 amended the ERA 1996 to set out the instances where an employee[14] may be protected from both the consequences of breaching any obligations of confidence[15] and from any detriment he may have suffered as a result of making a disclosure. Section 43A states that a disclosure must relate to one of the specified categories of subject matter set out in the Act (a "qualifying disclosure"),[16] *and* the disclosure must then be made in a specified manner.[17] The worker must then have suffered a detriment. A qualifying disclosure is one which, in the *reasonable belief* of the worker making the disclosure, (*i.e.* the test is subjective), tends to show one or more of the following[18]:

- That a criminal offence has been committed or is likely to be committed.
- That a person has failed, is failing or is likely to fail to comply with any legal obligation to which he or she is subject.
- That a miscarriage of justice has occurred, is occurring or is likely to occur.
- That the health and safety of any individual has been, is being or is likely to be endangered.
- That the environment has been or is likely to be damaged, or.
- That the information tending to show any of the above has been, is being or is likely to be deliberately concealed.

The appropriate methods of disclosure are set out in sections 43C to 43H. The provisions seek to ensure that the person responsible for the "relevant failure"[19] is the person to whom the disclosure should be

---

[12] *Speed Seal Products Ltd v. Paddington* [1986] 1 All E.R. 91, CA; *Lord Advocate v Scotsman Publications Ltd*, 1989 S.C. (HL) 122.

[13] *Faccenda Chicken Ltd*, above; and *Liverpool Victoria Friendly Society Ltd v. Houston* (1900) 3 F. 42. The memorisation need not be deliberate: *SBJ Stephenson Ltd v. Mandy* [2000] I.R.L.R. 233.

[14] The provisions are not limited to employees but extend to "workers": s.43K

[15] s.43J.

[16] s.43B.

[17] ss.43C to 43H.

[18] s.43B.

[19] See s.43L

addressed rather than the worker going straight to, *e.g.* the media. The six kinds of disclosure that are potentially protected are:

- A disclosure in good faith to the worker's employer or to another person responsible for the wrongdoing—s.43C.
- A disclosure to a legal adviser—s.43D.
- A disclosure in good faith to a Minister of the Crown where the worker or his employer is appointed under an enactment by a Minister of the Crown—s.43E.
- A disclosure to the relevant prescribed person—s.43F.[20] (1) Where the worker reasonably believes that he will be subjected to detriment by his employer if he makes the disclosure to his employer or the prescribed person, or (2) that there being no prescribed person he reasonably believes that the evidence relating to the relevant failure will be destroyed if he informs his employer, or (3) he has already made the disclosure to his employer or the prescribed person—s.43G. For any of the above conditions to apply the disclosure must also be made in good faith, with a genuine belief that the allegation is true, that the worker does not make any personal gain from the disclosure, and in all the circumstances of the case, it is reasonable for him to make the disclosure.[21]

If a worker claims that he has been unfairly dismissed by reason of him making a protected disclosure under section 103A, it is notable that he does not require one year's service nor is there any limit on the compensatory award. The worker is also protected from being subjected to action short of dismissal under section 47B.

In summary, where employment is continuing, the implied duty of fidelity is such that the employee must not misuse or disclose: (1) information which is imparted to him in confidence; or (2) specific trade secrets even although he knows the information by heart (*Faccenda Chicken Ltd*). The extent of the duty will vary depending on the nature of the contract and the public interest exception should be noted.

Confidential information after the contract ends

In the absence of an express term, is the (ex) employee under any 2.09 continuing duty once the contract of employment comes to an end? This is fully discussed in *Faccenda Chicken Ltd*. In this case F had left his position as Sales Manager of Faccenda Chicken Limited to set up in business selling chickens from refrigerated vans in the same area as FC Limited operated a very similar business. FC Limited alleged that P was unlawfully making use of their sales information which comprised names and addresses of the company's customers and their usual requirements; best route information for vans; customers preferred delivery times and days; and price structures. The company considered this package of

---

[20] See Public Interest Disclosure (Prescribed Persons) Order 1999 (S.I. 1999 No. 1549).
[21] See s.43G(3) for the factors to which regard should be had in determining the reasonableness of the disclosure

information was confidential. The Court of Appeal held that once the employment ceases, there is a continuing duty on an ex-employee not to use or disclose certain information but this obligation will only cover information that is of a sufficiently high degree of confidentiality so as to amount to a trade secret or its equivalent. It does not extend to cover information which is merely "confidential" in the sense that unauthorised disclosure during the course of the employment would be a breach of the duty of good faith.

Thus, it is essential to distinguish between information that amounts to a trade secret or its equivalent and information that is merely confidential and that an employee is free to use to his advantage once his employment has ended. This is by no means an easy task; the Court of Appeal in *Faccenda Chicken* did set out some guidelines for identifying trade secrets although it made it clear that it is necessary to consider all the circumstances of a case and that these guidelines are simply some of the matters which should be taken into account. Specific note should be made of the following:

1. the nature of employment—employment where the employee habitually handled "confidential" information may impose a higher duty of confidentiality;
2. the nature of the information—was it akin to a trade secret and did only a limited number of employees have access to that kind of information?;
3. did the employer impress on the employee the confidentiality of the information at the time?; and
4. can the "secret" be easily isolated from other information which the employee is free to use or disclose? If the "secret" cannot be easily isolated the inference will be that it is not protectable after the contract comes to an end.

2.10   In the *Faccenda Chicken* case the employer was particularly anxious to protect pricing and discount information. It was agreed by the parties that the package of sales information contained some material which was not confidential. The Court of Appeal held that the price information was not clearly severable from the rest of the sales information; that none of the sales information was obviously secretive or sensitive; that the information was necessarily required by salesmen in order to do their work and readily committed to memory; that the information was generally known to junior level employees; and that no express instructions had ever been given that the sales information was to be treated as confidential. The Court concluded that neither the sales information as a whole nor the price information in isolation fell into the category of trade secrets. However, it should also be noted that the Court of Appeal did accept that in some circumstances the price information could be the equivalent of a trade secret (for example, the price in a tender document or the price to be charged for a new model of car in production).

The reasoning in the *Faccenda Chicken* case has been followed in Scotland.[22]

---

[22] *Harben Pumps (Scotland Ltd) v. Lafferty*, 1989 S.L.T. 752; *Malden Timber v. McLeish*, 1992 S.L.T. 727.

In *Symbian Ltd v. Christensen*[23] it was held that an employee who is placed on garden leave is relieved from his duty of good faith and fidelity as the employment relationship is thereby brought to an end. However since the contract continue to regulate the parties' relationship while the employee was on garden leave he could be prevented from working for a competitor by virtue of the clause in his contract requiring that the employee did not concern himself with any other business or occupation while he was employed by the plaintiffs.

EXPRESS COVENANTS

The general rule is that all contractual restraints on an ex-employee's 2.11 freedom to work where he or she pleases are void as being in restraint of trade and contrary to public policy unless they can be shown to be reasonable. A restraint may be found to be reasonable and therefore enforceable if it gives adequate, but no more than adequate, protection to the legitimate interests of an employer. The exclusion of competition *per se* is not a legitimate interest for protection because public policy demands that trade shall be free.[24] The first question to be asked, therefore, is whether the employer has rights that require protection. This is to be judged by looking at the nature of the employer's business and the employee's position within that business.[25] The rights for which an employer may in principle seek protection are: (1) trade connections, suppliers, customer base[26]; and (2) trade secrets and other confidential information.[27]

It is important that a distinction is made between information that can be regarded as, in some sense, the employer's property and that which has become part of the employee's general knowledge and "know how". Simply by working, an employee will develop skills and enhance his experience and general knowledge; he is perfectly entitled to put these attributes to the use of a new employer.[28] Moreover, where the true skills and art of a job lie in the make up of the person performing (his personality, ability to get on with others, etc.), the employer will not be able to establish a proprietary right in customer connections built up by the employee as a result of these personal qualities.[29]

The Court of Appeal suggested in *Faccenda Chicken* that the duty of fidelity would be broken where an employee *deliberately* memorised confidential information, *e.g.* a list of clients. However, "Many true and vital trade secrets in the strict sense, including such things as the ingredients of chemical compounds and other sophisticated products must rest firmly in the minds of those who have worked with them and been interested in them, ready for recall". The use by an ex-employee of

---

[23] [2001] I.R.L.R. 77, CA.

[24] *Nordenfelt v. Maxim Nordenfelt Guns and Ammunition Company* [1894] A.C. 535, HL; *Scottish Farmers Dairy Company (Glasgow) Ltd v. McGhee*, 1933 S.C. 148.

[25] *Herbert Morris Ltd v. Saxelby* [1916] 1 A.C. 688, HL.

[26] *Scottish Farmers Dairy Company*, above.

[27] *A. & D. Bedrooms v. Michael*, 1984 S.L.T. 297.

[28] *FSS Travel & Leisure Systems Ltd v. Johnson* [1998] I.R.L.R. 382, CA.

[29] *Cantor Fitzgerald (U.K.) Ltd v. Wallace* [1992] I.R.L.R. 215, QB.

confidential information gained from his former employer will not be exempt from the nexus of confidentiality just because it is information he innocently absorbed while employed as opposed to information he learned with a deliberate intention to misappropriate.[30] Clearly, there exists a fine dividing line between the information that can be protected and that which cannot.[31]

Is the restraint reasonable and in the public interest?

2.12　　Assuming the employer has a legitimate interest to protect, the court will then seek to determine whether the restriction contained in the restrictive covenant is reasonable between the parties and in the public interest. In making this assessment the court will examine the length of time the restriction will last, the area it will cover and the capacity in which it will affect the employee.

Geographical restriction

2.13　　Where the purpose of the restrictive covenant is to protect trade secrets the employer may be able to support a wider geographical restriction than can be sustained where the employer's aim is the protection of business connections. Thus, in one case[32] a management trainee had agreed to a restrictive covenant which prevented him from taking up employment with a competitor of his employer, Bluebell Apparel (which produced Wrangler jeans) in any capacity whatsoever for a period of two years after the termination of employment. He took up employment with Levi Strauss and although there was no geographical limitation contained in the covenant it was upheld on the basis that it was reasonable for the protection of Wrangler's trade secrets. The court recognised that the manufacturing of jeans was a world wide business and stated that the prohibition against disclosing trade secrets was worthless unless accompanied by a restriction preventing the employee from entering the employment of rivals.

Protection of business connections

2.14　　The courts are likely to be even more critical of covenants which purport to protect client or trade connections. In *Spencer v. Marchington*[33] the restraint imposed on the former employee of an

---

[30] *SBJ Stephenson Ltd v. Mandy* [2000] I.R.L.R. 233, QBD. The relevant distinction between what is the employer's property and what is the employee's property is to be found in the speech of Lord Shaw in *Herbert Morris Ltd v. Saxelby* [1916] 1 A.C. 688 at 714.

[31] See *Jack Allen (Sales and Service) Ltd v. Smith* [1999] I.R.L.R. 19, OH for the tests that must be satisfied where an *interim* interdict is sought. See also *Oil Technics Ltd v. Thistle Chemicals Ltd*, 1997 S.L.T. 416 and *Osborne v. BBC*, 2000 S.C. 29 for the position where a pursuer seeks to interdict a third party from using or publishing information which was rendered confidential by an agreement to which the defender was not party. Any interdict must accurately specify the information to which it applies: *International Computers Ltd v. Eccleson*, 2000 G.W.D. 28–1074.

[32] *Bluebell Apparel Ltd v. Dickinson*, 1978 S.C. 16; 1980 S.L.T. 157. This case can be contrasted with *Commercial Plastics Ltd v. Vincent* [1964] 3 All E.R. 546, CA; and *Greer v. Sketchley Ltd* [1979] I.R.L.R. 445, CA. Cf. *Scully UK Ltd v. Lee* [1998] I.R.L.R. 259, CA where it was noted by the Court of Appeal that with business becoming increasingly global, a clause that seeks to restrict an employee's future activities beyond the UK will not necessarily be unreasonable.

[33] [1988] I.R.L.R. 392.

employment agency purported to prevent the individual from carrying on an employment agency within a radius of 25 miles of one of the offices where she was employed. It was held that this restriction was more than was required to protect the defendant's legitimate interests given that only one of the customers of the relevant office was to be found in an area of more than 20 miles radius from the office. The court was not willing to sever the offending restriction or to recast it so as to render it enforceable. In another case involving an employment agency[34] the covenants in the contract of employment of a Branch Manager and consultant to the agency were held to be invalid in circumstances where the geographical area was limited to a radius of 1,000 metres of the branch at which they worked. Although this radius was small the location of the branch where they worked meant that the area covered most of the City of London. It is therefore extremely important that in selecting geographical limits the scope of the restraint thus created is examined carefully. A similar approach has been taken in Scotland.[35]

Covenants may also be unenforceable because they seek to protect too wide a base of trade connections in some other respect. In one Scottish case[36] the restriction on the employee was that he should not work for any previous or present client of his employer's group of companies for a period of 18 months after the termination of his employment with his employing company. The court held that the previous clients of the employer could no longer be regarded as a protectable interest. There were no current commercial connections to be protected in relation to this group of clients and the company. The court was also concerned that there was no area limit on the restriction, given that the ex-employee had only worked in Scotland and that the restriction prevented the employee from dealing with clients of the group rather than the employing company itself. In the end the court concluded that the restriction was unreasonably wide and therefore void.[37]

Office Angels v. Rainer-Thomas[38] is a good example of a court studying the stated purpose of a covenant and its practical effect. The stated purpose of the covenant was to protect the goodwill of the clients of the company. As previously indicated it provided that the employee could not operate an employment agency within a 1,000 metre radius of the branch at which he worked. The court, however, noted that the business carried on by Office Angels Limited was carried on almost entirely over the telephone and that therefore where a new business might be located would be immaterial and would not protect the goodwill of Office Angels Limited. The court also made clear that where the employer expressly states a purpose for a restrictive covenant he is not permitted at a later date to add to or amend that purpose. The employers had attempted to argue that the purpose of the covenant was also to protect their connections with temporary workers. The court regarded this as a

---

[34] *Office Angels v. Rainer-Thomas* [1991] I.R.L.R. 214, CA followed in *FSS Travel & Leisure Systems Ltd v. Johnson* [1998] I.R.L.R. 382.

[35] *Dallas v. Simpson*, 1989 S.L.T. 454.

[36] *Hinton & Higgs UK Ltd v. Murphy,* 1988 S.C. 353; [1989] I.R.L.R. 519.

[37] See also *Marley Tile Company Ltd v. Johnstone* [1982] I.R.L.R. 75, CA; *Attwood v. Lamont* [1920] 3 K.B. 571, CA at 577; and *Routh v. Jones* [1947] 1 All E.R. 758, CA.

[38] [1991] I.R.L.R. 214, CA.

separate interest from the protection of customer goodwill. The court was also satisfied that a non-solicitation clause rather than a non-employment clause would have protected the goodwill without having the same adverse effects on trade and on the employee's ability to earn his living. This made it more difficult for the employer to argue that a restrictive covenant on non-employment should be upheld.

In another recent case, the principles derived from Office Angels were applied by the Court of Appeal in holding that a non-solicitation clause preventing the employee from soliciting the trade of the employer's customers with whom he dealt is not bound to be held invalid just because there is no time-limit on the past period when such dealings took place. A non-solicitation clause which is restricted to customers with whom the employee has in the past been in personal contact is capable of amounting to a reasonable restraint for the protection of the employer's business.[39]

Protection for a group of companies

2.15   It is interesting to speculate whether restrictive covenants can ever protect not just the interests of the employer but of the group of employers of which the company forms part. *Hinton & Higgs Ltd v. Murphy*[40] considers this point among others. Can the employer have a legitimate interest in protecting the trade connections not just of his particular company but of associated or subsidiary companies? In one case[41] the Lord Ordinary seemed prepared to "lift the veil" and treat the employing company and its subsidiaries as a single group for the purpose of examining the scope of a restrictive covenant which provided that the employee would not "be concerned or interested in any business in competition with the employer or of any subsidiary or associated company".

The categories of enforceability for restrictive covenants are not restricted to employer/employee relationships or to the sale of a business and are capable of applying between joint venturers.[42]

Transfer of undertakings

2.16   Because of the nature of restrictive covenants an interesting question arises in relation to a transfer of an undertaking. In another Scottish case, *Initial Supplies Limited v. McCall*[43] Lord Coulsfield expressed concern about the circumstances where a business in which an employee was employed was bought over by a company with a much larger group of clients and trade connections. The whole character of the restrictive covenant would thus change were it to apply automatically to the new employment by virtue of the Transfer of Undertakings (Protection of

---

[39] *Dentmaster (U.K.) Ltd v. Kent* [1997] I.R.L.R. 636.
[40] [1989] I.R.L.R. 519.
[41] *Group Four Total Security Ltd v. Ferrier*, 1985 S.C. 70.
[42] *Dawnay, Day & Co. Ltd v. De Braconier D'Alphen* [1997] I.R.L.R. 442, CA where there is a restrictive covenant in an agreement between undertakings, if the restriction has the effect of preventing, restricting or distorting competition, it may fall foul of the Competition Act 1998, see generally Whish, *Competition Law* (4th ed., 2000).
[43] 1990 S.C.L.R. 559.

Employment) Regulations 1981.[44] In this case the employer's application for an interim interdict to enforce the restrictive covenant was refused. In a more recent case in England[45] the Court of Appeal held that the key words in regulation 5 of the 1981 Regulations: "the contract shall have effect after the transfer as if originally made between the persons so employed and the transferee", have a retrospective effect in the sense that they are to be read as referring to the transferee as the owner of the business transferred. Accordingly, a restrictive covenant could be enforced against an employee if within a prohibited period, he did business with persons who had done business with the undertaking transferred. The plaintiffs in this case were deemed as a result of the transfer retrospectively to have been the owner.

Severability

If the clause in an employment contract acts as an unreasonable 2.17 restraint of trade the courts will refuse to rewrite it so as to convert it into a reasonable one. The clause will simply be struck out as unenforceable because the employer has tried to cast a net too wide in some respect. However, where restrictive covenants are drawn in such a way that they comprise a series of independent and severable obligations, the courts may "sever" or excise the offending portion and enforce the remainder of the covenant. This is sometimes called the "blue pencil" test; if the offending words can simply be deleted by a pencil line they are severable. It seems that this approach may be taken where the part which is left is an independent obligation, provided that the character of the covenant obligation stays the same. In a Scottish case[46] the Lord Ordinary was prepared to delete the words "or previous" from the wording of a restrictive covenant that related to "existing or previous" customers. He was clearly influenced by the fact that the covenant itself provided that it would remain valid if a part was deleted or if the period of its application was reduced. It was also stated that the parties agreed to abide by the covenant with any necessary modification. However, although the Lord Ordinary did accept the removal of the words "or previous" as a deletion it should be noted that this part of his judgment is probably obiter in that he had already concluded that the restriction was invalid and unenforceable for other reasons.

Some drafters include a clause in the agreement to the effect that, in the event that any such restriction should be found to be void but would be valid if some part thereof could be deleted or the period or area of application reduced, such restriction should apply with such modification as may be necessary to make it valid and effective. This is often known as an automatic amendment clause. However, such a clause was considered in one case in Scotland[47] in which Lord Coulsfield stated that he did not think that an express clause to the effect that the parties would be bound by a modified covenant enabled the court to do anything which

---

[44] S.I. 1981 No. 1794.
[45] *Morris Angel & Son Ltd v. Hollande* [1993] I.C.R. 71; *Credit Suisse First Boston (Europe) Ltd v. Padiachy* [1998] I.R.L.R. 504.
[46] *Hinton & Higgs Ltd v. Murphy* [1989] I.R.L.R. 519.
[47] *Living Design (Home Improvements) Ltd v. Davidson* [1994] I.R.L.R. 67.

could not have been done otherwise. Thus he stated: "It is recognised that even in the absence of such a clause the court can sever the unreasonable part of a restriction where that can be done simply by deleting that offending part without in consequence re-writing the contract or altering it's scope". Lord Coulsfield continued, quoting with approval the cautionary observations in *Mason v. Provident Clothing Company*[48] in which Lord Moulton stated that there should be severance only if the enforceable part is clearly severable and even so only where it is of trivial importance or technical and not part of the main import and substance of the clause. Applying that approach to the facts of *Living Design*, Lord Coulsfield concluded that the "however terminated" clause (see below) could not be regarded as trivial and was not therefore capable of severance. In a case that was not cited to Lord Coulsfield[49] the Privy Council suggested that "scope" in this context simply means the nature of the contract as a whole and accepted that severance is partly a question of the parties intentions.

2.18   A restrictive covenant can only be relied on and enforced by the employer if the employer himself has not breached the employment contract. For example, if an employee is dismissed without notice in a situation where such a dismissal is not justified the employer is in breach and therefore cannot rely on the restrictive covenant contained within the employment contract. In order to attempt to guard against these dangers some drafters insert a clause into the covenant stating that the restriction in the covenant will continue to apply after the termination of employment however that termination comes about and whether the termination is lawful or unlawful. Such a clause was considered in the Living Design case referred to above. Ms Davidson was Promotions Manager of Living Design, a company which sold double glazing throughout Scotland. In return for the sum of £5,000 she signed a covenant to the effect that she would not, within Scotland and the North of England, for a period of six months after the termination of her employment (however it came about whether lawful or unlawful) be directly engaged, concerned or interested in any capacity in any other business or trade that was substantially the same as the business carried on by the company or any of its subsidiaries. Ms Davidson then left Living Design's employment, each party claiming that the other was in breach. Living Design applied for interim interdict in terms of the restrictive covenant. However, Lord Coulsfield refused the application, following the statements made obiter by Scott J. in *Briggs v. Oates*[50] and held that a "restrictive covenant which is phrased so as to operate on the termination of the employment of an employee however that comes about and whether lawfully or not is manifestly wholly unreasonable".

In *Turner v. Commonwealth & British Minerals Ltd*,[51] it was held that payment of a sum to an employee to gain acceptance of a restrictive covenant does not obviate the need for the covenant to pass the test of reasonableness, though the fact that the payment was made will be taken

---

[48] [1913] A.C. 724.
[49] *Amoco Australian PTY Ltd v. Rocca Brothers Motor Engineering Company PTY Ltd* [1975] A.C. 561 at 578.
[50] [1990] I.R.L.R. 471.
[51] [2000] I.R.L.R. 114, CA.

into consideration.[52] Where the employer has paid a specific sum for a restrictive covenant subsequently held to be unenforceable, the sum may have to be repaid by the employee.[53]

In *Lux Traffic Control Limited v. Healey*[54] the covenant provided that the restrictions would continue to apply for a period of three years after the termination of the employee's contract "however such employment may be terminated". Lord Abernethy followed Living Design and held that the "however terminated" wording made the entire restriction unreasonably wide and recalled the interim interdict. Living Design was followed without any discussion of the different wording of the "however terminated" clause.[55]

In a more recent decision[56] on this issue the Court of Appeal has held that some earlier decisions including *Living Design* and *Lux Traffic Control* were wrongly decided. In *Rock Refrigeration Ltd v. Jones*[57] the contract of employment included a covenant expressed as operating upon determination of the contract "howsoever arising" or "howsoever occasioned". Mr Jones left the company to join a competitor. The Court of Appeal held that such a clause is not void from the beginning as an unreasonable restraint of trade. Instead, if there is a repudiatory breach of the contract by the employer then the employee is released from his obligations and the restrictive covenant cannot be enforced against him. The Court of Session reached the same conclusion by deciding that the phrase "howsoever caused" should not be construed as covering unlawful termination, reaffirming the decision in *Aramark*.[58] Some drafters also insert an express declaration in restrictive covenants to the effect that the parties agree that the covenant is reasonable. A court will not be bound by this, seeing it as an attempt to oust its jurisdiction. It must also not be forgotten that courts have a duty to enforce the public interest. This duty will override the parties' own declarations as to the reasonableness of the agreement.

Public interest

It should be borne in mind that even if a covenant represents a fair 2.19 balance between employer and employee it may be declared void in the public interest.[59] However, there is little authority on what will be construed to be against the public interest in this area. The case of *Initial Services v. Putterill*[60] concerned the implied duty of fidelity but it clearly has implications for express covenants as well. In *Bull v. Pitney Bowes Ltd*[61] there was a restriction in the employee's contract, which meant that if he took up employment with a competitor after retirement he would

---

[52] See also *TSC Europe (UK) Ltd v. Massey* [1999] I.R.L.R. 22, para. 49.
[53] *Credit Suisse First Boston (Europe) Ltd v. Padiachy* [1998] I.R.L.R. 504.
[54] 1994 S.L.T. 1153.
[55] But compare with *Aramark plc v. Sommerville*, 1995 S.L.T. 749 where similar wording produced a different result.
[56] *Rock Refrigeration Ltd v. Jones* [1996] I.R.L.R. 675.
[57] [1996] I.R.L.R. 675.
[58] *P.R. Consultants Scotland Ltd v. Mann* [1996] I.R.L.R. 188.
[59] *Nordenfelt v. Maxim Nordenfelt Guns and Ammunition Company* [1894] A.C. 535, HL.
[60] [1967] 3 All E.R. 145, CA.
[61] [1967] 1 W.L.R. 273.

lose his company pension. He did take up employment with an organisation regarded by his employer as being a competitor. This led to his pension being stopped. The court came to the conclusion that public interest was involved because the salary which he would require to receive from his new employers was higher than it would otherwise have been in that they had to compensate him for his loss of pension. As a result of this the prices the new employer would have to charge members of the public would be much greater. The restriction was thus seen to be against the public interest. The public interest is more generally involved in all restrictive covenants as the court must take account of it in determining the reasonableness of the restriction in the light of the principle that the public should have access to free market services.

Other sources of protection of employer's business interests

2.20   The rights of an employer and an employee to an invention made on or after June 1, 1978 are regulated exclusively by section 39 of the Patents Act 1977.

The employee's implied duty of fidelity is irrelevant to the determination of ownership of an invention. Section 42(2) renders unenforceable any contractual term which "diminishes the employee's rights" in inventions made by him after June 1, 1978 and after the date of the contract.[62] However, section 42(3) provides that section 42(2) must not be construed as in any way derogating from "any duty of confidentiality" owed by the employee to his or her employee. Thus, it may be difficult for an employee to exploit an invention if he or she made use of any confidential information in designing it.[63]

Copyright

2.21   The Copyright, Designs and Patents Act 1988 covers "literary, dramatic, musical or artistic works". Literary work includes computer programmes. The general rule is that the ownership of copyright in a work vests in the author. However, employees constitute a major exception to this principle as section 11(2) of the 1988 Act states that a work made by an employee "in the course of his employment" belongs to the employer, subject to any agreement to the contrary.[64] The author's moral rights to be identified as author or director are not infringed by anything done or authorised to be done by the author's employer where the copyright in the work was first vested in the employer.[65] Note that while moral rights are inalienable by the author *inter vivos*, under section 87, an author can waive his moral rights.

---

[62] *Greater Glasgow Health Board's Application* [1996] R.P.C. 207; *Harris' Patent* [1985] R.P.C. 19, quoted in *Staeng Ltd's Application* [1996] R.P.C. 183.

[63] See *Goddin and Rennie's Application* [1996] R.P.C. 141, OH.

[64] Proprietary remedies are to be distinguished from claims based on breach of confidence: *International Computers Ltd v. Eccleson*, 2000 G.W.D. 28–1074.

[65] See s.79(3) and s.82(1)(a) respectively and generally Cornish, *Intellectual Property* (3rd ed., 1999).

Law of delict

The law in relation to "passing off" can offer some protection to an   2.22
employer's business interests. There also exists a civil remedy in respect
of "inducing a breach of contract". This would cover the situation where
a third party induced an employee to break his contract of employment
by disclosing the employer's trade secrets or other confidential
information.

CHAPTER 3

SEX AND RACE DISCRIMINATION

INTRODUCTION

3.01 The Sex Discrimination Act 1975 (SDA) is the central United Kingdom legislative provision in the field of sex discrimination. The Race Relations Act 1976 (RRA) was modelled on the SDA. Accordingly, much of the case law decided under the SDA is useful in interpreting the RRA and vice versa, although a degree of care should be taken since, to date, the interpretation of the SDA has been influenced by E.C. law which has not played a significant role in the law governing racial discrimination. That position is very likely to change, given that Article 13 of the Treaty of Amsterdam states that the Council may take appropriate action to combat discrimination based on sex, racial or ethnic origin, religion or belief, disability, age or sexual orientation. Consequent upon this the Council has adopted a new Equal Treatment Framework Directive on Discrimination in Employment[1] and a Race Directive.[2]

The scope of both Acts extends far beyond the field of employment. Each establishes a regulatory Commission[3] with a range of powers including the ability to fund legal assistance for claimants[4] as well as making it unlawful to discriminate in the provision of services and education and in advertising. There are also provisions making it unlawful for trade unions,[5] training providers,[6] qualifying bodies[7] and employment agencies[8] to discriminate. However, the remainder of this chapter will focus on the legislative provisions of most relevance in the employment context.

---

[1] Directive 2000/78/EC. Those provisions relating to sexual orientation and religious discrimination must be implemented by December 2, 2003, those relating to age and disability discrimination must be implemented by December 2, 2006.

[2] Directive 2000/43/EC, to be implemented by July 19, 2003. See generally para. 3.38 et seq. below.

[3] SDA, s.53 establishes the Equal Opportunities Commission (EOC); RRA, s.43 establishes the Commission for Racial Equality (CRE).

[4] SDA, ss.56A–61, ss.67–75 and Sched. 3; RRA, ss.47–52, ss.58–67 and Sched. 1.

[5] SDA, s.12; RRA, s.11.

[6] SDA, s.14; RRA, s.13. See Lana v. Positive Action Training in Housing (London) Ltd [2001] I.R.L.R. 501, EAT, particularly in relation to the interaction between SDA s.14 and s.41(2) which is such that where an organisation agrees to provide or make available training, and does so by using another agency, the principal organisation will be liable for any act of discrimination which falls within the scope of that agency arrangement.

[7] SDA, s.13; RRA, s.12; see also Jepson and Dyas-Elliott v. Labour Party [1996] I.R.L.R. 116. A political party is likely to be a "qualifying body" under s.12 in terms of its relations with prospective local government candidates—Sawyer v. Ahsan [1999] I.R.L.R. 609, EAT.

[8] SDA, s.15; RRA, s.14.

WORKERS PROTECTED AGAINST DISCRIMINATION

Part 2 of the SDA and the RRA is headed "Discrimination in the 3.02 Employment Field". SDA, s.6 and RRA, s.4 prohibit discrimination against job applicants and employees[9] in relation to recruitment, job offer terms, access to opportunities for promotion, transfer or training and access to benefits, facilities and services.[10] In addition, dismissal due to sex or race or subjection to any other detriment is also unlawful. All of the foregoing applies to employment in establishments in Great Britain; an employee will be regarded as so employed unless s/he does his or her work wholly outside Great Britain.[11] There is a limited exception to the provisions of SDA, s.6 and RRA, s.4 where sex or race is a genuine occupational qualification for a particular job.[12] Thus, for example, if it was genuinely necessary to restrict access to a job to one sex or another for reasons of authenticity, privacy or decency or because of restrictions on accommodation in live-in jobs such action would fall within the genuine occupational qualification (GOQ) exception.[13]

"Employment" is defined in section 82(1) of the SDA and section 78 of the RRA as "employment under a contract of service or of apprenticeship or a contract personally to execute any work or labour". This definition of employment is wider than that which applies under the unfair dismissal provisions in ERA, the latter being confined to those under a contract of service or apprenticeship. In *Hugh Jones v. St John's College Cambridge*[14] it was held that although a research fellow was not employed under a contract of service she was engaged in the execution of work or labour in terms of section 82(1) and her treatment fell within the provisions of the SDA. In *Quinnen v. Hovells*[15] the EAT held "the concept of a contract for the engagement of personal work or labour, lying outside the scope of the master-servant relationship, is a wide and flexible one intended by Parliament to be interpreted as such". In this case a self-employed individual who worked on a commission only basis for a man who moved around department stores hiring a pitch to sell fancy goods, came within the terms of the SDA. The question also arose in *Gillick v. Roevin Management Services and B.P. Chemicals Ltd*[16] in

---

[9] A claim will survive the death of the applicant and rights will pass to the estate—*Harris (personal representative of Andrews deceased) v. Lewisham & Guy's Mental Health NHS Trust* [2000] I.R.L.R. 320, CA.

[10] While a claim of discrimination in relation to pay is specifically excluded from the SDA by s.6 (being dealt with instead under the EPA) such a claim may be made under the RRA—see *Wakeman and others v. Quick Corporation and another* [1999] I.R.L.R. 424, CA for an example of such a claim under the RRA.

[11] The Equal Opportunities (Employment Legislation) (Territorial Limits) Regulations 1999 (S.I. 1999 No. 3163) widened the coverage of the SDA which, prior to their coming into force, did not cover individuals who worked "mainly" outside Great Britain.

[12] SDA, s.7; RRA, s.5.

[13] SDA, s.7 and RRA, s.5 set out additional circumstances where sex or race may be a GOQ. See also *Neil v. Watts* and *Carlton v. Personnel Hygiene Services Ltd*, E.O.R. DCLD No. 3, p.2.

[14] [1979] I.C.R. 848.

[15] [1984] I.R.L.R. 227, EAT; In *Kelly v. Northern Ireland Housing Executive* [1998] I.R.L.R. 593, HL it was held that a partner in a firm of solicitors, who would be carrying out the work available, could fall within the definition.

[16] [1993] I.R.L.R. 437, EAT.

which an agency worker was held to be an employee of an employment agency for the purpose of the SDA. Her relationship with B.P., the company with whom she was placed, was governed by the provisions of section 9 of the SDA which covers discrimination against contract workers.[17] Section 9 applies not just to discrimination between men and women who are both contract workers, but also as between a contract worker and a full-time employee providing they are employed by the same principal.[18] *Patefield v. Belfast City Council*[19] exemplifies the application of section 9[20] in the context of pregnancy related sex discrimination.

Both the SDA and the RRA also prohibit discrimination in partnerships[21] and by or in relation to barristers and advocates.[22] In addition police officers are deemed to be employees for the purposes of the Acts.[23] While statutory office holders are excluded from the scope of the SDA[24] and RRA[25] it has been held that they may be "workers" who are in "employment" within the meaning of European Community law, and thus entitled to bring equal pay and sex discrimination complaints, notwithstanding that they do not fall within the definition of "employment" under domestic equal pay and sex discrimination legislation.[26]

DISCRIMINATION

3.03 Discrimination on the ground of sex or race can be either direct or indirect. Section 1(1)(a) of the SDA defines direct sex discrimination. It involves treating a woman less favourably on the ground of sex than a man is, or would be, treated.[27] The inclusion of the words "would be" makes it clear that it is perfectly legitimate to have a hypothetical comparator in a claim under the SDA, unlike the situation with the Equal Pay Act 1970[28] where a named comparator is required. In making the comparison required by the SDA the relevant circumstances in both cases must be the same or not materially different.[29] In other words, like must be compared with like so far as possible. The most obvious type of direct sex discrimination occurs when employers act upon stereotypical

---

[17] See RRA, s.7.

[18] *Allonby v. Accrington & Rossendale College* [2001] I.R.L.R. 364, CA.

[19] [2000] I.R.L.R. 664. See also *(1) Hansbury (2) Brook Street Bureau v. Electronic Data Systems Ltd* EAT/128/00, March 29, 2001.

[20] To be exact, the case deals with the equivalent Northern Ireland legislative provision which is in identical terms to SDA, s.9.

[21] SDA, s.11; RRA, s.10.

[22] SDA, ss.35A, 35B; RRA, ss.26A, 26B.

[23] SDA, s.17; RRA, s.16.

[24] SDA, s.85(2)

[25] RRA, s.75(2)

[26] *Perceval-Price v. Department of Economic Development* [2000] I.R.L.R. 380—tribunal chairmen of various descriptions were held to be workers under E.C. law.

[27] SDA, s.2, makes it clear that discrimination against men on the ground of sex is similarly unlawful.

[28] Hereinafter EqPA.

[29] SDA, s.5; *Chief Constable of West Yorkshire v. Vento* [2001] I.R.L.R. 124, EAT; *Shamoon v. Chief Constable of the RUC* [2001] I.R.L.R. 520, NICA.

assumptions about the likely behaviour of one sex[30] compared to the other or about one sex being particularly suited to a certain type of work or working environment.[31] Slightly less obviously a decision based upon a gender based criterion will also be directly discriminatory.[32] An example par excellence of such is a decision based upon the fact of a woman's pregnancy or her childbearing capacity. Since only women can become pregnant, adverse treatment on the ground of pregnancy will amount to direct sex discrimination.[33]

MARITAL DISCRIMINATION

Section 3 of the SDA makes it unlawful to discriminate directly or 3.04 indirectly against married persons in the employment field on the ground of their marital status. However, it should be noted that this section provides no remedy to those who suffer discrimination because they are single. This is because section 3 states "a person discriminates against a married person . . . if".[34] This may not comply with the requirements of European Community law and could be subject to challenge in the future. All that is said on the subject of sex discrimination in employment should be taken to apply equally to discrimination on the ground of marital status.

DIRECT RACIAL DISCRIMINATION

Direct racial discrimination occurs where, on racial grounds, a person 3.05 treats another less favourably than he treats or would treat others.[35] Adverse treatment on racial grounds includes treatment based upon "colour, race, nationality or ethnic or national origins".[36] A "racial group" means a group of persons defined by reference to any of the above criteria.[37]

Direct racial discrimination will occur if an individual is treated adversely because of another person's race. In *Showboat Entertainment Centre v. Owens*[38] the applicant, who was white, was dismissed from his job as manager of an amusement arcade for failing to comply with an instruction to exclude black people from the premises. It was held that the words "on racial grounds" are perfectly capable of covering any reason for an action based on race, whether it be the race of the complainant or of others. A complaint of direct racial discrimination by the manager was accordingly upheld.

---

[30] *Horsey v. Dyfed County Council* [1982] I.R.L.R. 395, EAT.
[31] See *Greig v. Community Industry* [1979] I.R.L.R. 158, EAT.
[32] *James v. Eastleigh Borough Council* [1990] I.R.L.R. 288, HL.
[33] *Webb v. EMO Air Cargo (U.K.) Ltd* [1993] I.R.L.R. 27, HL. See Chap. 5 for a more detailed discussion of discrimination and pregnancy/maternity.
[34] *Bick v. Royal West of England Residential School for the Deaf* [1976] I.R.L.R. 326, IT.
[35] RRA, s.1(1)(a).
[36] RRA, s.3(1).
[37] *ibid.*
[38] [1984] I.R.L.R. 7, EAT; see also *Weathersfield Ltd (t/a Van & Truck Rentals) v. Sargent* [1998] I.R.L.R. 14, EAT; aff'd [1999] I.R.L.R. 94, CA.

3.06　　The definition of "racial grounds" has generated a good deal of case law, much of which has focused on the concepts of "ethnic origin" and "ethnic group". In *Mandla v. Dowell Lee*[39] the House of Lords held that for a group to fulfil the definition of an ethnic group for the purposes of the RRA it had to regard itself as a distinct community by virtue of certain characteristics, two of which were essential. These were:

>　1. a long shared history, of which the group was conscious as distinguishing it from other groups; and
>　2. a cultural tradition of its own, including family and social customs and manners, often but not necessarily associated with religious observance.

Certain other characteristics were also held to be relevant to the assessment of whether an ethnic group existed. These were:

>　3. a common geographical origin or descent from a small number of common ancestors;
>　4. a common language although this did not necessarily have to be peculiar to the group;
>　5. a common literature peculiar to the group;
>　6. a common religion different from that of neighbouring groups; and
>　7. the characteristic of being a minority or being oppressed by a dominant group within a larger community.

The House of Lords held that Sikhs were a distinct ethnic group and therefore protected by the Act.

　　Similarly, it has been held that Jews are an ethnic group[40] as are Gypsies.[41] As far as Rastafarians are concerned they have been held not to be an ethnic group.[42] The case law suggests that Muslims will be viewed as a religious rather than racial group. However, often discrimination against individuals who are Muslims will be found to be based on race.

3.07　　The issue of whether the Scots (and English) are members of a "racial group" for the purposes of the RRA has been examined by the EAT in Scotland in *Northern Joint Police Board v. Power*[43] and *BBC Scotland v. Souster.*[44]

　　In the Power case the employment tribunal found that an Englishman fell to be considered within the ambit of the definition of "racial group" and specifically within the scope of the concept of "national origins". Under reference to *Ealing London Borough Council v. Race Relations Board*[45] the EAT examined the distinction between "nationality" (which it considered has a juridical basis pointing to citizenship) and "national

---

[39] [1983] I.R.L.R. 209, HL.
[40] *Seide v. Gillette Industries Ltd* [1980] I.R.L.R. 427, EAT.
[41] *Commission for Racial Equality v. Button* [1989] I.R.L.R. 8, CA.
[42] *Dawkins v. Crown Suppliers (PSA)* [1993] I.R.L.R. 284, CA.
[43] [1997] I.R.L.R. 610, EAT.
[44] 2001 S.C. 458; [2001] I.R.L.R. 150.
[45] [1972] A.C. 342.

origins". It considered that citizens of the constituent parts of the United Kingdom could properly be regarded as of British nationality. In looking at the phrase "national origins" the EAT stated:

> [w]hat has to be ascertained are identifiable elements, both historically and geographically, which at least at some point in time reveals the existence of a nation. Whatever may be difficult fringe questions to this issue, what cannot be in doubt is that both England and Scotland were once separate nations. That, in our opinion, is sufficient to dispose of the matter, since thereafter we agree with the proposition that it is for each individual to show that his origins are embedded in such a nation, and how he chooses to do so requires scrutiny by the Tribunal hearing the application . . . There is therefore no need for the tests . . . in *Mandla* . . . with regard to the question of groups based on ethnic origins in relation to the issue of national origins, since the former by definition need not have, although it might have, a defined historical and geographical base.

In *Souster* the Inner House upheld the decision of the EAT that the applicant could make a relevant claim of racial discrimination under the umbrella of "national origins" in circumstances where he considered that the fact that he was English had been taken into account by the BBC when it failed to extend his contract as the presenter of "Rugby Special". In so doing they rejected the argument that the phrase "national origins" in section 3(1) RRA was limited to nationality in the legal sense and thus to citizenship acquired at birth. The Inner House further agreed with the EAT that the applicant could not bring a claim on the basis that he had been discriminated against on the grounds of his English *ethnic* origins as neither the Scots nor the English can be described as an "ethnic group" for the purposes of the Act. It held that a distinctive racial element is required for recognition as an ethnic group.

The irrelevance of discriminatory motive

A discriminatory motive or intention is not required to establish direct 3.08 sex or racial discrimination.[46] In *James v. Eastleigh Borough Council*[47] the House of Lords held that the test which should be applied in assessing whether there was direct discrimination was the "but for" test. Would the applicant have received the same treatment from the respondent but for his or her sex?

Causation

The fact that the race or sex of an individual was an important factor 3.09 in an employer's decision is enough to found a discrimination claim. It is not necessary that the employer's decision should be based solely on a sex linked or racial consideration.[48]

---

[46] *R. v. Birmingham City Council, ex p. Equal Opportunities Commission (No. 1)* [1989] I.R.L.R. 173, HL.

[47] [1990] I.R.L.R. 288, HL.

[48] *Owen and Briggs v. James* [1982] I.R.L.R. 502, CA.

DEFINITION OF INDIRECT DISCRIMINATION

3.10 With effect from October 12, 2001, as a result of the provisions of the Sex Discrimination (Indirect Discrimination and Burden of Proof) Regulations 2001[49] there are two definitions of indirect discrimination under the SDA. The one which is applicable will depend upon the provisions of the Act upon which reliance is placed. Section 1(1)(b) of the SDA contains the definition of indirect discrimination which has been in force since the SDA was first enacted. It states:

"(1) A person discriminates against a woman in any circumstances relevant for the purposes of any provision of this Act if—
   (a) . . .
   (b) he applies to her a **requirement or condition** which he applies or would apply equally to a man but—
      (i) which is such that the proportion of women who can comply with it is considerably smaller than the proportion of men who can comply with it, and
      (ii) which he cannot show to be justifiable irrespective of the sex of the person to whom it is applied, and
      (iii) which is to her detriment because she cannot comply with it."

However, as a result of the provisions of the 2001 Regulations this definition no longer applies in cases under Part II of the Act, which deals with discrimination in the employment field, to discrimination by or in relation to barristers and advocates[50] or to discrimination in the provision of vocational training.[51] In such cases an amended definition of indirect discrimination applies which is set out in section 1(2) SDA. This specifies that indirect discrimination will occur where a person applies to a woman a **"provision, criterion or practice"** which he would apply equally to a man but:

   (i) which is such that it would be to the detriment of a considerably larger proportion of women than of men, and
   (ii) which he cannot show to be justifiable irrespective of the sex of the person to whom it is applied, and
   (i) which is to her detriment.

This amended definition of indirect discrimination implements within domestic law some of the provisions of the E.C. Burden of Proof Directive.[52] The replacement of the words "requirement or condition" with "provision, criterion or practice" is significant; it means that a wider category of actions by employers (or providers of vocational education) will be caught within the definition than was previously the case. (See

---

[49] S.I. 2001 No. 2660.
[50] ss.35A and 35B, SDA.
[51] Under Pt III, SDA.
[52] Directive 98/52/EC.

para. 3.12 below for discussion of the narrow judicial construction given to the words "requirement or condition" in the past.) The reference to the comparative "proportions" of men and women who can comply with a particular provision, criterion or practice suggests that the revised definition will still require statistical evidence to be produced in relation to relative proportions in the vast majority of cases (unless the matter is so clear that the relevant proportions are within the knowledge of the tribunal).

Section 1(1)(b) of the RRA states that a person discriminates against another if: 3.11

> (a) . . .
> (b) he applies to that other a requirement or condition which he applies or would apply equally to persons not of the same racial group as that other but—
>> (i) which is such that the proportion of persons of the same racial group as that other who can comply with it is considerably smaller than the proportion of persons not of that racial group who can comply with it; and
>> (ii) which he cannot show to be justifiable irrespective of the colour, race, nationality or ethnic or national origins of the person to whom it is applied; and
>> (iii) which is to the detriment of that other because he cannot comply with it.

While the Burden of Proof Directive only applies in the area of sex discrimination the provisions of the E.C. Race Directive (Directive 2000/43/EC), which must be implemented within domestic law by July 2003, specify that indirect discrimination will occur where "an apparently neutral provision, criterion or practice would put persons of a racial or ethnic origin at a *particular* disadvantage compared with other persons, unless that provision, criterion or practice is objectively justified by a legitimate aim and the means of achieving that aim are appropriate and necessary". This wording differs from that in the Burden of Proof Directive (and the implementing domestic Regulations) which, as noted previously, states that indirect sex discrimination will occur where "an apparently neutral provision, criterion or practice disadvantages a *substantially higher proportion* of the members of one sex" unless objective justification can be shown. The Government has stated that the reason for the difference in wording is related to the fact that some E.U. Member States do not, and are reluctant to begin, collecting statistics relating to racial origin. In these circumstances the responsible Parliamentary Under-Secretary has stated that the RRA will be amended to allow a prima facie case to be made by the introduction of expert evidence where statistical evidence is unavailable. He suggested that the number of persons who would benefit from this change is "small".

Given that the Race Directive makes it clear that it must be possible to challenge indirectly discriminatory "provisions, criteria or practices" rather than just a "requirement or condition" it is clear that the current definition of indirect racial discrimination in domestic law will require to be amended so that it is identical in nature, in this respect, to the amended definition of indirect sex discrimination introduced by the Sex Discrimination (Indirect Discrimination and Burden of Proof) Regulations 2001.

Virtually every sub-clause of the definition of indirect discrimination in the RRA and the previous definition in the SDA has been subjected to intense judicial scrutiny over the years. While it is impossible to mention all of the important case law in this area the following will hopefully serve to exemplify the main issues which have arisen and those which remain unresolved.

Requirement or condition

3.12   In examining the concept of what will amount to a "requirement or condition" the following analysis sets out some of the case law under the SDA. As noted above, the legislation now refers to the wider concept of a "provision, criterion or practice". However, the previous case law does exemplify some of the problems caused by the more narrowly focused definition which still applies to non-employment related claims under the SDA and to all claims under the RRA in the meantime.

It is clear that the requirement or condition (now provision, criterion or practice under the employment based provisions of the SDA) imposed by the employer must be applied to both sexes/all races. If it is gender/racially based this will amount to direct discrimination.[53]

One of the key debates in this area has focused upon whether the requirement or condition imposed must be an absolute requirement (*i.e.* considered to be necessary to obtain the job or benefit in question). The issue arose starkly in the case of *Perera v. Civil Service Commission*,[54] a case under the RRA. Mr Perera was born and educated as a lawyer in Sri Lanka and passed the English Bar examinations. He applied unsuccessfully for a post as a Legal Assistant in the Civil Service. He claimed indirect discrimination, arguing that the factors taken into account by the selection board were whether the applicant had experience in the United Kingdom, had a good command of the English language, had British nationality or intended to apply for it, and the applicant's age. He submitted that while failure to meet one of these criteria in itself might not have been a bar to selection, a candidate who met none of the above criteria had no chance of selection and that accordingly the selection board had applied a requirement that candidates should have these qualities. He argued that it was more difficult for those from his racial group to meet such a requirement. The employment tribunal held that it was not enough to show that the selection board took account of one or more factors that candidates of Mr Perera's racial group were less likely to possess, since the lack of any one of the factors could be off-set by a "plus" factor. To succeed, Mr Perera had to establish that the lack of these factors constituted an absolute bar to selection to demonstrate that a requirement or condition had been imposed and he had failed to do so. The Court of Appeal, confirming this decision stated that a requirement or a condition means a "must"—something that has to be complied with. As none of the four

---

[53] *James v. Eastleigh Borough Council* [1990] I.R.L.R. 288, HL.
[54] [1983] I.R.L.R. 166, CA.

factors identified amounted to a requirement or condition in the sense
that the lack of it would be an absolute bar the claim was dismissed.
The issue arose again in *Meer v. London Borough of Tower Hamlets.*[55] 3.13
In this case the employer used 12 criteria for long listing, which included
experience in Tower Hamlets. The applicant did not meet this criterion
and claimed that it indirectly discriminated against those of Indian
origin. Both the employment tribunal and EAT, following *Perera,*
dismissed the complaint on the ground that lack of Tower Hamlets
experience was not an absolute bar to selection. On appeal, it was held
that *Perera* was binding and could not be distinguished in any way
although Balcombe L.J. stated that there were strong arguments that the
absolute bar construction of requirement or condition might not be
consistent with the object of the Act and that the law as stated by *Perera*
might need to be reformed. The *Perera* line was followed by the EAT in
Scotland in the sex discrimination case of *Connolly v. Strathclyde
Regional Council.*[56]

This approach can be compared with the one taken *in Tickle v.* 3.14
Governors of Riverview CF School and Surrey County Council[57] where the
employment tribunal rejected the suggestion that a requirement or
condition had to be an absolute bar to found an indirect discrimination
claim. It distinguished *Perera* on the basis that it was a race rather than a
sex discrimination case and held that "all English law is now subject to
European Community law and wherever it is possible, English law
should be interpreted so as to comply with European Community law. It
is clear from the decision of the European Court of Justice in *Bilka-
Kaufhaus GmbH v. Weber von Hartz*[58] that the requirement or condition
need not be absolute".

This whole issue was reconsidered by the EAT in Scotland in *Falkirk* 3.15
Council v. Whyte.[59] In this case the employer had stated that management training and supervisory experience were "desirable" (rather than
specifying that they were necessary) for a promoted management post in
Corntonvale prison. However, the employment tribunal held that in
practice, given how the interview panel operated, they were decisive
factors in the Corntonvale selection and that: "Applying a liberal
interpretation under the wide approach of Community law to sex
discrimination, the tribunal therefore decided that in effect these were
requirements and conditions which fell within the meaning of those
terms in section 1(1)(b) of the Act". The tribunal went on to find that
the requirement had a disproportionate impact on women who were
mostly in basic grade posts and that it was not justifiable on an objective
balance between its discriminatory effect and the employer's needs.

On appeal it was argued that the tribunal had erred in treating the
factors in question as a "requirement or condition". It was submitted
that on the basis of *Perera* a factor can only be a "requirement or
condition" if a failure to comply with it is an absolute bar to obtaining
the post in question. The EAT rejected the appeal, holding that it was

---

[55] [1988] I.R.L.R. 399, CA.
[56] EAT/1039/94, unreported.
[57] E.O.R. DCLD No. 10, p.1.
[58] [1987] I.C.R. 110.
[59] [1997] I.R.L.R. 560, EAT.

open to the employment tribunal to give a liberal interpretation to what the SDA means by "requirement or condition" and that if a factor is "material and it is shown otherwise that qualifying for the particular factor is more difficult for women than for men in the appropriate workplace, we do not see why that should not be a condition or requirement in terms of the legislation in relation to applications for the post, particularly when the relevant factor or factors turn out to be decisive". The EAT went on to "observe in passing that if the case turned upon whether or not the relevant factors to become a require-ment or condition had to be an absolute bar to qualification for the post in question, we would not be inclined to follow the race discrimination cases and, in particular, *Perera*". It can thus be seen that, as a result of more liberal judicial interpretation in which reliance was placed upon E.C. law, there was a movement in SDA cases towards the broader categories which are now set out in statute.

3.16   Over the years there has also been some judicial debate on whether there are certain features of a job which are integral, fundamental aspects of the job rather than amounting to specific requirements or conditions imposed upon the job. An argument of this type found favour in *Clymo v. Wandsworth London Borough Council*.[60] Ms Clymo was a branch librarian. She took maternity leave and after the birth of her child asked if she could job-share her post with her husband. The respondent refused on the basis that it considered that a senior job with management responsibilities could not be shared. The EAT held there could be no requirement or condition to work full-time where the very nature or grade of job required full-time attendance. However, despite *Clymo*, the general principle that holds is that a requirement or condition can be any obligation of service, however fundamental to a job, including a requirement that a job be performed on a full-time basis.

In a number of cases, specific reference has been made to the fact that the words "requirement" and "condition" should be given a wide inter-pretation. This can be seen in *Home Office v. Holmes*.[61] Ms Holmes was employed as a full-time executive officer. She applied to work part-time because she had two young children. The Home Office had a general policy that executive officers were not allowed to work on a part-time basis and it refused her request. The employment tribunal found that a requirement or condition to work full-time had been applied to her and that the proportion of women who could comply with that requirement was considerably smaller than the proportion of men, because of women's family commitments. The Home Office appealed arguing that the number of hours worked was part of the job itself, not a requirement or condition. Rejecting this the EAT held there was no basis for giving the words "requirement" or "condition" a restrictive interpretation in light of the policy underlying the Act. Similarly, in *Clarke and Powell v. Eley (IMI) Kynoch Limited*[62] the EAT held that the purpose of the legislation was to eliminate practices which had a disproportionate adverse impact on women and that the words "requirement" or "condition" should not therefore be given a restricted interpretation.

---

[60] [1989] I.R.L.R. 241, EAT.
[61] [1984] I.R.L.R. 299, EAT.
[62] [1982] I.R.L.R. 482, EAT.

Despite the decision in *Clymo* there is now little doubt that if an 3.17 employer insists that a job should be done on a full-time basis this will be seen as the imposition of a requirement (now best described as a 'criterion or practice' under the amended definition) falling within the terms of the SDA. The employer can attempt to justify the use of such a criterion or practice although recent case law, such as *Given v. Scottish Power plc*,[63] suggests that this is not necessarily an easy task for employers. Here, a female Supervisor asked to job-share on her return from maternity leave. The employer did allow ordinary team members to job-share but the request was rejected because Mrs Given held a supervisory position. After several requests had been rejected she resigned. The employer argued that the requirement to work full-time was justified because of the supervisory nature of the position. However, the employment tribunal held that the applicant had been indirectly discriminated against on the grounds of sex and marital status and awarded £35,000 in compensation since it found the discrimination to have been intentional.[64]

Generally, it is submitted that employers faced with job-share/part- 3.18 time requests from women who seek such employment due to domestic commitments should treat the requests seriously and sensitively making significant efforts to meet them. Employers who insist on a particular job being done on a full-time basis should ensure that such a practice is objectively justifiable. Those who seek to impose a blanket policy of full-time working for certain types or grades of work may well find themselves facing indirect discrimination claims.

The requirement to work on a full-time basis is one that is reasonably 3.19 easy to identify. However, in other cases, more nebulous requirements (in terms of the old definition) have been accepted as falling within the terms of the legislation. In particular, in *Watches of Switzerland v. Savell*,[65] the requirement formulated by Mrs Savell was that in order to be promoted she had to satisfy the vague, subjective, and unadvertised promotion procedure of the company. This was held to be capable of being a requirement or condition in terms of the SDA. The applicant led expert evidence to demonstrate that a subjective promotion procedure has an adverse impact on women. She also showed the existence of sub-conscious bias against women and a tendency to overlook them when making promotions. Accordingly, it was held that she had suffered indirect discrimination.

By way of further example, the imposition of an age restriction on a post[66] and of a mobility clause[67] have both been held to have resulted in indirect sex discrimination. Similarly, the imposition of a particular shift system may also amount to indirect sex discrimination.[68] It is submitted

---

[63] EAT/12/97.

[64] See *also MacMillan v. Edinburgh Voluntary Organisations Council* (Case No. 3522/940) and note that Given was decided prior to the Sex Discrimination and Equal Pay (Miscellaneous Amendment) Regulations 1996 (S.I. 1996 No. 438)—see later in this chapter.

[65] [1983] I.R.L.R. 141, EAT.

[66] *Price v. Civil Service Commission (No. 2)* [1978] I.R.L.R. 3, IT.

[67] *Meade-Hill and NUCPS v. British Council* [1995] I.R.L.R. 478, CA.

[68] *London Underground Ltd v. Edwards (No. 2)* [1997] I.R.L.R. 157, EAT; aff'd [1998] I.R.L.R. 364 CA, *Hale and Clunie v. Wiltshire Healthcare NHS Trust* (DCLD No. 39, Spring 1999, p.1).

that employers should consider very carefully the practices which they apply (to take on board the amended definition which applies under the SDA and which will apply shortly under the RRA) and job requirements which they impose in respect of new posts and those which already exist within the organisation with a view to ensuring that these can be objectively justified.

3.20   So far as indirect racial discrimination is concerned it has, for example, been found to be justifiable to forbid a beard on grounds of hygiene[69] and to require employees to wear protective head gear.[70] A requirement that labourers complete application forms in English in their own handwriting[71] when the job itself did not involve any writing and a requirement that students who have not been ordinarily resident in the European Community for three years pay higher fees[72] have been held not to be justifiable.

"Can comply"

3.21   Case law has established over the years that the phrase "can comply" means "can in practice" rather than "can in theory". The leading case on this point is *Mandla v. Dowell Lee*.[73] This was a case under the RRA in which the applicant alleged that the defendant private school and its headmaster had indirectly discriminated against him by refusing to offer him a place at the school unless he removed his turban and cut off his hair in conformity with school rules regarding uniform. The House of Lords made it clear that the words "can comply" mean "can in practice comply" or "can comply consistently with the customs and cultural conditions of the racial group". They did not mean "can physically comply". A literal reading of the word "can" in section 1(1)(b) would deprive Sikhs and members of other groups of much of the protection which Parliament evidently intended the Act to afford to them. This approach can be compared with the one adopted by the EAT in *Clymo*. While the EAT held that the words "can comply" meant "can comply in practice", it went on to hold that because the applicant and her husband could afford a child minder and because child minders were available in London, the applicant was able to comply in practice with the requirement to work full-time. However, *Clymo* is not readily followed.

Pool for comparison

3.22   The definition of indirect sex discrimination involves a comparison of the proportion of each sex who can comply with the particular requirement or condition at issue. A similar comparative exercise must, of course, be done in a racial discrimination case (although see the comments at paragraph 3.11 about changes likely to be made by 2003). This requires the identification of the appropriate pool for comparison purposes which has been held to be a matter of fact for the tribunal.[74]

---

[69] *Singh v. Rowntree Mackintosh Ltd* [1979] I.R.L.R. 199, CA.
[70] *Singh v. British Rail Engineering* Ltd [1986] I.C.R. 22, EAT.
[71] *Isa and Rashid v. BL Cars* (1981) COIT 1103/125, unreported. See also *Sunner v. Air Canada* (EOR, DCLD No. 36, p.5).
[72] *Orphanos v. Queen Mary College* [1985] I.R.L.R. 349, HL.
[73] [1983] I.R.L.R. 209, HL.
[74] *Kidd v. DRG (U.K.) Ltd* [1985] I.R.L.R. 190, EAT.

However, it is often extremely difficult to identify the appropriate pool. For example, if an employer requires a job to be done on a full-time basis and an applicant seeks to show that an indirectly discriminatory criterion or practice has been applied what is the appropriate pool for the comparison? Is it working women as a whole in the United Kingdom, those qualified in the national work force to do the job in question, or those qualified to do the job within the local area, etc.?

Scottish tribunals have tended to use national statistics when considering, for example, recruitment cases about part-timers but the approach varies depending on the type of case. For example, in *Pearse v. City of Bradford Metropolitan Council*[75] the applicant claimed the selection arrangements for the post of senior lecturer were indirectly discriminatory. The applicant was a part-time lecturer and the senior lecturer post was only open to full-time workers within the college. At the employment tribunal she identified the "pool" as all men and women employed at the college and showed that only 21.8 per cent of female staff were employed full-time compared with 46.7 per cent of male staff. However, the respondent chose a pool of all suitably qualified people employed at the college and the tribunal preferred this pool. Since the applicant presented no statistics on the preferred pool the tribunal dismissed her claim. On appeal, the EAT held the employment tribunal was entitled to find the correct pool for comparison was all men and women with appropriate qualifications for the vacant post.[76]

It is clear from case law that the appropriate pool will vary depending on the type of claim that is brought. In some cases the national workforce may form a statistical base, for others the pool may be much more restricted. It may be necessary in some cases to have statistical information on various possible pools to hand and to present this to the tribunal.

Disparate impact—"considerably smaller proportion" or "considerably larger proportion" (under the amended definition in the SDA)

It has been held in *Staffordshire County Council v. Black*.[77] that it is a question of fact for the employment tribunal whether a considerably smaller proportion of one sex can comply with a requirement or condition imposed. In this case the EAT held that the employment tribunal had not erred in finding that the proportion of female teachers over age 50 employed by the County Council who could comply with the requirement to be full-time for the purpose of calculating maximum pension service credit (89.5 per cent) was not "considerably smaller" than the proportion of male teachers over age 50 who were full time (97 per cent). The EAT refused to accept the employee's submission that "considerably smaller" meant no more than "worthy of consideration". It held that the words "considerably smaller" are ordinary words in common usage. There were more women than men full-time teachers over age 50 in absolute terms and a difference of 7.5 percentage points, 3.23

---

[75] [1988] I.R.L.R. 379, EAT.
[76] See also *Mawkin v. Alien and Elliott* (Case No. 07494 91), unreported; and *Jones v. University of Manchester* [1993] I.R.L.R. 218, CA.
[77] [1995] I.R.L.R. 234, EAT.

in context, did not support the proposition that a considerably smaller proportion of women than men could meet the requirement imposed. Further, the EAT held that the test for identifying disparate impact under E.C. law was the same as under the SDA, *i.e.* the tribunal should identify the condition which was applied and ask whether the proportion of women who could comply with it is considerably smaller than the proportion of men.[78] The same type of approach is likely to be taken in considering whether a considerably larger proportion of women than men suffer a detriment by the imposition of a particular provision, criterion or practice.

3.24   In *R. v. Secretary of State for Employment, ex p. Seymour-Smith and Perez*[79] the issue of disparate impact is analysed fully. This case involved a challenge to the two years service qualification in respect of the right to claim unfair dismissal. It was argued that the imposition of this requirement was indirectly discriminatory, in breach of the provisions of the Equal Treatment Directive and Article 119 (now Article 141) of the E.C. Treaty, since the proportion of women who could comply with it was considerably smaller than the proportion of men as at 1991 (when the two individual applicants in the case were actually dismissed) and it was a requirement which could not be justified. Statistical evidence showed that between 1985 and 1991 the proportion of men who had two or more years service at 16 or more hours per week with their current employer ranged from 72 per cent to 77.4 per cent whereas the proportion of women in this category ranged from 63.8 per cent to 68.9 per cent. The House of Lords referred a number of questions to the ECJ on the construction of Article 119 (now Article 141) including, "What is the legal test for establishing whether a measure adopted by a Member State has such a degree of disparate effect as between men and women as to amount to indirect discrimination for the purposes of Article 119 (now Article 141) of the E.C. Treaty unless shown to be based upon objectively justified factors other than sex?"[80] In response the ECJ stated that it was a matter for the national court to determine whether the statistics were valid and could be taken into account (issues such as the number of individuals covered and whether they might illustrate for-tuitous phenomenon could be considered). Thereafter, the correct test was to ask whether the available statistics indicated that a considerably smaller proportion of women than men could meet the requirement of the two year rule. If so this would be prima facie evidence of indirect discrimination although the employer could then seek to show that the rule was objectively justified. The Court also pointed out that if there was a lesser but persistent and relatively constant disparity between the sexes in terms of meeting the requirement of the rule this could also amount to indirect discrimination. It was a matter for the national court to draw conclusions from the statistics. On reference back to the House of Lords their Lordships agreed with the Court of Appeal (Lord Slynn and Lord Steyn dissenting on this issue but not in relation to the issue of

---

[78] See also *Greater Manchester Police Authority v. Lea* [1990] I.R.L.R. 372, EAT.

[79] [1995] I.R.L.R. 464, CA; [1997] I.R.L.R. 315, HL; [1999] I.R.L.R. 253, ECJ; *No. 2* [2000] I.R.L.R. 263, HL.

[80] Note also *R. v. Secretary of State for Trade and Industry, ex p. Unison* [1996] I.R.L.R. 438, DC.

objective justification) that the two year requirement was prima facie discriminatory, being impressed with the "persistent and relatively constant disparity" between the proportions of men and women who could meet the requirement between 1985 and 1991. Over the six year period from 1985 to 1990 inclusive the ratio of men and women who qualified was roughly 10:9 although the disparity began to diminish in 1991 and continued to do so in 1992 and 1993.

Detriment

"Detriment" simply means personal disadvantage.[81]   3.25

Justification

In the early days of the SDA and RRA the EAT equated justifiability 3.26 with necessity rather than convenience. However, the test was substantially diluted by the decision in *Ojutiku and Oburoni v. Manpower Services Commission*.[82] This was a race case in which the Court of Appeal ruled that it was not essential for an employer to prove that the requirement was necessary for the good of the business but rather that: "if a person produces reasons for doing something which would be acceptable to right thinking people as sound and tolerable reasons for so doing then he has justified his conduct". The ECJ has adopted a much stricter test under Community law; in *Bilka-Kaufhaus GmbH v. Weber von Hartz*[83] it held that a discriminatory provision would only be justified if: "the means chosen for achieving that objective corresponded to a real need on the part of the undertaking, are appropriate with a view to achieving the objective in question and are necessary to that end".

Subsequently, the House of Lords in *Hampson v. Department of Education and Science*[84] affirmed the test formulated by the Court of Appeal that "justifiable requires an objective balance to be struck between the discriminatory effect of the condition and the reasonable needs of the party who applies the condition". The *Bilka-Kaufhaus* test was applied by the House of Lords in *R. v. Secretary of State for Employment, ex parte Equal Opportunities Commission*.[85]

That a redundancy policy is on its face gender neutral, even though its effect is that the proportion of women who can comply with it is considerably smaller than men, (or, under the new definition, that a considerably larger proportion of women than men suffer a detriment as a result of the policy) does not mean that it is justifiable. On the contrary, the very fact that a policy is gender-neutral will bring section 1(1)(b) into operation. The policy must then be objectively justifiable.[86]

Burden of proof

There is no doubt that until the Sex Discrimination (Indirect Discrimi- 3.27 nation and Burden of Proof) Regulations 2001 came into force on

---

[81] *MOD v. Jeremiah* [1979] I.R.L.R. 436, HL.
[82] [1982] I.R.L.R. 418, CA.
[83] [1987] I.C.R. 110.
[84] [1989] I.R.L.R. 69, HL.
[85] [1994] I.R.L.R. 176, HL.
[86] *Whiffen v. Milham Girls' School* [2001] I.R.L.R. 468.

October 12, 2001 the burden of proving that discrimination had occurred lay firmly on the applicant in all types of discrimination cases. However, employment tribunals and courts increasingly recognised that it is not usual to find clear and incontrovertible evidence of discrimination, although the way in which the recognition of this difficulty has been formulated by certain chairmen and judges has led to some confusion.[87]

3.28   Over the last decade the guidance formulated by Neill L.J. in *King v. The Great Britain-China Centre*,[88] has been widely relied upon by employment tribunals charged with assessing whether an applicant has effectively discharged the burden of proving that discrimination has occurred:

1. It is for the applicant to make out his or her case. If she does not prove her case on the balance of probabilities she will fail.
2. It is important to bear in mind that it is unusual to find direct evidence of discrimination. Few employers would be willing to admit discrimination even to themselves. In some cases the discrimination will not be intentional but based on the assumption that the individual will not fit it in.
3. The outcome of the case therefore usually depends on what inferences it is proper to draw from the primary facts found by the Tribunal. These inferences can include any inferences it is just and equitable to draw in accordance with section 65(2)(b) of the RRA (s.74(2)(b) of the SDA) from an evasive or equivocal reply to a questionnaire used under section 65 of the RRA (s.74 of the SDA).
4. Usually a finding that a person has been treated differently from others and a finding of difference in race or sex will point to the possibility of discrimination. In such a case the Tribunal will look to the employer for an explanation. If no explanation is put forward or the tribunal considers it to be inadequate or unsatisfactory it will be legitimate for the Tribunal to infer unlawful discrimination.
5. It is unnecessary and unhelpful to introduce the concept of a shifting evidential burden of proof. At the conclusion of all the evidence the tribunal should make findings as to the primary facts and draw such inferences as they consider proper from those facts. They should then reach a conclusion on the balance of probabilities, bearing in mind both the difficulties which face persons who complain of unlawful discrimination and the fact that it is for the complainant to prove his or her case.[89]

The guidance set out in King underpins the approach of the Court of Appeal in the much more recent case of *Anya v. University of Oxford*[90] in

---

[87] See *Oxford v. Department of Health and Social Security* [1977] I.R.L.R. 225, EAT.
[88] [1991] I.R.L.R. 513, CA.
[89] Note also *Glasgow City Council v. Zafar* [1998] I.R.L.R. 36, HL.
[90] [2001] I.R.L.R. 377, CA.

which the Court of Appeal emphasised that little direct discrimination is overt or even deliberate. Inferences must be drawn from the circumstances surrounding a particular decision and, where appropriate, from the history of events between the parties. The case involved an allegation that a doctor had not been appointed to a particular post because of his race. He alleged that the evidence showed a preconceived hostility towards him which was indicative of racial bias. The Court of Appeal held that the employment tribunal had erred in failing to draw any conclusion as to where the truth lay in respect of prior events put in evidence by the applicant and what, if anything, it indicated in terms of racial bias. It had also failed by not recording any inferences or conclusions from the fact that, in breach of the University's Equal Opportunities policy, no person specification was drawn up until ten minutes before the interview and no references were taken up. The tribunal also erred in directing itself that if an employer behaves unreasonably towards a black employee, it is not to be inferred, without more, that the reason for this is attributable to the employee's colour in that the employer might well behave just as unreasonably to a white employee. The Court of Appeal made it clear that unreasonable behaviour may well justify an inference of racial bias if there is nothing else to explain it. A theoretical possibility that the employer might behave equally badly to staff of all races was not enough to negate the possibility of such an inference being drawn—that would require evidence that the employer did actually treat all employees in such a fashion.

The difficulties which can arise in proving that discrimination has 3.29 occurred have now been acknowledged in a statutory context by the provisions of the Sex Discrimination (Indirect Discrimination and Burden of Proof) Regulations 2001. Regulation 5 inserts a new section 63A into the SDA which applies to any complaint presented to an employment tribunal.[91] The effect of this section is that where a complainant proves facts from which the tribunal could conclude, in the absence of an adequate explanation, that the respondent has committed an act of unlawful discrimination (or is to be treated as having committed such an act under the provisions governing vicarious liability) then the tribunal must uphold the complaint unless the respondent proves that he did not commit (or is not to be treated as having committed) such an act. A provision to like effect is introduced to govern the burden of proof in sheriff court actions.[92] While the 2001 Regulations only amend the SDA, it should be noted that article 8 of the Race Directive requires similar provisions to be introduced with regard to the burden of proof in complaints of race discrimination by October 2003.[93]

As the Government sees it the amendment of the provisions in the SDA governing burden of proof will make very little difference in practice because it considers that tribunals have operated in a way which broadly reflects this section over the last 10 years as a result of the guidance given by the Court of Appeal in *King*. This view is expressed in

---

[91] s.63 SDA — the new provisions will apply to any case which had not been determined by October 12, 2001.
[92] s.66A.
[93] Directive 2000/43/EC.

a guidance document issued by the Cabinet Office.[94] However, the position is not as straightforward as this might suggest. The guidance document states that:

"U.K. tribunals already have an established practice of drawing an inference of discrimination if an employer fails to produce evidence that satisfies them that there has been no breach of the principle of equal treatment—House of Lords, *Zafar v. Glasgow City Council*."[95]

That is not, however, what *Zafar* says given that the House of Lords held in that case that the tribunal had misdirected themselves in considering that they were *bound* in law to draw an inference of discrimination on racial grounds in the absence of any other satisfactory non-racial explanation for the differential treatment of the applicant by his employer. According to the House of Lords in *Zafar* the guidance given in *King v. The Great Britain-China Centre* as to how inferences of discrimination can be properly drawn, which says that if the tribunal considers the explanation to be inadequate or unsatisfactory it will be *legitimate* for it to infer that the discrimination was on racial grounds, should in future be applied in discrimination cases of race or sex discrimination. The remarks of the EAT in *Khanna v. Ministry of Defence*[96] and *Chattopadyay v. Headmaster of Holloway School*[97] to the effect that such inferences *"should"* be drawn, put the matter too high and should not be followed, according to their Lordships.

There is, however, a difference it is suggested between it being *legitimate* for a tribunal to draw an inference of discrimination where less favourable treatment is shown and the employer does not offer an adequate explanation and a tribunal being *bound* to draw such an inference as would seem to be required by the new statutory provisions. This distinction was one of the main points examined in the *Zafar* case.

SEXUAL AND RACIAL HARASSMENT

3.30 Sexual or racial harassment is in itself a detriment under the SDA and the RRA respectively. In the earliest case law under the legislation there had been suggestions that a person had to suffer dismissal or the like for there to be a detriment. One of the leading cases in this field is *Porcelli v. Strathclyde Regional Council*,[98] which involved serious sexual harassment of a female school laboratory technician by two male technicians. The defence mounted by Strathclyde Regional Council was that the two males would have treated a disliked male colleague just as badly. On appeal this was rejected and it was held that the question to be asked was: "Was the applicant less favourably treated on the grounds of her

---

[94] "Clarity in the Sex Discrimination Act: Workplace Guidance on the Burden of Proof Directive" available at www.cabinet-office.gov.uk.

[95] [1998] I.R.L.R. 36.

[96] [1981] I.R.L.R. 331, EAT.

[97] [1981] I.R.L.R. 487, EAT.

[98] [1986] I.R.L.R. 134, CS.

sex than a man would have been treated?" It was not a defence to state that a male colleague would have been treated unpleasantly if the form of unpleasantness in such a case would not have been sex specific. *Porcelli* also makes it clear that it is not necessary that an act of sexual harassment betrays a sexual motivation on the part of the person concerned. It may well be that the behaviour is motivated by bullying for example.[99]

A single act of harassment can be enough to establish liability although it is a question of fact and degree.[1]

It is also clear that a woman is entitled to work on the basis that 3.31 certain kinds of behaviour which others might find offensive are acceptable to her while others are not. In other words, she is entitled to draw a line and should make clear that she is doing so. Furthermore, a woman is entitled to find certain behaviour acceptable from male A but to find it unacceptable from male B.[2] Increasingly, employment tribunals have been making use of the European Commission Recommendation[3] and Code of Practice on the Protection of the Dignity of Women and Men at Work[4] which defines sexual harassment as "unwanted conduct of a sexual nature, or other conduct based on sex affecting the dignity of women and men at work". The Code sums up the position admirably: "The essential characteristic of sexual harassment is that it is unwanted by the recipient, that it is for each individual to determine what behaviour is acceptable to them and what they regard as offensive. Sexual attention becomes sexual harassment if it is persisted in once it has been made clear that it is regarded by the recipient as offensive, although one incident of harassment may constitute sexual harassment if it is sufficiently serious".[5]

It is also worth bearing in mind that harassment or a failure to 3.32 properly investigate a complaint of harassment may result in a breach of contract. In *Reed v. Bull Information Systems and Stedman*[6] a manager carried out a course of conduct which was found to amount to sexual harassment. As well as breaching the SDA this conduct was also held to amount to a fundamental breach of the implied duty of trust and confidence. The employer's failure to investigate the applicant's complaints of harassment was also sufficient to justify a finding of breach of trust and confidence by the employer.

The interaction between the SDA and common law is also evident in the decision of the House of Lords in *Waters v. Commissioner of Police of the Metropolis*[7] which confirms that an employer is liable under the law of

---

[99] See also *Rarity v. Jarvie Plant Ltd* [1990] I.R.L.R. 3, EAT.

[1] *Bracebridge Engineering Ltd v. Darby* [1990] I.R.L.R. 3, EAT; *Wakefield v. The Automobile Association*, E.O.R. DCLD No. 6, p.5; *Insitu Cleaning Ltd v. Heads* [1995] I.R.L.R. 4, EAT.

[2] *Johnstone v. Fenton Barns (Scotland) Ltd* (1990) E.O.R. DCLD No. 5, p.7.

[3] Recommendation 91/131/EEC.

[4] See *Wadman v. Carpenter Farrer Partnership* [1993] I.R.L.R. 374, EAT; *Felstead v. Denis's Coaches and Travel*, E.O.R. DCLD No. 20, p.4.

[5] For a case in which the applicant's sexual harassment claim failed because she had failed to make it clear that certain behaviour was unwanted see *Chaudry v. Scottish Asian Action Committee*, E.O.R. DCLD, 35 Spring 1998, p.3.

[6] [1999] I.R.L.R. 299, EAT.

[7] [2000] I.R.L.R. 720.

negligence for injury caused by harassment and/or victimisation where the employer knows or ought to know that harassment/victimisation is taking place but fails to take reasonable steps to prevent it. In this case Lord Hutton expressed the view that "a person employed under an ordinary contract of employment can have a valid cause of action in negligence against her employer if the employer fails to protect her against victimisation and harassment which causes physical or psychiatric injury. This duty arises both under the contract of employment and under the common law principles of negligence."

Vicarious liability

3.33   One of the main issues which requires to be considered in a harassment case is whether the harasser is acting in the course of his employment. The pertinent section of the SDA is section 41(1)[8] which states that: "Anything done by a person in the course of his employment shall be treated for the purposes of this Act as done by his employers as well as by him". The leading case on this issue is *Jones v. Tower Boot Company Limited*.[9] The applicant, whose mother was white and whose father was black, worked for the respondent for a month in 1992 until he resigned. During that time he was subjected to a number of incidents of racial harassment from work colleagues. One employee burned his arm with a hot screwdriver, metal bolts were thrown at his head, his legs were whipped with a piece of welt, someone stuck a notice on his back bearing the words "chipmunks are go" and he was called names such as "chimp", "monkey" and "baboon". The employment tribunal which heard Mr Jones's racial discrimination complaint held that the employer was liable on the basis that the employees were acting in the course of their employment within the meaning of section 32(1) of the RRA. However, the EAT overturned this decision, holding that the phrase "in the course of employment" had a well-established meaning in law and that the nub of the test was set out in Salmond on Torts as "whether the unauthorised wrongful act of the servant is so connected with that which he was employed to do to be a mode of doing it". The EAT concluded that the acts complained of could not by any stretch of the imagination fall within that definition. The Court of Appeal restored the decision of the employment tribunal. It considered that the EAT had erred in applying the common law test of vicarious liability. For the purpose of section 32 of the RRA and section 41 of the SDA the words "in the course of employment" should be interpreted in the sense in which they are employed in everyday speech and not restrictively by reference to the principles established in respect of an employer's liability for the torts of his employee. The sections should be given a wide interpretation, given that the policy of the legislation was to deter racial and sexual harassment in the workplace through the widening of the net of responsibility beyond the guilty employees themselves. Employers were supplied with a reasonable steps defence which could exonerate the conscientious employer who had taken reasonable steps to prevent the

---

[8] See RRA, s.32(1).
[9] [1997] I.R.L.R. 168, CA.

harassment. In relation to this last point it should be noted that section 41(3) of the SDA and section 32(3) of the RRA provide employers with a defence if they can prove that they took such steps as were reasonably practicable to prevent employees doing acts of the type in respect of which complaint is made.[10]

In *Cannife v. East Riding of Yorkshire Council*[11] the issue arose of whether an employer can rely on this defence if it can be shown that there was nothing that the employer could have done to prevent the act in respect of which complaint is made. It was held by the EAT that the proper approach is:

1. to identify whether the respondent took any steps at all to prevent the employee from doing the act or acts complained of in the course of employment;
2. having identified what steps, if any, they took, to consider whether there were any further acts, they could have taken, which were reasonably practicable.

The issue of whether the doing of any such acts would have prevented the acts of discrimination was worth addressing but not determinative either way. Even if the steps did not have any realistic chance of success, "if in fact it was reasonably practicable for them to be done, they should have been done. That is the purpose of this legislation, and that is the difficult eye of the needle through which a respondent employer who seeks to avoid a vicarious liability must travel in order to avoid that liability". An employer who takes all reasonably practicable steps will avoid liability even if those steps do not actually prevent an act of discrimination (that is the very essence of the defence) but an employer who has not taken reasonable steps will not avoid liability simply by showing that, even if it had, the act of discrimination would still have occurred. Had the tribunal decision been upheld in this case it would have meant that the more outrageous the act of harassment the less likely it would be that the employee would have a remedy against the employer—that would not accord with the purpose of the legislation.

It should be borne in mind that behaviour which occurs outwith the workplace may still be found to be in the "course of employment". In *Chief Constable of the Lincolnshire Police v. Stubbs*[12] it was held that events which occurred in a pub and at a party were within the course of employment. The EAT considered that when there is a social gathering of work colleagues, it is entirely appropriate for the tribunal to consider whether or not the circumstances show that what was occurring was an extension of their employment. Each case will depend upon its own facts and the tribunal's exercise of judgment as an industrial jury.

---

[10] See also *Lister v. Hesley Hall Ltd* [2001] I.R.L.R. 472, HL for discussion of the fact that the conventional test in Salmond is less than satisfactory within the employment context even at common law.

[11] [2000] I.R.L.R. 555, EAT.

[12] [1999] I.R.L.R. 81, EAT.

Liability for the acts of third parties

3.34   Employers of individuals who are harassed can, in certain circumstances, be liable for the actings of third parties. This can occur where the employer causes or permits the harassment to occur in circumstances where he can control whether it happens or not. The tribunal must ask itself whether the event in question was something which was sufficiently under the control of the employer that he could, by the application of good employment practice, have prevented it or reduced its extent.[13]

Aiding Unlawful Acts

3.35   Under section 33 of the RRA and section 42 of the SDA, a person who knowingly aids another person to do something which is unlawful under the Act is to be treated for the purposes of the legislation as him/ herself doing an unlawful act of the like description. In *Anyanwu v. South Bank Student Union*[14] the House of Lords held that the expression "aids" in section 33(1) of the RRA is a familiar word in everyday use bearing no technical or special meaning in this context. A person aids another if he helps or assists, or cooperates or collaborates with him. He does so whether or not his help is substantial and productive, provided the help is not so insignificant as to be negligible. The word indicated the provision of assistance to another which "helped" the carrying out of an unlawful act rather than "caused" it. However, for a claim to succeed, something more than a general attitude of helpfulness and co-operation is needed.[15]

Victimisation

3.36   Both the SDA and the RRA also contain provisions which offer a degree of protection to those who complain of discrimination or who assist others in so doing. Section 4 of the SDA and section 2 of the RRA specify that a person (the discriminator) will discriminate against another person (the person victimised) if he treats that other person less favourably than he treats or would treat others and does so because the person has:

1. brought proceedings against the discriminator or any other person under the SDA, EqPA or RRA;
2. given evidence or information in connection with proceedings brought against the discriminator or any other person under the SDA, EqPA or RRA;
3. otherwise done anything under or by reference to the SDA, EqPA or RRA in relation to the discriminator or any other person; or
4. alleged that the discriminator or any other person has committed an act which would amount to a contravention of the SDA, EqPA or RRA (although the allegation need not make reference to any particular Act).

---

[13] *Burton and Rhule v. De Vere Hotels Ltd* [1996] I.R.L.R. 596, EAT.
[14] [2001] I.R.L.R. 305, HL.
[15] *Hallam v. Cheltenham Borough Council* [2001] I.R.L.R. 312, HL.

The above protection will also apply if the discriminator treats a person less favourably than others because he knows the person intends to do one of these things or suspects that the person has done or intends to do one of these things.

The victimisation provisions were rather restrictively interpreted for many years after the coming into force of the SDA and RRA, particularly in *Cornelius v. University College of Swansea*[16] where it was held that a person claiming victimisation under section 4 of the SDA must be able to show not only that she was victimised for bringing proceedings but that she was victimised because she brought proceedings under the SDA. This decision was criticised for adding a hurdle which is at the very least contrary to the spirit and intention of the provisions. Similarly in *Aziz v. Trinity Street Taxis Ltd*[17] the Court of Appeal suggested that to succeed with a victimisation claim an applicant would require to show that the respondent was consciously motivated by the fact that the applicant had done an act under or by reference to the RRA. However in *Nagarajan v. London Regional Transport*[18] the House of Lords pointed out that conscious motivation was not necessary to establish direct discrimination; the reason why a discriminator acted on racial grounds was irrelevant in such circumstances. Their Lordships considered that there was no good reason why a different approach should be adopted in relation to victimisation. In so far as the *Aziz* case suggested that a motive consciously connected with the race relations legislation was necessary to establish victimisation it was incorrect.

Chief Constable of West Yorkshire Police v. Khan[19] considered the issue of an appropriate comparator for someone who claims that he/she has been victimised for bringing a complaint under the RRA. Here, Sergeant Khan brought a claim under the RRA, claiming that he had been discriminated against on racial grounds in respect of an application for promotion to inspector. Before his case was heard he applied for a promoted post in another force. A reference request was received but the Chief Constable refused to provide a reference on the basis that he might prejudice his own case before the tribunal. Sergeant Khan added a victimisation claim to his tribunal application. The original claim under the RRA was ultimately dismissed but the victimisation claim was upheld. An appeal to the EAT by the employer was dismissed. On further appeal, the employer argued that the tribunal had erred by not choosing as a comparator (the "other person" for the purpose of section 2(1)) someone who had brought proceedings of some other type against the Chief Constable. It was also argued that the tribunal had erred by holding that the employer had acted "by reason" of the fact that Sergeant Khan had brought proceedings under the RRA.

The Court of Appeal dismissed the appeal holding that, given the purpose of section 2 to protect those who bring proceedings under the RRA, in assessing whether there has been less favourable treatment the appropriate comparison is with the way in which other employees would

---

[16] [1987] I.R.L.R. 141, CA.

[17] [1988] I.R.L.R. 204, CA.

[18] [1998] I.R.L.R. 73, CA; rev'd [1999] I.R.L.R. 572; [2000] 1 A.C. 501, HL.

[19] [2000] I.R.L.R. 324, CA, House of Lords decision delivered October 11, 2001, IDS Brief 697, p.3.

normally be treated. The "relevant circumstance" in this case was the request for the reference and the correct approach was to look at what was requested rather than the reason for not providing it. The correct approach was to compare the way Sergeant Khan was treated with the manner in which other employees in relation to whom a reference had been requested would normally be treated. Looked at in this way the decision of the tribunal was correct. It also held that in assessing whether someone has been victimised "by reason" that he or she has done an act within section 2 of the RRA all that is required is the proper application of the "but for" test, rather than a conscious motive or intention to discriminate. In the present case, the tribunal had correctly taken the view that if it had not been for the proceedings brought under the Act, a reference would have been provided.

On further appeal the House of Lords saw the case as raising three main issues. These were:

(1) Who was the appropriate comparator for determining whether K had been less favourably treated than others?
(2) Was K actually treated less favourably than an appropriate comparator?
(3) If so, was the reason for the treatment the fact he had done a "protected" act under the RRA?

In considering the appropriate comparator the House of Lords noted that two different approaches had been adopted in previous cases. One approach involved comparing the complainant with someone who has done a similar act—if the complainant had made a complaint to a tribunal under the RRA the comparator would be an employee who had made a complaint to a tribunal under another statute. This approach would allow an employer to victimise someone who had brought a claim under the RRA if he could victimise someone who had brought a claim under some other piece of legislation. The House of Lords rejected the idea that this was a valid comparator, holding instead that the appropriate comparator was quite simply someone who had not done a protected act (such as bringing a claim of race discrimination).

On the issue of less favourable treatment the House of Lords held that K had been treated less favourably because he had been refused a reference, whereas another employee who did not have a discrimination claim pending before the tribunal would have received one.

However, on the third issue, the House of Lords disagreed with the approach adopted by the Court of Appeal. In particular their Lordships did not accept that the "but for" test could be applied in the manner suggested by the Court of Appeal. Each judge concluded that K had not been victimised because he had done a protected act, although, they each reached that conclusion by a slightly different route. What was crucial, however, was that the reason for the refusal to provide a reference was not because K had brought proceedings. Rather, it was because the provision of a reference might compromise the Chief Constable's handling of the case brought against him. This was seen as a crucial distinction, it being considered important that an employer should be able to act reasonably to protect his position in proceedings without being open to a claim of victimisation. It was the Chief

Constable's concern that giving a reference might compromise the handling of the case rather than the fact that K had done a protected act which was the real reason for the refusal to provide a reference. This did not amount to victimisation.

In *Ledeatte v. London Borough of Tower Hamlets*[20] the EAT emphasised that an employee wishing to show that she had been victimised contrary to the provisions of the RRA had to show that the individuals who mistreated her had actual knowledge of the protected act. Without such knowledge it could not be shown that the less favourable treatment was "by reason that" the employee had done a protected act.

Post-Employment Victimisation and Discrimination

The issue of whether protection against victimisation and discrimina- 3.37 tion extends to acts carried out after the employment has come to an end has been a source of controversy. In *Coote v. Granada Hospitality Ltd*[21] the ECJ held that if there was no judicial protection from measures which an employer took after the employment had ended, in retaliation for equal treatment proceedings brought by a worker during the course of employment, employees might be deterred from bringing such proceedings. Whilst there was an express requirement in the Equal Treatment Directive that Member States provide protection against dismissal as a reaction to equal treatment proceedings brought by employees, the scope of the protection which the Directive required Member States to provide extended also to other measures, such as those taken by an employer to prevent an ex-employee from obtaining alternative employment (in this case failing to provide a reference). On remit back, the EAT[22] held that the SDA could be interpreted in a manner which gave effect to the provisions of the Directive. However, this judgment has been narrowly interpreted as applying only to victimisation claims under the SDA rather than to acts of sex discrimination occurring after the employment relationship has ended.[23] Furthermore, it has been held that there is no protection under the RRA in respect of acts of discrimination or victimisation which occur after the employment relationship has ended. The argument that, as a result of the decision in *Coote,* post-employment claims for victimisation fell within the scope of the RRA was rejected by the EAT in *D'Souza v. London Borough of Lambeth.*[24] The EAT considered that it was bound by the decision of the Court of Appeal in *Adekeye v. The Post Office (No. 2)*[25] in which it had been held that the RRA did not cover post employment victimisation. However, the EAT suggested that the Court of Appeal might wish to review the decision in *Adekeye* in light of the decision of the ECJ in *Coote.*

---

[20] IRLB 649, September 2000.

[21] Case C-185/97 [1998] I.R.L.R. 656, ECJ.

[22] *Coote v. Granada Hospitality Ltd (No. 2)* [1999] I.R.L.R. 452, EAT.

[23] *Relaxation Group v. Rhys Harper* [2000] I.R.L.R. 810, EAT; aff'd [2001] I.R.L.R. 460, CA, confirms that the protection against post-employment victimisation does not extend to a claim of discrimination brought after the cessation of employment.

[24] IDS Brief 669, Sept 2000.

[25] [1997] I.R.L.R. 105, CA.

INFLUENCE OF EUROPEAN COMMUNITY LAW

3.38 There are a number of E.C. law concepts that require to be understood prior to any discussion of European discrimination case law. It is also necessary to briefly summarise the main pieces of community legislation which have an impact in the field of discrimination in employment:

1. Article 141 (formerly 119) of the E.C. Treaty states that: "each member state shall ... ensure and subsequently maintain the application of the principle that men and women should receive equal pay for equal work". The concept of pay has been widely defined by the ECJ which has held, for example, that a statutory redundancy payment is pay within the meaning of Article 141.[26]

2. Four Directives are of central importance in this field—directives are legislative provisions directed at Member States which are instructed to import their terms into domestic law:

   (a) Directive 75/117 is otherwise known as the Equal Pay Directive. It has been held by the ECJ that this Directive "is principally designed to fulfil the practical application of the principle of equal pay outlined in Article 119 of the Treaty (and) in no way alters the content or scope of that principle as defined in the Treaty".[27]

   (b) Directive 76/207 is known as the Equal Treatment Directive. It puts into effect the principle of equal treatment for men and women as regards access to employment, training, working conditions and conditions governing dismissal.

   (c) Directive 2000/78/EC is a Framework Directive on Equal Treatment in Employment.[28] It requires Member States to introduce domestic measures which make it unlawful to discriminate on the grounds of sexual orientation, age, disability, and religion or belief.

   (d) Directive 2000/43/EC is known as the Race Directive. It seeks to lay out a framework for combating discrimination on the grounds of racial or ethnic origin with a view to implementing the principal of equal treatment.[29]

3.39 Before going on to examine the effect of this legislation it is necessary to grasp the concepts of direct applicability and direct effect. If a piece of community legislation is directly applicable this means that it acquires

---

[26] *Barber v. GRE Assurance Group* [1990] I.R.L.R. 240, ECJ.

[27] *Jenkins v. Kingsgate (Clothing Productions) Ltd* [1981] I.R.L.R. 228, ECJ; *Biggs v. Somerset County Council* [1996] I.R.L.R. 203, CA.

[28] Directive 2000/78/EC. Those provisions relating to sexual orientation and religious discrimination must be implemented by December 2, 2003, those relating to age and disability discrimination must be implemented by December 2, 2006.

[29] Directive 2000/43/EC, to be implemented by July 19, 2003.

legal force in the legal systems of the Member States as soon as it forms part of Community law and as it stands. In other words, it requires no further implementation to be effective within domestic legal systems. The Articles which make up the E.C. Treaty are good examples of directly applicable provisions.

If a provision of Community law has direct effect this means, in essence, that it gives rights which can be enforced before national courts and the ECJ in certain circumstances. To be directly effective a piece of Community legislation must be clear and precise, embody an unconditional obligation and not be subject to further implementation by the Member State.[30] It would be easy to assume that this means that directives do not have direct effect because they are, in effect, instructions to Member States to introduce legislation within a specified time to ensure that the rights and duties set out in the directive become part of the domestic law of the Member States. However, such an assumption would be incorrect since the ECJ has made it clear that if a Member State has not taken the steps required to implement a directive within the time set down within it, that directive will then gain the attribute of direct effect if it meets the above conditions.[31] 3.40

There is a further complication in that there are two kinds of direct effect—vertical and horizontal. A piece of legislation with horizontal direct effect can be used directly between private individuals and by individuals against the state or what is known as an "emanation of the state". Legislation which has vertical direct effect can be used by individuals only against a Member State or an emanation of the state.[32] Treaty articles which have direct effect have both horizontal and vertical direct effect. This means that, for example, Article 119 (now 141) can be used both against private employers and against state bodies. Directives only have vertical direct effect (an attribute gained after the time for their implementation has elapsed). The consequence is that state employees can use the Equal Treatment Directive against their employer while private sector employees cannot make use of this Directive against their employer. That, of course, places private sector employees at a disadvantage.

It is important to grasp these fundamental concepts if one is to have an understanding of the relevant case law. The Armed Forces pregnancy dismissal case of *Leale and Lane v. Ministry of Defence*[33] relied on the fact that the applicants could use the Equal Treatment Directive against their state employer. Subsequently, thousands of other women who had been dismissed from the armed services because they became pregnant lodged claims on the same basis.[34] 3.41

---

[30] *Van Duyn v. Home Office* [1975] 3 All E.R. 190, ECJ.

[31] *Marshall v. Southampton and South-West Hampshire Area Health Authority (No. 1)* [1986] I.R.L.R. 140, ECJ.

[32] See *Foster v. British Gas plc* [1990] I.R.L.R. 353, ECJ; and *Griffin v. South West Water Services Ltd* [1995] I.R.L.R. 15, Ch D, for discussion of the type of organisation which can be so described.

[33] Unreported, settled prior to hearing in the High Court.

[34] The women claimed sex discrimination, on the basis that the MOD had breached the Equal Treatment Directive. Unfair dismissal complaints could not be made at the time since the armed services were exempt from unfair dismissal legislation throughout the entire period when the policy of automatic dismissal on the ground of pregnancy was in force.

Another example of the Equal Treatment Directive being used against an emanation of the state is found in *Marshall v. Southampton and South-West Hampshire Area Health Authority (No. 1)*.[35] Ms Marshall was made to retire at 60 while men in the same employment could work until 65. At that time the SDA allowed discrimination between men and women with regard to compulsory retirement age. Ms Marshall was an employee of the state and the ECJ held that she was able to rely upon the vertical direct effect of the Equal Treatment Directive which did not allow such discrimination and which the Government had failed to implement.

3.42   Given this obvious disparity in the treatment of public and private sector employees the case of *Francovich v. Italian Republic*[36] is worthy of note. In that case the ECJ held that a Member State may be required to make good the loss suffered by an individual as a result of its failure to take all necessary steps to achieve the result required by a directive. Certain conditions must be met before such a right of action will arise: (1) the result required by the directive must include the conferring of rights for the benefit of individuals; (2) the content of these rights must be able to be determined by reference to the provisions of the directive; and (3) a causal link must exist between the state's breach of its obligation and the damage suffered by the person affected.

Francovich is an important decision that develops the principle set out in a number of European Court decisions of the need to ensure "full and effective" protection of Community law rights. In *Brasserie du Pecheur SA v. Germany*[37] and *R. v. Secretary of State for Transport, ex parte Factortame*[38] the ECJ extended the right to a remedy in the event of breach of Community law by a Member State. Any breach of Community law, whether directly effective or not, may found a damages claim if the breach is sufficiently serious and the requirements set out in *Francovich* are met. A breach is sufficiently serious if the Member State has "manifestly and gravely disregarded the limits on its discretion".[39]

3.43   The ECJ has made it clear that United Kingdom courts must give precedence to directly effective Community law where there is any conflict between it and domestic law.[40] In *Preston v. Wolverhampton Health Care NHS Trust*[41] the Court of Appeal expressed the principle thus: "The legal technique which is used for resolving . . . a conflict between domestic and Community law is for the court to disapply that part of domestic law which conflicts with Community law". Furthermore United Kingdom law must be interpreted so as to conform with Community law if that is at all possible.[42] This duty was emphasised by

---

[35] [1986] I.R.L.R. 140, ECJ.

[36] [1992] I.R.L.R. 84; [1995] I.C.R. 722, ECJ.

[37] [1996] I.R.L.R. 267, ECJ.

[38] *ibid.*

[39] *Brasserie du Pecheur SA v. Germany* [1996] I.R.L.R. 267, ECJ.

[40] *R. v. Secretary of State for Transport, ex p. Factortame* [1996] I.R.L.R. 267, ECJ.

[41] [1997] I.R.L.R. 233, C.A. the House of Lords subsequently made a reference to the ECJ in this case: [1998] I.R.L.R. 197 HL; [2000] I.R.L.R. 506 ECJ; [2001] I.R.L.R. 237 HL. However, this summary of the way in which Community law works was not under challenge.

[42] *Pickstone v. Freemans plc* [1988] I.R.L.R. 357, HL; *Von Colson and Kamann v. Land Nordrhein-Westfahen* [1986] 2 C.M.L.R. 430, ECJ.

the ECJ *in Marleasing SA v. La Comercial Internacional de Alimentacion SA*[43] when it stated: "the national court asked to interpret national law is bound to do so in every way possible in the light of the text and aim of the Directive to achieve the results envisaged by it". In *Litster v. Forth Dry Dock and Engineering Co. Ltd*[44] the House of Lords confirmed that United Kingdom courts are under a duty to give a purposive construction to regulations passed for the purpose of complying with directives. In that particular case this principle led to the court inserting words in the TUPE Regulations since this was necessary to ensure that the regulations complied with the requirements of the Acquired Rights Directive.[45]

Jurisdiction to hear complaints under European Community law

Normally, employment tribunals are given jurisdiction to hear cases by specific provisions under legislation. For example, the SDA provides that employment tribunals shall have jurisdiction to hear employment claims under that Act.[46] There are no specific provisions which state the forum in which complaints based upon Community law are to be heard. For years, employment tribunals simply acted on the basis that they had jurisdiction to deal with these claims. However, the whole matter was thrown into the spotlight by the case of *Secretary of State for Scotland and Greater Glasgow Health Board v. Wright and Hannah*.[47] An employment tribunal held that it did have jurisdiction to hear a claim based on Community law in circumstances where the relevant domestic law did not apply due to a specific exclusion in the domestic provisions and the EAT dismissed an appeal against this finding, stating that there is no doubt that an employment tribunal has jurisdiction to apply the provisions of Article 119 (now 141) and the Directive when an originating application is based on domestic legislation which is found to provide no remedy. In *Rankin v. British Coal Corporation*[48] the EAT stated that the reason why employment tribunals have jurisdiction to hear Community law claims is set out in *Shields v. Coomes E. (Holdings) Ltd*[49]; it is to be assumed that Parliament intended tribunals to apply Community law since appeals from tribunals lie to the EAT and thence to the civil appeal courts which are under a duty to apply Community law. It must be assumed that courts and tribunals should all apply the same law. However, doubt has now been cast on this principle by the decision of the Court of Appeal in *Biggs v. Somerset County Council*[50] which held that Article 119 (now 141) does not provide the basis for a separate claim for compensation for unfair dismissal but "even if such a separate basis of claim existed it would not fall within the jurisdiction of an

3.44

---

[43] [1992] E.C.R. I-4135.
[44] [1989] I.R.L.R. 161, HL.
[45] Directive 77/187.
[46] SDA, s.63.
[47] [1991] I.R.L.R. 187, EAT.
[48] [1993] I.R.L.R. 69, EAT.
[49] [1978] ICR 1159, CA.
[50] [1996] I.R.L.R. 203, CA.

employment tribunal". It is clear from *Biggs* and from *Preston v. Wolverhampton Health Care NHS Trust*[51] that the prevailing judicial view is that Community law does not provide individuals with "free standing" rights (contrary to the line adopted by the EAT in Scotland in *Rankin*). Instead, Community law rights must be accessed through domestic law, with Community law supplementing or supplanting domestic law as necessary.

3.45   This leads to the further question of what jurisdictional rules apply to such claims. For example, is there a time-limit for making a claim to an employment tribunal where an applicant seeks to rely upon Community law? The Treaty itself does not deal with the matter but there has been much case law on this point in recent years.[52] The basic principle which holds is that in the absence of Community rules on the subject, it is for the domestic legal system of each Member State to determine the procedural conditions governing actions at law intended to ensure the protection of rights which individuals derive from the direct effect of Community law, provided that such conditions are not less favourable than those relating to similar actions of a domestic nature nor framed so as to render virtually impossible the exercise of rights conferred by Community law.[53] So far as reliance upon directives is concerned it has been held that no time-limit can be applied against an applicant until the state has fully implemented the provisions of the directive within national law. It will only be at this point that individuals will be in a position to fully know their rights.[54] It was for this reason that so many women were able to make claims against the MOD in respect of their dismissal on the ground of pregnancy which had occurred in many cases years before they commenced proceedings. The State had failed to implement the provisions of the Equal Treatment Directive within domestic law so far as the armed services were concerned since it had specifically excluded service personnel from the protection offered by the SDA.

The position with regard to the impact of Article 141 and the jurisdictional rules which apply to its use in domestic courts will be discussed in Chapter 4 which considers equal pay law.

Community law and the rights of part-time workers

3.46   Many of the most important discrimination cases in which Community law has had a major impact have focused upon the rights of part-time workers. Just as in domestic law, Community law recognises the concept of indirect discrimination and this has been of great significance in the

---

[51] [1997] I.R.L.R. 233, CA.

[52] See, for example, *McKechnie v. UBM Building Supplies Southern Ltd* [1991] I.R.L.R. 283, EAT; *Stevens v. Bexley Health Authority* [1989] I.R.L.R. 240, EAT; *Hughes v. Strathclyde Regional Council and Churclier v. Strathclyde Regional Council* [1990] E.O.R. DCLD No. 6, p.4; *Rankin v. British Coal Corporation* [1993] I.R.L.R. 69, EAT.

[53] *Emmott v. Minister for Social Welfare and Att.-Gen.* [1991] I.R.L.R. 387, ECJ; *Johnston v. Chief Constable of the Royal Ulster Constabulary* [1998] N.I. 188; *Preston v. Wolverhampton Healthcare NHS Trust (No. 2)* [2001] I.R.L.R. 237 HL.

[54] *ibid.*

landmark cases in this area. One of those is *R. v. Secretary of State for Employment, ex parte Equal Opportunities Commission.*[55] The central issues in this case were the conditions governing the right to bring an unfair dismissal complaint and/or a complaint for a statutory redundancy payment which were set out at that time in the Employment Protection (Consolidation) Act 1978.[56] These conditions required a claimant to have worked 16 hours or more per week for two years or five years if the employee worked between eight and 16 hours per week. The EOC challenged the more onerous requirement imposed on those working under 16 hours, claiming that it was contrary to Community law because it indirectly discriminated against women who form the vast majority of part-time workers in the United Kingdom. The House of Lords held that no objective justification had been shown for the hours per week qualifying thresholds in the EP(C)A. Declarations were made that:

1. The provisions of the EP(C)A whereby employees who worked for fewer than 16 hours per week were subject to different conditions in respect of qualification for redundancy pay from those which apply to employees who work for 16 hours per week or more were incompatible with Article 119 of the Treaty of Rome and the Equal Pay Directive; and
2. The provisions of the EP(C)A whereby employees who worked for fewer than 16 hours per week were subject to different conditions in respect of the right to compensation for unfair dismissal from those which applied to employees who work for 16 hours per week or more were incompatible with the Equal Treatment Directive.

The decision was important not just in relation to the rights of part-time 3.47 workers but for establishing the principle that claims based upon an assertion that United Kingdom law is in breach of Community law in some respect can be brought before United Kingdom courts by way of an application for judicial review. After the EOC case the Government quickly introduced the Employment Protection (Part-time Employees) Regulations 1995[57] to remove the distinctions in the EP(C)A based on hours worked per week.

The EOC case left some doubt about whether unfair dismissal compensation was pay under Article 119. This issue was referred to the ECJ by the House of Lords in *R. v. Secretary of State for Employment, ex parte Seymour-Smith & Perez.*[58] (See Chap. 4.)

PART-TIME WORKERS

The rights of part-time workers continues to be a subject which engages 3.48 the attention of both the ECJ and the other community institutions.

---

[55] [1994] I.R.L.R. 176, HL.
[56] Hereinafter EP(C)A.
[57] S.I. 1995 No. 31.
[58] [1997] I.C.R. 371, HL.

In *Gerster v. Freistaat Bayern*[59] the ECJ held that, where many more women than men work part-time, national regulations requiring part-time employees to complete a period of employment more than one-third longer than that completed by their full-time counterparts in order to have approximately the same chance of promotion are contrary to the ETD if there is no special link between length of service and acquisition of a certain level of knowledge and experience.[60]

On December 15, 1997 the E.U. Labour and Social Affairs Council adopted the Part Time Workers' Directive.[61] This directive gives part-time workers the right "not to be treated in a less favourable manner than comparable full time workers solely because they work part time" unless any such differential treatment can be "justified on objective grounds". The Directive has now been implemented in the United Kingdom by the Part-Time Workers (Prevention of Less Favourable Treatment) Regulations 2000.[62]

PREGNANCY AND SEX DISCRIMINATION

3.49 Community law has also played a significant role in establishing the principle that adverse treatment on the ground of pregnancy amounts to sex discrimination. This area is examined more fully in Chapter 5.

DISCRIMINATION ON THE GROUND OF GENDER REASSIGNMENT

3.50 In *P v. S and Cornwall County Council*[63] the ECJ decided that the Equal Treatment Directive protected a transsexual who was dismissed because of gender reassignment. It reasoned that the scope of the directive is not confined simply to discrimination based on the fact that a person is one or other sex. A person who suffers adverse treatment because of gender reassignment is treated unfavourably by comparison with persons of the sex to which he or she was deemed to belong before undergoing gender reassignment. This, it was held, was discrimination based essentially, if not exclusively, on the sex of the person concerned and was in breach of the Equal Treatment Directive.

Following upon this decision an employment tribunal decided in *Reed v. Chessington World of Adventures Ltd*[64] that the SDA can be construed so that the principles set out in *P v. S* apply to a private sector employer. This decision was the subject of an appeal[65] and the EAT upheld the decision that the SDA can be construed so as to cover unfavourable treatment on grounds of an intention to undergo gender reassignment.

---

[59] [1997] I.R.L.R. 699, ECJ.
[60] See also *Kording v. Senator fur Finanzen* [1997] I.R.L.R. 710, ECJ.
[61] Directive 97/81.
[62] S.I. 2000 No. 1551.
[63] [1996] I.R.L.R. 347, ECJ.
[64] Unreported, London South Industrial Tribunal, decided July 31, 1996.
[65] [1997] I.R.L.R. 556, EAT.

Consequent upon the decisions in *P v. S* and *Reed* the SDA was amended by the Sex Discrimination (Gender Reassignment) Regulations 1999.[66] The Department for Education and Employment has also produced a Guide to the Regulations which provides guidance and good practice examples.

Section 82 of the SDA defines "gender reassignment" as "a process which is undertaken under medical supervision for the purpose of reassigning a person's sex by changing physiological or other characteristics of sex, and includes any part of such a process". This definition is wide, and will clearly include the early stages of the process prior to any surgical or other specific medical intervention, such as hormone treatment.

Regulation 2 is the key provision; it inserts a new section 2A into the SDA which makes it unlawful for a person ("A") to discriminate against another person ("B") by treating B less favourably than he treats or would treat other persons "on the ground that B intends to undergo, is undergoing or has undergone gender reassignment". This is clearly a provision which covers *direct* discrimination. The fact that an "intention" to undergo gender reassignment is enough to gain protection from discrimination means, it is submitted, that it is not, in fact, necessary for there to be any medical involvement before the protection applies. Accordingly, an individual who is dismissed or harassed or treated in some other "less favourable" manner simply because he/she announces that he/she intends to undergo a process of gender reassignment will be able to make a claim. The scope of protection is thus wider than that which was mooted in the Consultation Paper which preceded the Regulations. There it was suggested that "a specific request to the medical profession to intervene" could mark the onset of protection. It is not clear from the Regulations whether the intention to undergo gender reassignment must be specifically communicated to the employer or whether the protection will apply from the point that the employer knew *or ought reasonably to have known* of the intention.

The words "would treat" make it clear that a hypothetical comparator can be used while the words "on the ground that" suggest that the usual rule of causation in discrimination cases will apply, *i.e.* on the basis of *Owen and Briggs v. James*[67] it will not be necessary to show that the sole reason for the discrimination is gender reassignment. It will be enough to show that this was an "important factor" in the decision in respect of which complaint is made.

The comparison which is to be made in assessing whether discrimination has occurred is between a transsexual and "other persons". This is actually wider that the comparison used by the ECJ in *P v. S* which was between the transsexual and "persons of the sex to which he or she was deemed to belong before undergoing gender reassignment". Section 5(3) of the SDA is amended to make it clear that the comparison of the cases of a transsexual and "other persons" must be such "that the relevant circumstances in the one case are the same, or not materially different, in the other".

---

[66] S.I. 1999 No. 1102.
[67] [1982] I.R.L.R. 502, CA.

It is clear from section 2A of the SDA (derived from Regulation 2) that the areas in which discrimination is prohibited are employment, vocational training and discrimination against barristers and advocates. Although it is not specifically mentioned in the Regulations the vicarious liability provisions which apply to sex discrimination will also apply to discrimination on the ground of gender reassignment.

Section 2A(3) deals specifically with the comparison which is to be made in relation to absence caused by the fact that a person is undergoing gender reassignment. For these purposes "B" will be treated less favourably than others in relation to arrangements made for absence if:—

(a) he is treated less favourably than he would be if the absence was due to sickness or injury, or

(b) he is treated less favourably than he would be if the absence was due to some other cause and, having regard to the circumstances of the case, it is reasonable for him to be treated no less favourably.

Subsection (3)(a) means that if employees are allowed a certain number of days off due to sickness or injury before a sanction of any type is applied then a transsexual undergoing gender reassignment is entitled to the same number of days for the purposes of gender reassignment. It is clear from the use of the word "or" that subsection (3)(b) provides an alternative basis on which a discrimination claim may be founded. In effect it means that even if a person undergoing gender reassignment is treated no less favourably than someone who is absent as a result of illness a claim could still succeed if the transsexual can establish that he/she was treated less favourably than someone who was absent for a reason other than illness and that this less favourable treatment was unreasonable. Absence for a reason other than illness could cover time allowed off for sabbaticals or time off to nurse a sick relative.

While at first glance it might be tempting to compare the status of an individual undergoing gender reassignment with that of a pregnant employee such a comparison is not particularly apt so far as these Regulations are concerned. It is clear from the above provisions that a direct comparison is allowed between sickness and the process of undergoing gender reassignment. That comparison is not allowed if one is considering the treatment of a pregnant woman (see *Brown v. Rentokil Ltd*[68]—not possible to apply a uniform absence rule to sick employees and employees off sick as a result of pregnancy.) The DEE Guide states "As with any major treatment, there is always a small possibility that complications arising as a result of medical treatment for transsexualism could result in a prolonged incapacity for work. If incapacity continues beyond the normal expectations for the process undergone, a transsexual employee could be retired on medical grounds in the same way as any other person who becomes unfit for duty".

Whether it is permissible under Community law to dismiss a transsexual due to gender reassignment connected absence on the same basis as one would dismiss an employee whose absence is due to illness is almost certainly an issue which will come before the courts in due course.

---

[68] [1998] I.R.L.R. 445, ECJ.

Regulation 3 amends the SDA to make it unlawful to discriminate in relation to pay and other contractual terms and conditions on the ground of gender reassignment. However, it is made clear that, while transsexuals are entitled to access to a sick pay scheme, it will not be discriminatory to cease paying them if an employee off work due to sickness or injury would also cease to receive payment.

Regulation 4 contains extensive and complex GOQ provisions which are inserted into the SDA as section 7A and 7B. There are two categories of GOQ set out. The first, which is set out in section 7A, essentially is that which was already to be found in section 7 of the SDA where a person's sex is regarded as a GOQ for a job. Thus it will be possible to claim that "being a man" or "being a woman" is a GOQ for a job. If the employer can show that and that the treatment of the person undergoing gender reassignment is "reasonable in view of the circumstances described in the relevant paragraph of s.7(2) and any other relevant circumstances" then treatment which would otherwise have been unlawful will not be so. (Section 7(2) SDA contains various provisions where being of one or other sex will be regarded as GOQ, *e.g.* for reasons of physiology (excluding strength and stamina), authenticity, privacy or decency etc.—see s.7(2) for more detail)).

The Guide states: "There are very few instances in which a job will qualify for a GOQ on the ground of sex. However, exceptions may arise such as where considerations of privacy and decency or authenticity are involved. This could include, for example, a job which requires the job holder to model clothes, or work in the presence of people who are in a state of undress". The Guide also makes it clear that "employers should be aware that failure to recruit a person to whom gender reassignment grounds apply and who is living and presenting in their 'new' sex may be considered unreasonable and lead to claims of discrimination by those aggrieved. The onus will be on the employer to show that he or she acted reasonably in the circumstances". The difficulty is that the Regulations themselves do not define who is a "man" and who is a "woman" nor do they give any indication when sex is to be regarded as changed during the process of reassignment. The GOQ exceptions under section 7A will not apply where the duties in question can reasonably be carried out by existing employees.

Section 7B SDA sets out four "supplementary" GOQs (which can still be used even where there are other employees who can carry out the duties in question). These are:

(a) the job involves the holder of the job being liable to be called upon to perform intimate physical searches pursuant to statutory powers;

(b) the job is likely to involve the holder of the job doing his work, or living, in a private home and needs to be held otherwise than by a person who is undergoing or has undergone gender reassignment, because objection might reasonably be taken to allowing such a person—

    (i) the degree of physical or social contact with a person living in the home, or

    (ii) the knowledge of intimate details of such a person's life, which is likely, because of the nature or circumstances of the job or of the home, to be allowed to, or available to, the holder of the job;

(c) the nature or location of the establishment makes it imprac-
    ticable for the holder of the job to live elsewhere than in
    premises provided by the employer, and—
    (i) the only such premises which are available for per-
        sons holding that kind of job are such that reason-
        able objection could be taken, for the purpose of
        preserving decency and privacy, to the holder of the
        job sharing accommodation and facilities of either
        sex whilst undergoing gender reassignment, and
    (ii) it is not reasonable to expect the employer either to
        equip those premises with suitable accommodation
        or to make alternative arrangements; or
(d) the holder of the job provides vulnerable individuals with
    personal services promoting their welfare, or similar per-
    sonal services, and in the reasonable view of the employer
    those services cannot be effectively provided by a person
    whilst that person is undergoing gender reassignment.

Paragraphs (c) and (d) apply only in relation to discrimination against a
person who intends to undergo or is undergoing gender reassignment.
(The difficulty is that the Regulations do not specify when the process
ends. Groups representing transsexuals state that, particularly for female
to male transsexuals it may never be possible for some men to assert that
their treatment is finished.) It follows that the exceptions set out at (a)
and (b) apply even to those who have completed the gender reassignment process.

The issue of whether a male to female transsexual can be lawfully
excluded from serving as police officer, under GOQ provisions in section
7 SDA has been considered by the EAT in *Chief Constable of West
Yorkshire Police v. A and Secretary of State for Education and Employment*.[69] It was held that such a person could lawfully be excluded under
the GOQ provisions governing privacy and decency, given the need for
police officers to conduct physical searches and the legislative regime
applying thereto. The reasoning of the EAT is complex and the full
decision should be consulted for the detailed rationale of the decision.

Special provision is made in relation to employment for the purposes
of an organised religion.[70]

Additional Points to Note from the Guide

The following points are drawn for the Guide issued by the DEE.

- Equal opportunities policies which refer to discrimination
  on the ground of sex should also refer to discrimination on
  the ground of gender reassignment.
- It should not be expected that job applicants and inter-
  viewees will necessarily wish to disclose transsexual status. It
  is not a question which should be asked at interview where

---

[69] EAT/661/99 and EAT/213/00, heard July 3, 4 and 5, 2001, unreported at the time of
writing.
[70] See SDA, s.19.

no GOQ exception exists. However, where an exception may apply job applicants/interviewees would be expected to disclose transsexual status.

- In managing a sex transition the employer should discuss with the employee how they would like to handle the situation. This might include agreeing the point when individuals will commence using single sex facilities in their new gender, agreeing a dress code for the transition, how and when colleagues will be informed and by whom, when personal details such as name etc. are expected to change.

- Where reasonable and practical it is good practice for an employer to update their personnel records to ensure they reflect current name, title and sex. Where it is necessary to retain records showing original name, sex etc. (for example for pension or N.I. purposes) access should be restricted to those who require the information for the performance of their duties.

- Employers who have corporate insurance benefits should advise underwriters of a transsexual employee's status since the policy may be invalidated if a major fact such as gender reassignment is not disclosed. The employer should tell the employee in advance that the information is being disclosed.

DISCRIMINATION ON THE GROUND OF SEXUAL ORIENTATION

It was widely predicted, following upon the decision of the ECJ in *P v. S*, 3.51 that the arguments put forward for the applicant before the ECJ in *Grant v. South West Trains Ltd*[71] would also succeed. Ms Grant was denied travel concessions for her long term same sex partner when a man in a long term relationship with a woman, even although they were unmarried, would have been granted the concessions for his partner. Ms Grant claimed that this amounted to discrimination, contrary to the EqPA, the Equal Treatment Directive and Article 119 (now 141). The employment tribunal considered that the decision in *P v. S* was "persuasive authority for the proposition that discrimination on the ground of sexual orientation [was] unlawful" and referred various questions to the ECJ. The ECJ had no difficulty in holding that the concessions amounted to pay for the purposes of Article 119 (and that therefore the Equal Treatment Directive was not relevant). However, it went on to hold that since a male worker living with a same sex partner would also have been denied the concession there was no discrimination on the ground of sex. It considered that "in the present state of the law within the community, stable relationships between two persons of the same sex are not regarded as equivalent to marriages or stable relationships outside marriage between persons of the opposite sex. Consequently, an employer is not required by Community law to treat the situation of a person who has a stable relationship with a partner of the same sex as equivalent to that of a person who is married to or has a stable relationship outside marriage with a partner of the opposite sex".

---

[71] [1998] I.R.L.R. 206, ECJ.

The Inner House has recently had reason to re-assert the position set out in *Grant* that discrimination on the grounds of sexual orientation is not discrimination on the grounds of sex for the purposes of the SDA, in *MacDonald v. MoD* although the decision was by a majority rather than being unanimous.[72] The case involved the dismissal of a gay man from the armed services because of his sexual orientation. The Court of Session, overturning the decision of the EAT, held that the word "sex" in the SDA was not ambiguous and could not be interpreted to include "on grounds of sexual orientation" as well as meaning "gender". Furthermore, contrary to the decision of the EAT, the interpretation of "sex" in the SDA as not including sexual orientation was not incompatible with any right derived from the European Convention on Human Rights. Interestingly, however, there was a difference of opinion between their Lordships as to who the relevant comparator should be under section 5(3) of the SDA. Lords Kirkwood and Caplan were of the orthodox opinion that the relevant comparator was a woman who was sexually attracted to members of her own sex. On this reasoning there was no difference between the way the applicant and a comparable woman would have been treated. However Lord Prosser was of the opinion that the relevant comparator should be a heterosexual woman, being a woman who wanted to do exactly the same thing as the complainant, *i.e.* have or want to have a male partner—that would be the same factual circumstance while the circumstance of a woman having or wanting a female partner would be analogous rather than being "the same". He considered that the approach adopted by the majority involved an unjustified gloss upon the words of section 5(3), and entailed a comparison with a woman in circumstances which might broadly be comparable, but which are not "the same or not materially different". He was of the view that in deciding how to treat any individual, those who applied the policy were concerned with the gender of that individual and any partner. It followed, in his view that the policy was discriminatory on the ground of sex.[73]

This debate, which has been ongoing for some time, will be rendered irrelevant shortly given that the E.C. Framework Directive[74] on the elimination of discrimination in employment extends to the prevention of discrimination on the grounds of sexual orientation. The Directive must be implemented in domestic law by December 2003.

The foregoing should not be taken as indicative that Mr McDonald was found to have no remedy in relation to his discharge from the RAF. It was expressly acknowledged by counsel for the Ministry of Defence that the MOD had breached the respondent's rights under Article 8 (right to respect for private life), in combination with Article 14 (no discrimination in respect of rights under the ECHR) of the ECHR. This follows upon the decision of the European Court of Human Rights in *Smith and Grady v. U.K.*[75] which led to the MOD lifting its ban on gay men and lesbian women serving in the armed forces.

---

[72] [2001] I.R.L.R. 431.
[73] See *Pearce v. Governing Body of Mayfield Secondary School* [2000] I.R.L.R. 548, EAT for a further example of the comparison favoured by the majority in *McDonald* being used.
[74] 2000/78/EC.
[75] [1999] I.R.L.R. 734.

MECHANICS OF PURSUING A DISCRIMINATION COMPLAINT

Employment related complaints under the SDA and RRA should be 3.52 made to an employment tribunal within three months of the act of discrimination.[76] It is possible for the employment tribunal to extend the time-limit where it is "just and equitable"[77] to do so. In deciding what is just and equitable a tribunal is entitled to take into account anything which it judges to be relevant.[78] There has been an ongoing debate about the effect which pursuit of an internal grievance or appeal may have upon the issue of whether it would be just and equitable to allow a claim lodged outwith the three month period to be heard. In *Aniagwu v. London Borough of Hackney*[79] the EAT held that a tribunal had erred in failing to take into account the applicant's explanation for late lodging which was that he had lodged an internal appeal against the allegedly discriminatory decision and hoped that the matter might be resolved internally. The EAT thought that every tribunal, if asked, would consider it sensible to seek redress of a grievance through internal proceedings before resorting to litigation. In these circumstances the EAT substituted a decision that it was just and equitable that A's claim should be heard. However, in *Robinson v. Post Office*[80] the EAT emphasised that *Aniagwu* did not establish a proposition of broad applicability to the effect that whenever there was a delay in lodging a claim it could be excused by the fact that an internal procedure was being utilised and had not been exhausted. Delay on account of an incomplete internal appeal was just one of the factors to be put in the balance. In this case the applicant had known the time-limit and ignored the advice of his trade union in relation to it. It was a matter for the tribunal to decide what weight to attribute to various matters. This approach can be contrasted with that of the EAT in the Scottish case of *Grimes v. Strathclyde Fire Brigade*[81] in which Lord Johnson states that "the decision in *Aniagwu* is both correct and powerful and we support it".

In considering when an act of discrimination took place an act extending over a period is to be treated as done at the end of the period.[82] An act extends over a period of time if it takes the form of some policy, rule or practice in accordance with which decisions are taken from time to time. A succession of specific instances can indicate the existence of a practice which in turn can constitute a continuing act extending over a period.[83]

The position with regard to time-limits for claims founded on Community law is, as discussed earlier in this chapter, more complex.[84]

---

[76] SDA, ss.63 and 76; RRA, ss.54 and 68.

[77] SDA, s.76(1); RRA, s.68(1).

[78] *Hutchison v. Westward Television Ltd* [1977] I.R.L.R. 69, EAT. The decision in *Ministry of Defence v. Wood* (EAT/1156/99, unreported) under the SDA is worth noting simply because the EAT upheld the decision of a Tribunal that the claim should be allowed to proceed, despite the fact that it was some seven and a half years out of time.

[79] [1999] I.R.L.R. 303, EAT.

[80] [2000] I.R.L.R. 804, EAT.

[81] Unreported, EAT/801/00, heard January 17, 2001.

[82] SDA, s.76(6); RRA, s.68(7). See *e.g. Cast v. Croydon College* [1998] I.R.L.R. 318, CA.

[83] *Owusu v. London Fire and Civil Defence Authority* [1995] I.R.L.R. 574, EAT.

[84] See Chap. 4 for time-limit in Community law based equal pay claims.

APPEALS

3.53 Appeals from employment tribunals lie on a point of law to the EAT and thence to the Court of Session and the House of Lords. It is possible for any tribunal or court to refer questions to the ECJ concerning the interpretation of Community law for a preliminary ruling in terms of Article 234 (previously 177) of the E.C. Treaty.

THE QUESTIONNAIRE PROCEDURE

3.54 Under the authority of section 74 of the SDA and section 65 of the RRA it is possible for a complainant to send a questionnaire to the respondent in a case at any time prior to lodging of an employment tribunal application or within 21 days of an application being lodged.[85] These questionnaires, commonly known respectively as SD74s and RR65s, allow a complainant to question a respondent on his reasons for doing any relevant act or on any other matter which is or may be relevant. The questions and any replies are admissible as evidence and if it appears to a tribunal that a respondent deliberately, and without reasonable excuse, failed to reply within a reasonable period or that his reply was evasive or equivocal, the tribunal may draw any inference from that fact that it considers it just and equitable to draw, including an inference that the respondent committed an unlawful act.[86] Judicious use of such questionnaires can be extremely helpful to a complainant's case.

REMEDIES

3.55 There are three remedies which an employment tribunal can utilise if it considers that it is just and equitable to do so in the event that it finds that a sex or race discrimination complaint is well founded[87]: (1) an order declaring the rights of the parties in relation to the act to which the complaint relates; (2) an order requiring the respondent to pay compensation to the complainant which can include compensation for injury to feelings and which is to be calculated in the same way as damages in reparation for breach of statutory duty; and (3) a recommendation that the respondent take within a specified time action appearing to the tribunal to be practicable for the purpose of obviating or reducing the adverse effect on the complainant of any act of discrimination to which the complaint relates. (If a respondent, without reasonable justification, fails to comply with a recommendation the tribunal can increase the amount of compensation awarded or make an order for compensation to be paid if this was not done in the first place.)

---

[85] Sex Discrimination (Questions and Replies) Order 1975 (S.I. 1975 No. 2048), Art. 5 Race Relations (Questions and Replies) Order 1977 (S.I. 1977 No. 842), Art. 5.
[86] SDA, s.74; RRA, s.65.
[87] SDA, s.65; RRA, s.56.

COMPENSATION FOR DIRECT AND INTENTIONAL INDIRECT DISCRIMINATION

The compensation provisions in respect of direct and intentional indirect 3.56
sex and race discrimination differ from the provisions applicable in the
event of unintentional indirect discrimination. So far as direct and
intentional indirect discrimination is concerned it has always been
possible since the SDA and RRA came into force for compensation to
be awarded both in respect of injury to feelings and financial loss
occasioned by the act of discrimination (for example, lost wages can be
awarded if the act of discrimination involves dismissal, failure to recruit
or failure to promote to a higher paid job) but for many years the total
compensation which could be awarded was capped by statute. All this
changed, however, as a result of the case of Ms Helen Marshall. As
discussed previously, Ms Marshall was compulsorily retired by her
employer at the age of 60 although male colleagues were allowed to
work on to age 65. Ms Marshall argued that this treatment was
discriminatory and in breach of the Equal Treatment Directive. The ECJ
agreed[88] and, in a landmark decision, held that Ms Marshall was entitled
to rely on the direct effect of the Directive since she was employed by an
emanation of the state and the state had failed to implement the
directive within the required time-limit. The case was then referred back
to the original tribunal which had heard it some years before for
compensation to be awarded.

In calculating compensation, the employment tribunal proceeded to 3.57
award the sum of £19,405 as it considered the statutory limit on
compensation set down by section 65 of the SDA at that time did not
provide an adequate remedy as required by Article 6 of the Equal
Treatment Directive. Article 6 states that Member States are required to
introduce into their national legal systems "such measures as are
necessary to enable all persons who consider themselves wronged . . . to
pursue their claims by judicial process". Of the sum awarded, £7,710 was
interest from the date of the act of discrimination, since the tribunal held
that such an award was necessary to ensure an adequate remedy. The
employer appealed against this decision and it was overturned by the
EAT which held that compensation was restricted to the maximum
under the SDA. The House of Lords referred the matter to the ECJ.
The ECJ held that the object of the Directive was to "arrive at real
equality of opportunity" and this cannot be attained "in the absence of
measures appropriate to restore such equality when it has not been
observed".[89] Accordingly, the fixing of an upper limit on awards did not
constitute proper implementation of Article 6 since it limited the
amount of compensation to a level which was not necessarily consistent
with the requirement of ensuring real equality of opportunity by
adequate reparation for loss sustained. In assessing compensation,
factors such as the effluxion of time and the effect that this had on the
value of the award had to be taken into account. In these circumstances,

---

[88] *Marshall v. Southampton and South-West Hampshire Area Health Authority (No. 1)*
[1986] I.R.L.R. 140, ECJ.
[89] *Marshall v. Southampton and South-West Hampshire Area Health Authority (No. 2)*
[1990] I.R.L.R. 481, ECJ.

an award of interest was to be regarded as an essential component of compensation for the purposes of restoring real equality of treatment. Shortly thereafter the Sex Discrimination and Equal Pay (Remedies) Regulations 1993[90] removed the limit on compensation and gave tribunals the power to award interest on the sums due for pecuniary loss and injury to feelings. Complex regulations now exist which set out exactly how interest is to be calculated in discrimination cases.[91]

Consequent upon the lifting of the compensation limit in sex discrimination cases the limit was also lifted in race cases by the Race Relations (Remedies) Act 1994.

3.58   The impact of *Marshall v. Southampton and South-West Area Health Authority (No. 2)*[92] is seen in the compensation which was awarded to ex-servicewomen dismissed from the Armed Services on the grounds of pregnancy. However in *Ministry of Defence v. Cannock*[93] the EAT set out guidelines for calculating compensation in discrimination cases and the application of these reduced the amount of compensation awarded in subsequent MOD cases. In a less than scientific approach the EAT suggested that when assessing compensation, employment tribunals should keep "a sense of due proportion". This, it was suggested, involved looking at the individual components of any award and then looking at the total to make sure that the total seems a sensible and just reflection of the chances which had been assessed. The decision in *Cannock* has been heavily criticised for being based more on public opinion than the requirements of the law.[94]

3.59   The likely level of award for injury to feelings in any given case can be difficult to predict. In 1999 the average award for injury to feelings in a sex discrimination case was £3,787 with the median award being £2,125. The highest award was £37,500. In race cases the average award for injury to feelings was £5,297 with the median award being £3,000. The highest award was £30,000.[95] In *Virdi v. The Commissioner of Police of the Metropolis*[96] an employment tribunal awarded £100,000 for injury to feelings together with an additional sum of £25,000 for aggravated damages to a police officer discriminated against on the ground of race.[97]

More generally, it is important to note that compensation is only awarded in a minority of the discrimination cases which are heard by employment tribunals.

COMPENSATION FOR UNINTENTIONAL INDIRECT DISCRIMINATION

3.60 Until very recently it was not possible for compensation to be awarded in cases of unintentional indirect sex discrimination. This could lead to grave injustice because it meant that if a woman, for example, lost her

---

[90] S.I. 1993 No. 2798.

[91] See Employment Tribunals (Interest on Awards in Discrimination Cases) Regulations 1996 (S.I. 1996 No. 2803).

[92] [1990] I.R.L.R. 481, ECJ.

[93] [1994] I.R.L.R. 509, EAT.

[94] For a judicial re-examination of *Cannock* see *Ministry of Defence v. Hunt* [1996] I.R.L.R. 139, EAT and *Ministry of Defence v. O'Hare (No. 2)* [1997] I.C.R. 306, EAT.

[95] See E.O.R. No. 93, September/October 2000, p.11.

[96] E.O.R. DCLD No. 47, Spring 2001, p.1.

[97] See *ICTS (UK) Ltd v. Tchoula* [2000] I.R.L.R. 643, EAT for further discussion of awards for injury to feelings in the context of the categorisation of cases into groups.

job as a result of such discrimination no sum could be awarded in respect of loss of wages. Increasingly, tribunals appeared minded to find that indirect discrimination was intentional.[98]

In *McMillan v. Edinburgh Voluntary Organisations Council*[99] tribunal 3.61 found that the applicant had suffered loss as a result of unintentional indirect sex discrimination. It accepted that the provisions of the SDA which at that time prevented it awarding financial compensation were contrary to the Equal Treatment Directive, having regard to the decision in *Marshall v. Southampton and South-West Area Health Authority (No. 2)*.[1] However, it held that since the applicant was not employed by an emanation of the state she could not rely on the direct effect of the Directive and that it was not able to award any compensation. On appeal it was argued that it was possible to construe the SDA to accord with the requirements of the Directive but the EAT held that this was not possible without distorting the meaning of the domestic legislation. Shortly thereafter the Sex Discrimination and Equal Pay (Miscellaneous Amendments) Regulations 1996[2] were laid and came into force on March 25, 1996. These Regulations amended section 65 of the SDA to allow compensation to be awarded for unintentional indirect discrimination. However, compensation can only be awarded if the tribunal makes such an order declaring the rights of the parties and/or recommendation as it would have made if it did not have the power to award compensation and thereafter still considers it is just and equitable for compensation to be awarded.[3] In other words, compensation is to be a remedy of last resort. So far as unintentional indirect racial discrimination is concerned it remains the case that compensation cannot be awarded.[4]

COMPENSATION FOR PSYCHIATRIC INJURY

In *Sheriff v. Klyne Tugs (Lowestoft) Ltd*[5] the Court of Appeal held that an 3.62 employment tribunal has jurisdiction to award damages for personal injury caused by the statutory tort (delict) of discrimination. This includes damages for both physical and psychiatric injury. It follows from this that if a complainant can show that the act of discrimination has led to psychiatric illness, and not just to emotional distress (which is compensated for by damages for injury to feelings) then a further head of damages will be available in the employment tribunal. Unlike in action for negligence, however, it does not appear that the applicant has to prove that it was reasonably foreseeable that the conduct in question would cause psychiatric injury. According to Stuart-Smith L.J. "all that needs to be established is the causal link" between the act of discrimination and the injury. However, he suggests that in employment tribunal

---

[98] For examples, see *London Underground v. Edwards* [1995] I.R.L.R. 536, EAT and *Given v. Scottish Power*, E.O.R. DCLD No. 24, p.1.
[99] [1998] I.R.L.R. 364, CA.
[1] [1990] I.R.L.R. 481, ECJ.
[2] S.I. 1996 No. 438.
[3] SDA, s.65(1B).
[4] RRA, s.57(3).
[5] [1999] I.R.L.R. 481, CA.

cases involving claims of injury to health as well as injury to feelings it would be appropriate for a medical report to be obtained. *HM Prison Service v. Salmon*[6] contains discussion of the manner in which employment tribunals should go about assessing damages for psychiatric injury

RECOMMENDATIONS

3.63 Recommendations must contain a time-limit for implementation[7] and if they recommend changes in practice these must be such as to affect the applicant.[8] Case law reveals that tribunals have made a variety of recommendations. For example, in *Morris v. Scott and Knowles*[9] the tribunal recommended that the respondent restore the full-time working hours of the applicants. In *Steel v. Union of Post Office Workers (No. 2)*[10] the tribunal recommended that the respondent backdate the applicant's seniority which had been adversely affected by discriminatory action. However, where recommendations have been made in promotion cases that an applicant should be promoted to the next available suitable vacancy these have been struck down[11] on the basis that the legislation does not allow positive discrimination and that if the recommendations were implemented this could lead to discrimination against other candidates.

COMPROMISE AGREEMENTS/CONTRACTS AND ACAS SETTLEMENTS

3.64 Normally a term in a contract which purports to exclude or limit any provision of the SDA, EqPA or RRA is unenforceable. However, this rule does not apply to an ACAS conciliated settlement or to a compromise contract which fulfils the requirements set out in section 77 of the SDA or section 72 of the RRA. Compromise agreements are now commonly used where an applicant who has access to independent advice, as defined in these sections, wishes to enter into an agreement to settle a complaint outwith the tribunal. The vast majority of discrimination complaints are, in fact, settled without the need for a tribunal hearing.

PROPOSALS FOR REFORM OF EQUALITY LAW

3.65 "Equality: a new framework—report of the independent review of the enforcement of UK anti-discrimination legislation",[12] produced by the Cambridge Centre for Public Law and the Judge Institute of Management Studies at Cambridge University, is described by Lord Lester of

---

[6] [2001] I.R.L.R. 425, EAT.

[7] *Prestcold v. Irvine* [1980] I.R.L.R. 267, EAT.

[8] *Bayoomi v. British Railways Board* [1981] I.R.L.R. 431, IT; *Turton v. MacGregor Wallcoverings Ltd* [1977] I.R.L.R. 249, IT.

[9] [1976] I.R.L.R. 238, IT.

[10] [1978] I.R.L.R. 198, IT.

[11] See *British Gas v. Sharma* [1991] I.R.L.R. 101, EAT; and *O'Mara v. Scottish Agricultural College,* IDS Brief 461, January 1992, EAT.

[12] For discussion of this report see E.O.R. No. 93, September/October 2000, p.40–45.

Herne Hill Q.C. as a "profound study of what is wrong with the existing laws, and of what can and should be done to develop an accessible legislative framework". The report sets out more than 50 recommendations for change, including a proposal that there should be a single Equality Act, "written in plain language so as to facilitate comprehension"[13] which would cover discrimination on the ground of "sex, race, colour, ethnic or national origin, religion or belief, disability, age, sexual orientation, or other status". It also recommends that there should be a single Equality Commission for Britain covering all grounds of unlawful discrimination.

---

[13] Recommendation 1.

CHAPTER 4

EQUAL PAY

INTRODUCTION

4.01 Domestic law governing the right of a worker to receive equal pay (and equality in respect of other contractual terms) to that received by a worker of the opposite sex[1] doing the same or very similar work, or work of equal value (whether previously formally rated as such or not) is set out in the Equal Pay Act 1970.[2] However, domestic law has been considerably influenced and supplemented by European Community equal pay law which is found principally in Article 141 of the Treaty of Rome and the Equal Pay Directive.[3] The interaction of domestic and Community law in this area is considered below. Despite the existence of this body of law there is still a substantial gap between the average earnings of men and women. In 2000 the average gross hourly earnings of women in full-time employment (excluding overtime) were 81.6 per cent of men's. Women's average gross weekly earnings (including overtime) were 74.7 per cent of men's.[4] Much of this disparity is accounted for by the fact that women and men still tend to be concentrated in different jobs and those jobs typically done by women often have lower status and pay than jobs typically held by men.[5]

EUROPEAN COMMUNITY EQUAL PAY PROVISIONS

4.02 At this stage it may be helpful to give a broad outline of the Community law provisions which govern the right to equal pay without discrimination on the ground of sex before examining domestic legislation and the interaction of these two bodies of law.

ARTICLE 141 OF THE TREATY OF ROME

4.03 Article 141 (formerly 119) requires Member States to ensure and maintain "the application of the principle that men and women should

---

[1] Although the Equal Pay Act is framed with reference to women and their treatment relative to men, EqPA, s.1(13) makes it clear that it applies equally in the converse case of men and their treatment relative to women.

[2] Hereinafter EqPA.

[3] Directive 75/117.

[4] New Earnings Survey 2000.

[5] See Equal Opportunities Commission Code of Practice on Equal Pay for further discussion.

receive equal pay for equal work". Pay is defined as "the ordinary basic or minimum wage or salary and any other consideration, whether in cash or in kind, which the worker receives, directly or indirectly, in respect of his employment from his employer". The ECJ has held that Article 141 has direct effect, giving rise to rights which can be enforced by individuals before national courts and tribunals.[6] Since the right originates from a Treaty Article, rather than a Directive, it can be relied upon by both private and public sector employees.

THE EQUAL PAY DIRECTIVE

The Equal Pay Directive[7] makes it clear that the principle of equal pay 4.04 outlined in Article 141 means that for the same work, or for work to which equal value is attributed, all discrimination on grounds of sex is to be eliminated with regard to all aspects and conditions of remuneration. However, it has been held that this provision is principally designed to facilitate the practical application of the principle of equal pay set out in Article 141 and that it in no way alters the scope or content of that principle as set out in the Treaty.[8] The Directive also requires Member States to ensure that all laws, regulations and administrative provisions conform with the principle of equal pay and to introduce a judicial process to enable individuals to make claims arising from an alleged breach of the principle.

In *Biggs v. Somerset County Council*[9] it has been held that the EPD does not create any new or separate rights from those conferred by Article 141 while in *Preston v. Wolverhampton Healthcare NHS Trust*[10] it was held that the EPD does not have direct effect in any circumstances because Article 141 already provides a remedy to those seeking equal pay for equal work: "The doctrine of direct vertical effect has been developed in order to prevent the State from taking advantage of its own failure to enact a Directive into its national law. Where the national law does provide a remedy the doctrine of direct vertical effect does not come into play".[11]

There is a good deal of overlap between the protection provided by domestic and Community law. However, in some situations Community law may provide more extensive protection.[12] In these circumstances, the Community law standard, where it is relied upon by an individual, must prevail: "Community law is now part of our law: and, whenever there is any inconsistency, Community law has priority. It is not supplanting English law. It is part of our law which overrides any other part which is inconsistent with it".[13]

---

[6] Case 43/75 *Defrenne v. Société Anonyme Belge de Navigation Aérienne (Sabena)* [1976] I.C.R. 547, ECJ (known as *Defrenne (No. 2)*).

[7] Hereinafter EPD.

[8] *Jenkins v. Kingsgate (Clothing Productions) Ltd* [1981] I.R.L.R. 228, ECJ.

[9] [1996] I.R.L.R. 203, CA.

[10] Heard with *Fletcher v. Midland Bank plc* [1997] I.R.L.R. 233, CA.

[11] *per* Lord Justice Schiemann at para. 59.

[12] For example, see the cases set out below which deal with the range of comparators allowed in an equal pay claim where Article 141 is utilised.

[13] *per* Lord Denning in *Macarthys Ltd v. Smith* [1980] I.R.L.R. 210, CA See also *Amministrazione delle Finanze dello Stato v. Simmenthal Spa (No. 2)* [1978] E.C.R. 629, ECJ.

4.05   For a considerable number of years there was much debate about
whether Article 141 (and indeed other provisions of Community law
with direct effect) gave rise to "free-standing" rights[14] or whether it
operated largely within the confines of domestic law, simply operating to
disapply any barriers or limitations of domestic law where Article 141
gave more extensive rights. This debate is often characterised as one
between the dualist and monist approaches to the way in which
Community law operates. In both *Biggs* and *Barber v. Staffordshire
County Council*[15] the Court of Appeal has made it clear that the latter
approach is to be preferred.[16] In both cases the leading judgment was
given by Lord Justice Neill who considered that the approach of the
EAT in *Biggs* was the correct one:

> "I believe the true position to be as was explained by Mummery J
> in his valuable judgment in *Biggs v. Somerset County Council* . . .
> where he summarised the position as follows at p.459, paragraph
> 71:
>
> (a) The employment tribunal has no inherent jurisdiction.
>   Its statutory jurisdiction is confined to complaints that
>   may be made to it under specific statutes, such as the
>   Employment Protection (Consolidation) Act 1978, the
>   Sex Discrimination Act 1975, the Race Relations Act
>   1976, the Equal Pay Act 1970 and any other relevant
>   statute. We are not able to identify the legal source of
>   any jurisdiction in the tribunal to hear and determine
>   disputes about Community law generally.
>
> (b) In the exercise of its jurisdiction the tribunal may apply
>   Community law. The application of Community law
>   may have the effect of displacing provisions in domestic
>   law statutes which preclude a remedy claimed by the
>   applicant. In the present case the remedy claimed by
>   the applicant is unfair dismissal. That is a right con-
>   ferred on an employee by the Act of 1978 and earlier
>   legislation. If a particular applicant finds that the Act
>   contains a barrier which prevents the claim from suc-
>   ceeding but that barrier is incompatible with Com-
>   munity law, it is displaced in consequence of superior
>   and directly effective Community rights.
>
> (c) In applying Community law the tribunal is not assuming
>   or exercising jurisdiction in relation to a 'free-standing'
>   Community right separate from rights under domestic
>   law. In our view, some confusion is inherent in or
>   caused by the mesmeric metaphor, 'free-standing'.
>   'Free-standing' means not supported by a structural

---

[14] See *Rankin v. British Coal Corporation* [1993] I.R.L.R. 69, EAT, a decision of the
EAT in Scotland which adopted the approach, subsequently held incorrect, that Article
119 gave "free-standing" rights.

[15] [1996] I.R.L.R. 209, CA.

[16] See *Alabaster v. Woolwich plc and Secretary of State for Social Security* [2000] I.R.L.R.
754, EAT for an example of this approach in operation.

framework, not attached or connected to another structure. This is not a correct description of the claim
asserted by the applicant. She is not complaining of an
infringement of a 'free-standing' right in the sense of an
independent right of action created by Community law,
unsupported by any legal framework or not attached or
connected to any other legal structure. Her claim is
within the structural framework of the employment
protection legislation, subject to the disapplication of
the threshold qualifying provisions in accordance with
the EOC case".[17]

This approach has the consequence that all of the procedural conditions
governing domestic law claims will also apply in cases where Community
law is relied upon, unless these conditions are themselves contrary to the
provisions of Community law.[18]

Article 141 and the concept of pay

The word "pay" has been interpreted very broadly in a number of ECJ   4.06
decisions. So far as Community law is concerned, virtually any benefit
derived from the employment relationship, whether contractual or not,
appears to be encompassed within the definition of "pay". An example
of this broad approach is to be found in *Gillespie v. Northern Health and
Social Services Board*[19] which considered whether statutory and contractual maternity pay fell within the concept of pay for the purposes of
Article 141 (previously 119):

"The definition in the second paragraph of Article 119 provides
that the concept of pay ... includes all consideration which
workers receive directly or indirectly from their employers in
respect of their employment. The legal nature of such consideration is not important for the purposes of the application of Article
119 provided that it is granted in respect of employment (see
Garland v. British Rail Engineering Ltd, 12/81 [1982] IRLR 111,
paragraph 10).
Consideration classified as pay includes, inter alia, consideration
paid by the employer by virtue of legislative provisions and under a
contract of employment whose purpose is to ensure that workers
receive income even where, in certain cases specified by the
legislature, they are not performing any work provided for in their
contracts of employment (see *Arbeiterwohlfahrt der Stadt Berlin E.
V. v. Botel*, C–360/90 [1992] IRLR 423, paragraphs 14 and 15; also
Kowalska v. Freie und Hansestadt Hamburg, C–33/89 [1990] IRLR
447, paragraph 11, and *Barber v. Guardian Royal Exchange
Assurance Group Ltd*, 262/88 [1990] IRLR 240, paragraph 12).

---

[17] At para. 22.
[18] See below for discussion of possible conflicts relating to time-limits for making an
equal pay claim and remedies for breach of the principle of equal pay including *Preston v.
Wolverhampton Healthcare NHS Trust* [2000] I.R.L.R. 506, ECJ; [2001] I.R.L.R. 237, HL.
[19] [1996] I.R.L.R. 214, ECJ.

It follows that since the benefit paid by an employer under legislation or collective agreements to a woman on maternity leave is based on the employment relationship, it constitutes pay within the meaning of Article 119 of the Treaty and Directive 75/117".[20]

4.07 Similarly, it would appear that benefits derived from occupational pension schemes are to be viewed as pay[21] as are contributions to a pension scheme paid by the employer[22] and concessionary travel facilities.[23] It matters not, for the purposes of Article 141[24], that the "payment" in respect of which a claim is made is non-contractual[25] so long as it derives from the employment relationship. Redundancy pay, whether contractual or statutory, is also covered by Article 141. This was made clear in *Barber v. Guardian Royal Exchange Assurance Group*[26] where the ECJ held that:

> "[T]he concept of pay, within the meaning of the second paragraph of Article 119, comprises any other consideration, whether in cash or in kind, whether immediate or future, provided that the worker receives it, albeit indirectly, in respect of his employment from his employer . . . Accordingly, the fact that certain benefits are paid after the termination of the employment relationship does not prevent them from being in the nature of pay, within the meaning of Article 119 of the Treaty.
>
> As regards, in particular, the compensation granted to a worker in connection with his redundancy, it must be stated that such compensation constitutes a form of pay to which the worker is entitled in respect of his employment, which is paid to him upon termination of the employment relationship, which makes it possible to facilitate his adjustment to the new circumstances resulting from the loss of his employment and which provides him with a source of income during the period in which he is seeking new employment.
>
> It follows that compensation granted to a worker in connection with his redundancy falls in principle within the concept of pay for the purposes of Article 119 of the Treaty".[27]

4.08 The ECJ has held that compensation for unfair dismissal falls within the concept of "pay" for the purposes of Article 141.[28]

---

[20] At paras 12—14.

[21] See in particular Case C-262/88 *Barber v. Guardian Royal Exchange Assurance Group* [1990] I.R.L.R. 240 where it was held that a pension paid under a contracted out occupational scheme constituted "pay".

[22] *Worringham and Humphreys v. Lloyds Bank* [1981] I.R.L.R. 178, ECJ.

[23] *Garland v. British Rail Engineering* [1982] I.R.L.R. 111, ECJ.

[24] Previously Art. 119.

[25] Case C–360/90 *Arbeiterwohlfahrt der Stadt Berlin E.V. v. Botel* [1992] I.R.L.R. 423, ECJ.

[26] [1990] I.R.L.R. 240, ECJ.

[27] At paras 12–14. See also *Lewen v. Denda* [2000] I.R.L.R. 67, ECJ, where it was held that a Christmas bonus paid to staff as an incentive or as a reward for loyalty would constitute "pay" under article 141.

[28] *R v. Secretary of State for Employment, ex parte Seymour-Smith and Perez* [1999] I.R.L.R. 253, ECJ; *(No. 2)* [2000] I.R.L.R. 263, HL.

Pensions and Article 141

Claims based upon Article 141 have had a particularly significant 4.09
impact in the area of pension equality and there are a number of
important ECJ decisions in this field.

As previously noted, it has been clear since *Barber v. Guardian Royal
Exchange Assurance Group*[29] that occupational pension benefits are pay
for the purposes of Article 141. Article 141 does not prohibit an
employer reducing a woman's occupational pension from age 60 on the
ground that she will receive a state pension while not reducing a man's
pension until age 65.[30] The provision of survivor's benefits falls within
the scope of Article 141. However, equal treatment is not required for
periods of service prior to May 17, 1990. Accordingly, full equality
between men and women will not be achieved for some years to come.[31]

Unequal employer contributions in funded occupational pension
schemes, based on the use of actuarial factors differing according to sex,
taking account of the fact that women live on average longer than men,
do not fall within the scope of Article 141. The funding arrangement
chosen by the employer to secure the adequacy of the funds necessary to
cover the costs of the pensions promised is also outwith the concept of
pay.[32]

The right to join a pension scheme falls within Article 141 of the E.C. 4.10
Treaty and is therefore subject to the prohibition of discrimination laid
down by that article. Accordingly, in considering the position of part-
time workers excluded from a pension scheme, the ECJ stated that this
contravened Article 141 where it could be shown that the exclusion
affected a greater number of women than men, unless the employer
could show that the exclusion was objectively justified by factors which
were unrelated to sex. This right to equal treatment in relation to joining
an occupational pension scheme can be relied upon from April 8, 1976,
being the date when the court held for the first time that Article 141 had
direct effect.[33]

Article 141 precludes an employer who adopts measures necessary to
comply with *Barber* from raising the retirement age for women to that of
men in relation to periods of service completed between May 17, 1990
and the date on which those measures come into force. As regards
periods of service completed after the latter date Article 141 does not
prevent an employer from taking that step. In other words, in achieving
equality between men and women in respect of pension rights, there is
nothing under Community law to stop employers from increasing
pension ages rather than reducing pension ages.[34]

---

[29] [1983] I.R.L.R. 240, HL.

[30] *Birdseye Walls Ltd v. Roberts* [1994] I.R.L.R. 29, ECJ.

[31] *Ten Oever v. Stickling Bedrifspensioenfonds voor het Glazenwassers en Schoonmaak-bedrijf* [1993] I.R.L.R. 601, ECJ.

[32] *Neath v. Hugh Steeper Ltd* [1994] I.R.L.R. 91, ECJ.

[33] *Fisscher v. Voorhuis Hengelo BV en Stichting Bedrifpensioenfonds voor de Detailhandel* [1994] I.R.L.R. 662, ECJ; and *Vroege v. NCIV Instituut voor Volkshuisvesting BV en Stichting Pensioenfonds NCIV* [1994] I.R.L.R. 651, ECJ.

[34] *Smith v. Avdel Systems Ltd* [1994] I.R.L.R. 602, ECJ.

4.11   Article 141 can be relied upon by both employees and their dependants against the trustees of an occupational pension scheme. Trustees
are bound by Article 141 as well as employers.[35] Transfer benefits, when
an employee moves to another pension scheme, and lump sum benefits
when an employee takes early retirement, are not covered by the equal
treatment principle, since their value depends on the arrangements
chosen.[36] It is therefore for the transferee scheme to fund the elimination of any discriminatory effect suffered by the employee as a result of
an inadequate transfer of funds arising from discriminatory treatment, in
respect of service from May 17, 1990, while the worker was a member of
the transferor scheme.[37]

Article 141 precludes red circling the rights of female employees in
respect of service after May 17, 1990. It does not allow an occupational
pension scheme to maintain in force after May 17, 1990 (the date of the
Barber judgment) a condition as to retirement age differing according to
sex, even where this is done with the intention of protecting the rights of
existing female members to have a retirement age lower than that for
men. Once discrimination in pay has been found to exist post May 17,
1990 the only proper way of complying with Article 141 is to grant the
persons in the disadvantaged class the same advantages as those enjoyed
by persons in the favoured class.[38]

Article 141 and maternity pay

4.12   Article 141 has also been relied upon, with a limited degree of success,
by those seeking to challenge the fact that women on maternity leave
generally receive something less than their normal income. The specific
issue of whether women on maternity leave should be entitled to receive
their full normal salary was considered in *Gillespie v. Northern Health
and Social Services Board*,[39] a claim brought under Article 141, the EPD
and the Equal Treatment Directive.

The applicants claimed to have suffered discrimination on the ground
of sex because, during maternity leave, they did not receive full pay and
had not received the benefit of a backdated pay rise awarded during
their maternity leave period. The ECJ had no difficulty in holding that
benefit paid by the employer under legislation or a collective agreement
to a woman on maternity leave was pay for the purposes of Article 141
and the EPD. The Court pointed out that discrimination involves the
application of different rules to comparable situations or the application
of the same rule to different situations. However, it went on to hold that
women taking maternity leave are in a special position which requires
them to be afforded special protection but which is not comparable to
that of a man or a woman actually at work. It also pointed out that the
Pregnant Workers Directive,[40] which was passed after the women lodged

---

[35] *Coloroll Pension Trustees Ltd v. Russell* [1994] I.R.L.R. 586, ECJ.

[36] This is an extension of the reasoning in *Neath v. Hugh Steeper Ltd* [1994] I.R.L.R. 91,
ECJ.

[37]   *Coloroll Pension Trustees Ltd v. Russell* [1994] I.R.L.R. 586, ECJ.

[38] *Van den Akker v. Stickling Shell Pensioenfonds* [1994] I.R.L.R. 616, ECJ.

[39] [1996] I.R.L.R. 214, ECJ.

[40] Directive 92/85, hereinafter PWD.

their claims, makes it clear that all that women are entitled to is payment of an adequate allowance. The Court held that at the material time neither Article 141 nor the EPD required that women should continue to receive full pay during maternity leave. Nor did either of these provisions lay down any specific criteria for determining the amount of benefit to be paid during maternity leave, although the amount payable could not be so low as to undermine the purpose of maternity leave, namely the protection of women before and after giving birth.[41] So far as the ETD was concerned, the Court held that this was not relevant. The benefit paid during maternity leave, fell within the scope of Article 141 and the EPD. It could not, therefore, be covered by the Equal Treatment Directive as well. The preamble of the Equal Treatment Directive makes it clear that it does not apply to pay within the meaning of Article 141.

With regard to the question of whether a woman on maternity leave 4.13 should receive the benefit of a backdated pay rise awarded after the maternity leave commenced in respect of an earlier period the court answered this in the affirmative. It held that the principle of non-discrimination required that a woman who is still linked to her employer by a contract of employment or by an employment relationship during maternity leave should, like any other worker, benefit from any pay rise, even if backdated, which is awarded between the beginning of the period when entitlement to maternity pay is assessed and the end of the maternity leave. To deny such an increase is discriminatory since, if the worker had not been pregnant, she would have received the pay rise. In response to this decision the government amended the Statutory Maternity Pay (General) Regulations 1986 by inserting an new Regulation 21(7) which states "In any case where a woman receives a backdated pay increase which includes a sum in respect of a relevant period, normal weekly earnings shall be calculated as if such a sum was paid in that relevant period even though received after that period". However, in *Alabaster v. Woolwich plc and Secretary of State for Social Security*[42] the EAT held that this regulation did not fully implement the terms of the decision in *Gillespie*. In particular, it provides for an increase in the calculation of normal weekly earnings only where a pay increase is backdated, whereas the European Court's decision draws no distinction between backdated and immediate pay increases. In addition, the European Court did not tie in the pay increase to the "relevant period" for calculating statutory maternity pay as defined in regulation 21(3). *Gillespie* covered any pay increase, from the date on which it took effect, between the beginning of the "relevant period" to the end of the maternity leave.

---

[41] *Gillespie* was referred back to the NICA for consideration of whether the pay received by Mrs Gillespie (which was in excess of SMP levels) was so low as to undermine the purpose of maternity leave. It was held ([1997] I.R.L.R. 410, NICA) that the provision in the Pregnant Workers Directive to the effect that maternity pay "shall be deemed adequate" if the employee receives at least the amount she would have received had she been off sick was a reference to statutory sickness benefit levels rather than contractual sick pay and that since Mrs Gillespie received more than SSP her maternity pay was not such as to undermine the purpose of maternity leave.

[42] [2000] I.R.L.R. 754, EAT.

4.14   The reasoning in *Gillespie* is less than clear. It could equally have been
held that if the worker had not been pregnant she would still have been
receiving full pay! The ramifications of the decision that Mrs Gillespie
was entitled to the benefit of the pay increase since its denial would
discriminate against her in "her capacity as a worker" are still being
worked through. In *Iverson v. P & 0 Ferries (Dover) Ltd*,[43] decided shortly
after *Gillespie*, an employment tribunal took a broad view of what will
amount to discrimination against a woman on maternity leave in her
"capacity as a worker", holding that a woman was entitled to accrue
holidays during the period of extended maternity absence (*i.e.* the period
beyond the 14 (now 18) week maternity leave period), although it should
be noted that the comparison which was made in this case was with a
man on sick leave rather than a man still at work (as in *Gillespie*).

4.15   In *Boyle v. Equal Opportunities Commission*[44] the ECJ confirmed that
women on maternity leave are to be treated as in a class of their own—
they are entitled to the protection of the PWD during that period but
cannot compare their treatment, under the ETD or for pay purposes, to
a man off work sick. However, it is contrary to Article 141 to deprive a
woman who is absent from work as a result of a pregnancy related
illness, prior to the commencement of her maternity leave, of full pay
when workers absent as a result of other types of illness would receive
full pay; such treatment is based essentially on the fact of pregnancy and
is inherently discriminatory.[45]

4.16   In *Abdoulaye and Others v. Regie Nationale des Usines Renault SA*[46] the
ECJ was asked to consider a collective agreement which provided that
women on maternity leave received a bonus of FFr 7,500 as well as full
pay, such a bonus being held to amount to pay by the ECJ for the
purposes of Article 119 (now 141). Male workers considered this
provision was discriminatory since the same bonus was not offered to
new fathers. The employer argued that the bonus was designed to offset
the occupational disadvantages which arise for female workers as a result
of their absence from work, such as missing out on promotion and
training.

The ECJ pointed out (in line with *Gillespie, Boyle* etc) that the
principle of equal pay presupposes that the male and female workers
whom it covers are in comparable situations. However, women on
maternity leave are not in a comparable situation to men at work since
there are occupational disadvantages inherent in maternity leave which
arise as a result of being away from work. There was, therefore no
discrimination in relation to the payment of the bonus.

4.17   The issue of pay during parental leave has also been considered by the
ECJ in *Lewen v. Denda*.[47] Here, Mrs Lewen's maternity leave ended on
September 6, 1996 at which point she went on parental leave until July
12, 1999 (this being allowed under German law). In German law the

---

[43] IDS Brief 577, November 1996, p.17; aff'd [1999] I.C.R. 1088, EAT.
[44] Case C 411/96 [1998] I.R.L.R. 717.
[45] Case C-66/96 *Hoj Perdersen* [1999] I.R.L.R. 55, ECJ.
[46] [1999] I.R.L.R. 811.
[47] [2000] I.R.L.R. 67.

contract is regarded as "suspended" during such a period of leave. Mrs Lewen did not receive a Christmas 1996 bonus because she was not in "active" employment on December 1, although she worked earlier in the year. She claimed that this breached Article 119 (now 141).

The ECJ held that if the Christmas bonus was retroactive pay for work performed, refusal to award a bonus, even one reduced proportionately, to workers on parental leave who worked during the year in which the bonus was granted, on the sole ground that their contract of employment was suspended when the bonus was granted, placed them at a disadvantage as compared with those whose contract was not suspended at the time of the award. This amounted to discrimination within the meaning of Article 119 (141), since female workers were far more likely to be on parental leave when the bonus was awarded than male workers. The ECJ also confirmed that periods during which mothers are prohibited from working (for example, around the time of the birth of the child) must be counted for this purpose as periods worked. To exclude such periods for the purpose of awarding a bonus retroactively for work performed would discriminate against a female worker since, had she not been pregnant, those periods would have had to be counted as periods worked.

However, the ECJ considered that the position was different where the bonus was subject only to the condition that the worker was in active employment when it was awarded, and did not constitute retroactive pay for work performed. In such circumstances a worker who exercised a statutory right to take parental leave was in a special situation, which could not be compared to that of a man or woman at work. It followed that Article 141 did not make it unlawful to refuse to pay a Christmas bonus to a woman on parental leave where the award of such a bonus was subject to the sole condition that the worker must be in active employment when it was awarded. The approach in *Lewen* bears obvious similarities to that in *Gillespie*.

THE EQUAL PAY ACT 1970

The EqPA came into force in 1975 at the same time as the Sex Discrimination Act 1975.[48] The five year period between the date of Royal Assent and the commencement of the Act was to give employers the opportunity to ensure, on a voluntary basis, that their pay practices and policies met with the requirements of the legislation. The Act has been amended subsequently, principally by the SDA itself and the Equal Pay (Amendment) Regulations 1983.[49] It is a short but unwieldy piece of legislation; its complexity and the protracted nature of proceedings cause grave problems for applicants. Cases can take many years to reach a conclusion, particularly where reliance is placed on Community law. One extreme example is the case of *Enderby v. Frenchay Health Authority*[50] which was ongoing for 14 years. Although the lead claim of Mrs Enderby

4.18

---

[48] Hereinafter SDA.
[49] S.I. 1993 No. 1794.
[50] [1993] I.R.L.R. 591, ECJ.

was settled in 1997, various claims by other applicants which had been conjoined with hers were still continuing in 2000.[51]

The Equal Opportunities Commission[52] made detailed proposals for changing the legislation in 1990. It received a reply from the Government to these proposals in 1993 which rejected many of the key suggestions put forward (including the suggestion that collective claims be introduced).

4.19   Frustrated in its attempts to persuade the Government to strengthen the EqPA the EOC has, in the past, urged the European Commission to take legal action against the United Kingdom, claiming that: "British Equal Pay legislation was uniquely unworkable and continued to fail to meet EEC Equal Pay obligations". In particular, the EOC suggested that complainants are denied effective access to judicial protection as required by Article 2 of the EPD and that the United Kingdom has failed to ensure equal pay contrary to Article 6 of the EPD which obliges each Member State to take effective measures to ensure that the principles of equal pay are applied.[53] While no action appears to have been taken in response to this complaint there was an increased acceptance towards the end of the 1990s that steps had to be taken to improve the working of the EqPA. In December 1999 the Government issued a consultation document[54] containing proposals which were aimed at ensuring "that equal pay cases are quicker, easier and fairer for everyone". It was hoped that the changes proposed, which were largely procedural in nature, would diminish the gender pay gap which stood at 18 per cent in 1999 (having reduced from 37 per cent at the point when the Equal Pay Act was enacted). Some of the changes have been introduced, principally by the Employment Tribunals (Constitution and Rules of Procedure) Regulations 2001[55] which streamline the special rules applicable in equal value cases,[56] while others remain to be implemented. In mid 2001 the Government announced that it would be encouraging employers to undertake and act upon pay reviews, designed to achieve equal pay for women on a voluntary basis rather than introducing a legislative requirement to undertake such reviews, the latter course being desired by the EOC.

The head note of the EqPA states that it is "an Act to prevent discrimination, as regards terms and conditions of employment between men and women". The EqPA focuses on contractual terms of employment including, but not limited to, those concerning pay. This is in contrast to the SDA which is concerned with non-contractual matters. In other words, the two Acts are mutually exclusive although they both deal with sex discrimination and "should be construed and applied as a harmonious whole".[57] Care must be taken to ensure that a discrimination complaint is made under the appropriate legislation. Occasionally,

---

[51] *Evesham v. North Hertfordshire Health Authority and Secretary of State for Health* [2000] I.R.L.R. 257, CA.

[52] Hereinafter EOC.

[53] Request to the Commission of the European Communities by the Equal Opportunities Commission for Great Britain in Relation to the Implementation of the Principle of Equal Pay.

[54] "Towards Equal Pay for Women", Department of Education and Science.

[55] S.I. 2001 No. 1170.

[56] See Sched. 3 of the Regulations.

[57] *E. Coomes (Holdings) Ltd v. Shields* [1978] I.R.L.R. 263.

cases are dismissed on the basis that they have been raised under the SDA rather than the EqPA and vice versa. It should be noted that the coverage of Article 141 is wider than that of the EqPA since it covers non-contractual payments. However, this does not mean that domestic law is out of step with Community law since non-contractual claims can be made under the SDA.

DIRECT AND INDIRECT PAY DISCRIMINATION

In *Ratcliffe v. North Yorkshire County Council*[58] the House of Lords, in considering whether the distinction between direct and indirect discrimination was relevant in interpreting the EqPA, made the following obiter remarks: **4.20**

"There has been much argument in this case as to the relationship between s.1 of the Act of 1970 and s.1 of the Sex Discrimination Act 1975. The latter distinguishes between (a) a case where an employer on the ground of her sex treats a woman less favourably than he treats or would treat a man, and (b) a case where the employer applies to a woman a requirement or condition which he applies or would apply equally to a man, but which is such that the proportion of women who can comply with it is considerably smaller than the proportion of men who can comply with it and which the employer cannot show to be justifiable irrespective of the sex of the person to whom it is applied and which is to the detriment of a woman because she cannot comply with it. The first '(a)' is commonly referred to as 'direct' discrimination, the latter '(b)' as 'indirect' discrimination. It is submitted that this distinction must be introduced equally into the Act of 1970. For my part I do not accept that this is so. There is no provision in the Act of 1975 which expressly incorporates the distinction into the Act of 1970 even though Schedule 1 to the Act of 1975 incorporated a number of amendments into the Act of 1970 and even though Part II of that Schedule set out the Act of 1970 in full in its amended form. In my opinion the Act of 1970 must be interpreted in its amended form without bringing in the distinction between so-called 'direct' and 'indirect' discrimination."

It would be easy to be misled by the foregoing dicta. It is clear that both the EqPA and Article 141 have been repeatedly applied in situations which could reasonably be characterised as involving indirect discrimination as well as those involving direct discrimination. Many important judgments of the ECJ support the proposition that adverse treatment of part-time workers which affects their pay can amount to a breach of Article 141. For example, in *Bilka-Kaufhaus GmbH v. Weber von Hartz*[59] the ECJ held that the exclusion of part-time workers (principally

---

[58] *North Yorkshire County Council v. Ratcliffe* [1995] I.R.L.R. 439, HL at para. 19 *per* Lord Slynn of Hadley.
[59] [1986] I.R.L.R. 317, ECJ.

women) from an employer's pension scheme was in breach of Article 119 (now 141), unless the employer could show that the exclusion was objectively justified by factors unrelated to any discrimination on the ground of sex.[60]

The House of Lords revisited its dicta in *Ratcliffe* in *Strathclyde Regional Council and Others v. Wallace and Others*.[61] Giving the leading judgment, Lord Browne-Wilkinson stated that in *Ratcliffe*:

> "[T]his House expressed the view, obiter, that the Equal Pay Act 1970 has to be interpreted without introducing the distinction between direct and indirect discrimination drawn by section 1 of the Sex Discrimination Act 1975. That dictum must not be carried too far. Whilst there is no need to apply to the Equal Pay Act 1970 the hard and fast statutory distinction between the two types of discrimination drawn in the Sex Discrimination Act 1975, this House did not intend, and had no power, to sweep away all the law on equal pay under article 119 laid down by the European Court of Justice . . . The law on article 119, whilst recognising that in many cases there is a de facto distinction between direct and indirect discrimination, does not draw the same firm legal demarcation between the two as does the Sex Discrimination Act 1975."

4.21 Whilst this area of law is undoubtedly complex, the crucial fact to bear in mind is that both domestic and European equal pay law do cover situations which we might traditionally conceptualise as indirect discrimination as well as situations giving rise to direct discrimination.

However, it is clear from the decision in *Enderby v. Frenchay Health Authority and Secretary of State for Health*[62] that what might be characterised as indirect discrimination in terms of Article 141 is much more widely defined than under domestic law. Specifically, it would appear that there is no need to identify a "requirement" or "condition" to succeed under Community law. *Enderby* concerned equal value claims by senior speech therapists. Dr Pamela Enderby claimed that she was employed on work of equal value with male principal grade pharmacists and clinical psychologists employed in the National Health Service. At the relevant time, her annual pay as a chief grade III speech therapist was £10,106, while that of a principal clinical psychologist was £12,527 and that of a Grade III principal pharmacist was £14,106. The pay of speech therapists generally was up to 60 per cent less than that of pharmacists. Speech therapy was a predominantly female occupation while pharmacists and psychologists at the relevant grades were principally male. For the purpose of the reference to the ECJ it was agreed that the jobs were of equal value. The ECJ held: "if the pay of speech therapists is significantly lower than that of pharmacists and if the former

---

[60] See also *Rinner-Kuhn v. FWW Speual-Gebaudereinigung GmbH & Co. KG* [1989] I.R.L.R. 493, ECJ; *Kowalska v. Freie und Hansestadt Hamburg* [1991] I.R.L.R. 222, ECJ; *Gerster v. Freistaat Bayern* [1997] I.R.L.R. 699, ECJ; *Kording v. Senator fur Finanzen* [1997] I.R.L.R. 710, ECJ; Case C-281/97 *Krüger v. Kreiskrankenhaus Ebersberg* [1999] I.R.L.R. 808, ECJ.
[61] [1998] I.R.L.R. 146, HL.
[62] [1993] I.R.L.R. 591, ECJ.

are almost exclusively women while the latter are predominantly men, there is a prima facie case of sex discrimination, at least where the two jobs in question are of equal value and the statistics describing that situation are valid".[63]

THE EQUALITY CLAUSE

The key to the EqPA is section 1(1) which implies (unless there is 4.22 already an express clause) into every contract of employment an equality clause.[64] Section 1 (2) goes on to explain what an equality clause actually is and the consequences of its inclusion in the contract of employment. An equality clause "is a provision which relates to terms (whether concerned with pay or not) under which a woman is employed" and which has an effect in three different situations:

1. Where the woman is employed on "like work" with a man.[65] Broadly speaking, "like work" comparisons involve a man and a woman carrying out the same jobs or jobs which are broadly similar where the differences (if any) between what the woman does and what the man does are not of practical importance in relation to terms and conditions of employment.[66]
2. Where the woman is employed on "work rated as equivalent with that of a man".[67] A comparison of this type requires a job evaluation study to be in existence.
3. Where the woman is employed on "work of equal value to that of a man".[68] The equal value provisions of the Act were added as a result of the finding in *Commission of the European Communities v. United Kingdom of Great Britain and Northern Ireland*[69] that the United Kingdom was in breach of Community legislation by making equal pay for work of equal value depend on the existence of a job evaluation study (which would require the permission and co-operation of the employer).

---

[63] At para. 16.

[64] "Employed" is widely defined by s.1(6)(a) of the EqPA as: "employed under a contract of service or of apprenticeship or a contract personally to execute any work or labour, and related expressions shall be construed accordingly". By s.1(8), Crown Servants, unless statutory officeholders, are within the scope of the Act, although the exclusion of office holders was successfully challenged in *Perceval-Price v. Department for Economic Development* [2000] I.R.L.R. 380, CA (NI) in which it was held that the exclusion was contrary to the provisions of Article 141 and the ETD. While domestic law could not be read in a manner which made it compatible with Community law it should be read as if the offending exclusion was deleted. Overseas employees are excluded since employment must be at an establishment in Great Britain, although the provisions of the SDA, s.10 should be noted on this point.

[65] EqPA, s.1(2)(a).

[66] EqPA, s.1(4).

[67] EqPA, s.1(2)(b).

[68] EqPA, s.1(2)(c).

[69] [1982] I.R.L.R. 333; [1982] I.C.R. 578, ECJ.

4.23 In each of these cases the two (or more—there is nothing to stop an applicant comparing herself to a number of male employees) individuals compared must be real rather than hypothetical[70] and employed "in the same employment". A woman is entitled to select the man or men with whom she wishes to be compared.[71]

In the event that the foregoing conditions are fulfilled, leading to a comparison being made which is sanctioned by the Act, the effect of the equality clause will be to modify the woman's contract, if necessary, to ensure that each of her contractual terms is no less favourable than that of her comparator.[72] It should be particularly noted that it is each term of the contract which is equalised by the equality clause. If a contract contains terms relating to basic pay and to benefits in kind such as the use of a car, sick pay, cash bonuses and the like these cannot all be lumped together on the basis that they constitute one overall term relating to the total remuneration under the contract.[73] Accordingly, a woman employed on work of equal value is entitled to the same basic hourly wage and overtime rates as her comparator, irrespective of the fact that she receives better holiday and sickness benefits[74] or a shift allowance for working unsociable hours.[75] However, an applicant's entitlement to have the relevant term of her contract of employment modified so as to be not less favourable than that of her male comparator means that her salary should be matched to that of her comparator, rather than that she should be placed on the pay scale for his post at a level appropriate to her actual years of service.[76]

4.24 If the comparator's contract becomes more favourable in any respect the equality clause will operate to modify the woman's contract to ensure equality again prevails. It should be noted that once the contract has been modified in accordance with an equality clause it is then a contract providing remuneration at the higher rate and remains so modified even if the male comparator subsequently leaves the job or is promoted.[77] An alleged breach of the equality clause by the employer will give rise to the possibility of a complaint under the Act.

"Same Employment"

4.25 The definition of "same employment" is set out in section 1(6) of the EqPA which states that: "men shall be treated as in the same employment as a woman if they are men employed by her employer or any associated employer at the same establishment or establishments in

---

[70] In other words, unlike the SDA it is not possible for a woman to compare herself with a hypothetical man. She must identify an actual male employee (or employees) with whom she compares herself.

[71] *Ainsworth v. Glass Tubes and Components Ltd* [1977] I.R.L.R. 74; [1977] I.C.R. 347, EAT.

[72] It should be noted that there are limited terms of employment in respect of which an equality clause does not operate—see EqPA, s.6.

[73] *Hayward v. Cammell Laird Shipbuilders Ltd* [1988] I.R.L.R. 257, HL.

[74] *ibid.*

[75] *Jämställdhetsombudsmannen v. Örebro läns landsting* [2000] I.R.L.R. 421, ECJ. See also Case C-381/99 *Brunnhofer v. Bank der Österreichischen Postsparkasse AG* [2001] I.R.L.R. 571, ECJ.

[76] *Evesham v. North Hertfordshire Health Authority and Secretary of State for Health* [2000] I.R.L.R. 257, CA.

[77] *A. M. Sorbie v. Trust Houses Forte Hotels Ltd* [1976] I.R.L.R. 371, EAT.

Great Britain which include that one and at which common terms and conditions of employment are observed either generally or for employees of the relevant classes". Furthermore, section 1(6) states that: " 'Two employers' are to be treated as associated if one is a company of which the other (directly or indirectly) has control or if both are companies of which a third person (directly or indirectly) has control".

The above definition was examined in detail by the House of Lords in 4.26 the case of *British Coal Corporation v. Smith*.[78] In this case 1,286 women employed by British Coal as canteen workers and cleaners claimed equal pay for work of equal value, comparing themselves with surface mine workers and clerical workers. The claimants were employed at 47 different establishments and their comparators were employed at 14 different establishments. At the Court of Appeal stage it was held that "common terms and conditions" meant "the same" terms and conditions rather than terms and conditions which are "broadly similar" or "to the same overall effect". On this interpretation, section 1(6) permitted a choice of a male comparator from a separate establishment, if the terms and conditions of employment for men of the relevant class at his establishment were the same as those of men of the relevant class employed at the establishment where the woman making the comparison worked. Since there were different conditions regarding an incentive bonus and concessionary coal at the various establishments the definition within section 1(6) had not been met, according to the Court of Appeal.

The House of Lords reversed the Court of Appeal, holding that "common terms and conditions of employment" within the meaning of section 1(6) means terms and conditions which are substantially comparable on a broad basis, rather than the same terms and conditions. There was in this case material on which the tribunal could base its finding that the applicants and their comparators were in the same employment because the terms and conditions of the comparators were governed by national agreements, even though there were local variations relating to the incentive bonus and concessionary coal.[79]

It has been held that Article 141 of the Treaty of Rome allows a wider 4.27 range of comparisons to be made than those allowed by the EqPA. As noted above, where the applicant is relying on Article 141, as well as the EqPA, the rights arising under the more expansive provisions of Community law must prevail.[80] In particular, in *Scullard v. Knowles and Southern Regional Council for Education and Training*[81] the EAT held that Article 141 of the E.C. Treaty allows equal pay comparisons between those employed in the "same service" and does not restrict comparators to those in the "same employment", as defined in section 1(6). In this case Ms Scullard was employed by the second respondent (SRCET) as a Further Education Unit Manager, the second respondent being an independent voluntary association of local education authorities established for the purpose of co-ordinating the work of colleges of further education and exchanging information about further education.

---

[78] [1996] I.R.L.R. 399, HL.
[79] See also *Leverton v. Clwyd County Council* [1989] I.R.L.R. 28; [1989] I.C.R. 33, HL for analysis of the meaning of EPA, s.1(6).
[80] *Biggs v. Somerset County Council* [1996] I.R.L.R. 203, CA.
[81] [1996] I.R.L.R. 344, EAT.

There are 12 further education units in Great Britain, ultimately funded by the Department of Education and Employment. Ms Scullard brought an equal pay claim, comparing herself to male unit managers employed by other councils, all of whom received higher salaries for the same or similar work (she was the only woman employed as a unit manager). The employment tribunal had dismissed her complaint on the ground that her male comparators were not employed "in the same employment". The tribunal held, in considering whether the applicant and her comparators were employed by "associated employers" that neither SRCET nor the other regional advisory councils were "companies" and therefore her comparators could not be employed by "associated employers". On appeal, it was argued that she was entitled to bring her complaint on the basis of Article 141 of the E.C. Treaty.

The EAT held that the class of comparator defined in section 1(6) is more restricted than that which applies under Article 141. According to *Defrenne v. Sabena (No. 2)*[82] the question was whether the applicant and her comparators were employed "in the same establishment or service". This provided for a wider class of comparators than that contained in section 1(6) and overrode the provisions of section 1(6).

Accordingly, this decision makes it possible for equal pay comparisons to be made between public sector organisations with common terms and conditions which fall outside the scope of section 1(6) because they are not associated employers in the sense of one company controlled by another. The EAT lays emphasis on whether the work is carried out in the same service, a test which appears to focus attention on the nature of the work rather than on the status of the employer.

4.28 Similarly, in *Hayes and Quinn v. Mancunian Community Health Trust and South Manchester Health Authority*[83] an employment tribunal held that dental surgery assistants employed by one trust were allowed under Article 141 to compare themselves with a senior dental technician who was employed by a different trust because they were all employed in the same "service". The tribunal accepted that the applicants were not entitled to make a comparison with the senior dental technician under the EqPA because they were not "in the same employment", neither the trust nor the health authority being companies within the definition of "associated employers" under the EqPA. However, the tribunal considered that a comparison could be made given that the "second respondent Authority and the NHS Trust are, or were, all under the control of the Secretary of State for Health in a way which is entirely analogous to the scheme under the (Equal Pay) Act for Associated Companies . . . all these corporations have to report to the Secretary of State. At all stages the Secretary of State is able to define their areas of operation".

4.29 In *South Ayrshire Council v. Morton*[84] the issue arose again of the linkage between different public authorities which are engaged in the provision of the same service in the context of an Article 141 claim. The applicant employees were all primary teachers, female and male, claiming equal pay with secondary teachers. Ms Morton, who was employed by South Ayrshire Council, named as one of her comparators a male

[82] [1976] E.C.R. 455, ECJ.
[83] DCLD No. 29, August 1996, p.9.
[84] [2001] I.R.L.R. 28, EAT.

teacher employed by Highland Council. A preliminary issue arose as to whether such a cross employer comparison could be made. The Employment Tribunal held that such a comparison was allowed. The employer appealed to the EAT which noted that while each local authority in Scotland employs its own staff, including teachers, over the period to which the complaint related the salary scales of teachers were set by the Scottish Joint Negotiating Committee (SJNC), a body working under the general control of the Secretary of State (as he then was). These scales were applied throughout Scotland in the primary and secondary sectors. The essential question for the EAT was "whether or not there was sufficient connection in a loose and non-technical sense between" the employment of the two individuals concerned. The Employment Tribunal had reached the conclusion after hearing detailed evidence that, in reality, there was no local control of a teacher's pay and conditions. Under statute various obligations were imposed on local authorities in their role as education authorities. Common standards were set and if they were not met then the Secretary of State had the power to intervene. Education authorities, in effect, administered their functions to some extent on behalf of the Secretary of State and were answerable to him. In these circumstances the tribunal considered that there was sufficient community of interest for the whole structure of education to be regarded as a "service". It followed that the cross authority comparison should be allowed to proceed. The EAT considered that the Tribunal had applied the correct test and were entitled to reach this conclusion. The appeal was therefore dismissed.

4.30 The range of possible comparators in an equal pay case also arose in *Diocese of Hallam Trustee v. Connaughton*.[85] JC was employed as Director of Music for the Diocese from January 1990. When she resigned in September 1994 her salary was £11,138. Her post was advertised at a salary of £13,434 but when the successful applicant, a man, was appointed in January 1995 he received a salary of £20,000. JC claimed that she had the right to equal pay with her successor in that his work and hers were of equal value. The employment tribunal held as a preliminary point that it had jurisdiction to hear the claim because the applicant was entitled to rely on Article 141 in order to make a comparison with her successor. The EAT dismissed an appeal by the employer, holding that the employment tribunal had correctly concluded that the applicant was entitled to rely upon Article 141 to claim equal pay with her male successor. Although the EqPA defines an equality clause in terms of comparisons with male employees contemporaneously in the same employment the decision of the ECJ in *Macarthys Limited v. Smith*[86] provided support for the applicant's contention that she was entitled to rely on her male successor as a comparator given that his contract was so proximate to her own. It has also been held that Article 141 allows a woman to compare herself with her predecessor in employment.[87]

4.31 The ECJ is to be given the opportunity to consider again the scope of the comparisons which can be made under Article 141 as a result of this issue being referred by the Court of Appeal in *Lawrence v. Regent Office*

---

[85] [1996] I.R.L.R. 505, EAT.
[86] [1980] I.C.R. 672, CA.
[87] *Albion Shipping Agency v. Arnold* [1981] I.R.L.R. 525; [1982] I.C.R. 22, EAT.

Care Ltd.[88] Here, the applicants had been employed by the local authority. During that time an equal value test case brought by some of the applicants comparing their work with other local government employees was ultimately successful.[89] They had then been transferred to a new employer as a result of a contracting out process. However under their new employer they were asked to work at lower rates than were observed by the council. They brought an equal pay claim, relying upon Article 141 of the E.C. Treaty, citing current employees of the council whose work was rated as of equal value to their own under a local government job evaluation study. The EAT[90] held that in order to bring an equal pay claim the applicant and the comparator must be, in a loose sense, in the same establishment or service, even although it is not necessary for the same entity to be employer of both applicant and comparator or for the employer to be associated. It held that this condition was not met and that there was nothing to distinguish this case from any other in which an applicant claimed equal pay with someone employed by another company, not necessarily even in the same industry. However, the Court of Appeal decided to ask the ECJ whether Article 141 allowed employees who were now employed by private contractors, including former employees of a county council, to bring an equal pay claim in which they compared themselves with current employees of the council whose work had been rated as of equal value to their own. The Court has also asked the ECJ to consider whether an applicant who seeks to place reliance on the direct effect of Article 141, can do so only if the respondent employer is in a position where he is able to explain why the employer of the chosen comparator pays his employees as he does.

4.32   It is likely that the ECJ referral in *Lawrence* will be heard with *Allonby v. Accrington & Rossendale College*[91] which raises the issue of whether someone employed initially by the respondent as a part-time, hourly-paid lecturer on a series of fixed term contracts, who was then told that she would have to leave the employment of the college and register with a specific employment agency if she wished to continue working at the college, with a resultant loss of income, can compare herself under Article 141 with a male full-time lecturer employed by the college. The Court of Appeal held that the employment tribunal had not erred in finding that the college and ELS were not associated employers within the meaning of section 1(6) because neither had control of the other. However they referred to the ECJ the question of whether Article 141 entitled the claimant to bring an equal pay claim against the employment agency on the basis that when she lectured at the college, she and the male lecturer were employed in the same establishment or service for the purposes of Article 141, even though they are employed under contracts with different entities.

Having selected a man in the same employment, a woman who wishes to make a claim under the EqPA must then show that she is engaged in like work, work rated as equivalent or work of equal value.

---

[88] [2000] I.R.L.R. 608, CA.
[89] See [1995] I.R.L.R. 439, HL.
[90] [1999] I.R.L.R. 148, EAT.
[91] [2001] I.R.L.R. 364, CA.

LIKE WORK

Section 1(4) of the EqPA makes it clear that it is necessary for a woman 4.33
relying on the like work provisions to show both that (1) her work is the
"same" or "broadly similar" to that of her comparator and that (2) the
differences (if any) in the things that she and her comparator do (*i.e.* the
tasks that they each perform) are not of practical importance in relation
to terms and conditions of employment.[92] These two stages are separate
and it is the work which the individuals actually do rather than the work
which the employee might be required to do under the contract which is
to be examined.[93] It is a question of fact for the tribunal whether the
work compared is the same or broadly similar. A broad brush approach
should be taken[94] in examining whether the nature of the work is similar.
It is only at the second stage above that there will need to be an
assessment of the similarity of the tasks performed.[95] If the tasks
performed differ there must then be an assessment of whether these
differences are of any practical importance in relation to the terms and
conditions of employment of the individuals being compared. Do these
differences explain the disparity in terms? If there are significant
differences in the tasks performed by the woman and her male compara-
tor(s) that may lead the tribunal to conclude that they are not engaged
on "like" work.[96] Even if "like" work is established the differences may
allow the employer to succeed in establishing a section 1(3) defence (see
below).

However, in the context of what amounts to "like" work, the decision 4.34
of the ECJ in *Angestelltenbetriebsrat der Wiener Gebietskrankenkasse v.
Wiener Gebietskrankenkasse*[97] should be noted. While this is a decision
on the interpretation of Article 141 it may well impact upon the
interpretation of domestic law. In essence, the case serves to confuse
rather than clarify the concept of "like work". It concerned the pay of
psychotherapists employed by the Vienna Area Health Fund, some of
whom had trained first as psychologists and some of whom were doctors
of medicine. Those qualified as doctors were placed on a significantly
higher salary scale, the majority of the lower paid workers being women.

---

[92] *Capper Pass Ltd v. Lawton* [1976] I.R.L.R. 366, EAT.
[93] *Waddington v. Leicester Council for Voluntary Services* [1977] I.R.L.R. 32; [1977] I.C.R.
266, EAT. See also *Electrolux Ltd v. Hutchinson* [1976] I.R.L.R. 410; [1977] I.C.R. 252,
EAT; and *E. Coomes (Holdings) Ltd v. Shields* [1978] I.R.L.R. 263, CA on this latter point.
[94] *Dorothy Perkins Ltd v. Dance* [1977] I.R.L.R. 226, EAT.
[95] *Waddington*, above.
[96] See *Maidment and Hardacre v. Cooper and Co. (Birmingham) Ltd* [1978] I.R.L.R. 462
for an example of a case where a tribunal held that although the applicants were engaged
on work of a broadly similar nature to that of their comparators there were differences
between the jobs which were of practical importance in relation to terms and conditions
and therefore the applicants had failed to meet the definition of "like" work. See *National
Coal Board v. Sherwin and Spruce* [1978] I.R.L.R. 122; [1978] I.C.R. 700, EAT for a case
where it was held that if a man and a woman do the same work the fact that they do it at
different times should be disregarded for the purpose of determining whether they were
employed on "like" work and *British Leyland (U.K.) Ltd v. Powell* [1978] I.R.L.R. 57, EAT
for a case where it was held that the differences in tasks between the individuals compared
were not of practical importance in relation to terms and conditions.
[97] Case C-309/97 [1999] I.R.L.R. 804, ECJ.

In the clinic which gave rise to the claim being made, six psychologists, five of whom were women, were employed as psychotherapists together with six doctors, one of whom was a woman.

A claim for equal pay was made and various questions were referred to the ECJ. The one dealt with in the judgment of the Court concerned whether the two types of psychotherapists could be said to be employed in the "same work" for the purpose of Article 141 of the E.C. Treaty. The Court agreed with the Advocate General that professional training is not merely a factor which may amount to an objective justification for paying differential rates. It considered that it was also a possible criterion for determining whether the "same work" was actually being performed. The ECJ concluded that although the doctors and psychologists employed as psychotherapists performed seemingly identical activities in treating their patients (for which the same fee was charged by the clinic) they would draw upon knowledge and experience acquired in their different disciplines. In addition the ECJ noted that the national court had emphasised that the doctors were qualified to perform other tasks in the field which were not open to the psychologists who could only perform psychotherapy. The ECJ therefore considered that "the term 'the same work' does not apply, for the purposes of Article 119 [now 141] . . . where the same activities are performed over a considerable length of time by persons the basis of whose qualification to exercise their profession is different". While one can perhaps understand the ECJ's reasoning in this particular case, if there was evidence that the nature of the qualifications held by individuals had a definite, marked effect on the nature and scope of the work actually done by the two groups it is very difficult to accept the proposition that possession or lack of professional qualifications will, as a matter of course, be of practical importance in relation to whether two individuals are performing like work. It is submitted that it will be much more usual for such a factor to amount to possible justification where there is unequal pay for equal work.

WORK RATED AS EQUIVALENT

4.35 A woman is entitled to equal pay if she is employed on work rated as equivalent to that of a man. Section 1(5) of the EqPA makes it clear that a woman is to be regarded as employed on work rated equivalent to that of any men "if, but only if, her job and their job have been given an equal value, in terms of the demand made on the worker under various headings (for instance effort, skill, decision) on a study undertaken with a view to evaluating" jobs to be done by some or all of the employees in an undertaking or if the jobs "would have been given an equal value but for the evaluation being made on a system setting different values for men and women on the same demand under any heading". In other words, a job evaluation study must have been undertaken and this must either have rated the woman's job as of equal value to that of her comparator or would have rated the jobs as of equal value but for the fact that sex discrimination was built into the scheme.

A job evaluation scheme must be "analytical" to comply with the 4.36 requirements of section 1(5).[98] In *Eaton Ltd v. Nutall*[99] the EAT stated that section 1(5) can only apply to a "valid" job evaluation study:

> "It seems to us that subsection (5) can only apply to what may be called a valid evaluation study. By that, we mean a study satisfying the test of being thorough in analysis and capable of impartial application. It should be possible by applying the study to arrive at the position of a particular employee at a particular point in a particular salary grade without taking other matters into account except those unconnected with the nature of the work. It will be in order to take into account such matters as merit or seniority, etc., but any matters concerning the work (e.g., responsibility) one would expect to find taken care of in the evaluation study. One which does not satisfy that test, and requires the management to make a subjective judgment concerning the nature of the work before the employee can be fitted into the appropriate place in the appropriate salary grade, would seem to us not to be a valid study for the purpose of sub-section (5)".[1]

The *Eaton* judgment also includes an appendix which sets out the main types of job evaluation studies in use.

If two jobs are given different points in an evaluation exercise but 4.37 rated as within the same salary grading at the end of the job grading exercise it is reasonable to regard them as "rated as equivalent" within the meaning of section 1(5).[2]

It should be noted that if a woman makes an equal value claim under section 1(2)(c) of the EqPA and the employer has carried out a valid job evaluation exercise the Act deems that it shall be taken there are no reasonable grounds for the tribunal to hold that the jobs are of equal value.[3] That is the Act, in fact, bars equal value comparisons where the jobs have already been evaluated as unequal as long as there are no reasonable grounds to determine that the evaluation was made by reference to a job evaluation system which was in itself discriminatory.[4] This provision was applied in *Henderson v. Jaguar Cars Ltd*[5] where it was held that the tribunal can only examine the nature of the scheme and not its application. Where one is faced with a gender neutral scheme which is applied in a discriminatory fashion the remedy lies under the SDA.

---

[98] *Bromley v. H. & J. Quick Ltd* [1988] I.R.L.R. 456, CA.
[99] [1977] I.R.L.R. 71, EAT.
[1] At para. 13.
[2] *Springboard Sunderland Trust v. Robson* [1992] I.R.L.R. 261; [1992] I.C.R. 554, EAT.
[3] EqPA, s.2A(2).
[4] *Bromley v. H. & J. Quick Ltd* [1988] I.R.L.R. 456, CA establishes that where an employer seeks to rely on s.2A the onus is on the employer to show that there has been a job evaluation study which satisfies the requirements of s.1(5) and that there are no reasonable grounds for determining that the evaluation was tainted by sex discrimination. For guidance from the ECJ on job evaluation and sex discrimination, see *Rummler v. Dato-Druck GmbH* [1987] I.R.L.R. 32, ECJ.
[5] DCLD No. 11, p.1.

WORK OF EQUAL VALUE

4.38 If a woman is engaged on "like" work with her comparator or work "rated as equivalent" she must make her claim under section 1(2)(a) or section 1(2)(b) of the EqPA respectively. It is only where neither of these claims is appropriate that an equal value claim should be made.[6]However, a woman employed on "like" work or "work rated as equivalent", within the meaning of the legislation, with one man is not precluded from claiming that she is employed on work of equal value to that of another man.[7]

Given that in an equal value claim an applicant is entitled to compare her job with entirely different jobs performed by her male comparators (for example, a female cook could compare her work with that of a painter and/or thermal insulation engineer and/or a joiner[8] one might expect that a substantial number of equal value complaints would be made annually, particularly given the extent of sex segregation in the British labour market. However, this is not the case. On average, over the last decade, between 30 and 40 employers per annum in the United Kingdom have been involved in equal value claims, although the number of applications lodged is always higher since it is not uncommon for multiple applications to be made against a single employer.

4.39 In large part these statistics are explained by the fact that the law governing the right to claim equal pay for work of equal value is particularly complex. It has been subject to much criticism, especially in relation to the protracted nature of proceedings when an equal value claim is made.[9]For example, *Smith v. British Coal Corporation*[10] involved equal value claims which first began to be submitted in December 1985. Various preliminary issues were still be considered in 1996. Lord Slynn, in his judgment in the House of Lords in that case said: "that these proceedings have taken such an extraordinary amount of time is much to be regretted". He went on to say that such delay "defeats an essential purpose of the legislation if employees cannot enforce within a reasonable time such rights (if any) as they have to remedy inequality of remuneration".

Prior to July 1996 an employment tribunal had no power to decide the question of whether particular jobs were of equal value by itself. The tribunal was required to refer the matter to an independent job evaluation expert, selected from a panel of experts maintained by ACAS, except in very limited circumstances where it considered that there were "no reasonable grounds" for determining that the jobs were of equal value.[11] Lord Bridge has described the process involved as "lengthy, elaborate and . . . expensive".[12] As a result of an amendment to the Act,

---

[6] EqPA, s.1(2)(c).

[7] *Pickstone v. Freemans plc* [1988] I.R.L.R. 357, HL.

[8] This was the exact comparison made by the successful applicant in *Hayward v. Cammell Laird Shipbuilders Ltd* [1988] I.R.L.R. 257, HL.

[9] See *Enderby v. Frenchay Health Authority and another* [1993] I.R.L.R. 591, ECJ— ongoing for 14 years, not completed until 2000.

[10] Case No. 31708/85, which is reported as *British Coal Corporation v. Smith* [1996] I.R.L.R. 404, HL on a preliminary point.

[11] EqPA, s.2A(1)(b).

[12] *Leverton v. Clywd County Council* [1989] I.R.L.R. 28, HL.

made by regulation 3 of the Sex Discrimination and Equal Pay (Miscellaneous Amendments) Regulations 1996,[13] section 2A(1)(a) of the EqPA now allows the tribunal to determine the question of whether work is of equal value itself. This change was introduced in an effort to reduce the length of time taken to adjudicate on claims. However, given the complexity of the task involved it is likely that independent experts will continue to be involved in the vast majority of equal value cases. Furthermore, a tribunal will err if it dismisses an equal value complaint because there are no reasonable grounds for determining that the work of the applicants is not of equal value to that of their comparators, and thus that there is no basis for commissioning an independent expert's report, if it does so without giving the parties an opportunity to adduce their own expert evidence.[14]

Special rules of procedure exist for use only in equal value claims. 4.40 These detailed rules, which are to be found in Schedule 3 of the Employment Tribunals (Constitution and Rules of Procedure) (Scotland) Regulations[15] amend the Principal Rules in Schedule 1 for the purposes of an equal value claim. All references are therefore to Schedule 1 as amended by the provisions of Schedule 3. Assuming that an expert report is sought, the expert has to carry out, in effect, a job evaluation study in respect of the applicant and her comparators.[16] The report is normally admitted in evidence[17] although it is open to the tribunal to determine that it should not be admitted on certain specified grounds.[18] At any time after the tribunal has received the report a party may call one witness (only) to give evidence on the question which the tribunal has asked the independent expert to consider.[19] If the report is admitted by the tribunal there is only limited scope for a party to give evidence upon or question any witness on a matter of fact upon which the conclusion of the report is based.[20]

MULTIPLE APPLICATIONS

From time to time, a substantial number of equal pay claims based on 4.41 identical facts are lodged against a single employer by a group of applicants. While there is no formal "test case" procedure set out in the rules of procedure it is normal for the tribunal, in association with the parties, to seek to identify a selection of representative cases to proceed to a full hearing. Thereafter, if these claims are dismissed and an applicant in the group, whose case was not heard, seeks to proceed with her claim her application is likely to be struck out as "vexatious". This situation arose in *Ashmore v. British Coal Corporation*[21] where the Court of Appeal held that the employment tribunal had correctly exercised

---

[13] S.I. 1996 No. 438.
[14] *Wood v. William Ball Ltd* [1999] I.R.L.R. 773, EAT.
[15] S.I. 2001 No. 1170.
[16] *Leverton v. Clwyd County Council* [1989] I.R.L.R. 28, HL.
[17] 2001 Regulations, Schedule 1, r.10A (17).
[18] Schedule 1, r.10A(18).
[19] Schedule 1, r.11(2B).
[20] Schedule 1, r.11(2C).
[21] [1990] I.R.L.R. 283, CA.

their discretion to strike out the appellant's equal pay claim on grounds that her attempt to have the claim listed for hearing was an abuse of process and therefore "vexatious", in circumstances in which her claim had been sisted pending the determination of sample cases raising similar factual issues and those issues had been determined in favour of the employer.[22] The court went on to explain that where sample cases have been chosen so that the tribunal can investigate all the relevant evidence as fully as possible, and findings have been made on that evidence, it is contrary to the interests of justice and public policy to allow those same issues to be litigated again, unless there is fresh evidence which justifies reopening the issue. The 2001 Tribunal Rules of Procedure allow for two or more originating applications to be presented in a single document by applicants who claim relief arising out of the same set of facts. This may assist in the administration of multiple applicant equal pay claims and serve to underline the position adopted in *Ashmore*.

THE GENUINE MATERIAL FACTOR OR DIFFERENCE DEFENCE

4.42   Section 1(3) of the EqPA sets out a defence for an employer faced with an equal pay claim. In the case of a claim under the like work or work rated as equivalent provisions the employer must show that the difference in pay is "genuinely due to a material factor which is not the difference of sex", and that factor **must** be a "material difference" between the woman's case and that of the man.[23] In an equal value claim the defence requires the employer to prove that the variation is "genuinely due to a material factor which is not the difference of sex" and that factor **may** be such a material difference.[24]

4.43   The distinction in wording between section 1(3)(a) and section 1(3)(b) is of limited practical effect. Historically, it would appear that the difference arose because the Government of the day wished to ensure that an employer faced with an equal value claim could rely on a material factor other than sex which was not a "material difference between the woman's case and the man's". It was stated at the time that what the Government had in mind were "circumstances where the difference in pay is not due to personal factors between the man and the woman, but rather to skill shortages or other market forces".[25] This distinction was derived from the case of *Fletcher v. Clay Cross (Quarry Services) Ltd*[26] in which the Court of Appeal examined what was encompassed by the phrase "material difference". Lord Denning stated that:

> "The issue depends on whether there is a material difference (other than sex) between her case and his. Take heed to those words: 'between her case and his'. They show that the Tribunal is

---

[22] See 2001 Regulations, Schedule 1, r.15(2).
[23] EqPA, s.1(3)(a).
[24] EqPA, s.1(3)(b).
[25] EqPA, s.1(3)(b).
[26] [1978] I.R.L.R. 361, CA, paras 12—13.

to have regard to her and to him—to the personal equation of the woman as compared to that of the man—irrespective of any extrinsic forces which led to the variation in pay. As I said in *E Coomes (Holdings) Ltd v. Shields* [1978] IRLR at page 266, the sub-section applies when 'the personal equation of the man is such that he deserves to be paid at a higher rate than the woman'. Thus the personal equation of the man may warrant a wage differential if he has much longer length of service, or has superior skill or qualifications; or gives bigger output or productivity; or has been placed, owing to down-grading, in a protected pay category, vividly described as 'red-circled'; or to other circumstances personal to him in doing his job.

But the Tribunal is not to have regard to any extrinsic forces which have led to the man being paid more. An employer cannot avoid his obligations under the Act by saying: 'I paid him more because he asked for more', or 'I paid her less because she was willing to come for less'. If any such excuse were permitted, the Act would be a dead letter. Those are the very reasons why there was unequal pay before the Statute. They are the very circumstances in which the Statute was intended to operate."

The section 1(3)(b) defence open in an equal value case was worded to ensure that the tribunal was entitled to take into account the "extrinsic forces" which the Court of Appeal had held were not to be considered in a like work/work rated as equivalent case.

However, in the like work case of *Rainey v. Greater Glasgow Health Board*[27] the House of Lords considered that the approach in Fletcher was unduly restrictive. Lord Keith of Kinkel examined what was meant by the phrase "material difference" and the nature of the factors which might amount to such: 4.44

"The difference must be 'material', which I would construe as meaning 'significant and relevant', and it must be between 'her case and his'. Consideration of a person's case must necessarily involve consideration of all the circumstances of that case. These may well go beyond what is not very happily described as 'the personal equation', *i.e.* the personal qualities by way of skill, experience or training which the individual brings to the job. Some circumstances may on examination prove to be not significant or not relevant, but others may do so, though not relating to the personal qualities of the employer. In particular, where there is no question of intentional sex discrimination whether direct or indirect (and there is none here) a difference which is connected with economic factors affecting the efficient carrying on of the employer's business or other activity may well be relevant."[28]

In these circumstances there would appear to be very little difference between the factors which can amount to a defence under section 1(3)(a) and those falling within section 1(3)(b). However, it should be noted that 4.45

---

[27] [1987] I.R.L.R. 26, HL.
[28] At para. 14.

while differences between the tasks performed by the woman and her male comparator will not usually be relevant in a like work claim to establishing a defence under section 1(3)(a), since their significance will already have been assessed in considering whether the provisions of section 1(4) are met, it has been held that differences in demands between jobs can be relevant for the purpose of section 1(3) as well as in relation to the issue of whether the two jobs are of equal value.[29]

Section 1(3) requires the employer to prove, on the balance of probabilities,[30] not only that the variation is genuinely due to (*i.e.* caused by[31]) a material factor but also to prove that this is not due to the difference of sex.[32] If the factor relied upon is tainted by discrimination the defence will not succeed.[33] This is clear from the decision of the House of Lords in *Ratcliffe v. North Yorkshire County Council.*[34]

4.46　　This was a "work rated as equivalent" claim under the EqPA. The applicants were three female school catering assistants. In 1987 their jobs were assessed under a local authority job evaluation scheme as being of equal value to those performed *inter alia* by gardeners and refuse collectors, which were male dominated occupations. The vast majority of catering assistants were, as one might expect, women who found that the hours of work were compatible with their domestic responsibilities.

From 1988 the women were paid on an equal basis with their male comparators in accordance with NJC Conditions. In 1989 the Council was required to put the school meal service out to Compulsory Competitive Tendering (CCT). A Direct Service Organisation (DSO) was duly formed and the Council's territory was divided into six areas for bidding purposes. Only the DSO tendered for area one but the area two contract was awarded to an outside commercial contractor which had substantially lower labour costs than the DSO.

In order to compete effectively for the remaining four contracts the DSO manager decided that he had to reduce labour costs. Accordingly, the catering assistants were made redundant in July 1991 and re-employed a month later on lower hourly rates and less beneficial holiday and sick pay provision. Their male comparators remained on NJC conditions. In their application to the employment tribunal the three applicants claimed that they had been treated less favourably than their comparators and that a clause should be implied in their contracts of employment which entitled them to the same terms and conditions as their comparators. The DSO defended the applications by arguing *inter alia* that the variation between the applicants' contracts and those of their comparators was genuinely due to a material factor which was not the difference of sex.

4.47　　The employment tribunal accepted that for the DSO to compete effectively the cost of meals had to be reduced, necessitating a reduction in labour costs of 25 per cent. It was also accepted that the DSO manager, had to have regard to the market forces and, in particular, that

---

[29] *Davies v. McCartneys* [1989] I.R.L.R. 439, EAT.
[30] *National Vulcan Engineering Insurance Group Ltd v. Wade* [1978] I.R.L.R. 225, CA.
[31] *Methven v. Cow Industrial Polymers Ltd* [1980] I.R.L.R. 289, CA.
[32] *The Financial Times Ltd v. Byrne (No. 2)* [1992] I.R.L.R. 163, EAT.
[33] *British Coal Corporation v. Smith* [1996] I.R.L.R. 399, HL.
[34] [1995] I.R.L.R. 439, HL.

because of the low pay in the catering industry in general, and particularly in those areas where women were exclusively employed, he could not afford to continue to engage staff on NJC terms, conditions and pay".

By a majority, the employment tribunal concluded that:

1. The applicants were on less favourable terms because the DSO manager had decided that it was necessary to reduce them in order to compete effectively in the open market. This decision arose from "his perception of market forces in a market which is virtually exclusively female doing work which is convenient to that female workforce and which, but for the particular hours and times of work, that workforce would not be able to do . . . It was clear to Mr Tillbrook, that it was a work force that would, by and large, continue to do the work, even at a reduced rate of pay", the alternative being no work or work with a commercial catering organisation on poorer terms in any event.

2. It was clear that both the DSO and the employees were "over the proverbial 'barrel' due to the fact that competitors only employed women and, because of that, employed them on less favourable terms than the Council did previously . . . That may well have been a material factor but it was certainly a material factor due to the difference of sex arising out of the general perception in the United Kingdom, and certainly in North Yorkshire, that a woman should stay at home to look after the children and if she wants to work it must fit in with that domestic duty and the lack of facilities to enable her, easily, to do otherwise".[35]

Accordingly, the majority concluded that there had been direct discrimination and that the employer had failed to show that the variation between the contracts was due to a material factor which was not the difference of sex. The minority member held that the requirements of the compulsory competitive tendering process did amount to a material factor defence which was unrelated to sex.

On appeal the EAT concluded that the employment tribunal had failed to clearly direct itself in relation to section 1(3) of the EqPA, which sets out the material factor defence, and remitted the matter back to another employment tribunal. On further appeal the Court of Appeal held that the Council had established a material factor defence in that: "The need to compete with a rival bid was unconnected with the difference of sex between potential male and female employees". In reaching this conclusion, the Court of Appeal also made it clear that the distinction between direct and indirect discrimination set out in the SDA should also form the basis of any analysis under the EqPA.

On further appeal the House of Lords held that the EqPA: "must be interpreted . . . without bringing in the distinction between so called 'direct' and 'indirect' discrimination". The central question under the EqPA was whether equal treatment had been accorded to men and

4.48

---

[35] [1996] I.R.L.R. 439, at para. 9.

women on like work/work rated as equivalent. The work of the applicants and their comparators had been rated as equivalent and they were entitled to a declaration in their favour unless a material factor defence was established. In analysing that issue it was held that the employment tribunal had been entitled to come to the conclusion reached by the majority:

> "The women could not have found other suitable work and were obliged to take the wages offered if they were to continue with this work . . . The fact is that the employer re-engaged the women at rates of pay less than those received by the male comparators and no material difference other than the difference of sex has been found to exist between the cases of the women and the male comparators".[36]

4.49 In reaching that conclusion the court was implicitly recognising that if, in a sex segregated labour market, there is a female dominated work force which, due to force of gender-related circumstances, commands low rates of pay which are reduced further in order to compete with a competitor who also has a female dominated work force, the women are being paid less because they are women. Although the court was conscious of the difficulties faced by the employer in seeking to compete with a rival tenderer it considered that: "to reduce the women's wages below that of their male comparators was the very kind of discrimination in relation to pay which the Act sought to remove".

In these circumstances it is unlikely that employers involved in the compulsory competitive tendering of services, which are provided by work forces dominated by women, will be able to defend an equal pay claim on the basis that wages had to be reduced to allow the employer to compete effectively in the market place and thereby retain the contract.[37]

4.50 There has been a string of conflicting decisions over the years on whether, in establishing a material factor defence, it is sufficient for the employer to show that the cause of the variation was untainted by sex discrimination or whether the employer must also be able to show a good and sufficient reason for the variation in pay even where the absence of sex discrimination has been demonstrated. Put another way, does the employer need to be able to objectively justify the difference in pay?

4.51 In *Barber v. NCR (Manufacturing)*[38] the EAT held that there may be a cause for a variation which does not amount to a material factor:

> "In our view, there is a small, but critical, difference between saying that the variation is genuinely due to a material factor other than sex, on the one hand, and saying that the cause of the variation was free from sex discrimination, on the other. It seems

---

[36] At para. 24.

[37] See *Lawrence v. Regent Office Care* [2000] I.R.L.R. 608, CA which raises the issue of whether a comparison can be made between a worker who remains in the employment of the original employer and one who transfers over to an employer which is awarded a contract in a contracting out exercise.

[38] [1993] I.R.L.R. 95, EAT.

to us that these expressions do not have the same meaning, and that there may well be a 'cause' for a variation which is not a 'material factor' other than the difference of sex."[39]

This approach would lead one to suggest that care must be taken by an employer to ensure that reliance is not placed upon a factor which might once have been a material factor but which no longer amounts to such. For example, in *Benveniste v. University of Southampton*[40] a female lecturer claimed equal pay for like work with three male lecturers. The employer argued that it had a material factor defence since the female employee had been taken on at a time of financial constraint and the university could not afford to pay her more at that time. However, it was accepted that the financial constraints no longer existed and in these circumstances it was held that the section 1(3) defence had "evaporated" when the constraints were removed. However, a question now arises in light of the decisions in *Wallace* and *Marshall (No. 1)* (see below) as to whether such circumstances might now be considered as amounting to a sufficient defence.

It is permissible for an employer seeking to establish a section 1(3) 4.52 defence to rely upon a variety of factors which, taken together, explain the difference in pay between the woman and her comparator.[41]

In *Rainey*[42] the House of Lords suggested that in order to discharge the onus placed on him by section 1(3) an employer must demonstrate objectively justified grounds for the difference in pay between the woman and the man and that the decision of the European Court of Justice in *Bilka-Kaufhaus v. Weber von Hartz*[43] to this effect must be accepted as authoritative.[44] The decision of the ECJ in *Enderby*[45] also supports this proposition. Applying a principle derived from case law under the SDA, in all situations where objective justification has to be shown this will involve an objective balance being struck between the discriminatory effect of any requirement or condition imposed and the reasonable needs of the employer.[46]

Bearing in mind the dictum in the *Ratcliffe*[47] case that the distinction between direct and indirect discrimination has no place in the interpretation of the EqPA one might expect that any attempt to rely on a section 1(3) defence would involve the employer having to objectively justify any difference in pay between the complainant and her comparators. This analysis would be supported by the reasoning in *British Coal Corporation v. Smith*[48] where no distinction between direct and indirect

---

[39] At para. 10.

[40] [1989] I.R.L.R. 122, CA.

[41] For example, see *Strathclyde Regional Council v. Wallace* [1998] I.R.L.R. 146, HL.

[42] [1987] I.R.L.R. 26, HL.

[43] [1986] I.R.L.R. 317, ECJ.

[44] The relevant test to be applied in assessing whether the defence is available is examined in *Leverton v. Clwyd County Council* [1989] I.R.L.R. 28, HL. In that case Lord Bridge considered that the appropriate criteria to be considered were those of reasonable necessity and objective justifiability when examining whether a s.1(3) defence applies.

[45] [1993] I.R.L.R. 591, ECJ.

[46] *Hampson v. Department of Education and Science* [1989] I.R.L.R. 69, CA.

[47] *Ratcliffe v. North Yorkshire County Council* [1995] I.R.L.R. 591, ECJ.

[48] [1996] I.R.L.R. 399, HL.

discrimination was made and it was held that the employer had to show that the "justification" for the difference in benefits received by the women and their male comparators satisfied "objective criteria".

4.53   However, in *Tyldesley v. TML Plastics Ltd*[49] the EAT held that in the absence of any suggestion of indirect discrimination no requirement of objective justification arises. It was sufficient to meet the defence that the explanation for the differential put forward by the employer was accepted as the cause of the difference or was a sufficient influence to be significant and relevant whether or not the explanation was objectively justified. According to the EAT, the comments in *Rainey* on the need for objective justification were restricted to claims of indirect pay discrimination. It followed, said the EAT, that a careless mistake, which could not possibly be objectively justified, could amount to a defence, provided that the tribunal was satisfied that the mistake was genuine and of sufficient influence to be significant. If a genuine mistake would suffice to establish the defence so, according to the EAT, would a genuine perception, whether reasonable or not, about the need to engage an individual with particular skills or experience and to pay him accordingly.

This decision was approved by the Court of Session in *Strathclyde Regional Council v. Wallace*.[50] In this case, nine female teachers were performing the job of a principal teacher but none had actually been appointed to that position. They formed part of a much larger group (81 men and 53 women) who were unpromoted but claimed to be carrying out principal teacher duties.

4.54   The nine women brought equal pay claims, identifying at least one male comparator who had been appointed as a principal teacher and was receiving a salary appropriate to that responsibility. The employment tribunal found that the applicants had been performing like work.

The employers argued that the variation in pay between the applicants and their male comparators was due to a combination of material factors, including the fact that the promotion structure was established by statute, that posts had to be filled after competition and that financial constraints limited the number of promoted posts available.

The employment tribunal took the view, however, that the employers had not established a material factor defence. The tribunal noted that the employer's "underlying theme was that they had no intention to discriminate. It is however quite clear that it is not sufficient for the employer to show that he did not intend to discriminate". The tribunal noted that the statutory promotion structure had a degree of flexibility, so that it did not "necessarily" prevent the applicants being appointed principal teachers. This factor did not, therefore, satisfy section 1(3). So far as financial constraints were concerned, bearing in mind the size of the respondent's operations and of its budget the tribunal said that it "did not consider that financial circumstances offered the respondents a material factor defence".

4.55   On appeal to the EAT, it was argued that the tribunal had erred by requiring the employers to demonstrate an "objective justification" for the use of the factor in question. The EAT took the view that the

[49] [1996] I.R.L.R. 395, EAT.
[50] [1996] I.R.L.R. 670, CS.

tribunal had not done this, but instead, quite legitimately, had decided that the factors relied upon by the employer had not actually caused the difference in pay.

On further appeal, the Court of Session held that the employment 4.56 tribunal had erred by searching to see whether there was objective justification for the aspects of the system of working on which the employers relied. The EAT erred, therefore, in upholding the decision of the employment tribunal. The Court went on to hold that the proper approach to be adopted when employers rely upon section 1(3) was that set out by the EAT in *Tyldesley v. TML Plastics Ltd*: a difference in pay explained by a factor not itself a factor of sex or tainted by sex discrimination should, in principle, constitute a valid defence. It considered that the difference in treatment between the applicants and their male comparators was not on the ground of sex, but was due to the employers' system of promotion coupled with financial constraints. These constituted material factors. The employment tribunal had misdirected itself by judging the fairness of the employers' system of promotion. The employment tribunal had also erred in holding that the employers could not justify their defence upon financial grounds in that the additional amount involved was relatively small compared with their total educational budget. That the employers might have been able to find the additional sum did not mean that the employment tribunal was entitled to reject financial circumstances as being a material factor.

Lord Weir went on to suggest that if the employers had been required to objectively justify their actions, then the tribunal's decision would have been correct. However, he considered that this was not something which the employers had to establish.

On further appeal to the House of Lords[51] it was held that, read 4.57 without reference to authority, the words of section 1(3) did not present any great difficulty. To establish a defence an employer was required to show that the difference in pay was 'genuinely' due to a factor which was (a) material and (b) not the difference of sex. The requirement of genuineness would be met if the employment tribunal came to the conclusion that the reason put forward by the employer was not a sham or a pretence. A factor would be regarded as material if the employer could show that it was causally related to the difference in pay, *i.e.* that it was a significant factor. The employer would also have to show that the difference of sex was not a factor relied upon. (In this particular case this matter presented no difficulty for the employer since it was an agreed fact that the disparity in pay had nothing to do with gender). On a straightforward application of section 1(3) it was considered that the employer had established a material factor defence. The question of justification will only arise, it was held, where a factor relied upon by the employer is gender discriminatory. In other words, provided that there is no element of sex discrimination, an employer will establish a material factor defence by identifying the factors which it alleges have caused the disparity in pay, proving that those factors are genuine and proving that they were causally relevant to the disparity. The House of Lords also

---

[51] [1998] I.R.L.R. 146, HL.

pointed out that the purpose of the EqPA is to eliminate sex discrimination not to achieve fair wages.[52]

4.58   The House of Lords took the same approach in *Glasgow City Council v. Marshall*[53] in which female instructors in a special school compared themselves with male teachers in the school who were better paid. The instructors claimed that, although they lacked formal teaching qualifications, they were doing like work with the teachers and this was held to be so by the tribunal which heard the case, the lack of qualifications not being found important and there being no difference in the work being done or in the skills and knowledge required to do it. The tribunal also held that the employer had not succeeded in establishing a material factor defence under section 1(3) of the EqPA. On eventual appeal to the House of Lords it was emphasised that from the outset of the case the employer had referred to statistics showing the breakdown by sex of instructors and teachers and relied upon the absence of sex discrimination. The applicants did not challenge the absence of sex discrimination. The ET, however, had considered that "to demonstrate lack of sex discrimination in the matter of disparity of remuneration ... is nothing to the point". Lord Nicholls (leading judgment) summarised the position thus: "In short, the effect of the industrial tribunal's decision was that, even in a case where the absence of sex discrimination was demonstrated, some good and sufficient reason must exist for the variation in pay. If none was proved, the claim succeeded. The question for your Lordships' house is whether this was a proper interpretation of section 1(3)".

Lord Nicholls could understand why the instructors felt aggrieved that teachers doing the same job were paid more but he had "more difficulty in understanding how, in the absence of sex discrimination, this perceived unfairness is said to be caught and cured by a statute whose object, according to its preamble, is to prevent discrimination between men and women as regards terms and conditions of employment". He was of the view that if the approach of the tribunal was correct this would mean that in a case where there is no suggestion of sex discrimination, the equality clause (imported into every contract by s.1 of the Act) would still operate. "That would be difficult to reconcile with the gender-related elements of the statutory equality clause. The equality clause is concerned with variations in pay or conditions between a woman doing like work with a man and vice versa. But if the equality clause were to operate where no sex discrimination is involved, the statutory starting point of a gender-based comparison would become largely meaningless. On this interpretation of the Act, what matters is not sex discrimination. What matters is whether, within one establishment, there is a variation in pay or conditions between one employee doing like work with another employee. The sex of the employees would be neither here nor there, save that to get the claim off the ground the chosen comparator must be of the opposite sex." Lord Nicholls did not accept that the EqPA was intended to have that result. He considered that the Act worked by creating a rebuttable presumption of sex

---

[52] For further discussion see *Glasgow City Council v. Marshall and Others,* 1998 S.C. 274; aff'd [2000] I.R.L.R. 272, HL.

[53] [2000] I.R.L.R. 272, HL

discrimination which arose once a woman showed that she was doing like work or work of equal value to man but was paid less. The burden then passed to the employer to show that the explanation for the variation is not tainted by sex. To do this the employer has to satisfy the tribunal on several matters:—

1. The proffered explanation or reason is genuine and not a sham or pretence.
2. The less favourable treatment is due to this reason—in this sense the factor must be a "material" factor, *i.e.* significant and relevant.
3. The reason is not "the difference of sex"—this phrase embraced both direct and indirect discrimination.
4. The factor relied upon is a "material" difference, *i.e.* a significant and relevant difference between the woman's case and the man's case.

Analysed thus it was apparent that an employer who satisfied the tribunal with regard to the third requirement was under no obligation to prove a "good" reason for the pay disparity. According to the House of Lords if there is any evidence of sex discrimination, such as evidence that the difference in pay has a disparately adverse impact on women the employer will be called upon to satisfy the tribunal that the difference in pay is objectively justifiable. However, if the employer proves the absence of sex discrimination he is not obliged to justify the pay disparity. All the other judges agreed with Lord Nicholls although Lord Slynn made one further remark which perhaps encapsulates the decision in a nutshell: "This is plainly in essence a claim that the pay is not fair: and not a claim that the pay is unequal because of discrimination between the sexes. As such it does not fall within the Equal Pay Act 1970".

Interestingly, Counsel for the employer sought to reopen the "like work" point on the basis of *Angestelltenbetriebsrat der Wiener Gebietskrankenkasse v. Wiener Gebietskrankenkasse*[54] although he was not allowed to do so since the point had not been taken in the lower courts.

The approach taken in *Marshall* can be contrasted with that of the ECJ in *Brunnhofer v. Bank der österreichischen Postsparkasse*[55] in which the court suggests that "an employer may validly explain [a] difference in pay" by providing "objectively justified reasons unrelated to any discrimination based on sex and in conformity with the principle of proportionality". This was a direct discrimination case and it appears from the decision that this test is set out as generally applicable in equal pay cases. There is no suggestion that the requirement to have an objectively justified and proportionate reason is restricted to cases of indirect discrimination. Given that *Brunnhofer* was decided after *Marshall* it remains to be seen whether the approach in *Marshall* will now be subject to challenge.

---

[54] [1999] I.R.L.R. 804, ECJ.
[55] Case C–381/99 [2001] I.R.L.R. 571, ECJ.

SPECIFIC SECTION 1(3) DEFENCES

4.59 Employers have sought to rely on a wide range of matters as "material factors". The following are simply examples:

Market forces

4.60   Extrinsic forces, such as difficulty in recruiting staff at a particular point in time, leading to the need to offer employment on higher than "normal" salaries can be a genuine material factor causing a pay differential.[56] However, the market forces argument will not succeed if it is tainted because the market itself is founded on discriminatory practices.[57]

Personal factors

4.61   Differences in qualifications, seniority, length of service, experience, skill levels, flexibility (in the sense of being willing and able to work variable shift patterns), etc., can be material factors causing a difference in pay between a woman and her comparator.[58] However, factors of this type may disadvantage women as a group (*i.e.* they may be indirectly discriminatory) and employers must be sure that they can objectively justify differences in pay as a result of such factors.

Grading systems

4.62   A pay differential between a woman and her comparator can be defended if the reason for it is that they are in separate grading or pay scales, the use of which is untainted by sex discrimination.[59] However, if women predominated on one scale or grade and men on another that could raise the suspicion that the grading/scale structure was being used to disguise discrimination.[60]

Separate pay/Collective bargaining systems

4.63   It has been held that the fact that the pay of a female complainant and her male comparator is determined by reference to separate collective bargaining processes will not in itself amount to a defence to a claim, even where it is shown that there is no discrimination within each of the processes. In *British Coal Corporation v. Smith*[61] the variation in terms between surface mineworkers (all men) and canteen workers and cleaners (principally women) originated in separate pay bargaining structures. However, the House of Lords held that the original tribunal

---

[56] *Rainey*, above.

[57] *Ratcliffe*, above.

[58] *Rainey*, above.

[59] *Waddington v. Leicester Council for Voluntary Services* [1977] I.R.L.R. 32, EAT.

[60] See, for example, *Electrolux Ltd v. Hutchinson* [1976] I.R.L.R. 410, EAT where the employer sought to rely on the fact that the woman was on grade 1 while her comparator was on grade 10. However, it emerged that 599 of the 600 female employees were on grade 1 while all male employees were on grade 10. It was held that the grading structure was being used to underpin discrimination in pay.

[61] [1996] I.R.L.R. 399, HL.

had not erred in holding that the simple existence of separate pay structures was not in itself a defence. It was for the tribunal to decide whether the justification for the differences in contractual terms satisfied objective criteria unrelated to sex. In *Enderby*[62] the ECJ held:

> "The fact that the respective rates of pay of two jobs of equal value, one carried out almost exclusively by women and the other predominantly by men, were arrived at by collective bargaining processes which, although carried out by the same parties, are distinct, and, taken separately, have in themselves no discriminatory effect, is not sufficient objective justification for the difference in pay between those two jobs".

Post *Wallace* it is submitted that the same decision would almost certainly be reached, given the proportion of women and men covered by the relevant collective agreements—this would be perceived as a factor which was (indirectly) discriminatory and the employer would therefore have to objectively justify its position to meet the defence.

Red circling

An employer may be able to establish a section 1(3) defence where the 4.64 difference in pay between the applicant and her male comparator is due to the fact that the man has a personally protected salary for a particular reason (for example, he may have performed a more highly paid job which became redundant and accepted an alternative post, which would normally attract a lower salary, on the basis that his old salary was protected) and the employer can show that women and men who are not in the red circled group are treated the same.[63] However, such a defence will not succeed if the current disparity in salary levels is due to earlier discrimination which had excluded women from the red circle when it was formed.[64] The defence may also fail where there is prolonged maintenance of the red circle arrangement since this would be a factor for the tribunal to consider in assessing whether the burden of proving the statutory defence has been met.[65]

Financial constraints

Where an individual is paid less than the norm due to financial 4.65 constraints this could amount to a material factor defence when a comparison is made between that individual and another who is employed at the normal rate for the job. However, it is questionable whether the employer can rely on this factor once the circumstances giving rise to the difference in pay no longer exist—in essence, it might be difficult to show that the variation was genuinely due to this factor.[66]

---

[62] C–127/92 [1993] I.R.L.R. 591, ECJ, at para. 23. See also *British Road Services Ltd v. Loughran* [1997] I.R.L.R. 92, NICA.

[63] *Snoxell and Davies v. Vauxhall Motors Ltd; Charles Early & Witney Marriot Ltd v. Smith and Ball* [1977] I.R.L.R. 123, EAT.

[64] *Snoxell and Davies; Charles Early & Witney Marriot Ltd* [1997] I.R.L.R. 123, EAT.

[65] *Outlook Supplies Ltd v. Parry* [1978] I.R.L.R. 12, EAT. See also *United Biscuits Ltd v. Young* [1978] I.R.L.R. 15, EAT, in respect of circumstances which can lead to the failure of a red circling defence.

[66] *Benveniste v. University of Southampton* [1989] I.R.L.R. 122, CA.

Mistake or error

4.66   A genuine administrative error can amount to a section 1(3) defence.[67]

Hours of work

4.67   The fact that a woman works part-time while her male comparator works full-time will not in itself amount to a material factor defence. If part-time workers are treated less favourably than full-time workers in relation to pay this will normally be in breach of the EqPA and Article 141, where a substantially smaller proportion of women than men work full-time unless the pay differential can be objectively justified on grounds which are unrelated to sex. This will require the national court to hold that the measures adopted by the employer (which have given rise to prima facie discrimination) correspond to a real need on the part of the undertaking, are appropriate with a view to establishing the objectives pursued and are necessary to that end.[68]

Place or time of work

4.68   Regional variations in pay (for example, London weighting allowances) can amount to a material factor defence[69] as can differences in hours of work which are marked by the payment of shift premiums, although care must be taken to ensure that there is no discrimination in the allocation of geographical postings and shift working which attracts premium payments, since such would prevent the establishment of the defence.

STAGE IN PROCEEDINGS WHEN THE SECTION 1(3) DEFENCE CAN BE EXAMINED

4.69   In an equal value case the tribunal is permitted, on the application of a party, if it considers it appropriate to hear evidence and submissions in respect of any genuine material factor defence relied upon prior to deciding whether to refer the case to an independent job evaluation expert.[70] In other words, the defence can be examined at the outset of the case, if the tribunal agrees to the request, and, if it is established, the case will be dismissed at that point.[71] If the employer fails at the outset to persuade the tribunal that there is a genuine material factor defence he cannot argue his defence again after the report of the independent expert is received.

---

[67] *Young v. University of Edinburgh* [EAT 244/93, June 14, 1994, unreported]; and *Tyldesley v. TML Plastics Ltd* [1996] I.R.L.R. 395.

[68] *Bilka-Kaufhaus GmbH v. Weber von Hartz* [1986] I.R.L.R. 317, ECJ.

[69] *Navy, Army and Air Force Institutes v. Varley* [1976] I.R.L.R. 408, EAT.

[70] Employment Tribunals (Constitution and Rules of Procedure) (Scotland) Regulations 2001, Sched. 1, r.11(2E).

[71] *McGregor v. General Municipal Boilermakers and Allied Trades Union* [1987] I.C.R. 505, EAT.

TIME-LIMIT FOR MAKING AN EQUAL PAY COMPLAINT

In *British Railways Board v. Paul*[72] it was held that there was no time-limit for making a claim to an employment tribunal under the EqPA (unless the complaint arose as a result of a reference to the tribunal by the Secretary of State under section 2(2) or a court under section 2(3) in which case the time-limit was six months from the date the individual ceased to be employed in the employment, in terms of section 2(4)). However, in *Etherson v. Strathclyde Regional Council*[73] the approach in *Paul* was rejected and it was held that the time-limit for making a claim to the employment tribunal is six months from the date of termination of the employment to which the complaint relates. *Preston v. Wolverhampton Healthcare NHS Trust* raised the issue of whether the six month time-limit was applicable in a claim in which reliance was placed upon Article 141 of E.C. Treaty. This issue, amongst others, was referred to the ECJ by the House of Lords. The ECJ[74] held that such a limitation period was not contrary to the requirements of Community law provided that it not less favourable for actions based on Community law than for those based on domestic law. On reference back to the House of Lords[75] it was held that the six month time-limit for lodging applications was not less favourable than the time-limit for comparable domestic claims. In relation to when the time-limit starts to run where there are intermittent contracts of service without a stable employment relationship, it was held that the period of six months under section 2(4) runs from the end of each contract of service. It was considered that this does not violate Community rules as to effectiveness and equivalence. However, where such contracts are concluded at regular intervals in respect of the same employment in a stable employment relationship, the six month period runs from the end of the last contract forming part of that relationship. This latter situation might arise commonly in professions such as teaching where contracts of temporary staff may be terminated at the end of one term and started at the beginning of the next.

In *National Power Plc v. Young*[76] the Court of Appeal held that the EAT had been correct to conclude that the word "employment" in section 2(4), which provides that an equal pay claim cannot be brought if the applicant has not been "employed in the employment" to which the claim relates within the six months preceding the date of the claim, does not relate to the particular job on which the woman bases her claim to an equality clause but rather to the contract of employment itself.

The civil courts have a concurrent jurisdiction under the EqPA in respect of which the ordinary time-limits for making a contractual claim apply. However, a court can decline jurisdiction in certain circumstances[77] and it is, in fact, very rare for EqPA claims to be lodged or heard in the civil courts.

4.70

---

[72] [1988] I.R.L.R. 20, EAT.
[73] [1992] I.R.L.R. 392, EAT.
[74] [2000] I.R.L.R. 506, ECJ.
[75] *Preston (No. 2)* [2001] I.R.L.R. 237, HL.
[76] [2001] I.R.L.R. 32, CA.
[77] See EqPA, s.2(3).

4.71 Community law does not specify a particular time-limit for making a claim based upon Article 141. In *Rewe-Zentralfinanz eG and Rewe-Zentral AG v. Landwirtschaftskammer für das Saarland*[78] the ECJ held that:

> "In the absence of Community rules on this subject, it is for the domestic legal system of each Member State to designate courts having jurisdiction and to determine the procedural conditions governing actions at law intended to ensure the protection of the rights which citizens have from the direct effect of Community law, it being understood that such conditions cannot be less favourable than those relating to similar actions of a domestic nature".

It is this principle which prevailed in *Preston* before the ECJ and on subsequent reference back to the House of Lords.

REMEDIES

4.72 Two remedies are available to those who bring a successful claim under the EqPA. First, the tribunal will issue a declaration that the equality clause in the contract has modified the term in the woman's contract which is less favourable than the clause of a similar kind in the comparator's contract. Secondly, the tribunal is entitled to make an award of arrears of remuneration (this will happen where there is a difference in the money paid to the applicant and her comparator) or damages (this will happen where there is a difference in contractual benefits).[79] However, section 2(5) of the EqPA makes it clear that no payment can be awarded in respect of a time earlier than two years before the date on which the proceedings were instituted. The issue of whether this restriction on damages, monetary award, is compatible with the requirements of Community Law was referred to the ECJ by the EAT in *Levez v. T.H. Jennings (Harlow Pools) Ltd (No. 1)*,[80] being a case in which the applicant had actually been misled by the employer about the salary paid to her male comparator, thereby delaying her decision to make an equal pay claim. The ECJ held that it was contrary to Community law to limit entitlement to arrears of remuneration or damages for breach of the principle of equal pay to a period of two years prior to the date on which the proceedings were instituted, where there was no possibility of extending that period in the event of the delay in bringing the claim being attributable to misrepresentation of the comparator's pay on the part of the employer. Leaving aside cases where misrepresentation has occurred the ECJ held that a national rule under which entitlement to arrears of remuneration is restricted to the two years preceding the date on which the proceedings were instituted did not make the exercise of rights conferred by Community Law either

---

[78] [1976] E.C.R. 1989 at 1997.

[79] Under reg. 3(1) of the Sex Discrimination and Equal Pay (Remedies) Regulations 1993 (S.I. 1993 No. 2798) the tribunal has a discretion to award interest on arrears of remuneration or damages.

[80] [1996] I.R.L.R. 499, EAT.

virtually impossible or excessively difficult. However, the principle of "equivalence" also had to be satisfied—Community law rights should not be subject to more onerous restrictions than similar domestic claims. It was for the national court to decide whether the principle of equivalence was satisfied. On reference back to the EAT,[81] it was held that the restriction under section 2(5) was incompatible with E.C. law in that it breached the principle of equivalence. Comparable actions, such as breach of contract, unlawful deductions from wages or discrimination on grounds of race or disability, all gave rise to more favourable compensation provisions. It was held that the six year limitation period applicable to claims for breach of contract in England was the appropriate limitation to be applied to compensation. In Scotland the relevant period is five years.[82] The Government indicated in December 2000 that it intended to amend the EqPA accordingly.

In *Magorrian v. Eastern Health and Social Services Board*[83] the ECJ has 4.73 held that in a claim based upon Article 141 for recognition of the claimants' entitlement to join an occupational pension scheme Community law precludes the application of a national rule under which entitlement is limited to a period which starts to run from a point in time two years prior to commencement of proceedings in connection with the claim. *Magorrian* was viewed by the ECJ as a case about full and equal access to an occupational pension scheme rather than as a case, strictly speaking, concerning entitlement to benefits arising under a scheme. The decision of the ECJ in *Magorrian* was available to the House of Lords when it heard the appeal in *Preston*. However, it was considered that *Magorrian* was not so decisive of the issues raised by *Preston* in relation to section 2(4) and (5) as to avoid the need to make a reference to the ECJ.

Like *Magorrian*, *Preston* involved consideration of whether the two 4.74 year limitation imposed by section 2(5) of the EqPA was compatible with the requirements of Community law where a claim was made under Article 141 for retrospective access to a pension scheme by workers deprived of such access as a result of their part-time status. The ECJ emphasised that the claim was not to obtain arrears of benefits under the scheme but to obtain retroactive membership for the purpose of future rights to benefits. The limitation on retroactive membership was judged to strike at the very essence of the rights conferred by the Community legal order, making it impossible in practice for individuals to exercise their Community law rights. As such the two year limitation on retrospective scheme membership, which is set out in section 2(5)of the EqPA, being read with effect from April 6, 1978 with regulation 12 of the Occupational Pension Schemes (Equal Access to Membership) Regulations 1976,[84] was held to be incompatible with Community law. On reference back to the House of Lords[85] it was held that the respondents could not rely on the two year rule in section 2(5) to prevent the applicants from retroactively gaining membership of the

---

[81] [1999] I.R.L.R. 764, EAT
[82] Prescription and Limitation (Scotland) Act 1973, s.6.
[83] [1998] I.R.L.R. 39, ECJ.
[84] S.I. 1976 No. 142.
[85] [2001] I.R.L.R. 237, HL.

pension scheme for the period of employment back to April 8, 1976[86] or to the date of commencement of employment, whichever was later, or from receiving pension benefits from such schemes which would otherwise have been due to be paid in the period after the application to the tribunal, calculated so as to take into account their service since April 8, 1976, so long as relevant pension contributions were paid by the applicants. The ramifications of this decision are still being worked through. Thousands of cases are still before employment tribunals. Many of them are likely to settle. However, the door is still open for an employer to seek to objectively justify the past exclusion of part-time workers from a pension scheme.

EQUAL PAY CODES OF PRACTICE

4.75 The EOC has issued a Code of Practice on equal pay which is admissible before employment tribunals in equal pay and sex discrimination cases. The aim of the code, which came into force on March 26, 1997, is to provide practical guidance and recommend good practice to those with responsibility for pay arrangements within organisations. As well as giving a basic outline of both domestic and European equal pay law the code sets out the practical implications of the law for employers and provides guidance on the process of pay review and the identification of discriminatory elements in pay systems. It also provides guidance on drawing up an equal pay policy and provides an example of such a policy.

4.76   In a separate initiative the European Commission has also issued a Code of Practice on the implementation of equal pay for work of equal value for women and men.[87] It points to continuing differentials between the pay of women and men in both manual and non-manual work across Europe. Various factors are highlighted as causative of these gaps. These include vertical and horizontal segregation of jobs held by women and men with typically women's jobs being generally less well paid and a tendency for sectors of the economy in which men predominate to offer pay additions such as bonuses.

The E.C. code is similar in many respects to the EOC code; both recommend that the way to tackle sex discrimination in pay is to review payment systems for sex bias although the E.C. code offers greater detail so far as the pay review process is concerned.

The evaluation of the effect of such codes in achieving the objective of equal pay is likely to be a long term process.

THE EQUAL PAY TASK FORCE

4.77 The EOC commissioned a group of independent experts from business, trade unions and the equal opportunities field, as an Equal Pay Task Force, to review the working of the equal pay legislation and the barriers

---

[86] The date of the ECJ judgment in *Defrenne v. Sabena (No. 2)*.
[87] COM (96) 336 Final.

to the achievement of equal pay. The report of the Task Force was published in February 2001.[88] In relation to the issue of pay discrimination, which is estimated to be the cause of 25–50 per cent of the pay gap, the Task Force recommends that the most effective measure is to require employers to carry out equal pay audits of their workforce at regular intervals. However, the Government has rejected that proposal[89] and suggests instead that it will encourage employers to undertake and act on pay audits on a voluntary basis. A Women's Employment Pay Review is to be set up to work alongside the EOC in building support for various voluntary measures designed to reduce the pay gap.

---

[88] "Just Pay", a summary of which can be downloaded from the EOC website at www.eoc.org.uk.
[89] See IDS Brief 684, May 2001, p.18 for more detail.

CHAPTER 5

PREGNANCY, MATERNITY, PARENTAL LEAVE AND TIME OFF FOR DEPENDANTS

MATERNITY RIGHTS—THE CURRENT LEGISLATIVE PROVISIONS

5.01 The law governing maternity leave and pay has changed dramatically over the course of the last decade as a result of the introduction of domestic legislation to implement the Pregnant Workers Directive[1] and consequent upon case law developments emanating from the ECJ.

THE CURRENT MATERNITY LEAVE PROVISIONS

5.02 The current maternity provisions are to be found in sections 71 to 75 of the Employment Rights Act 1996,[2] as substituted by section 7 of the Employment Relations Act 1999,[3] and in the Maternity and Parental Leave etc. Regulations 1999.[4] The framework set out in the 1996 Act is skeletal in nature with the practical specification of the rights and obligations of employees and employers being left to the Regulations.

There are three periods of maternity leave which may be available to a woman: ordinary maternity leave; compulsory maternity leave and additional maternity leave (in that order). The earliest that ordinary maternity leave can commence is the beginning of the eleventh week before the expected week of childbirth (EWC)[5] unless childbirth occurs before that date in which case maternity leave will commence on the day on which childbirth occurs.[6] Childbirth is defined as meaning the birth of a living child or the birth of a child, whether living or dead, after 24 weeks of pregnancy.[7] It should be noted that maternity leave is only available to "employees" with "employee" being defined as someone who has entered into a contract of service or apprenticeship. This is a narrower definition than is found in a number of other statutory provisions (for example, the SDA 1975, RRA 1976 or DDA 1995).[8]

---

[1] Directive 92/85.

[2] Hereinafter ERA. Note also ss.55–57 which gives all women the right to paid time off for ante-natal appointments.

[3] Which substitutes the provisions found in Pt I of Sched. 4 of the 1999 Act for those found previously in Pt VIII, Employment Rights Act 1996.

[4] S.I. 1999 No. 3312, hereinafter the MPL Regulations 1999.

[5] reg. 4(2), MPL Regulations 1999.

[6] reg. 6(2), MPL Regulations 1999.

[7] reg. 2, MPL Regulations 1999.

[8] See Chap. 1 for further detail.

Clearly, individuals who are self-employed will not qualify for the statutory right to maternity leave.

Ordinary Maternity Leave (OML)

All employees whose EWC began on or after April 30, 2000,[9] and who 5.03 satisfy the conditions set out in regulation 4 of the MPL Regulations 1999, are entitled to 18 weeks ordinary maternity leave,[10] irrespective of length of service or whether the employment is temporary or permanent.[11]

The regulation 4 entitlement to OML is dependent upon satisfaction of the following conditions:—

At least 21 days before the date on which the woman intends to start her OML (or, if that is not reasonably practicable, as soon as reasonably practicable) she notifies the employer:

(a) that she is pregnant (note this does not have to be notification in writing, unlike the previous provisions in the 1996 Act);
(b) of the EWC (by means of a medical certificate if the employer requests one)—same as previous provisions;
(c) of the date on which her OML is to commence (in writing if the employer requests this)—same as previous provisions.

However, in the event that the woman is absent from work wholly or partly because of pregnancy in the six week period before the EWC, her OML will commence automatically, irrespective of the wishes of the employee or employer.[12] The 21 day notification period is, obviously, not required in such circumstances but the employee will not be entitled to OML unless she notifies the employer as soon as reasonably practicable (in writing if so requested)[13] that she is absent from work wholly or partly because of pregnancy.[14] In the event that OML begins because the woman has given birth, to qualify for the period of leave she must notify the employer (in writing if so requested) as soon as reasonably practicable that she has given birth.[15] In the Consultation paper issued prior to the formulation of the MPL Regulations 1999 the Government suggested that if a woman failed to give the required notifications prior to the commencement of OML the start of the leave would be delayed until 21 days after the day on which the correct notifications should have been given. (In other words, a 21 day notice period will be imposed). It also

[9] reg. 3(1), MPL Regulations 1999.

[10] Unless the end of the "compulsory maternity leave" period would be later, in which case OML will end when the compulsory leave period ends, or the OML period is ended by dismissal in which case OML ends on the date of dismissal.

[11] However there are specific requirements which govern the entitlement to statutory maternity pay, for which, see below.

[12] reg. 6(1)(b). In Case C–411/96 *Boyle v. Equal Opportunities Commission* [1998] I.R.L.R. 717, ECJ, the automatic triggering of maternity leave was held not to be contrary to, or incompatible with, the Pregnant Workers Directive or the Equal Treatment Directive.

[13] reg. 4(5).

[14] reg. 4(3)(b).

[15] reg. 4(4)(b).

suggested that a woman who started her leave without giving the required notifications could be treated as being absent without authority. In fact, the final version of the Regulations did not include provisions dealing expressly with the consequences of failure to give the required notice. However, it is submitted that if an employee attempted to commence OML without giving the required notice, an employer would be entitled to insist upon it and delay the commencement of the leave accordingly (subject to the provisions governing automatic commencement of leave and the need to ensure the period of compulsory leave is honoured). If the employee insisted on being absent, without having given the requisite notice, then, logically, her absence will be unauthorised which could justify disciplinary action. While it might be argued that a dismissal in such circumstances would be automatically unfair, as being related to maternity leave,[16] this argument has not yet been tested. In any event, such a dismissal might, in the circumstances, be viewed as unfair under normal unfair dismissal principles.

Compulsory Maternity Leave (CML)

5.04   Section 72 of the ERA, read with regulation 8 of the MPL Regulations 1999, specifies that a woman must take two weeks "compulsory" maternity leave commencing with the date of birth of the child. This requirement, which stems from the Pregnant Workers Directive also formed part of the pre-1999 provisions, although it was rather more obscure, being found only in an statutory instrument. The current provisions perhaps make it rather more explicit that the onus is on the employer not to allow the woman "to work". As with the previous provisions an employer who breaches this requirement will be guilty of a criminal offence, punishable by a fine. It is immaterial where the work is done or what it involves.

The period of compulsory leave is to fall within the OML period[17] If necessary that period could be extended but it is difficult to envisage this being required since the baby would need to be more than a month overdue before such an extension would be required!

Additional Maternity Leave (AML)

5.05   An employee who is entitled to OML and who has been continuously employed by her employer for a period of at least one year at the beginning of the eleventh week before the EWC is entitled to AML.[18] AML will commence on the day after the last day of the OML period.[19] Under the pre-1999 maternity leave provisions a woman with the continuous service then required was entitled to the "right to return" to work within the period ending 29 weeks after the beginning of the week in which childbirth occurred. A woman who wished to exercise the right to return to work was required to notify her employer in writing that she intended to exercise her right to return prior to her maternity leave

---

[16] ERA 1996, s.99.
[17] s.72(3). Also note s.205 of the Public Health Act 1936 which prohibits women who work in factories from returning to work for four weeks after having given birth.
[18] ERA 1996, s.73 and reg. 5 of the MPL Regulations 1999.
[19] reg. 6(3), MPL Regulations 1999.

commencing. Under the current provisions there is no requirement for the employee to inform her employer before her OML commences that she intends to exercise her right to AML. It will be presumed that she intends to take her AML unless she notifies the employer of an intention to return early.

However, an employer is entitled to write to an employee no earlier that 21 days before the end of her OML period, asking her to notify him in writing of:

(a) the date on which childbirth occurred;
(b) whether she intends to return to work after the AML period.

The employee is required to respond within 21 days normally (reasonably practicable extension available).[20]

The provisions of regulations 19 and 20 (which, *inter alia*, protect the employee against detriment on the ground that she took AML (reg. 19) and provide for automatic unfair dismissal if the reason for the dismissal is connected to taking AML (reg. 20)) will not apply to employees who have failed to comply with a written request from their employer in terms of regulation 12.[21] A "Regulation 12 letter" must warn the employee of the above consequences of a failure to respond and it must also tell the employee how to calculate when her AML period will end.

In the Consultation paper issued prior to the MPL Regulations 1999, the Government proposed that when a woman failed to respond to an employer's request for the date of childbirth and confirmation that she was intending to return to work after AML the employer should be able to take "appropriate disciplinary action". However, there is no provision to this effect in the Regulations.

Under the pre-1999 provisions if an employer wrote to an employee asking her to confirm whether she intended to return and she failed to reply within 14 days she lost her statutory right to return. This draconian penalty does not form part of the current maternity leave regime.

The AML period continues until the end of the period of 29 weeks beginning with the actual week of childbirth[22] unless AML is ended by dismissal in which case the date of dismissal marks the end of AML.[23]

STATUS OF EMPLOYEE ON MATERNITY LEAVE

Ordinary Maternity Leave

Section 71(4) of the ERA 1996 makes it clear that employees absent 5.06 from work during OML are to be treated for all purposes (with one exception) as if they were not absent at all. Rights are not simply preserved; they continue to accrue. Thus, if a woman has a company car with an element of private use she should be permitted to retain that car

---

[20] reg. 12(1), MPL Regulations 1999.
[21] reg. 12(2), MPL Regulations 1999.
[22] reg. 7(4), MPL Regulations 1999.
[23] reg. 7(5), MPL Regulations 1999.

during the 18 week period. Similarly, holiday entitlement continues to accrue over this time. The entitlement to the benefit of her terms and conditions of employment extends to all matters connected to her employment, except "remuneration" whether or not they arise under her contract of employment. In other words, a benefit should continue under the contract even if it is not contractual in nature. In considering this entitlement there is no question of the female employee having to compare herself with how a sick man would be treated during a period of absence. "Remuneration" is narrowly defined in regulation 9 of the MPL Regulations 1999 as including "only sums payable to an employee by way of wages or salary". During the Committee Stage of the Bill, the Minister of State, in discussing these provisions, stated that "During ordinary maternity leave, contractual holiday arrangements accrue. A period of ordinary maternity leave counts towards the qualifying period for statutory holidays under the Working Time Regulations".

A woman is also bound by any obligations which arise under her terms and conditions during OML, except those which would be inconsistent with the fact that she is on maternity leave.[24]

Additional Maternity Leave

5.07 The pre-1999 provisions made it difficult to determine whether women absent from work who had the "right to return" had a subsisting contract of employment at all. In various cases it was suggested that a "ghost" contract existed or that that the contract of employment had been "suspended".[25]

In the Consultation paper which preceded the Employment Relations Act 1999 and the MPL Regulations 1999 the Government acknowledged that at that point it was "unclear whether women on additional maternity leave [were] 'employees' for legal purposes". It also accepted that it was not "clear which contractual benefits apply while a woman is on maternity leave". It determined that in these circumstances the new provisions would ensure that the contract of employment continued throughout AML unless either party to the contract expressly ended it or it expired. That commitment has been followed through in the statutory provisions. Specifically, section 73(4) of the ERA 1999 states that an employee on AML will be entitled, to the extent prescribed in Regulations, to the benefit of the terms and conditions of employment which would have applied had she not been absent. She will be similarly bound, to the extent prescribed, by obligations arising under those terms and condition and will be entitled to return from leave to a job of a prescribed kind. Section 73(5) specifies that "terms and conditions of employment" include matters connected with the employee's employment whether contractual or not but does not include "remuneration".

However, in the 1999 Regulations the Government significantly restricted the contractual rights and duties which subsist during the AML period. Specifically regulation 17 states that an employee who takes AML[26] is entitled to the benefit of her employer's implied obligation of

---

[24] ERA 1996, s.71(4)(b).
[25] For discussion of the status of the contract of employment under the old law see *Halfpenny v. IGE Medical Systems Ltd* [2001] I.R.L.R. 96.
[26] Or parental leave—see later in this chapter.

trust and confidence and to any terms and conditions relating to notice of termination of employment, compensation in the event of redundancy and disciplinary and grievance procedures. Similarly, she is bound by her implied obligation of good faith, and any express obligation to her employer prohibiting the disclosure of confidential information, the acceptance of gifts or other benefits or participation in any competing business.

It should be noted that where an employee is entitled under her contract of employment or otherwise to rights corresponding to OML or AML but which are more favourable than those laid down by statute, regulation 21 of the MPL Regulations 1999 provides that she need not choose whether to exercise just her statutory rights or just those otherwise conferred. While she cannot exercise both rights separately she may "take advantage of whichever right is, in any particular respect, the more favourable". So, for example, if the employer's scheme allowed for greater contractual rights to accrue during the period corresponding to AML than are specified by statute the employee would be entitled to take advantage of these more beneficial provisions.

MATERNITY SUSPENSION

Section 66 of the ERA 1996 specifies that an employee may be 5.08 suspended by her employer, with pay, for designated health and safety reasons on the ground that she is pregnant, has recently given birth or is breastfeeding. The provisions governing maternity suspension are complex.[27] It should be noted that maternity suspension will only be necessary if altering the employees working conditions and hours of work to avoid the risk is not possible and suitable alternative work is not available.[28] Suspended employees are entitled to full pay.[29]

PROTECTION AGAINST DETRIMENT

Previously the only protection afforded to employees who were subjected 5.09 to action short of dismissal in connection with their pregnancy was to bring a claim of sex discrimination. While this right remains, there is now protection against action short of dismissal for reasons specified in section 47C of the ERA 1996, read with regulation 19 of the MPR Regulations 1999. Regulation 19(2) contains the protected reasons, and is in identical terms to regulation 20(3) which renders automatically unfair a dismissal for any of the protected reasons (see below). There is no definition of what constitutes a "detriment" but the protection is wide, an employee being entitled not to be subjected to "any detriment by any act, or any deliberate failure to act, by her employer" for any of

---

[27] See the Management of Health and Safety at Work Regulations 1999 (S.I. 1999 No. 3242), especially reg. 16.

[28] ERA 1996, s.67.

[29] See *British Airways (European Operations at Gatwick) Ltd v. Moore and Botterill* [2000] I.R.L.R. 296, EAT for a discussion of the maternity suspension provisions and the provision of alternative work.

the protected reasons. If the detriment amounts to a dismissal however, then the act of the employer is excluded from the ambit of regulation 19, falling instead within the scope of regulation 20.[30] Since these provisions also apply to detriment related to parental leave and time off for dependants they are discussed in more detail later in the chapter.

PROTECTION AGAINST DISMISSAL

5.10 Section 99 of the ERA 1996, read with regulation 20 of the MPL Regulations 1999, makes it automatically unfair to dismiss an employee for specified reasons including a reason connected to pregnancy, childbirth, maternity or any type of maternity leave. No qualifying period of service is required to benefit from this protection. Since these provisions also apply to dismissal for a reason connected to parental leave or time off for dependants they will be discussed later in this chapter.

REDUNDANCY WHILE ON MATERNITY LEAVE

5.11 Section 74 of the ERA 1996, read with regulation 10 of the MPL Regulations 1999, deals with the situation where, during OML or AML, it is not practicable by reason of redundancy for the employer to continue to employ a woman under her existing contract of employment. If there is a suitable available vacancy, the employee is entitled to be offered alternative employment on terms which are not substantially less favourable to her than if she had continued to be employed under the previous contract. If regulation 10 is not complied with, then the employee will be regarded as unfairly dismissed. In other words, the dismissal will be automatically unfair.[31]

Regulation 20(2) provides that a redundancy dismissal will be automatically unfair under section 99 of the ERA 1996 where the principal reason for *selecting* the employee for redundancy is for one of the reasons in regulation 20(3)[32] and it is shown that the circumstances giving rise to the redundancy apply to one or more employees in the same undertaking who hold similar positions to the employee who was made redundant but who were not dismissed.

It should be noted that where the employee is dismissed, but it is not for any of the reasons listed in regulation 20(3) or section 99 of the ERA, then, although the dismissal of the employee will not be regarded as automatically unfair, the employee may still bring a claim for unfair dismissal under section 98 of the ERA 1996.[33] In such circumstances the

---

[30] reg. 19(4).

[31] reg. 20(1)(b), MPL Regulations 1999.

[32] Since these are the same reasons as apply under s.99 of the ERA 1996 they will be discussed in more detail below.

[33] See Chap. 11. An employee who is absent from work after the expiration of her period of maternity leave for a pregnancy related reason and who is dismissed for this reason may still be automatically treated as unfairly dismissed: *Caledonia Bureau Investment & Property v. Caffrey* [1998] I.R.L.R. 110, EAT. The EAT admitted that it had engaged in a "purposive" construction of s.99 of the ERA 1996 and the correctness of the decision has been questioned—see Editorial, August 1998 I.R.L.R..

employee will require to fulfil the requirement of having one year's continuous service to make such a claim.

THE RIGHT TO WRITTEN STATEMENT OF REASONS FOR DISMISSAL OF A PREGNANT WOMAN

A woman dismissed at any time either while she is pregnant or, after 5.12 childbirth in circumstances in which her OML or AML terminates by reason of dismissal, has an automatic entitlement to a written statement of reasons for her dismissal.[34] No request is necessary and no qualifying period of service is required to benefit from this provision. The sanction for failure by an employer to comply with this requirement is two weeks pay.[35]

RETURNING TO WORK AFTER OML OR AML

Ordinary Maternity Leave

Under section 71(4)(c) of the ERA 1996 an employee is entitled to 5.13 return from OML to the job in which she was employed before her absence. This right includes the right to return on terms and conditions, including those relating to seniority, pension and similar rights, which are not less favourable than those which would have applied had she not been absent.[36] No notice is required to return to work after the 18 week period of OML: the employee may simply turn up for work on the first day after the 18 weeks. However if she intends to return before the end of the 18 week period, she must give her employer at least 21 days notice of the date on which she intends to return.[37] If she does not do so the employer is entitled to postpone her return to the date which will ensure that he has received 21 days notice although this cannot be a date which is later that the end of the OML period.[38] If an employee who is notified that her return date is postponed under these provisions decides to return before the "postponed" return day the employer is not obliged to pay her.[39]

Additional Maternity Leave

An employee who has taken AML is entitled to return from leave to 5.14 the job in which she was employed before her absence, or, if it is not reasonably practicable for the employer to permit her to return to that job, to another job which is both suitable and appropriate for her in the circumstances.[40] The right is to return on terms and conditions as to remuneration not less favourable than those which would have been

---

[34] ERA, s.92(4).
[35] ERA, s.93(2).
[36] ERA, s.71(7).
[37] reg. 11(1), MPL Regulations 1999.
[38] reg. 11(2) and (3), MPL Regulations 1999.
[39] reg. 11(4), MPL Regulations 1999.
[40] reg. 18(2), MPL Regulations 1999.

applicable to her had she not been absent from work at any time from the commencement of her ordinary maternity leave period. So far as seniority, pension and similar rights are concerned these should be as they would have been had her employment prior to her AML been continuous with her employment following her return to work (subject to the rules in the Social Security Act 1989 governing equal treatment under pension schemes in a maternity situation). In relation to other terms and conditions these should be no less favourable than those which would have applied had she not been on AML.[41]

Like OML no notice is required where the employee intends to return to work after her period of AML. However, again as with OML, 21 days notice is required where the employee intends to return early from AML[42] and the employer can postpone the return to ensure that such notice is given unless that would lead to return being delayed until after the end of the AML.

Under the previous maternity provisions an employer could postpone the employee's return after the equivalent of AML by up to four weeks, subject to notifying her in advance of the reasons for this. An employee was entitled to postpone her return for up to four weeks for medical reasons. However, postponement on such grounds is no longer permissible. If an employee is sick at the end of her maternity leave (whether OML or AML) and thus cannot return on the expected date then the employer's normal rules on sick leave should apply.

MATERNITY PAY

5.15 The Social Security Contributions and Benefits Act 1992[43] and the Statutory Maternity Pay (General) Regulations 1986[44] have been amended in respect of women who were expecting their babies on or after October 16, 1994, so that, although women will not be entitled to their remuneration during their OML or AML, most of them will have the right to receive Statutory Maternity Pay (SMP) or Maternity Allowance instead. A woman who is actually performing work under a contract of service is ineligible for a payment of SMP in respect of any week in which she undertakes work.[45] Those women who have 26 weeks service at the fifteenth week before the baby is due and meet certain minimum earnings and notification requirements will qualify for SMP.[46] This is payable at two rates: 90 per cent of average weekly earnings for the first six weeks and a flat statutory rate for the following 12 weeks. Those women who are self-employed or who do not qualify for SMP for any other reason may qualify for maternity allowance. To qualify for this allowance individuals must have worked and made 26 weeks national insurance contributions in the 66 weeks preceding the week in which the baby is due. Unlike the position with regard to OML, to qualify for SMP

---

[41] reg. 18(5), MPL Regulations 1999.
[42] reg. 11(2), MPL Regulations 1999.
[43] Hereinafter SSCBA.
[44] S.I. 1986 No. 1960, hereinafter 1986 Regulations.
[45] SSCBA, s.165(4).
[46] SSCBA, s.164(2).

it is necessary for a medical certificate to be produced no later than the end of the third week of the maternity pay period, unless for "good cause" she could not provide the certificate at that point.[47] No SMP will be paid unless the employer receives the medical evidence.

MATERNITY PAY AND SEX DISCRIMINATION

One area of controversy in recent years has been the interaction between 5.16 the law governing equal pay and maternity pay. The case of *Gillespie v. Northern Health and Social Services Board*[48] is of particular note. This is dealt with more fully in Chapter 4.[49]

PROPOSED CHANGES TO MATERNITY LEAVE AND PAY

In 2001 the Trade and Industry Secretary acknowledged that the current 5.17 legislation governing maternity leave and pay is "a minefield of qualification periods and dates, variable leave lengths, different calculation periods and short notification requirements". Having consulted widely, the Government produced a set of proposals for a new statutory framework although some of the detail of what is proposed may yet change. Crucially, it is proposed that all women should be entitled to 26 weeks OML, regardless of length of service, and that women who qualify for SMP should be entitled to AML of 26 weeks. Those women who have completed 26 weeks' continuous service ending with the fifteenth week before the EWC, and whose average earnings in the 26 weeks up to and including the notification week are at least equal to the lower earnings limit for national insurance contributions, will qualify for SMP which will be paid throughout OML. It is also proposed that the trigger provisions which lead to the automatic commencement of OML, due to absence for a pregnancy related reason, should operate after the beginning of the fourth week before the EWC and that the notification periods under the legislation should all be 28 days (instead of, for example, 21 days for an early return from OML or AML). In the March 2001 Budget it was confirmed that there will be:

- an increase in the flat rate of Statutory Maternity Pay (SMP) and Maternity Allowance from its present rate of £62.20 a week to £75 a week from April 2002 and to £100 a week from April 2003;
- an extension of the period of maternity pay at this enhanced rate from 18 weeks to 26 weeks from April 2003;

---

[47] 1986 Regulations, reg. 22(1). See also Statutory Maternity Pay (Medical Evidence) Regulations 1987 (S.I. 1987 No. 235). The certificate must be produced by the thirteenth week of the maternity pay period at the very latest.

[48] [1996] I.R.L.R. 214, ECJ.

[49] Note also *Gillespie (No. 2)* and *Todd v. Eastern Health and Social Services Board* [1997] I.R.L.R. 410, NICA on the issue of comparisons between sick pay and maternity pay—this decision has been criticised for its rather superficial approach to the type of comparisons which may be valid, see in particular E.O.R. No. 74, July/August 1997.

- the right to two weeks' paid paternity leave from 2003, paid at the same flat rate as SMP;
- from 2003, paid adoption leave when a child is first placed with a family, to allow one of the adoptive parents to take leave for the same period and paid at the same rate as SMP.

Further changes are expected to be announced during the course of 2001.

PREGNANCY AND SEX DISCRIMINATION

5.18 The statutory scheme governing maternity leave is complex enough. However, a further layer of complexity is added by the impact of sex discrimination law in this area.

The SDA was used for a number of years by women who did not have sufficient service to qualify for the right to return under the provisions of the EP(C)A. If a woman in this position who had been refused time off to have a baby or who had been dismissed because she was pregnant or needed time off for that reason could show that a man in "analogous circumstances (such as sickness)"[50] had been or would be treated more favourably, then it was possible to make out a case of direct sex discrimination.

As the law developed in this area, principally as a result of the impact of European Community law, there was a great deal of debate about whether a woman who had suffered a detriment as a result of pregnancy had to compare herself to a man to establish sex discrimination. It was argued that since only women can become pregnant detrimental treatment on that ground must amount to sex discrimination and there was no need to consider how a man in analogous circumstances would be treated. Indeed, the point was that there were no analogous circumstances to pregnancy which was gender specific. This argument was initially repelled by courts hearing claims based upon domestic law.

5.19   The issue of whether such a comparison was necessary to found a sex discrimination claim under the Equal Treatment Directive was considered by the ECJ in *Dekker v. Stichting Vormingscentrum Voor Jonge Volwassen Plus*[51] and *Hertz v. Aldi Marked*.[52] In *Dekker* it was held that unfavourable treatment on the ground of pregnancy was direct discrimination on the ground of sex. The Court considered that pregnancy was a condition unique to women so that where it could be shown that unfavourable treatment was on the ground of pregnancy, that treatment was, by definition, on the ground of sex. A reason which applied "exclusively to one sex" was inherently discriminatory. Since discrimination on the ground of pregnancy was discrimination on the ground of sex *per se*, there was no need to compare the treatment of a pregnant woman with that of a hypothetical man.

In this case an employer had refused to employ Mrs Dekker, who was judged to be the most suitable person for the job, because she was

---

[50] *Hayes v. Malleable Mens Working Club and Institute* [1985] I.R.L.R. 367, EAT.
[51] [1991] I.R.L.R. 27, ECJ.
[52] [1991] I.R.L.R. 31, ECJ.

pregnant and this would have certain financial consequences for the employer. The ECJ held that "a refusal to employ because of the financial consequences of absence connected with pregnancy must be deemed to be based principally on the fact of the pregnancy. Such discrimination cannot be justified by the financial detriment that would be suffered by the employer during the woman's maternity leave". The Court emphasised that if the reason for the employer's decision "resides in the fact that the person concerned is pregnant, the decision is directly related to the applicant's sex. Viewed in this way it is of no importance . . . that there were no male applicants".

In *Hertz* the Court adopted a similar line but this case concerned the   5.20 dismissal of a woman, long after her maternity leave had ended, as a result of lengthy absence occasioned by an illness which had its origin in pregnancy. In these circumstances the Court held:

> "[I]n regard to an illness which appears after maternity leave, there is no reason to distinguish an illness which has its origin in pregnancy or confinement from any other illness. Female and male workers are equally exposed to illness and although certain problems are specifically linked to one sex or the other, the only question is whether a woman is dismissed for absence due to illness on the same conditions as a man. If sickness absence would lead to dismissal of a male worker under the same conditions, there is no direct discrimination on grounds of sex".[53]

Accordingly, the male comparator remained appropriate in certain limited circumstances.

Thereafter the issue came before the House of Lords in *Webb v. EMO*   5.21 *Air Cargo (U.K.) Ltd.*[54] Here, a woman was dismissed when she told her employer that she was pregnant since she had been taken on in the first instance to cover for another employee who was going on maternity leave although she had been told that she would be kept on permanently thereafter. The employer argued that the dismissal was not because of pregnancy *per se* but because Mrs Webb would not be able to provide the cover for her absent colleague which was needed.[55] The House of Lords held that while it was discrimination to dismiss because of pregnancy itself Mrs Webb had not been dismissed because she was pregnant but because she could not provide the necessary cover. In these circumstances her treatment had to be compared with that of a man in analogous circumstances for the purposes of the SDA. However, the House of Lords also decided that a reference would be made to the ECJ asking that Court to consider whether it is discrimination on grounds of sex contrary to the Equal Treatment Directive for an employer to

---

[53] At paras 16–17.
[54] [1993] I.R.L.R. 27.
[55] See *O'Neill v. Governors of St Thomas More RCVA Upper School* [1996] I.R.L.R. 372 for a case which examines whether it is possible to draw a distinction between pregnancy dismissal per se and dismissal because of the particular circumstances relating to the pregnancy such as the fact that the dismissed employee in this case was an R.E. teacher and the father of the child was a R.C. priest; in this case the EAT held that such a distinction was legally erroneous.

dismiss a female employee in the sort of situation which existed in the present case. It was considered that the reference was necessary because:

> "The European Court of Justice did not, in the *Dekker* and *Hertz* cases, have to consider the situation where a woman, on account of her pregnancy, will not be able to carry out, at the time when her services are required, the particular job for which she is applying or for which she has been engaged. The two decisions did not give any clear indication whether in such a situation the Court would regard the fundamental reason for the refusal to engage the woman or for dismissing her as being her unavailability for the job and not her pregnancy. In the event of the European Court deciding that the latter was the correct view for the purposes of Directive 76/207, it would be necessary for the House of Lords to consider whether it was possible to construe the relevant provisions of the Sex Discrimination Act in such a way as to accord with that decision".[56]

In the event, the ECJ did decide that Mrs Webb's treatment was in breach of the Equal Treatment Directive and that she had suffered discrimination. It considered that:

> "Since pregnancy is not in any way comparable with a pathological condition, and even less so with unavailability for work on non-medical grounds, there can be no question of comparing the situation of a woman who finds herself incapable by reason of pregnancy of performing the task for which she was recruited with that of a man similarly incapable for medical or other reasons. Nor can dismissal of a pregnant woman recruited for an indefinite period be justified on grounds relating to her inability to fulfil a fundamental condition of her contract of employment".[57]

5.22 After the decision of the ECJ in *Webb* the Inner House of the Court of Session held in *Brown v. Rentokil Limited*[58] that an employee had not suffered sex discrimination when she was dismissed while pregnant after a period of pregnancy related illness. In this case the employer had a rule that all employees absent for a period of 26 weeks were dismissed. The rule had been enforced against a man. Thereafter, Mrs Brown was dismissed under the rule. Her absence was as a result of pregnancy related illness. The Court of Session held that this was a dismissal as a result of illness rather than a dismissal on the ground of pregnancy. Since there was evidence that a man absent for a similar period would have been treated in the same way there was no discrimination.

5.23   After the Court of Session hearing in *Brown* the case of *Webb* (No. 2) was referred back to the House of Lords by the ECJ which then held that the only way of construing the more precise test of unlawful discrimination set out in section 1(1)(a) and section 5(3) of the SDA to accord with the ruling of the ECJ, was to hold that: "in a case where a

---

[56] At para. 23.
[57] [1994] E.C.R. I-3567 at para. 24; [1994] I.R.L.R. 482.
[58] [1995] I.R.L.R. 211, CS.

woman is engaged for an indefinite period the fact that the reason why she will be temporarily unavailable for work at a time when to her knowledge her services will be particularly required is pregnancy is a circumstance relevant to her case, being a circumstance which could not be present in the case of a hypothetical man".[59] The Court found that it was able to construe domestic legislation to accord with Community law by adopting this approach and accordingly held that Mrs Webb's dismissal had been in breach of the SDA.

Lord Keith's reasoning in relation to section 5(3) of the SDA is, to say 5.24 the least, opaque. If pregnancy is a circumstance which is relevant in the case of a woman which could not be present in the case of a man how can the relevant circumstances in the two cases be the same or not materially different, as is required by section 5(3)?

Obiter, the Court went on to point out that the ECJ had placed much emphasis on the fact that Mrs Webb's contract was for an indefinite duration. It was suggested that this gave rise to the possibility of a distinction between such a case and that of an individual recruited for a fixed term/temporary employment whose absence due to pregnancy would render her unavailable for the whole of the period she was required. Pregnancy, it was suggested, would not necessarily be a relevant circumstance in a case involving a failure to recruit or dismissal in such circumstances. Lord Keith went on to state that if such a situation was not distinguished it would tend to be perceived as unfair to employers and such as to bring the law of sex discrimination into disrepute. However, in subsequent cases this possible exception to the general principle was narrowly construed,[60] eventually being held to be irrelevant by the ECJ in *Tele Danmark A/S v. Handels-og Kontorfunktionaefernes Forbund i Danmark (HK)*.[61]

The *Brown* case was subsequently appealed to the House of Lords 5.25 which decided to refer a number of questions to the ECJ. The crucial issue raised was whether dismissal during the course of pregnancy as a result of absence caused by a pregnancy related illness amounts to sex discrimination contrary to the provisions of the Equal Treatment Directive. While someone in Mrs Brown's circumstances would now be protected by the law of unfair dismissal, irrespective of length of service, the issue raised remains of importance given that unfair dismissal compensation is still subject to a statutory cap while compensation for discrimination is not.[62]

A number of commentators suggested that the ECJ was bound to find in favour of Mrs Brown in light of its decision in *Webb*. However, after Brown was referred the ECJ handed down its decision in *Larsson v. Fotex Supermarked A/S*.[63] In this case it held that it was not sex discrimination *per se* to dismiss a woman after her maternity leave has

---

[59] [1995] I.R.L.R. 645, HL at para. 11.

[60] See, for example, *Caruana v. Manchester Airport plc* [1996] I.R.L.R. 378, EAT; failure to renew a fixed term contract because the employee would be unavailable for work at the date of its commencement due to pregnancy was sex discrimination.

[61] IDS Brief 696, November 2001, p.3.

[62] The cap on damages for unfair dismissal is currently £51,700: s.124 of the ERA 1996, as amended by the Employment Rights (Increase of Limits) Order 2001 (S.I. 2001 No. 21).

[63] (C–400/95) [1997] I.R.L.R. 643, ECJ.

ended because of absence due to a pregnancy related illness, even where the illness first appeared during pregnancy itself and the absence commenced at that time. The Court's reasoning in *Larsson* did not appear to sit at all well with the stance it adopted in *Webb*. In particular the Court expressed the view that the principle of equal treatment did not preclude account being taken of a woman's absence from work between the beginning of her pregnancy and the beginning of her maternity leave when calculating the period providing grounds for her dismissal under national law.

5.26   The inference to be drawn from the reasoning of the ECJ in *Larsson* was that the dismissal of a pregnant woman for absence caused by a pregnancy related illness was not sex discrimination *per se*. A comparison with a sick man required to be made. The reasoning in *Larsson* did not sit at all well with the statement of the ECJ in Webb that: "there can be no question of comparing the situation of a woman who finds herself incapable, by reason of pregnancy ... with that of a man similarly incapable for medical or other reasons".[64]

5.27   It was against this background that oral argument in *Brown* was heard at the ECJ. The case was heard by an 11 judge court (Larsson having been heard by a five judge chamber). In his subsequent opinion, the Advocate General made sweeping and trenchant criticisms of the decision in *Larsson,* suggesting that "The Court appears to maintain in *Larsson* a position contrary to what is to be inferred from a brief examination of its earlier judgments, but also directly to contradict the reading of those judgments which has been propounded over time both by its Advocate General and by the numerous authors who have commented on the judgments".[65] He went on to state that in his opinion the dismissal of a pregnant woman, on account of ill health caused by pregnancy, amounted to a breach of the ETD because it was based upon a gender specific circumstance.

The decision of the ECJ is of particular note in light of the fact that the Court, in a rare move, expressly overrules one of its previous decisions, namely *Larsson*. Against the background of the principles set out in *Dekker* and *Webb*, and the express statement in the ETD that "there shall be no discrimination whatsoever on grounds of sex"[66] the Court pointed out that, while pregnancy is not comparable to a pathological condition, it is a period during which disorders and complications may arise, some of which may compel a woman to rest completely for all or part of the pregnancy. These disorders and complications are risks inherent in the condition of pregnancy and are thus a specific feature of that condition. In these circumstances it was made clear that "dismissal of a woman during pregnancy cannot be based on her inability, as a result of her condition, to perform the duties which she is contractually bound to carry out". To hold otherwise, the Court said, would be to render the provision of the ETD ineffective. Accordingly, it held that:

> "dismissal of a female worker during pregnancy for absences due
> to incapacity for work resulting from her pregnancy is linked to the

---

[64] At para. 24.
[65] At para. 49.
[66] Art. 2(1), ETD.

occurrence of risks inherent in pregnancy and must therefore be regarded as essentially based on the fact of pregnancy. Such a dismissal can affect only women and therefore constitutes direct discrimination on grounds of sex".[67]

The Court also went on to make it clear that, contrary to *Larsson*, if a woman is absent due to pregnancy related illness during her pregnancy, maternity leave and thereafter, her absence during the period of pregnancy cannot be used subsequently to justify her dismissal. It is clear from the case law up to and including *Larsson* that absence during maternity leave cannot be taken into account in such circumstances.

So far as the "comparable man" is concerned, the ECJ reiterates in *Brown* that where pathological conditions caused by pregnancy or childbirth arise after maternity leave then any resulting absence should be treated in the same way as a male worker's absence due to incapacity for work. If that happens then there will be no discrimination on the ground of sex.[68] There is, of course, a logical inconsistency here which has been with us ever since the decision in *Hertz*. However, it is submitted that this long established triumph of pragmatism over logic is unlikely to be departed from in the future.

Brown, in effect, makes it clear that the entire period from the beginning of the pregnancy to the end of the maternity leave must be regarded as a "protected" period. Any absence which arises during the pregnancy as a result of the consequences of the pregnancy should be discounted if an employer is considering at any point whether the employee should be dismissed for absence. There is no place for the "comparable man" at this stage. Post maternity leave the "comparable man" will rematerialise. While the detriment suffered by Mrs Brown was dismissal, it is submitted that if a woman suffers any detriment in her employment as a result of the consequences of pregnancy this will almost certainly amount to sex discrimination.[69]

The extent to which European law protects pregnant women can be seen in the case of *Mahlburg v. Land Mecklenburg-Vorpommern*.[70] Here, Ms Mahlburg was employed as a operating theatre nurse on a fixed term contract from August 26, 1994 to August 31, 1995. She applied on June 1, 1995 for two permanent operating theatre nurse posts which had been internally advertised and which were to be taken up immediately. As at the date of application she was pregnant. The relevant German law specifies that pregnant women are not allowed to work in jobs where there is a risk of harm being caused to the baby or mother.[71] Given the risk of infection Ms Mahlburg was transferred to another internal post, remaining there until the end of her fixed term contract. On September 18, 1995 Ms Mahlburg was told that she had been unsuccessful with her

5.28

---

[67] At para. 24.

[68] See para. 25.

[69] See for example *Caisse Nationale D'Assurance Vieillesse des Travailleurs (CNAVTS) v. Thibault* [1998] I.R.L.R. 399, ECJ—denial of performance review on basis of significant period of absence from work during the review year held to breach ETD where reason for absence was maternity leave.

[70] Case C-207/98 [2000] I.R.L.R. 276, ECJ.

[71] There are comparable provisions in the U.K., see for example, the Management of Health and Safety at Work Regulations 1999 (S.I. 1999 No. 3242).

applications since "legal requirements" prohibited employers from employing pregnant women in areas where they would be exposed to risks from harmful substances.

Ms Mahlburg claimed that the employer had acted in breach of the ETD. The employer suggested that it was acting to protect the employee in accordance with national legislation and the provisions of Article 2(3) of the ETD which states that the provisions of the Directive are without prejudice to provisions concerning the protection of women, particularly as regards pregnancy and maternity. Ultimately, the matter was referred to the ECJ which pointed out that:—

1. The Court has held that dismissal of a pregnant woman recruited for an indefinite period cannot be justified on grounds of her inability to fulfil a fundamental condition of her employment contract *(Webb (No. 2))*.
2. A statutory prohibition on night time work by pregnant women cannot serve as a basis for terminating a contract for an indefinite period (*Habermann-Beltermann*[72]).
3. In accordance with *Thibault* the provisions of Article 2(3) ETD cannot be prayed in aid to support unfavourable treatment of women in relation to access to employment.

Accordingly, the ECJ held that it was not permissible for an employer to refuse to employ a pregnant woman on the ground that a legal prohibition would prevent her from working for the duration of her pregnancy in a post which was for an unlimited duration. The fact that the obligation to take on pregnant women in these circumstances might have financial consequences, in particular for small and medium sized undertakings, was not something which could be taken into account *(Dekker)*. A breach of the ETD had therefore been established.

5.29   The decisions of the ECJ in this area obviously require to be taken into account by domestic tribunals and courts called upon to consider whether pregnancy related discrimination, in breach of the SDA, has occurred.[73] In *Abbey National plc v. Formoso*[74] the applicant had been persuaded to remain in the employment of the respondent by her superior over an after-work drink. Some four months later rumours began to circulate in the respondent company to the effect that the applicant had said that her manager had taken her out for a meal that night and suggested that they should spend the night together. Ms Formoso denied any involvement in the rumours and indicated she was upset by them. On the same day she discovered that she was pregnant and the next day she visited her doctor and obtained a sick note which stated that she was unfit due to anxiety and pregnancy. The employer began to investigate the rumours and when the applicant returned to work on March 18 she was immediately suspended by reason of an allegation of gross misconduct to the effect that she had misled people about the night she went out for a drink with her manager. She was then

---

[72] Case 421/92 [1994] I.R.L.R. 364, ECJ.
[73] See, for example, *Healy v. William B Morrison and Sons* (IDS Brief 648, Nov 1999) for a classic example of the impact of *Brown v. Rentokil Ltd.*
[74] [1999] I.R.L.R. 222, EAT.

certified sick again. On June 17 she wrote to the employer indicating that she wished to commence maternity leave on July 22 and intended to return to work after the birth of the baby.

The employers decided to take disciplinary proceedings against Ms Formoso and took the view that it would be better if the matter was resolved before her maternity leave commenced. They asked her to attend a disciplinary hearing, but she declined on grounds that she and her doctor considered that she was emotionally unfit to attend such a meeting and was likely to remain so until after her pregnancy was over. Nevertheless, the disciplinary hearing took place on July 30, in the employee's absence. She was dismissed for gross misconduct. An internal appeal, again in her absence, was unsuccessful.

The applicant's claim under the SDA was upheld, the tribunal concluding that by July 30, her advanced state of pregnancy was "inevitably and inextricably linked to her emotional state". Thus her illness was related to her pregnancy and she had suffered a detriment when she could not attend the disciplinary hearing to defend herself. On appeal the EAT upheld the decision of the tribunal, pointing out that *Brown v. Rentokil Ltd* made it clear that dismissal of a woman at any time during her pregnancy for absence due to an illness resulting from that pregnancy is direct sex discrimination The EAT considered that where an applicant is prevented from defending herself at a disciplinary hearing due to her absence for a pregnancy-related reason, that is also sex discrimination.

In *McGuigan v. T G Baynes and Sons*[75] the employer (a firm of solicitors) failed to consult with the applicant over her impending redundancy, a prominent cause of that failure being the hope that the employee would decide not to return to work after maternity leave. This failure to consult was held by the EAT (overturning the employment tribunal) to amount to sex discrimination, given that the predominant cause of the failure was connected to the absence of the employee on maternity leave. In other words but for her absence on maternity leave (which was pregnancy related) the employer might well have consulted with her. The fact that the applicant might well have been made redundant even if there had been consultation did not mean that there had been no discrimination.

In *GUS Home Shopping Ltd v. Green and Mclauchlin*[76] the respondent employers had determined to make a number of employees redundant as a result of the merger of two separate places of business. In order to effect a smooth transfer, the employers introduced a discretionary loyalty bonus. Payment was contingent upon an orderly and effective transfer; co-operation and goodwill of the individual employee; and the employee remaining in the post to a certain date. The applicant employees did not receive any loyalty reward because one was on maternity leave while the other had a period of pregnancy-related sick leave followed by maternity leave. The employer considered that their absence prevented them demonstrating the necessary level of commitment. The tribunal found that the employees were not considered for the loyalty bonus as a result

---

[75] IRLB 622, August 1999.
[76] [2001] I.R.L.R. 75, EAT.

of their absence due to pregnancy and that the failure of the employers to recognise the special status given to women in such circumstances amounted to an act of direct sex discrimination. This decision was upheld on appeal to the EAT.

Contract Workers and Pregnancy Discrimination

5.30   The protection which is given to female workers who become pregnant under the SDA extends to contract workers.[77] In *Patefield v. Belfast City Council*[78] the applicant began work with a recruitment agency. In February 1995 she was sent by the agency to work for Belfast City Council as a clerk in the cemeteries office. In 1997 the agency lost its contract to supply temporary staff to the council and was replaced by another agency. At the request of the applicant's line manager at the council the new agency took her on to its books and she remained at work as usual.

In September 1997 Mrs Patefield became pregnant and told her supervisor that she intended to work until March. In February 1998 she wrote to the council informing them of her intention to be absent for the birth of her baby and stating that she intended to return to work. She asked for written confirmation that she could return to her "own job" following the birth. The council wrote back stating it could not give such confirmation since she did not work for the council "as an employee under a contract of employment" although it was also stated that she was not precluded from returning to a placement with them through the agency should one arise.

In August 1998 Mrs Patefield told the council in writing that she would be available to return to work on August 17. The council stated that while it recognised her right to return to work after maternity leave it was not possible for her to return to the cemeteries office as she had been replaced by a permanent council employee. It delayed her return and then offered an inferior post. She claimed sex discrimination. The provisions governing contract workers in the sex discrimination legislation in force in Northern Ireland are exactly the same as those found in section 9 of the SDA. *Inter alia* these make it unlawful for a principal to subject a contract worker to a detriment on the ground of sex. A tribunal found that Mrs Patefield was an employee of the agency but that the council, as principal, had discriminated against her as a contract worker. It was found that had she not gone off work on maternity leave she would have undoubtedly remained in post.

On appeal, the NICA upheld this decision. It accepted that in normal circumstances the council would have been able to replace Mrs Patefield with a permanent employee at any time while she was working there. It also acknowledged that it might seem paradoxical to hold that they could not do so while she was on maternity leave. However, it felt compelled to reach that conclusion in light of the decision in *Webb (No. 2)*, given that it had been found as a fact that Mrs Patefield would have remained in her post but for the fact that she went on maternity leave. By replacing her with a permanent employee when it knew that she wanted

---

[77] See SDA 1975, s.9
[78] IRLB 653, November 2000.

to return after the birth of her child the council had subjected Mrs Patefield to a detriment by effectively removing the possibility of her returning to post. Given that detriment arose as a result of the fact she took "maternity leave" it amounted to sex discrimination.

PARENTAL LEAVE

The Employment Relations Act 1999 introduced into domestic law for the first time a right to parental leave. In so doing the Government was seeking to implement the provisions of the Parental Leave Directive.[79] The 1999 Act substituted new sections 76—81 into the ERA 1996, which set out the basic right although it is left to the Secretary of State to flesh out the right and the qualifying conditions for entitlement by means of Regulations. This has been done in Part III of the Maternity and Parental Leave Regulations 1999.

5.31

As the law currently stands,[80] an employee who has been continuously employed for at least one year and who has, or expects to have, "responsibility" for a child born or adopted on or after December 15, 1999 is entitled to 13 weeks parental leave for each child.[81] While there is no mention of the date from which the one-year's continuous service is to be calculated, the DTI suggest that it should be calculated looking back from the day on which the employee wishes to commence the leave.[82] A week in any case will be a period of absence from work of equal duration to the period for which the employee is normally required to work.[83] In other words, an employee who normally works two days per week will be entitled to 26 days leave in total per child. (Averaging provisions apply in the event that there is a variable working week.) Leave for periods shorter than one week, where that is allowed under the leave scheme applicable in a particular workplace, will be aggregated until the employee has received 13 weeks in total.[84]

"Employee" is defined as someone who has entered into or works under a "contract of employment" which, in turn, is defined as "a contract of service or apprenticeship, whether express or implied".[85]

An employee has "responsibility" for a child if he/she is:

(a) someone who has parental responsibilities for a child under the Children (Scotland) Act 1995 or has acquired them in accordance with the provisions of that Act; or

(b) someone who has been registered as the child's father under the provisions of section 18(1) or (2) of the Registration of Births, Deaths and Marriages (Scotland) Act 1965.

---

[79] Council Directive 96/34/EC on the framework agreement on parental leave.

[80] The Government announced its intention in Autumn 2001 to amend the parental leave legislation to under its coverage—see para. 5.37 below.

[81] regs 13 and 14, MPL Regulations 1999. In the case of multiple births the employee will be entitled to 13 weeks leave for each child.

[82] URN 99/1193, available at www.dti.gov.uk.

[83] reg. 14.

[84] reg. 14(4).

[85] reg. 2.

This definition means that someone who simply co-habits with a birth parent will not be entitled to parental leave while a natural parent will be so entitled even if he/she does not live with the child. Parental leave is available to both parents but cannot be transferred between them.

Parental leave must be taken before the fifth birthday of the child, except in the case of a child who is adopted, in which case the leave must be taken in the five year period from the date of placement of the child, as long as that is before the eighteenth birthday of the child, or where the employer has postponed the leave until a date after the child's fifth birthday.[86] However, special provisions exist in relation to children in receipt of disability living allowance; in such a case parental leave can be taken up until the eighteenth birthday of the child.[87]

"Parental leave" is not defined in the 1999 Act but regulation 12 refers to "absence from work . . . for the purpose of caring" for a child. The Consultation Paper, which preceded the final version of the Regulations, indicated that the reasons for leave need not be connected to the child's health. It could cover, for example, time off to settle the child into a new playgroup.

Subsistence of contractual rights and obligations during parental leave

5.32   Parental leave is akin to AML in terms of the contractual rights and obligations which continue to exist during the parental leave period.[88] Just as with OML and AML there is no entitlement to remuneration during parental leave.[89] Special provisions have been made extending the availability of income support to those on very low incomes.[90]

Right to return after parental leave

5.33   Regulation 18(1) of the MPL Regulations specifies that an employee who takes parental leave for a period of four weeks or less (except where that is immediately after AML) is entitled to return from leave to the job in which s/he was employed before his/her absence. Employees who take parental leave for a period of more than four weeks are entitled to return to the same job or, if it is not reasonably practicable for the employer to permit him/her to return to that job, to another job which is both suitable for him/her and appropriate for him/her to do in the circumstances (*i.e.* an identical right to that available on return from AML).[91] Those employees who take parental leave immediately after AML are entitled to return to the same job unless it would not be have been reasonably practicable to let them do so after AML, and it remains not reasonably practicable to let them do so at the end of parental leave in which case they are entitled to return to a suitable job which is appropriate in the circumstances.[92]

---

[86] reg. 15, MPL Regulations 1999.

[87] *ibid.*

[88] reg. 17.

[89] ERA 1996, s.77(2)(b).

[90] See the Income Support (General) Amendment (No. 2) Regulations 1999 which came into force on January 5, 2000.

[91] reg. 18(2), MPL Regulations 1999.

[92] *ibid.*

Complaint to an employment tribunal

An employee has the right to complain to an employment tribunal if 5.34 an employer refuses to allow him/her to take parental leave or unreasonably postpones it. A complaint is to be made within three months unless "not reasonably practicable". Compensation is to be awarded which the tribunal considers is "just and equitable" bearing in mind "the employer's behaviour" and any loss sustained by the employee.[93]

Protection from detriment/automatically unfairness of dismissal for asserting the right

Individuals who take, or seek to take, parental leave are protected 5.35 from being subjected to a detriment for that reason and from unfair dismissal.[94] However, since the provisions which apply are also relevant to individuals who take time off for dependants they will be discussed in more detail later in this chapter.

Default Provisions/the Model Scheme

The Government is keen to ensure that there is scope for employers 5.36 and employees to agree how the right to parental leave should actually be implemented in practice, bearing in mind the needs of individual organisations. To that end, parental leave agreements may be decided between them and incorporated within contracts of employment by means of individual agreements or collective/workforce agreements (as defined in Sched. 1 of the MPL Regulations 1999), failing which the default provisions, set out in Schedule 2 of the Regulations, will apply.[95] Where there is a contractual agreement derived from a collective or workforce agreement the provisions may be more or less beneficial than the default scheme, as long as they comply with the floor of rights set out in the primary legislation and the Regulations.

The Government Consultation paper which preceded the final version of the MPL Regulations explains the position thus:

"Designing a Scheme
The scheme can be more generous than the provisions of the regulations.

Employees could be allowed to take their leave in the form of reduced hours working. An agreed scheme could allow people to take parental leave to care for children who are older than five or who were born or adopted before December 1999. But it cannot impose lower age limits or a later birth or adoption date. . . .

For each employee, the scheme must be given legal force by being written into the employee' s contract of employment. Existing employees must agree to the change, unless the contract provides for the terms of collective or workforce agreements to become part of employment contracts automatically. If this is not

---

[93] ERA 1996, s.80.
[94] regs 19 and 20, MPL Regulations 1999.
[95] reg. 16, MPL Regulations 1999.

done, or if no agreement is in place, the model scheme will automatically apply to the individual concerned."

The terms of the model/default scheme specify that:

- An employer can ask for such evidence as may be reasonably required of the employee's parental responsibility for the child in respect of whom leave is taken together with the child's date of birth (or date of placement for adoption) and, in the case of a child entitled to disability living allowance, proof of that fact.
- An employer is entitled to at least 21 days notice of commencement of leave together with specification of the start and end date of the period of leave.
- In the case of a father who wishes to take leave on the date of birth of a child the employer is entitled to notice of the EWC to be given at least 21 days in advance of the commencement of that week.
- An employer cannot postpone leave to be taken at the time of the birth or adoption of a child but can do so otherwise where the operation of the business would be unduly disrupted if the leave was taken. In these circumstances the employer must inform the employee within 7 days of the request for leave and allow the employee to take leave no later than 6 months after the start of the original proposed leave period.
- The maximum leave permitted in respect of one child in any one year is 4 weeks and leave must be taken in blocks of one week (whatever constitutes a week for the employee in question) or a multiple of that period (except where the child is entitled to disability living allowance).

Challenge to restriction of right to parental leave

5.37   It is notable (and controversial) that the Government gave the right to parental leave only to those responsible for children born on or after December 15, 1999. A challenge was mounted by the Trades Union Congress to this restriction on the basis that it did not comply with the Parental Leave Directive.[96] The High Court has referred the matter to the ECJ. However, the Government has already announced its intention to extend parental leave in 2001 to those parents with children under 5 who were born prior to December 15, 1999.

The Government has published draft amendment regulations, the consultation period in relation to these having ended on August 8, 2001. Under the proposals the parents of children who were under five on December 15, 1999 will be eligible for parental leave if they meet the other qualifying conditions. Under the statutory fall back scheme parents can take a maximum of four weeks leave in any one year. On this basis it will take more than three years for parents whose children were under

---

[96] See *R v. Secretary of State for Trade and Industry, ex parte Trades Union Congress* [2000] I.R.L.R. 565, QBD.

five on December 15, 1999 to take their newly acquired (at least so far as domestic law is concerned!) entitlement to parental leave. Accordingly, parents of children born or placed with them for adoption between December 15, 1994 and December 14, 1999 will be given a period of a little over three years to take their leave from the date on which the amendment regulations come into force. Furthermore, an employee will be deemed to meet the one year service requirement with a current employer if he/she had one year's service with a different employer at any time between December 15, 1998 and the date on which the new regulations come into force. If we assume that the amendment regulations come into force in December 2001 this means that parents of a child who was just under five in December 1999 will be able to take parental leave until the child is 10.

Further changes to be implemented

The Government has also announced that parental leave entitlement 5.38 of parents of disabled children is to be increased from 13 to 18 weeks from a date to be announced in 2001. From 2003, fathers will have the right to two weeks' paid paternity leave, paid at the same flat rate as SMP.

Time off for Dependants

Section 57A of the ERA 1996 (as inserted by the Employment Relations 5.39 Act 1999) gives an employee an entitlement to be permitted by his employer[97] to take a **reasonable** amount of time off in order to take action which is necessary:

(a) to provide assistance on an occasion when a dependant falls ill, gives birth or is injured or assaulted;
(b) to make arrangements for the provision of care for a dependant who is ill or injured;
(c) in consequence of the death of a dependant;
(d) because of the unexpected disruption or termination of arrangements for the care of a dependant; or
(e) to deal with an incident which involves a child of the employee and which occurs unexpectedly in a period during which an educational establishment which the child attends is responsible for him.

The right is dependent upon the employee telling the employer as soon as reasonably practicable about the reason for the absence and how long he/she expects to be absent (unless the employee cannot comply with the duty to inform the employer of the absence until after he/she has actually returned to work).[98]

---

[97] Presumably the provision is framed as an entitlement to be permitted to build in a degree of control by the employer.
[98] ERA 1996, s.57A(2).

A dependant is defined as a:

(1) spouse
(2) child
(3) parent
(4) a person who lives in the same house as the employee, otherwise than as a lodger, boarder, tenant or employee.[99]

For the purposes of (a) and (b) above a dependant will also include any person who reasonably relies on the employee:

(i) for assistance on an occasion when the person falls ill or is injured or assaulted, or
(ii) to make arrangements for the provision of care in the event of illness or injury.

For the purposes of (d) dependant includes any person who reasonably relies on the employee to make arrangements for the provision of care. In discussing the extent of the right Lord Sainsbury stated:

"We intend the right to apply where a dependant becomes sick or has an accident, or is assaulted, including where the victim is distressed rather than physically injured. It provides for reasonable time off, if an employee suffers a bereavement of a family member, to deal with the consequences of that bereavement, such as making funeral arrangements, as well as to take time off to attend the funeral. Employees will be able to take time off in the event of the unexpected absence of the carer, where the person is a dependant of the employee. so if the childminder or nurse does not turn up the employee will be able to sort things out without fearing reprisals at work. Employees may have to take time off to attend to a problem arising at their children's school or during school hours—for example if the child has been involved in a fight, where the child is distressed, or if the child has committed a serious misdemeanour which could lead to expulsion. Again, the provision will secure their right to do so."
He also stated that "in all cases, the right will be limited to the amount of time which is reasonable in all the circumstances of a particular case. For example, if a child falls ill with chickenpox the leave must be sufficient to enable the employee to cope with the crisis—to deal with the immediate care of the child and to make alternative longer term arrangements. The right will not enable a mother to take a fortnight off while her child is in quarantine".

Complaint to an employment tribunal

5.40   Section 57B of the ERA 1996 specifies that an employee may complain to an employment tribunal if his employer fails to permit him to take time off in accordance with section 57A. Such a complaint is to

---

[99] ERA 1996, s.57A(3).

be made within three months of the failure or, if this was not reasonably practicable, within such further period as the tribunal considers reasonable. As with denial of the right to take parental leave, it is open to the tribunal to make a declaration and to award such compensation as the tribunal considers just and equitable, having regard to the employer's default in failing to permit time off and any loss sustained by the employee.[1]

Employers may, of course give employees paid time off to deal with emergencies of the type covered by these provisions—indeed, many of them already do. However, employees now have a degree of comfort that they are not relying upon a "favour" by their employer (which may be bestowed in one case but not in another) when it comes to coping with problems that can arise in combining work with family caring commitments.

Leave for family and domestic reasons—protection from detriment

As a result of the provisions of section 47C of the ERA 1996 and 5.41 regulation 19 of the MPL Regulations 1999, an employee has the right not to be subjected to a detriment by her (or his, where appropriate) employer because:

(a) she is pregnant or has given birth;
(b) she is suspended from work on maternity grounds
(c) she took, or availed herself of the benefits of, OML[2]
(d) she took or sought to take AML, parental leave or time off for dependants
(e) she declined to sign a workforce agreement for the purpose of the MPL Regulations 1999
(f) she is a workforce representative, or a candidate for such a post, in terms of the MPL Regulations 1999 and has performed, or proposed to perform, any functions or activities in this role

For the purpose of regulation 19 "detriment" does not include dismissal. This is because regulation 20 specifically deals with dismissal for any of the above reasons.

An employee who considers that s/he has been subjected to a detriment, contrary to section 47C, is entitled to present a complaint to an employment tribunal. Such a complaint should be presented within three months of the act in respect of which complaint is made unless it was not reasonably practicable to do so.[3]

Leave for family reasons and unfair dismissal

As a result of the provisions of section 99 of the ERA 1996 5.42 and regulation 20 of the MPL Regulations 1999 a dismissal will be automatically unfair if the reason (or principle reason) for it is any of the

---

[1] ERA 1996, s.57B(3), (4).
[2] A woman will avail herself of the benefits of OML if she avails herself of the benefit of any of the terms and conditions of employment preserved over this period—reg. 19(3), MPL Regulations 1999
[3] ERA 1996, s.48.

reasons set out above (unless immediately before the end of her AML the number of employees employed by a woman's employer, added to the number employed by an associated employer did not exceed five and it was not practicable for the employer to permit her to return to the job she performed before her absence or a suitable alternative job). It will also be automatically unfair to dismiss a woman if, during OML or AML, it was not practicable to continue her employment by reason of redundancy and she was not offered suitable alternative employment which was available, the above exception applicable to small employers also applying in these cirumstances.[4] Under the provisions of regulation 20(2) an employee will also be regarded as unfairly dismissed if the reason for her dismissal is redundancy, if it is shown that the circumstances giving rise to the redundancy apply to one or more employees in the same undertaking holding similar positions who have not been dismissed and it is shown that the reason, or principle reason the employee was selected was one of those set out at (a) to (g) above.

However, it should be noted that a dismissal will not be automatically unfair if it is for one of the above reasons and the employer can show that, for a reason other than redundancy, it was not reasonably practicable for the employer to permit the employee to return to a job which was both suitable for her and appropriate in the circumstances and the employee accepts or unreasonably refuses such a job from an associated employer.[5]

---

[4] reg. 20(6), MPL Regulations 1996.
[5] reg. 20(7) and (8), MPL Regulations 1999.

CHAPTER 6

DISABILITY DISCRIMINATION

INTRODUCTION

The Disability Discrimination Act 1995,[1] which makes it unlawful to 6.01
discriminate in certain circumstances on the ground of disability, finally
received Royal Assent on November 8, 1995, the Government of the day
having been under considerable pressure for many years to plug what
was widely agreed to be a legislative gap in equality law. While the 1995
Act was not introduced in response to the requirements of European
Community Law it should be noted that the recently adopted Equal
Treatment Framework Directive on Discrimination in Employment[2]
does embrace discrimination on the ground of disability. The requirements of the directive in this area must be implemented within domestic
law by December 2, 2006 although the government has already indicated
an intention to expand the coverage of the DDA in certain respects, in
line with the requirements of the directive, by 2004. Of particular note in
this regard is the Government's intention to remove the exemption from
the Act's coverage of employers who employ fewer than 15 employees.[3]
It has also signalled its intention to bring the police and fire service
within the scope of the DDA, but not the armed forces.[4] It is unlikely,
however, given the scope of the Framework Directive, that it will have a
significant influence upon the DDA and its interpretation by domestic
courts.

While we shall focus exclusively on the employment related provisions
of the Act it should be noted that the DDA also covers discrimination in
relation to the provision of goods, facilities, services and premises,[5]
education,[6] and public transport[7] although some of these provisions are
not yet in force.[8]

The complexity of DDA and the regime it introduces cannot be 6.02
overestimated. In its final form it is also something rather different from
what had first been envisaged. This is perhaps illustrated most starkly by
the fact that when the Bill was introduced at the start of 1995 it had 37

---

[1] Hereinafter DDA.
[2] Directive 2000/78/EC.
[3] DDA, s.7.
[4] At the moment s.64(5), DDA excludes service as a police officer or firefighter from the
Act.
[5] Pt 3. See, *e.g. Rose v. Bouchet* [1999] I.R.L.R. 463, Sh.Ct.
[6] Pt. 4.
[7] Pt. 5.
[8] The final provisions which have yet to be implemented will come into force in 2004.

clauses and five schedules. When it received the Royal Assent on November 8, 1995 it had 70 sections and five schedules. This is to say nothing of the supporting regulations, guidance and codes of practice issued by the Secretary of State. Of particular importance is the Code of Practice issued by the Secretary of State under section 53(1)(a) of the Act and the Guidance notes issued by the Secretary of State under section 3.[9] Both provide helpful and practical guidance designed to assist in combating discrimination in employment and illuminate the working of the Act in practice. They are admissible in evidence in any proceedings before an employment tribunal or sheriff court and together they are invaluable in construing the provisions of the Act.

The Disability Rights Commission Act 1999

6.03   When the DDA was first passed it established the National Disability Council (NDC) which, unlike the EOC and the CRE, had no enforcement powers whatsoever nor was it able to fund legal assistance for those bringing claims under the Act. However, the Disability Rights Commission Act 1999 abolished the NDC, and created a Disability Rights Commission (DRC) in its place. Like the CRE and the EOC the DRC has a duty to work towards the elimination of discrimination and to promote equality of opportunity. It has similar powers to the EOC and the CRE relating to formal investigations, non-discrimination notices and offering legal assistance to applicants. It is interesting to note that it had a budget of £11 million for it first full year of operation (in addition to start up costs), this being just slightly less than twice the government grant to the EOC (£5.8 million). The DRC's website is highly developed and contains a great deal of useful information.[10]

THE EMPLOYMENT PROVISIONS IN THE DDA

6.04 The employment provisions of the Act, which came into force on December 2, 1996, make all United Kingdom employers of 15 or more employees liable for discriminating against disabled job applicants and employees in respect of selection arrangements, recruitment, the terms on which employment is offered, terms and conditions of employment, opportunities for promotion, transfer or training, employment benefits, dismissal or any other detrimental treatment.[11]

According to the EAT in *Commissioner of Police of the Metropolis v. Harley*[12] the reference to "dismissal" in section 4(2) of the Act does not include constructive dismissal, it being considered that, as a matter of ordinary language and having regard to the common law, the primary meaning of the term "dismiss" or "dismissal" related to the termination

---

[9] Under s.53A, DDA (which was inserted by s.9(1) of the Disability Rights Commission Act 1999) the Disability Rights Commission is authorized to prepare and issue Codes of Practice. None have been issued by the Commission at the time of writing although it should be noted that this power was only given to the Commission in April 2000.

[10] www.drc-gb.org.

[11] DDA, s.4, which is similar in many respects to the SDA, s.6.

[12] [2001] I.R.L.R. 263.

of the contract of employment by the unilateral act of the employer. The EAT did not consider that the concept was apt to embrace constructive dismissal, which involved an act of election by the employee. However, it should be noted that the EAT did not consider the EAT decision in *Derby Specialist Fabrication Ltd v. Burton,*[13] which considered exactly the same point under the Race Relations Act, with the opposite conclusion being reached, on the basis that there was no reason to give the word "dismissal" a narrow meaning so as to exclude constructive dismissal.

The 15 employee minimum,[14] continues to cause consternation, excluding as it does many United Kingdom employers, although it should be noted that until 1998 an employer had to employ at least 20 to come within the scope of the Act. As noted above, the Government, having consulted with small employers, is committed to removing the small employer exemption by 2004.

Unlike the SDA, the DDA itself gives no guidance on the question of associated employers; however, the EAT has made it clear that there is no scope for adding together separate workforces employed by the same employer in parent, holding or subsidiary companies.[15]

The definition of discrimination

Section 5 of the DDA sets out the definition of discrimination. 6.05 Discrimination will occur if: (a) for a reason which relates to a disabled person's disability, they are treated less favourably than others are treated or would be treated to whom the reason does not or would not apply; and, (b) the employer cannot show that the treatment in question is justified. Less favourable treatment will be justified: "If, but only if, the reason for it is both material to the circumstances of the particular case and substantial".[16] It will be noted immediately that, unlike the SDA and RRA, the definition does not rely upon the concepts of direct and indirect discrimination.. The question is simply whether there was less favourable treatment due to disability and, if there was, whether this can be justified. It follows that, unlike direct sex and race discrimination, direct[17] disability discrimination can be justified. So far as indirect discrimination is concerned, taking the wide definition of discrimination, which will occur where there is unfavourable treatment for a reason "which relates to a disabled person's disability", together with the duty to make reasonable adjustments (see later) it is submitted that acts which might be appropriately so described (in terms of the definitions used in the SDA and RRA) will fall within the scope of the DDA.

---

[13] [2001] I.R.L.R. 69.

[14] Set by s.7 as amended by Disability Discrimination (Exemption for Small Employers) Order 1998 (S.I. 1998 No. 2618).

[15] *Hardie v. CD Northern Ltd* [2000] I.R.L.R. 87, EAT; *Colt Group v. Couchman* [2000] I.C.R. 327, EAT.

[16] s.5(3).

[17] While the concepts of "direct" and "indirect" discrimination form no part of the definition of discrimination in the DDA the point still holds—if, on the ground that he has a disability, a person is treated less favourably than others this can be justified under the Act

The issue arises of the comparison which should be made for the purpose of establishing that a disabled person was treated less favourably than "others" in terms of this definition. In *Clark v. Novacold Ltd*,[18] the applicant was disabled by reason of a back injury. He was off work for a considerable period of time and was dismissed by reason of his absence level. Before the employment tribunal the employer argued successfully that the appropriate comparator was "somebody who could have been off work for the same length of time as the applicant, but for a non-disablement reason". The tribunal was satisfied that someone else off work for a similar period for a reason unconnected with disability would have been dismissed and that, accordingly, the applicant was not treated less favourably than another person who was not disabled in a similar set of circumstances.

The EAT agreed that the appropriate comparator was someone who had been off work for a similar period but for a reason unconnected to disability. So far as Mr Justice Morison was concerned "s5(1) is concerned with a comparative exercise which is designed , logically, to isolate the sole factor in issue". However, it should be noted that the DDA, unlike the SDA and RRA, does not require that the comparison "must be such that the relevant circumstances in the one case are the same, or not materially different, in the other".

In essence, had the EAT decision been allowed to stand this would have meant that the DDA could do no more than protect employees against discrimination on the ground that the employer had some kind of difficulty with the fact that the person was disabled *per se*. However, in the same way as an employer is unlikely to dismiss an employee simply because she is pregnant it is equally unlikely they will dismiss because of the fact of disability itself. It is the consequences of the disability which will lead to dismissal or the like. Scrutiny of the Parliamentary debates on the Bill strongly suggests that the approach taken by the EAT was not what was intended. It was repeatedly stated in Parliament that the definition in section 5(1) was widely drafted to cover direct and indirect discrimination. The approach taken by the EAT did not accord with that. On further appeal the Court of Appeal held that both the tribunal and the EAT had made the wrong comparison. The correct approach in deciding whether the reason for less favourable treatment does not or would not apply to others, is simply to identify others to whom the reason for the treatment does not or would not apply. The test of less favourable treatment is based on the reason for the treatment of the disabled person and not on the fact of his disability. Unlike the SDA and RRA, the DDA does not turn on a like-for-like comparison of the treatment of the disabled person and of others in similar circumstances. The persons who are performing the main functions of their jobs are "others" to whom the reason for dismissal of the disabled person (*i.e.* inability to perform those functions) would not apply.

---

[18] [1998] I.R.L.R. 420, EAT; rev'd [1999] I.R.L.R. 318, CA. See also *British Sugar Plc v. Kirker* [1998] I.R.L.R. 624, EAT.

Knowledge of disability

Does an employer need to know that an employee is disabled in order 6.06
to treat the employee less favourably for that reason? This issue was
considered in *H. J. Heinz and Co. Ltd v. Kenrick.*[19] The EAT concluded
that section 5(1) does not require the employer to have knowledge of the
disability as such, or as to whether its material features fall within
Schedule 1 to the Act, in order to be said to have acted for a reason
which relates to the disability. In so holding the EAT expressly disagreed
with an earlier decision of another division of the EAT in *O'Neill v.
Symm & Co. Ltd,*[20] which appeared to conclude that there cannot be less
favourable treatment for a reason that relates to a person's disability
within the meaning of section 5(1)(a) unless the employer has knowledge
of the disability or at least the material features of it. In *Heinz* the EAT
concluded that there was nothing in the statutory language which
required that the relationship between the disability and the treatment
should be judged subjectively through the eyes of the employer. The
correct test was the objective one of whether the relationship exists, not
whether the employer knew of it. This required employers to pause to
consider whether the reason for some dismissal that they have in mind
might relate to disability and, if it might, to reflect on the Act and the
Code of Practice before dismissing. Unless the test was objective, there
would be difficulties with credible and honest yet ignorant or obtuse
employers who fail to recognise or acknowledge the obvious. The EAT
also held that the reference to a reason "which relates to" the disabled
person's disability in section 5(1)(a) widens the description of the
reasons which may be relevant so as to include a reason deriving from
how the disability manifests itself even where there is no knowledge of
the disability as such.

The Employer's Defence of Justification

Once it has been established that the reason for the less favourable 6.07
treatment relates to the person's disability, the employer will then be
given the opportunity to show that the treatment in question is justified.
While the provisions governing burden of proof in the DDA have not
been amended consequent upon the implementation of the Burden of
Proof Directive in domestic law[21] the provisions of the Equal Treatment
Framework Directive state that "Member States must take necessary
measures to ensure that where a complainant establishes facts from
which it may be presumed that there has been direct or indirect
discrimination it shall be for the respondent to prove that there has been
no breach of the principle of equal treatment".[22] In these circumstances
it may be necessary for the DDA to be amended to ensure that it
accords with the requirements of the Directive in this respect. As noted
above the defence of justification will only be met if the reason for the
less favourable treatment "is both material to the circumstances of the

---

[19] [2000] I.R.L.R. 144, EAT.
[20] [1998] I.R.L.R. 233, EAT.
[21] See Chap. 3 for more detail—the E.C. Burden of Proof Directive only covers sex
discrimination cases.
[22] Art. 10, Directive 2000/78/EC.

particular case and substantial". Case law under the Equal Pay Act 1970 which examines the "material factor defence" allowed by that Act may be useful in assessing what is meant by "material" in the DDA. In *Rainey v. Greater Glasgow Health Board*[23] the House of Lords held that "material" means "significant and relevant". Parliamentary debates on the DDA indicate that "substantial" is meant to suggest more than "minor" or "trivial" but it does not necessarily mean a large, grand, or highly significant object.[24] In *H. J. Heinz Co. Ltd v. Kenrick*[25] the EAT held that the threshold for justification of disability discrimination under section 5(3) is very low. It noted that section 5(3) provides that treatment "is" justified if the reason for it is both "material to the circumstances of the particular case and substantial", not that it "can" or "may" be justified. That meant that the condition stipulated in section 5(3) was both necessary and sufficient. Taking account of what the Code of Practice says about the meaning of "material to the circumstances of the particular case and substantial", the EAT concluded that if the reason for the treatment relates to the individual circumstances in question and is not just trivial or minor, then justification has to be held to exist in a case in which the employer has no section 6 duty of reasonable adjustment. It also considered that absence of knowledge of the disability, while not preventing a finding of less favourable treatment on the ground of disability, may be highly material to justifiability under section 5(1)(b) or section 5(2)(b) or as to the steps to be considered or taken under section 6.[26]

The requirement for the reason to be "material" is likely to make it difficult for employers to defend decisions based on unnecessary job requirements (for example, a requirement for the job holder to possess a driving licence, where the job would not involve driving).

The EAT has considered the approach to be taken in assessing whether the defence of justification is met in *Baynton v. Saurus General Engineers Ltd*[27] in which it was held that the statutory sequence for establishing justification under section 5(1)(a) and section 5(3) is as follows:

(1) The disabled applicant shows less favourable treatment, such as dismissal, under sections 1(1)(a) and 4(2)(d).

(2) The respondent shows that that treatment, the dismissal, is justified if:

    (i) the reason for the dismissal is both material to the circumstances of the particular case and substantial, unless

    (ii) the employer is under a section 6 duty in relation to the applicant but fails without justification to comply with that duty, subject to the treatment being justified even if he had complied with the section 6 duty.[28]

---

[23] [1987] I.R.L.R. 26 approved in *Strathclyde Regional Council v. Wallace* [1998] I.R.L.R. 604, EAT.

[24] See para. 4.6 of the Code of Practice.

[25] [2000] I.R.L.R. 144, EAT.

[26] See discussion of the duty to make adjustments below.

[27] [1999] I.R.L.R. 604, EAT.

[28] See below for detailed discussion of the duty to make reasonable adjustments.

An employment tribunal, in applying the test of justification under section 5(3), must carry out a balancing exercise between the interests of the disabled employee and the interests of the employer. This followed from the fact that the reason for the discriminatory treatment must be "material to the circumstances of the case"; the EAT held that this must include the circumstances of both the employer and employee.

However, in assessing whether the reason for less favourable treatment is material and substantial, within the meaning of section 5(3), a tribunal is not permitted to make up its mind on justification on the basis of its own appraisal of the medical evidence and to conclude that the reason is not material or substantial because the medical opinion on the basis of which the employer's decision was made is thought to be inferior to a different medical opinion expressed to the tribunal even if the tribunal would have come to a different decision as to the extent of the risk. If a risk assessment is properly conducted and based on the informed opinion of suitably qualified doctors and produces an answer which is not irrational, then the employer's assessment will be unassailable. In *Jones v. Post Office*[29] the applicant was a mail delivery driver. For many years he suffered from a type of diabetes that was able to be treated with tablets and dietary adjustments. Following a heart attack his diabetes required to be treated with insulin. The Post Office's medical fitness standards dictated that employees who required insulin ceased all driving duties. After an internal review, the applicant was offered limited driving duties which were not to exceed two hours a day. The applicant complained to the tribunal that the medical evidence showed that there was no greater risk that he would suffer a hypoglycaemic episode with the developed form of diabetes than previously. He therefore contended that the employer's purported justification for imposing a daily limit of two hours was neither material or substantial. The tribunal preferred the applicant's medical witnesses and upheld his claim. This decision was reversed by the EAT with whom, on further appeal, the Court of Appeal agreed. The latter court took the opportunity to compare the function of an employment tribunal in considering this issue to the approach which it must take, using the "bad of reasonable responses test", in assessing the reasonableness of an employer's conduct for the purposes of unfair dismissal. It considered that "in both cases, the members of the tribunal might themselves have come to a different conclusion on the evidence, but they must respect the opinion of the employer, in the one case if it is within the range of reasonable responses and in the other if the reason given is material and substantial."

As commentators have pointed out this suggests that the justification test under the employment provisions of the DDA is in no way comparable to that under the race, sex equal pay and part-time workers legislation, all of which apply the concept of "objective justification" as developed by European Community Law. One can also foresee it being difficult to reconcile the *Jones* approach to justification with the terms of the Employment Framework Directive, which adopts the European law objective justification standard for indirect disability discrimination. It is understood that leave to appeal has been sought from the House of

---

[29] [2001] I.R.L.R. 384, CA.

Lords—if the case proceeds it is likely to be argued that the test is an objective one in which it is for a tribunal to make its own decision as to whether the reason has been shown to be "material" and "substantial".

As the EAT pointed out in *Baynton* the interrelationship between section 5 and 6 of the DDA is crucial so far as the issue of justification is concerned.[30] While many of the above concepts and principles will be familiar to those with knowledge of sex and race discrimination legislation it is when one turns to consider the provisions of section 6 of the DDA that one enters into alien territory.

The Duty to make Reasonable Adjustments

6.08   Section 6 of the DDA requires employers to take what might be described as affirmative action. Specifically, section 6(1) imposes a duty on employers where: (a) any arrangements made by or on behalf of an employer, or any physical feature of premises occupied by an employer, place a disabled person at a substantial disadvantage in comparison with persons who are not disabled, to take such steps as are reasonable in all the circumstances to prevent the arrangements or feature having that effect.

Sections 5 and 6 interact closely in that an employer will also discriminate against a disabled person, contrary to section 5(2), if he fails to comply with the duty under section 6 to make a reasonable adjustment and he cannot show that his failure is justified.[31] In *Morse v. Wiltshire County Council*[32] guidance was given as to how a case under section 5(2) should proceed.

It is necessary to decide whether there is a section 6(1) duty incumbent upon the employer in the particular circumstances of the case.[33]

If there is such a duty, the issue then arises of whether the employer has taken such steps as are reasonable in order to prevent the arrangements or features referred to in section 6(1) having the effect of placing the disabled person at a substantial disadvantage? Consideration should be given to the factors in section 6(3) and (4).

If, but only if, the employer has failed to comply with the duty to make reasonable adjustments, must it then be decided whether the employer has shown that the failure was justified in terms of section 5(4), *i.e.* it was for a material and substantial reason.

6.09   The duty to adjust is triggered when a disabled person is placed at a "substantial disadvantage"[34] as a job applicant or as an employee, by selection arrangements or working conditions, or by any physical feature

---

[30] There is further discussion of the justification defence in that context below.

[31] s.5(2).

[32] [1998] I.R.L.R. 352, EAT.

[33] According to the EAT in *Morse* "a s.6(1) duty does arise where a disabled person is dismissed. The words in s.6(2)(b) 'any . . . arrangements on which employment . . . is . . . afforded' are wide enough to cover arrangements in relation to whether employment continues or is terminated in our view, and we are entitled to take a purposive view of s.6 and to bear in mind that the valuable and specific protection which it offers in obliging an employer to see if he can take steps reasonably to avoid dismissing a disabled employee would be lost to many vulnerable employees at their time of greatest need if it did not apply to the question of dismissal".

[34] s.6(1).

of premises. It should be noted that the duty is owed to particular disabled persons ("the disabled person concerned"[35]) as and when the occasion arises rather than to all disabled people in advance of any requirement; *i.e.* there is no general duty to make adjustments to make employment more open and practicable for disabled people.

Section 6(3) of the DDA sets out examples of the steps which an employer may have to take in relation to a disabled person in order to comply with the duty to make reasonable adjustments. The list is not exhaustive but includes making adjustments to premises, allocating some of the disabled person's duties to another person, transferring the person to fill an existing vacancy, altering working hours or place of work, modifying instructions or reference manuals, providing supervision or a reader or interpreter.

Section 6(4) gives some guidance on determining when it will be reasonable for an employer to have to take a particular step. Factors which will be taken into account include the extent to which taking the step would actually prevent the disabled person being placed at a substantial disadvantage, the extent to which it is practicable for the employer to take the step, the financial and other costs likely to be incurred in taking the step, the disruption to activities of the employer which could be caused, the extent of the employer's financial and other resources, and the availability to the employer of financial or other assistance to take the step. In explaining the provisions of section 6(4) the responsible Minister made the following comments during the passage of the Bill:

(a) if the only adjustments possible could make no more than a small improvement to the output of someone who was significantly under-productive, then they might not be reasonable if they were costly or disruptive;

(b) it might not be reasonable for an employer needing an employee urgently to have to wait for adjustments to be made to allow a disabled person to be employed. It was suggested that this was more likely to be the case with smaller employers. Also an adjustment would not be reasonable if it was impossible because the employer would be in breach of health and safety or fire legislation were it to be made.

(c) Cost to the employer will include use of staff and other resources and disruption as well as direct monetary sums incurred.

(d) It is more reasonable for an employer with considerable resources to make an adjustment with a significant cost than for an employer with few resources. It would not normally be reasonable for an employer to spend fewer resources on retaining a disabled person than on recruiting a replacement.

The Government suggested at the time of the Bill's passage that the concept of what is "reasonable" will ensure that employers are not faced

---

[35] *ibid.*

with an undue cost burden in making adjustments. It was repeatedly pointed out in parliamentary debates that many adjustments will cost little or nothing. An oft repeated example was the possible allocation of a dedicated parking space, where one is available, facilitating access for a disabled person who has difficulty in walking long distances.

Kenny v. Hampshire Constabulary[36] examines the limits on the obligation of an employer to make reasonable adjustments. In this case the applicant had cerebral palsy and required toileting assistance involving intimate physical contact. He applied for a post and was considered to be the best candidate. The employer sought volunteers to assist the applicant but no-one came forward. It also sought to obtain a grant to allow it to employ a carer to assist the applicant. However, the administrative process associated with this was such that the employer decided it could not delay filling the post until a decision was made and it then withdrew the job offer. The applicant claimed that he had been discriminated against on the ground of disability and the employer had failed in its duty to make a reasonable adjustment. However, the EAT held that an employer's duty under section 6 to make a reasonable adjustment to arrangements on which employment is offered or afforded is restricted to "job-related" matters. Not every failure to make an arrangement which deprives an employee of a chance to be employed is unlawful.

The definition in section 6(2), which refers to "any term, condition or arrangements on which employment, promotion, a transfer, training or any other benefit is offered or afforded", directs employers to make adjustments to the way the job is structured and organised so as to accommodate those who cannot fit into existing arrangements.

The EAT did not consider that the duty extended to employers provide carers to attend to their employees' personal needs, such as assistance in going to the toilet; a line had to be drawn on the extent of the employer's responsibilities in providing adjustments to accommodate a disabled employee. Although an employer is required by section 6(1) to consider making physical arrangements for a disabled person to use the toilet and physical adjustments to accommodate the presence of a personal carer, the EAT considered that had Parliament intended to impose on employers the duty to cater for an employee's personal needs in the toilet it would have said so, and the Code of Practice would have laid out the criteria to be applied. However, the case was remitted to the tribunal to consider whether the respondent was justified, in accordance with section 5(1), in not waiting for the result of the application for a support worker before withdrawing the offer.

The approach which a tribunal should take in considering whether an employer has met its obligation to make reasonable adjustments under section 6 of the DDA in circumstances where the employee has suggested adjustments but the employer does not make them in light of medical opinion that the applicant remains unfit for work was considered by the EAT in *Fu v. London Borough of Camden*.[37] It was considered that a tribunal had erred by failing to consider the extent to which, if at

---

[36] [1999] I.R.L.R. 76, EAT.
[37] [2001] I.R.L.R. 186, EAT.

all, adjustments proposed by the applicant could have overcome the medical symptoms which otherwise prevented her return to work. According to the EAT, a decision of a tribunal which addresses the issue as to whether an employer was justified in not implementing reasonable adjustments because they would not enable the employee to return to work would almost inevitably examine the adjustments on the one hand and the symptoms which could or could not be relieved by such adjustments on the other. Section 6 required consideration not only of the adjustments proposed, but of the question as to whether they were reasonable and the further question as to whether the employers were justified in not implementing them in advance of the dismissal which had occurred in this case so as to avoid it.

When an employer seeks to rely upon the defence of justification, but has failed to comply with the duty of reasonable adjustment, his treatment of the person cannot be justified unless it would have been justified even if he had made the reasonable adjustment required.[38] The issue then arises of whether an employer can justify a dismissal in a case where it did not know that the applicant was disabled and therefore did not turn its mind to the issue of whether reasonable adjustments might be made. In *Quinn v. Schwarzkopf Ltd*[39] the applicant went on sick leave in the early 1990s. His condition was later diagnosed as rheumatoid arthritis. He was subsequently dismissed in 1998. The employee brought a complaint to an employment tribunal alleging disability discrimination against the employer in that it had failed to make reasonable adjustments. The tribunal held that, although the applicant was disabled in terms of the Act, since the employer did not know or consider whether he was disabled it could not have made reasonable adjustments and, the dismissal was justified. The EAT, sitting in Scotland, allowed the appeal, holding that an employer cannot attempt to discharge the onus of justifying disability discrimination where in fact he did not even apply his mind during the currency of the employment to what could be done in terms of making reasonable adjustments, due to his ignorance of the disability. The legislation does not contemplate attempts by employers on a hypothetical basis to justify an act subsequently held to be discriminatory which they did not at the time consider to be such, because they were unaware of the existence of the disability, by seeking to show that there was nothing in fact they could have done. The situation would be different, according to the EAT, if the employer was aware of the disability but did nothing because he reached the conclusion that there was nothing that could reasonably be done. In considering this decision it might usefully be noted that section 6(6) expressly provides that there is no such duty "if the employer does not know, and could not reasonably be expected to know . . . that the person has a disability". This decision is under further appeal.[40] It should be noted that the same division of the EAT appears to have moved way from the position it appeared to adopt in *Quinn* in *Callagan v. Glasgow City Council*.[41] In particular, the EAT states that "in so far as this Tribunal

---

[38] s.5(5).
[39] [2001] I.R.L.R. 67 EAT.
[40] See also *H J Heinz and Co Ltd v. Kenrick* for further discussion.
[41] EAT/43/01, heard August 28, 2001.

may have suggested in *Quinn v. Schwarzkopf* that justification can never occur if the employer is ignorant of the fact of disability at the relevant time that goes too far".

A somewhat different approach, to that in *Quinn,* on a related matter was taken by another division of the EAT in *British Gas Services Ltd v. McCaull.*[42] Here the applicant was a service engineer with the appellants. He was epileptic and had suffered an attack at the wheel, causing a road traffic accident as a consequence of which the appellant's vehicle was written off. The applicant was thereafter deemed to be incapable of a number of duties including driving, and unsupervised work. This precluded him continuing as a service engineer. He was told that the only available alternative work was as a clerk. The applicant did not wish to transfer to this post, which involved significant salary loss, and was dismissed on the grounds of capability. He subsequently claimed unfair dismissal and disability discrimination. As far as the latter claim was concerned an issue arose as to whether the appellant could justify its less favourable treatment of the applicant, under section 5(1) and its failure to make a reasonable adjustment on the basis that it had never viewed the applicant as disabled under the DDA nor considered that it was under a duty to make reasonable adjustments. According to the employment tribunal, "it could not be right for an employer wholly to disregard its duty under section 6 DDA and then to seek to justify their disregard by way of submissions ex post facto at the hearing". This is essentially a variation of the view espoused by the EAT in *Quinn.* However the EAT rejected this approach, emphasising its view that the test of whether the section 6 duty has been met is an objective one:

> "Upon analysis the tribunal seems to be running together a number of separate points. First, it seems to be saying that an employer must consciously consider what steps it would take in the context of its section 6 duty; in other words, it will be in breach of that statutory duty if it is unaware of the existence of that duty. In so far as the tribunal was saying that it was wrong in law. There is no automatic breach of the s.6 duty because an employer is unaware of that duty: the question is not one of such awareness but of what steps the employer took or did not take. A benevolent and conscientious employer with a disabled employee might well take all reasonable steps as contemplated by section 6 while remaining entirely ignorant of the statutory provision itself".

> "The test of reasonableness as set out in section 6(4) does not relate to what the employer considered but to what he did and did not do. Whether an employer considered any or all of the steps set out as examples (and no more than that) in section 6(3), the test remains an objective one under section 6: did he take such steps as is reasonable in all the circumstances of the case for him to have to take in order to prevent arrangements made by the employer from placing the disabled person at a substantial disadvantage in comparison with those who are not disabled? It is for the tribunal to

consider what steps the employer took and what steps he did not take and then to apply the statutory test".[43]

THE DEFINITION OF DISABILITY

Section 1 of the Act defines a "disabled person" as a person who has a 6.10 disability. Disability in turn is defined as "a physical or mental impairment" which has a substantial long-term adverse impact on a person's ability to carry out normal day to day activities. One is therefore normally looking for four key features before a person will be protected by the legislation:

(i) there must be a "physical or mental impairment";
(ii) the impairment must adversely effect the person's ability to carry out "normal day to day activities";
(iii) the adverse effect must be "substantial"; and
(iv) the adverse effect must be "long term".

In addition, those who "have had" a disability in the past are also covered by most of the Act's provisions, including those governing employment.[44] This was conceded by the Government during the passage of the Bill and ensures that the Act covers those with a past history of, for example, mental illness or cancer even where they are viewed as having fully recovered. However, the Act does not protect people who are discriminated against because they are incorrectly perceived to have a disability—this leaves without protection those who are impaired in some way, but not in a manner which falls within the Act's definition or those who are erroneously treated as having a disability (for example asymptomatic HIV sufferers).

Schedule 1 to the Act amplifies the definition given in section 1. The overall intention of the Government was stated to be to formulate a definition which included "every commonly accepted form of disability", yet excluded those "who are not fairly or generally recognised as disabled". In *Vicary v. British Telecommunications plc*[45] Morison J. cautioned against the influence of stereotypical conceptions that lead to assumptions as to a person's abilities or disabilities:

"Finally, we should wish to add for the consideration of employment tribunals in the future that a relatively small proportion of the disabled community are what one might describe as visibly disabled, that is people in wheelchairs or carrying white sticks or other aids. It is important, therefore, that when they are approaching the question as to whether someone suffers from a disability, they should not have in their minds a stereotypical image of a

---

[43] At paras 42 and 43, citing *Morse v. Wiltshire County Council* [1998] I.R.L.R. 352, EAT. See also *Hammersmith and Fulham LBC v. Farnsworth* [2000] I.R.L.R. 691, EAT where it is stated that knowledge on the part of the employer is irrelevant both to assessing whether there was less favourable treatment and justification.
[44] s.2.
[45] [1999] I.R.L.R. 680, EAT.

person in a wheelchair moving around with considerable difficulty. Such persons may well have a physical impairment within the meaning of the Act and are thus to be treated as disabled, but it of course does not follow that other persons who are not in such a condition are inherently less likely to have a physical or mental impairment of a sort which satisfies the terms of the legislation".

Schedule 1 to the Act attempts, in particular, to provide assistance with the definition of mental impairment. This is defined as including "an impairment resulting from or consisting of a mental illness only if the illness is a clinically well recognised illness". At committee stage the responsible Minister made it clear that what amounts to a clinically well recognised illness will be a question of fact, so that on occasion employment tribunals may have to evaluate conflicting expert medical evidence. It will require that "a reasonably substantial body of practitioners . . . accept that a condition exists" according to the Minister. Examples given of what is covered included schizophrenia,[46] manic depression and severe and extended depressive psychoses.[47] In *Rugamer v. Sony Music Entertainment and McNicol v. Balfour Beatty Management*[48] it was confirmed that where the disability relied upon is a mental impairment then the impairment must be "clinically well recognised". The definition will therefore not cover "moods or mild eccentricities".

In *Goodwin v. Patent Office*[49] the EAT issued detailed guidance on the approach to be adopted in considering whether an individual is disabled for the purposes of the DDA. In this case the applicant was a paranoid schizophrenic who was dismissed after female colleagues complained of disturbing behaviour. Although he had auditory hallucinations which interrupted his concentration, the employment tribunal held that he was not protected by the Act because it did not consider that his impairment had a substantial adverse effect on his normal day to day activities as required by section 1(1) of the DDA. It noted that Dr Goodwin was able to perform his domestic activities without assistance and to work to a satisfactory standard. The applicant appealed against the decision that he was not disabled within the meaning of the Act. The EAT upheld the appeal, noting that the applicant was unable to carry on normal day to day conversation with his colleagues. This was good evidence that his ability to concentrate and communicate effectively had been adversely affected to a significant degree.

Obiter the EAT made the following points:

- In most cases a directions hearing will be good practice
- Where expert evidence is to be presented proper advance notice should be given to the other party and a copy of the report presented
- The tribunal should adopt an inquisitorial or interventionist role — there is a risk of a "Catch 22" situation since some

[46] See, *e.g. Goodwin v. Patent Office* [1999] I.R.L.R. 4, EAT.
[47] *e.g. Edwards v. Mid Suffolk District Council* [2001] I.R.L.R. 190, EAT.
[48] Joined cases EAT/1385/99 and EAT/1487/99. See also *Kapadia v. London Borough of Lambeth* [2000] I.R.L.R. 14, EAT; aff'd [2000] I.R.L.R. 699, CA.
[49] [1999] I.R.L.R. 4, EAT.

disabled people may be unable or unwilling to accept that they have a disability

- The tribunal should adopt a purposive approach to construction, with due regard to the ordinary and natural meaning of words
- Explicit reference should be made to any provision of the Guidance issued by the Secretary of State which the tribunal has taken into account
- In assessing whether an individual is disabled the tribunal should ask:

  (1) Does the applicant have an impairment which is either mental or physical? Mental impairment includes an impairment which results from or consists of a mental illness provided that the mental illness is "clinically well-recognised". If there is doubt as to whether a mental illness falls within the definition, it would be advisable to ascertain whether the illness is mentioned in the World Health Organisation's International Classification of Diseases.

  (2) Does the impairment affect the applicant's ability to carry out normal day to day activities in one of the respects set out in Schedule 1, paragraph 4(1), and does it have an adverse effect? The Act is concerned with a person's ability to carry out activities. The fact that a person can carry out such activities does not mean that his ability to carry them out has not been impaired. The focus of the Act is on the things that the applicant either cannot do or can only do with difficulty, rather than on the things that the person can do.

  (3) Is the adverse effect substantial? "Substantial" means "more than minor or trivial" rather than "very large". The tribunal may take into account how the applicant appears to the tribunal to "manage", although it should be slow to regard a person's capabilities in the relatively strange adversarial environment as an entirely reliable guide to the level of ability to perform normal day to day activities. The tribunal should examine how an applicant's abilities have actually been affected whilst on medication and then consider the "deduced effects"—the effects which they think there would have been but for the medication—and whether the actual and deduced effects on ability to carry out normal day to day activities is clearly more than trivial.

Is the Adverse Effect Long-term?

Paragraph 1(2) of Schedule 1 enables regulations to be made which exclude certain conditions from the scope of the Act; that authority was subsequently utilised with the Disability Discrimination (Meaning of Disability) Regulations 1996[50] coming into force on July 30, 1996. These

---

[50] S.I. 1996 No. 1455.

make it clear that addiction to nicotine, alcohol or any other substance is not to be treated as an impairment under the Act, unless the addiction is acquired originally as the result of the administration of medically prescribed drugs or other medical treatment.[51] Also excluded from the definition of impairment under the Act are exhibitionism, voyeurism, a tendency to steal, set fires or physically or sexually abuse others.[52] Similarly, tattoos and decorative body piercing will not qualify as disfigurements for the purposes of the Act.[53]

GUIDANCE RELATING TO THE DEFINITION OF DISABILITY

6.11　Section 3 of the DDA enables the Secretary of State to issue guidance about matters to be taken into account in determining whether an impairment has a substantial adverse and long term effect on a person's ability to carry out normal day to day activities and specifies that any such guidance must be taken into account by courts and tribunals as appropriate. Subsequently a document entitled "Guidance on matters to be taken into account in determining questions relating to the definition of disability" was issued on July 25, 1996 under this section.

Part I of the document sets out general guidance on: (a) the main elements of the definition of disability; (b) exclusions from the definition; (c) the definition of "impairment"; and (d) protection given to those registered as disabled under the Disabled Persons (Employment) Act 1944.

6.12　Part II of the Guidance provides more specific advice on matters to be taken into account in determining questions relating to the definition of disability, going through each of the key concepts in the statutory definition and providing detailed commentary thereon. For example. Part II, section A of the Guidance focuses on the meaning of the word "substantial" and suggests that when considering whether an effect is a substantial adverse effect account should be taken of:

(a) The time taken by a person with an impairment to carry out a normal day to day activity and the way he or she carries it out, compared with what might be expected if he or she did not have the impairment.

(b) The cumulative effects of an impairment—it may be that an impairment does not have a substantial adverse effect on a person when each normal day to day activity is considered in isolation. However, it is perfectly possible that it could have a substantial adverse effect if one considers its impact overall on the person's ability to carry out the range of activities specified as normal day to day activities. Similarly it may be that the person has more than one impairment. In such cases, account must be taken of whether the impairments considered together have a substantial effect overall

---

[51] reg. 3.

[52] reg. 4.

[53] reg. 5. Though as is pointed out in para 1329 of *Harvey*, disfigurement caused by the *removal* of such acts of self-mutilation would not seem to be automatically excluded.

on the person's ability to carry out normal day to day activities.

In *Leonard v. Southern Derbyshire Chamber of Commerce*[54] the EAT considered the approach which should be adopted by tribunals in applying the provisions of the Guidance. Attention should be focused on what an applicant could not do or could only do with difficulty rather than on what she could do. This approach avoided the danger of a tribunal concluding that as there were still many things that an applicant could do the adverse effect could not be substantial. In this case it was held that the tribunal had erred in its approach to the applicant's evidence. It had taken examples from the Guidance of what she could do, such as being able to eat and drink, and catch a ball and then weighed that in the balance against what she could not do, such as negotiate pavement edges safely. The EAT considered that this was inappropriate, since her ability to catch a ball did not diminish her inability to negotiate pavement edges safely. The EAT also suggested that in a case of mental impairment, it is particularly important that a tribunal takes into account the matters set out in paragraphs C6 and C7 of the Guidance. Paragraph C6 notes that an impairment may indirectly affect a person and gives as an example that "the impairment might make the activity more than usually fatiguing so that the person might not be able to repeat the task over a sustained period". Paragraph C7 says that "where a person has a mental illness such as depression account should be taken of whether, although that person has the physical ability to perform a task, he or she is, in practice, unable to sustain an activity over a reasonable period".

The provisions of the Guidance in relation to each component of the definition of disability are examined below.

THE CONSTITUENT PARTS OF THE DEFINITION

Long term effect

Paragraph 2 of Schedule 1 specifies that an impairment will be viewed 6.13 as having a long term effect if: (a) it has lasted at least 12 months; or (b) the period for which it lasts is likely to be at least 12 months; or (c) it is likely to last for the rest of the life of the person affected. It is also made clear, in paragraph 2(2) of Schedule 1, that when an impairment ceases to have a substantial adverse effect on a person's ability to carry out normal day to day activities it is to be treated as continuing to have that effect if that effect is likely to recur.(This will cover people who have impairments where the effects fluctuate, such as arthritis or multiple sclerosis). *Greenwood v. British Airways plc*[55] examines the issue of the relevant point in time for determining whether an impairment qualifies as having a long term effect in that it is likely to recur. An employment tribunal had held that when Mr Greenwood's application for promotion was rejected he was not a disabled person because his condition

---

[54] [2001] I.R.L.R. 19, EAT.
[55] [1999] I.R.L.R. 600, EAT.

(depression) had ceased and was not likely to recur, even though it did recur in fact between the rejection of the application for promotion and the tribunal hearing. The EAT considered that this approach was erroneous, holding that in determining whether an impairment is "likely" to last for at least 12 months the "tribunal should consider the adverse effect of the applicant's condition up to and including the employment tribunal hearing". This decision has been the subject of some criticism, it being suggested that the "likelihood" of an impairment recurring should be assessed at the time of the alleged act of discrimination rather than with the benefit of hindsight. Looked at another way, surely the applicant has to be a disabled person as at the date of the act of discrimination in order to rely upon the Act?

Normal day to day activities

6.14   Paragraph 4 of Schedule 1 makes it clear that an impairment will only be taken to affect the ability of the person concerned to carry out normal day to day activities if it affects at least one of the following:

> (a) mobility;
> (b) manual dexterity;
> (c) physical co-ordination;
> (d) continence;
> (e) ability to lift, carry or otherwise move everyday objects;
> (f) speech, hearing or eyesight;
> (g) memory or ability to concentrate, learn or understand; or
> (h) perception of the risk of physical danger.

The EAT has held that what is a day to day activity is best left unspecified, such being easily recognised, but defined with difficulty. Inquiry should not be focused on a particular or special set of circumstances, either at work or home.[56] While "work" is not one of the day to day activities listed, evidence of the nature of the applicant's duties at work and the way in which they are performed may be relevant since the work performed may well include some day to day activities. However, the fact that someone is able to perform his/her duties at work does not necessarily mean that s/he is not a disabled person for the purposes of the Act.[57] In *Abadeh v. British Telecommunications plc*[58] it was argued that the applicant's ability to travel on the London Underground could not be categorised as a normal day to day activity since he did not work or live in London and that flying was not a day to day activity for him because his work did not involve plane travel. While the tribunal accepted this argument it was rejected on appeal by the EAT which held that if the activity was instead classified, as it should have been, as simply "using public transport" then this would amount to a normal day to day activity, the assessment being made without regard to whether the activity is normal to the particular applicant.

In this case, the tribunal should have found that travelling by Underground or plane were normal means of transport, and then gone

---

[56] *Goodwin v. Patent Office* [1999] I.R.L.R. 4, EAT.
[57] *Law Hospital NHS Trust v. Rush* [2001] I.R.L.R. 611.
[58] [2001] I.R.L.R. 23, EAT.

on to consider whether on the facts the applicant's inability to use such forms of public transport amounted to an impairment which had a substantial and long-term adverse effect. However, the EAT noted that, given the applicant never actually used the Underground, it was difficult to see how any potential inability to use that form of public transport could be regarded as having a substantial adverse effect upon him.

In *Ekpe v. Commissioner of Police of the Metropolis*[59] the EAT counselled against an over-elaborate analysis of the Guidance on disability when assessing what amounts to a day to day activity. It suggests that if one of the abilities or capacities listed in paragraph 4(1)(a) to (h) of Schedule 1 to the Act has been affected then it is almost inevitable that there will be some adverse effect upon day to day activities. What is "normal" for the purposes of the Act can be defined as anything which is not abnormal or unusual as a regular activity, judged by an objective population standard. In this case the tribunal had erred in discounting the fact that the applicant could not put rollers in her hair and could not always use her right hand to put on her make-up on the basis that neither of these were "normal day to day activities" because they were activities carried out exclusively by women. That reasoning which would exclude anything done by women rather than men and vice versa from the category of normal activity was plainly wrong. The tribunal had been led into error by determining what was normal on the basis of an assessment of whether 50 per cent or more of the population would do it rather than by asking whether the activity was abnormal or unusual.

SUBSTANTIAL ADVERSE EFFECT

Part II, section B of the Guidance on the Meaning of Disability 6.15 examines the meaning of "long term effect" while section C provides assistance on the meaning of the phrase "normal day to day activities". The following provide examples (there are many more in the guidance document itself) of what it would and would not be reasonable to regard as substantial adverse effects in relation to some of the day to day activities covered by the Act:

Mobility—inability to travel a short journey as a passenger in a vehicle or difficulty going up or down steps or stairs could reasonably be regarded as a substantial effect. It would not be reasonable to regard inability to travel in a car for a journey lasting more than two hours without discomfort as a substantial adverse effect.

Manual dexterity—it would be reasonable to regard as a substantial adverse effect the loss of function in one or both hands such that the person cannot use the hand or hands or inability to handle a knife and fork at the same time. It would not be reasonable to regard as a substantial adverse effect the inability to undertake activities requiring delicate hand movements, such as threading a needle.

Hearing—it would be reasonable to regard as a substantial adverse effect inability to hold a conversation with someone talking in a normal voice in a moderately noisy environment. It would not be reasonable to

---

[59] [2001] I.R.L.R. 605, EAT.

regard as a substantial effect inability to hold a conversation in a noisy place, such as a factory floor.

Memory or ability to concentrate, learn or understand—it would be reasonable to regard as a substantial adverse effect persistent inability to remember the names of familiar people such as family or friends. It would not be reasonable to regard as a substantial effect occasionally forgetting the names of a familiar person, such as a colleague.

In *Abadeh v. British Telecommunications plc*[60] the EAT issued a reminder to employment tribunals that while it may be necessary for skilled medical witnesses to give evidence to assist the tribunal's decision as to whether the applicant is suffering a "substantial" adverse effect, it is for the tribunal alone to determine, as a matter of law, whether the impairment is indeed "substantial". In this case it considered that the tribunal were over-influenced by the employers' regional medical officer's opinion of whether or not the impairments were "substantial" under the Act, and in effect adopted her assessment instead of making their own. This was an error, the tribunal being the sole arbiter of fact and the law.[61]

In *Kapadia v. London Borough of Lambeth*[62] the employment tribunal rejected a complaint where the applicant was alleging that he was disabled by reason of reactive depression. The tribunal recognised that his condition was a clinically well-recognised illness. However they decided that it had no more than a trivial effect on his normal day to day activities. This finding was reached even although the respondent had not called any medical witnesses to challenge the applicant's medical witnesses who had given evidence that there was an underlying disability which was concealed by medical treatment. The decision of the tribunal was reversed by the EAT, with whom the Court of Appeal agreed, on the basis that the evidence of the applicant's witnesses was credible and had not been challenged. However Pill L.J. pointed out that in some cases the tribunal will be perfectly entitled to reject uncontested medical evidence. The evidence could be rejected on a number of grounds, for example that the witness might have misunderstood the evidence or the questions put to her.[63]

Substantial Adverse Effect and Medical Treatment

6.16   It is worth noting that in most cases where medical treatment, medication or some other aid is used to control or correct an impairment which would otherwise be likely to have a substantial adverse effect on the person's ability to carry out normal day to day activities it is still to be treated as being such an impairment. In other words, people will not lose protection under the Act if their disability is successfully controlled or corrected (there is an exception to this principle governing those with a sight impairment "correctable by spectacles or contact lenses"[64]).

---

[60] [2001] I.R.L.R. 23, EAT.

[61] See also *Law Hospital NHS Trust v. Rush* [2001] I.R.L.R. 611, CS.

[62] [2000] I.R.L.R. 699, CA.

[63] *De Keyser Ltd v. Wilson* [2001] I.R.L.R. 324, EAT contains framework guidance as to how expert evidence should be collected in employment tribunal cases.

[64] It is submitted that the wording of this exception is such that it would also cover those who chose not to correct their impairment by using spectacles or lenses.

THE DISABILITY DISCRIMINATION (EMPLOYMENT) REGULATIONS 1996[65]

The above Regulations, made under the authority of sections 5 and 6 of 6.17 the DDA, came into force on December 2, 1996. They allow employers to justify, on cost grounds, less favourable treatment of a disabled employee in respect of pension and sick pay provision. They also provide a defence for employers who pay disabled employees less than others where that is in accordance with a performance related scheme.

CODE OF PRACTICE

Section 53(1) of the DDA authorises the Secretary of State to issue 6.18 codes of practice containing such practical guidance as he considers appropriate with a view to: (a) eliminating discrimination in the field of employment against disabled persons and persons who have had a disability; or (b) encouraging good practice in relation to the employment of disabled persons and persons who have had a disability.

A code falling under the provisions of section 53(1)(a) has been issued and came into force on December 2, 1996. The code is admissible in evidence in any proceedings under the Act and if any of its provisions appear to a court or tribunal to be relevant to a question arising in the proceedings it must be taken into account in determining that question. *Inter alia* the code confirms that:

(a) Persons who are self employed and who agree to perform work personally fall within the definition of "employee" and must therefore be counted in determining whether there are 15 or more employees for coverage purposes.

(b) An adverse reaction by other employees to working with a disabled person would not justify less favourable treatment because it is not substantial. The same would apply to an attempt to justify less favourable treatment on the basis that customers might feel uncomfortable dealing with a disabled employee.

(c) It would be reasonable for an employer to have to spend at least as much on an adjustment to enable the retention of a disabled person, including the provision of retraining, as might be spent on recruiting and training a replacement.

The Code helpfully provides a number of examples of specific situations, going on to explain whether the employers' action in each case might be considered to be in breach of the DDA.

SIMILARITIES BETWEEN THE DDA AND THE SDA/RRA

The DDA parallels the other discrimination legislation in certain 6.19 respects:

---

[65] S.I. 1996 No. 1456.

1. Employment claims are to be made to an employment tribunal within three months of the act giving rise to the complaint. The time-limit can be extended if it is just and equitable to do so.[66]

2. Unlimited financial compensation can be awarded and tribunals can make recommendations (including a recommendation that the employer make an adjustment in respect of the disabled person) and declarations as to the rights of parties.[67]

3. The extended definition of employment found in the other discrimination legislation is carried over to the DDA.[68]

4. The Act applies to discrimination against contract workers both by their employers and by the principals who hire them.[69]

5. Similar vicarious liability provisions exist.[70]

6. Similar victimisation provisions exist.[71]

7. Compensation for injury to feelings can be awarded.[72]

8. There is provision for a questionnaire procedure.[73]

9. ACAS is given similar duties to promote settlement of complaints.[74]

10. Compromise agreements can be used to settle complaints.[75]

11. Similar provisions exist in respect of discrimination by trade organisations, including trade unions.[76]

12. Employment tribunals and the Employment Appeal Tribunal can make restricted reporting orders where "evidence of a personal nature" is likely to be heard. This measure was introduced following a consultation exercise because of concerns that potential complainants with a history of mental illness or who were HIV positive or who had Aids, for example, would be deterred from bringing a complaint by the prospect of publicity during proceedings.[77]

13. The Secretary of State is empowered to issue codes of practice to eliminate discrimination and encourage good practice, such codes being admissible evidence in tribunal proceedings.[78]

14. Section 11 of the DDA contains provisions governing advertisements which suggest that an employer may seek to discriminate. However, it should be noted that these are likely to be much less effective than the advertising provisions in the sex and race discrimination legislation, given

---

[66] s.8 and Sched. 3. See, *e.g. Harvey v. Port of Tilbury (London) Ltd* [1999] I.R.L.R. 693, EAT.

[67] s.8.

[68] s.68.

[69] s.12. See, *e.g. MHC Consulting Services Ltd v. Tansell* [2000] I.R.L.R. 387, CA.

[70] s.58.

[71] s.55.

[72] s.8.

[73] s.56.

[74] Sched. 3.

[75] s.9.

[76] s.13.

[77] ss.62 and 63.

[78] s.53.

that there is no prohibition as such against publishing an advertisement which indicates an intention to discriminate. The provision applies where a disabled person has applied for employment and the employer has refused to offer him employment and has advertised the employment by way of an advertisement which has indicated or might reasonably be understood to indicate, that any application for the employment would, or might, be determined to any extent by reference to: (a) the successful applicant not having any disability or any category of disability which includes the complainant's disability; or (b) the employer's reluctance to take any action or to make reasonable adjustments. In these circumstances if a complaint is made to an employment tribunal, the tribunal hearing the complaint is to assume, unless the contrary is shown, that the employer's reason for refusing to offer the employment to the complainant was related to the complainant's disability. In other words, a discriminatory advertisement can be used in evidence to create a rebuttable presumption of discrimination. However, it remains to be seen how many disabled people who see an advert which suggests that they may well be discriminated against will proceed to apply for the job.

Positive Discrimination

It is worthy of note that the DDA does not protect non-disabled 6.20 people from being discriminated against because they do not have a disability. (This is unlike the position with the SDA which protects both men and women while the RRA protects members of any racial group.) The consequence of this is that positive discrimination in favour of disabled people would appear to be allowed. This arises from the fact that there is no right of complaint for a person who wishes to complain of discrimination arising from the fact that the individual concerned is not disabled. The exception to this principle would appear to be in respect of employment in local government. The Local Government and Housing Act 1989 precludes local authorities from acting non-commercially. Appointments to local government posts must be made on merit. Prior to the DDA coming into force, as a result of the quota system imposed by the Disabled Persons (Employment) Act 1944, local authorities had been able to positively discriminate in favour of disabled people. However, these provisions were repealed by the DDA and it is submitted that such positive discrimination is no longer allowed. It was emphasised however, during the Bill's passage, that the obligation to appoint the most suitable person for the job applies after reasonable adjustments have been made in respect of disabled candidates. The Parliamentary Under Secretary of State for Education and Employment suggested that local authorities "would be able to do virtually anything to encourage and enable disabled people to work for them, as long as they appoint the person who is most suitable for the job after they have made reasonable adjustments. He indicated that there would be no maximum for such adjustments and that if a local authority is prepared to invest a large sum of money in making provisions so that a disabled person is suitable for a job, that will be the authority's prerogative.

CHAPTER 7

PART-TIME AND FIXED TERM WORKERS

PART-TIME WORKERS

7.01 It is a fact of the British economy that the vast majority of those who work part-time are female. Until recently, part-time workers who were treated less favourably than full-time workers on the basis of their part-time status had no remedy unless they could show that the less favourable treatment amounted to indirect discrimination on the ground of sex.[1] Male part-time workers frequently had no remedy at all, usually being unable to satisfy the requirements imposed by section 1(1) (b) of the SDA. However, the position has now changed as a result of the Part-time Workers (Prevention of Less Favourable Treatment) Regulations 2000[2] which were laid before Parliament on May 3, 2000 and came into force on July 1, 2000. The Regulations obviate the need for those who are treated less favourably than others on the ground of their part-time status to bring themselves within the ambit of the complex provisions governing indirect sex discrimination; this is likely to be particularly helpful to male part-time workers. However, use of the Regulations, certainly in the first year of operation, has been less than one might have expected.[3]

The Regulations implement the Part-Time Work Directive[4] which, in turn, essentially adopted the Framework Agreement on part-time work reached by the European social partners (both sides of industry). The Directive should, in fact, have been implemented by April 7, 2000 but the draft Regulations were not made available until late January 2000 for consultation purposes. The consultation process led to a number of changes being made between the draft and final versions of the Regulations. Where these are significant comment is made below.

7.02 Of immediate note is the fact that the draft Regulations referred to "employees" while the final version of the Regulations makes reference to "workers". In a Press Release the Government indicated that it had "listened carefully to the strong arguments which emerged during . . . consultation . . ." and had decided to extend the measures from employees to workers "in order to help thousands of extra part-timers who are some of the most vulnerable members of the workforce".

---

[1] Successful indirect discrimination claims have been brought by both individuals and groups of employees under the SDA—see Chap. 3 for more detail.
[2] S.I. 2000 No. 1551.
[3] This is borne out by the statistical information available from the Employment Tribunal Service.
[4] Directive 97/81/EC.

It will undoubtedly have been pointed out to the Government that the restriction of coverage to "employees", as mooted in the draft Regulations, might well have been subject to challenge on the basis that it did not accord with the intent of the parent Directive. However, it should be noted that the right to claim unfair dismissal on the basis that the reason for dismissal is connected to the exercising of rights under the Regulations, or assisting others to do so, is restricted to employees.[5]

An "employee" is defined as someone who has entered into or works under a contract of employment[6] while a "worker" is an individual who has entered into or works under a contract of employment or any other contract (whether express or implied) whereby the individual undertakes to do or perform personally any work or services for another party to the contract whose status is not that of a customer or client of any profession or business undertaking carried out by the individual.[7] This brings within the scope of the Regulations some casual workers and home workers who might conceivably have been excluded otherwise.

Full-time and Part-time workers—who falls into which category?

Regulation 2(1) and (2) define how full-time and part-time workers are to be identified for the purposes of the Regulations. In essence, someone will be a full-time worker if he/she is paid wholly or in part by reference to time worked and his/her employer treats him/her as a full-time worker, having regard to the "custom and practice" of the employer.[8] Similarly, a part-time worker will be someone who is paid wholly or partly by reference to time worked and whose employer treats him/her as a part-time worker, having regard to the employer's custom and practice.[9] This is, obviously, a flexible definition which leaves room for debate and confusion, not to mention avoidance strategies on the part of an employer. It means that someone working X hours could be a full-time worker when working for one employer and a part-time worker when working for another employer. 7.03

Less favourable treatment is not allowed unless justified

The basic underlying principle in the final version of the Regulations remains the same as that set out in the first draft Regulations—part-time workers should not be treated less favourably *because* of their part-time status than comparable full time workers in relation to contractual terms or by being subject to any other detriment. Treatment should be on a pro-rata basis (unless application of that principle would be "inappropriate") although the employer has the right to objectively justify any differential treatment.[10] 7.04

So far as the issue of objective justification is concerned the Notes issued by the DTI which accompany the Regulations specify that less favourable treatment will only be justified on objective grounds if it can be shown that the less favourable treatment:

---

[5] reg. 7(1).
[6] reg. 1(2).
[7] reg. 1(2).
[8] reg. 2(1).
[9] reg. 2(2).
[10] reg. 5.

1. is to achieve a legitimate objective, for example a genuine business objective;
2. is necessary to achieve that objective; and
3. is an appropriate way to achieve the objective.

Who will be a comparable full-time worker?

7.05   To establish a claim a part-time worker must be able to compare his/her treatment with that of a "comparable full-time worker". Regulation 2(4) specifies that a full-time worker will be an appropriate comparator if, at the time when the alleged less favourable treatment takes place, both workers are:

(a) (i) employed by the same employer under the same type of contract, and
     (ii) engaged in the same or broadly similar work having regard, where relevant, to whether they have a similar level of qualification, skills and experience; and

(b) the full-time worker works or is based at the same establishment as the part-time worker, or where there is no full-time worker working or based at that establishment who satisfies the requirements of sub-paragraph (a), works or is based at a different establishment and satisfies those requirements.

The terms of regulation 2 are such that they significantly limit the scope of permissible comparisons. Of particular note is the fact that a part-time worker is only able to compare him/herself with a full-time worker employed "under the same type of contract".

Regulation 2(3) sets out the circumstances in which employment will be treated as being under a different type of contract. In essence a distinction is made between "employees" and "workers" and between those engaged on a fixed term contract and those who are not. Those employed under a "contract of apprenticeship" are also to be treated as on a different contract from a "normal" full-time worker. It is not uncommon for part-time workers to be engaged on a different type of contract from that of full-time workers, even where the work which is done is identical or similar—where that is the case no valid comparison will be possible. The need to make this "like for like" comparison acts as an early stage barrier which will prevent a claim proceeding even where the detrimental treatment complained of is due to the fact that an individual works part-time and the employer is not able to justify the treatment in question. Another way of approaching this whole issue would have been to allow comparisons to be made between individuals on different types of contract with the employer being able to put forward the different nature of the two contracts as justification for the differential treatment. It would then be for a tribunal to decide whether the contractual differences *did* justify the differential treatment in question.

As currently framed, the Regulations provide something of an incentive to employers to engage part-time workers on different types of contracts from those which apply to full-time workers. That could be seen as undermining the purpose of the whole exercise, at least so far as the Framework Agreement is concerned, which was to ensure that part-time workers are treated in the same way as full-time workers unless a distinction in treatment can be justified.

It is also worth noting that, subject to what is said in paragraph 7.06 below, there is no scope for hypothetical comparisons to be made—in other words a part-time worker cannot argue that if there had been a comparable full-time worker employed then he/she would have been treated differently in respect of the matter giving rise to the complaint. Furthermore, a comparison is only allowed between individuals employed by the same employer. There is no scope for comparisons between associated employers, as there is in the Equal Pay Act 1970, nor for comparisons with workers employed by another employer. While the latter is not a phenomenon we may be used to in the United Kingdom it is more common in other European states where industry wide collective agreements are not unusual. The Framework Agreement actually states that "Where there is no comparable full-time worker in the same establishment, the comparison shall be made by reference to the applicable collective agreement or, where there is no applicable collective agreement, in accordance with national law, collective agreements or practice". It follows that the extent of the comparisons which could be made are likely to be wider in some other Member States than in the United Kingdom.

Overall, neither European sex discrimination law nor equal pay law adopts such a restrictive approach to the comparison which is permissible, the consequence being that few complainants will rely simply on the Regulations when bringing a claim unless they have no alternative.

Workers who move from full to part-time work

A new regulation[11] was added between the first and final version of 7.06 the Regulations to deal with the position of full-time workers who move to part-time work (whether under a new or varied contract). In these circumstances the worker will be able to compare their part-time conditions to those which applied under the previous full-time contract.[12]

Similarly, the final version of the Regulations contains a provision, which was not in the earlier draft version, dealing with the position of workers returning part-time after absence of less than 12 months who previously worked in a full-time capacity.[13] Workers in this situation who return to the same job or a job at the same level (whether under the same contract or not) on less than full-time hours are entitled to compare their part-time conditions with those which applied when they worked full time.

Both regulation 3 and 4 seek to protect those who move from full to part-time working from detriment, thereby potentially encouraging

---

[11] reg. 3.
[12] In effect, under regs 3 and 4, the part-time worker is entitled to act on the basis that there is a comparable full-time worker employed under the terms that applied to her/him immediately before s/he became part-time.
[13] reg. 4.

moves of this type. This is in accordance with the objectives of the parent Directive and was a matter which appeared to be completely overlooked in the first draft Regulations which were issued.

It is envisaged that those returning from maternity leave, parental leave, career breaks etc. will benefit from these provisions which allow for a form of self-comparison. However, it must be stressed that the Regulations do not give workers a legal right to move from full-time to part-time work. The Government has considered introducing such a right but, to date, has declined to do so. This contrasts with the situation in Germany where there is such a legal right.

Right to receive a written statement of reasons for less favourable treatment

7.07   A worker who considers that his employer may have breached regulation 5[14] is entitled to make a written request for a written statement giving particulars of the reasons for the treatment.[15] In the draft Regulations the employer was given 14 days to respond to such a request by providing a "written statement giving particulars of the reason for the treatment". That period has been increased in the final version of the Regulations to 21 days. The Government suggests that the increased period will give both parties a chance to establish the facts and lessen the likelihood of a claim being taken to an employment tribunal.

The extent of the information which should be provided by an employer in response to such a request is not specified. In the event that the treatment was related to the worker's part-time status the issue arises of whether the employer should simply make that bald assertion or set out any objective justification on which it relies in that event. It is submitted that the latter approach is more sensible, not least because the provision of more detailed information on the rationale for the less favourable treatment may lead to the worker deciding not to pursue a claim to an employment tribunal. Written statements of this type by an employer are specifically stated to be "admissible as evidence" in any proceedings and a tribunal is entitled to draw inferences from a statement which is "evasive or equivocal" (in the same manner as they currently do under the s.74, SDA and s.65, RRA questionnaire procedures).

Protection against victimisation

7.08   Regulation 7(1) specifies that "an employee" will be treated as automatically unfairly dismissed if the reason for the dismissal (or, where there is more than one, the principle reason) is one of those set out in regulation 7(3). No qualifying period of service is necessary to make such a claim[16] nor is there any upper age limit imposed in respect of applicants wishing to make such a claim.[17]

---

[14] *i.e.* the right not to be treated less favourably on the ground of part-time status.
[15] reg. 6.
[16] Sched., para. 2(2) to the Regulations, inserting s.108(3)(I) into ERA 1996.
[17] s.109(2)(I), ERA 1996.

Regulation 7(2) states that a "worker" has the right not to be subjected to a detriment by the employer which is done on a ground specified in regulation 7(3). Obviously "workers" are not able to claim unfair dismissal under the Employment Rights Act 1996, that being a right which is restricted to the narrow category of "employees". However, workers who lose their "employment" for a reason set out in regulation 7(3) would be able to make a claim under the detriment provision in regulation 7(2).

The reasons/grounds set out in regulation 7(3) are:

(a) that the worker has—

    (i) brought proceedings against the employer under these Regulations;

    (ii) requested from his employer a written statement of reasons under regulation 6;

    (iii) given evidence or information in connection with such proceedings brought by any worker;

    (iv) otherwise done anything under these Regulations in relation to the employer or any other person;

    (v) alleged that the employer had infringed these Regulations; or

    (vi) refused (or proposed to refuse) to forgo a right conferred on him by these Regulations, or

(b) that the employer believes or suspects that the worker has done or intends to do any of the things mentioned in subparagraph (a).

These provisions are very similar to those which apply in relation to victimisation under the discrimination statutes and, in common with those provisions, protection will not be given where an allegation that a right has been infringed is "false and not made in good faith".

In the event that the reason for the selection of an employee for redundancy is one of those set out in regulation 7(3) the resulting dismissal will also be automatically unfair.[18]

Vicarious liability

Regulation 11 is somewhat confusing as it fails to deal properly with 7.09 the intricacies of the distinction between workers and employees for the purposes of the Regulations. In essence, however, it makes an employer liable for the acts of his/her workers who are acting in the course of employment, unless the employer can show he/she took such steps as were reasonably practicable to prevent the worker doing such acts.[19] It also makes the employer liable in respect of any act done with the authority of the employer by any person acting as the agent of the employer. Again, this provision is similar to that found in discrimination statutes.

---

[18] Sched., para. 2(1) to the Regulations, inserting s.105(7E) into ERA 1996.

[19] Case law under the SDA and RRA will provide useful guidance in relation to the type of steps which would allow the employer to rely upon this statutory defence—see Chap. 3.

Special classes

7.10   Those in Crown employment, House of Commons/Lords staff, and police officers all come within the scope of the Regulations. Members of the armed forces are also covered except in relation to the right to claim unfair dismissal. Those holding judicial office do not fall within the scope of the Regulations.[20]

Complaint to employment tribunal

7.11   A worker who considers that his/her rights have been infringed under regulation 5 or 7(2) can make a complaint to an employment tribunal within three months of the date of the act in respect of which complaint is made.[21] If there is a series of similar acts then the time-limit will run from the last act in the series. The tribunal has a discretion to extend the time-limit where it considers that it is "just and equitable" to do so.

Regulation 8(6) specifies that "Where a worker presents a complaint under this regulation it is for the employer to identify the ground for the less favourable treatment or detriment".

Where a complaint is held to be well founded a tribunal can:

(a) make a declaration as to the rights of the complainant and the employer
(b) order the employer to pay compensation to the complainant
(c) make a recommendation that the employer take action which appears to the tribunal to be reasonable, within a specified period, to obviate or reduce the adverse effect on the complainant of any matter to which the complaint relates.

Any compensation which is awarded is to be such as the tribunal considers just and equitable in all the circumstances having regard to:

(a) the infringement to which the complaint relates, and
(b) any loss attributable to the infringement.

In the case of less favourable treatment (or subjection to a detriment) under regulation 5, the assessment of loss should have regard to the pro rata principle unless this is inappropriate. The loss will include any expenses reasonably incurred by the complainant as a result of the infringement and loss of any benefit which he/she might reasonably have expected to have had but for the infringement. Where there is an infringement of rights conferred by regulation 5, compensation is not to include a sum for injury to feelings.[22] By implication then, it would seem that where damages are awarded under regulation 7(2) (subjection to detriment for doing a "protected" act) compensation for injury to feelings can be awarded. However, it would appear that if you are dismissed for doing a "protected" act and make a complaint of unfair

---

[20] regs 12—17 inclusive.
[21] reg. 8.
[22] reg. 8(11).

dismissal under the provisions of the ERA 1996[23] you are *not* entitled to compensation for injury to feelings. In ascertaining loss the tribunal is entitled to take account of a failure to mitigate loss and in the event of the act complained of having been caused or contributed to by the actions of the complainant the tribunal is entitled to reduce compensation by such proportion as it considers to be just and equitable in the circumstances.[24] If an employer fails, without reasonable justification, to comply with a recommendation made by a tribunal the tribunal can make an order of compensation at that point or, if it has already made such an order, increase the amount of compensation awarded.[25]

Regulation 8(8) places a two year limit on the period which may be taken into account when establishing the loss of a worker who complains about the terms on which he/she is afforded access to an occupational pension scheme or about treatment under the rules of such a scheme. It is submitted that this is not legally sustainable given the terms of the decisions of the ECJ and House of Lords in *Preston v. Wolverhampton Healthcare NHS Trust*[26] and that the Regulations will require to be amended to deal with this point. In the meantime, workers who can, will bring a pension related complaint under equal pay law as well as under the Regulations.

Contracting out

Under the Regulations an employee cannot sign away his or her rights 7.12 to complain to an employment tribunal unless specific conditions are met. A compromise agreement or ACAS COT3 would therefore be strongly advisable if an employer is thinking of settling a complaint made under the Regulations.[27]

Non-statutory guidance

The Department of Trade and Industry has also issued a non-statutory 7.13 Guidance document with the Regulations to provide further information on complying with the law. It also offers examples of how to adopt best practice in relation to part-time working. The document is divided into two sections—Compliance Guidance and Best Practice Guidance.

The compliance section gives a number of examples of issues that should be addressed to comply with the Regulations, including:

- In the reorganisation of workloads, part-time workers should be not be treated less favourably than full-time workers, unless such treatment can be objectively justified.
- Previous or current part-time status should not of itself constitute a barrier to promotion to a post, whether that post is full or part-time.
- Part-time workers should be able to participate, on a pro rata basis in profit sharing or share option schemes and

---

[23] But not so if a complaint is made of victimisation under the SDA.
[24] reg. 8(12) and (13).
[25] reg. 8(14).
[26] See Chap. 4 for further discussion.
[27] reg. 9.

other benefits such as subsidised mortgages and staff dis-
counts, available for full-time staff, unless there are objective grounds for excluding them.
- Where a benefit, such as health insurance, cannot be applied
  pro rata, this is, in itself, not justification for denying it to
  part-time workers. Objective justification might include, for
  example, the disproportionate cost to the operation.

The Best Practice Guidance focuses on widening access to part time
work including best practice in dealing with requests to transfer from full
to part-time work and increasing the range of work which can be done
on a part-time basis. Factors relevant in considering a request to work
part-time are stated in the Guidance to include:

- Whether someone needs to be present in the post during all
  hours of work
- Whether the post can be filled as a job share
- Whether all the necessary work can be done in the hours
  requested
- Whether the job can be redefined to make it easier to do
  part-time
- Whether there is another job at a similar level the worker
  can do part-time
- How much it would cost to recruit and train a replacement
  if the worker left
- What benefits the organisation would obtain from a part-
  time arrangement
- The effect of such an arrangement upon other members of
  staff

In addition employers are advised to:

- Maximise the range of posts designated as suitable for part-
  time working or job sharing
- Effectively circulate information about vacancies
- Consider methods through which transfers between part-
  time and full-time work can be facilitated
- Monitor the organisation's use of part-time workers where
  possible
- Ensure the training is arranged in a way that is convenient
  to part-time workers

One particular matter covered in the Compliance section does help to
illuminate a potential difficulty which arises in relation to regulation
5(4). That regulation specifies that part-time workers do not have the
right to claim less favourable treatment if the employer denies them
premium overtime rates when they work beyond their part-time hours.
Overtime will only be payable once the part-time worker has exceeded
the number of hours which the comparable full-time worker is required
to work in the period. This is in accordance with the decision of the ECJ

in *Stadt Lengerich v. Helmig.*[28] However, neither this regulation nor *Helmig* dealt with the matter of premium payments for unsocial hours. It is not unusual for an employer to pay time and a half for week day overtime but to pay double time for weekend or other unsocial hours working. Is the part-time worker entitled to the unsocial hours premium? The Compliance Guidance suggests that "In special circumstances, special rates of pay apply. These may include bonus pay, shift allowances, unsocial hours payments or weekend payments. In these cases, part-time workers are entitled to the same hourly rate as a comparable full-time worker".

The Guidance document, which does provide useful assistance for employers, is available from the DTI.

FIXED TERM WORKERS

Fixed term workers merit particular consideration for two reasons. First, 7.14 the fact that they are on a fixed term contract has particular legal ramifications (for example, they may have waived their right to a redundancy payment on expiry of the fixed term). Secondly, figures from the E.U. Labour Force Survey indicate that the use of such contracts has been on the increase in recent years in Member States. This increased usage has been a catalytic force behind the development of E.U. legislation in this area.[29]

Put simply, under domestic law as it currently stands a fixed term 7.15 contract will exist when an employer and employee agree at the outset of the contractual term that it will end on a particular date. To qualify as a fixed term contract the duration of the contract must be certain. Contracts of this type can be confused with contracts for a particular purpose; this latter type of contract will be discharged when the purpose of the contract has been achieved, whenever that may be, this date being indefinite. Put this way, the distinction between the two types of contract may seem simple enough. However, there was a lack of clarity in respect of this distinction in case law authority for a time which was only resolved by the Court of Appeal in *Wiltshire County Council v. NATFHE.*[30] In considering conflicting authorities which existed at EAT level Lord Denning indicated that the view of Kilner-Brown J. in the case of *Ryan v. Shipboard Maintenance Ltd*[31] was to be preferred to that of Phillips J. (who had decided the *Wiltshire CC* case at EAT level). Lord Denning summarised the arguments as follows:

> "Phillips J said that a contract of employment which came to an end on the happening of an **uncertain** [author's emphasis] future event would be a contract for a 'fixed term'. For example, he said a contract of employment:

---

[28] Joined Cases C-399/92; C-409/92; C-425/92; C-34/93; C-50/93 and C-78/93; [1994] ECR I-5227; [1995] I.R.L.R. 216, ECJ.
[29] See the E.C. Fixed Term Work Directive (99/70/EC) which is discussed later in this chapter.
[30] [1980] I.R.L.R. 198, CA.
[31] [1980] I.R.L.R. 16; [1980] I.C.R. 88

'for the duration of the present government, or during the life of the present Sovereign, or for some other period capable of being determined by reference to prescribed tests.'
would be a contract for a fixed term.

That would be a very important extension of the words 'fixed term'. It was disapproved in the recent case of *Ryan v. Shipboard Maintenance Ltd* [1980] IRLR 16, [1980] ICR 88. Kilner-Brown J ventured to query the proposition of Phillips J. He declined to follow it. In that case a man was employed as a repairer on a ship, either in port or on the high seas. The job started and finished with the repairing of a ship, after which he received unemployment pay. The question was whether that was a contract for a fixed term or not. The appeal tribunal held it was not. Kilner-Brown J said:

' . . . we take the view that it is stretching the meaning of the words beyond the intention of Parliament to say that it covers an event which can be identified in character **but cannot be identified with a precise date in the future.**' " [author's emphasis]

By implication, Lord Denning agrees with Kilner-Brown J.'s position. He then went on to examine the provisions of what is now section 95(1)(b) of the Employment Rights Act 1996 which is in the following terms:—

95. Circumstances in which an employee is dismissed
(1) For the purposes of this Part an employee is dismissed by his employer if (and, subject to subsection (2) and section 96, only if)—
(a) . . .,
(b) he is employed under a contract for a fixed term and that term expires without being renewed under the same contract, or
(c) . . .

He considered that it was clear from the terms of the section that the legislature thought that in order to be a "fixed term" "there had to be a date stated at the beginning when the contract will expire". He also agreed with the proposition of the Court of Appeal in *Dixon v. BBC*[32] that ". . . a 'fixed term' is sufficiently satisfied if the contract is for a specific stated period".

When discussing what would amount to a contract for a specific purpose Lord Denning referred to the case of a seaman "who is engaged for the duration of a voyage—**and it is completely uncertain how long the voyage will last**" [author's emphasis].

7.16   In normal circumstances, a fixed term contract will terminate by effluxion of time. However, it should be noted that if a contract is specified to be for a fixed term but the employer has the right to terminate it by notice earlier than the term date it will still fall to be categorised as a fixed term contract.[33] In certain circumstances an

---

[32] [1979] I.C.R. 281.
[33] *Dixon v. British Broadcasting Corp* [1979] 2 All E.R. 112; [1979] I.R.L.R. 114; [1979] I.C.R. 281, CA.

employer is obliged to give an employee statutory notice even although the parties entered into a fixed term contract. Specifically, section 86(4) of the ERA states that where a contract is stated to be for a fixed term of one month or less but the employee concerned has actually been employed for three months or more the contract is to be treated as one of indefinite duration for the purposes of the statutory notice provisions set out in section 86. The wording of the provision is actually rather ambiguous—on one reading of it the section might appear to confer a general right to a contract for an indefinite period where there has been continuous employment for three months or more and a fixed term contract has been entered into for a month or less. However, it has been held that the scope of the subsection is constrained by the overall purpose of the section which deals with the right to a minimum period of notice. It is only in relation to rights arising under this section that the contract is to be considered as one of indefinite duration.[34]

As previously indicated the expiry of a fixed term contract without its 7.17 renewal is a dismissal for the purposes of Part X of the ERA 1996 which deals with unfair dismissal. However, the contract of apprenticeship deserves special mention in this context. An apprenticeship (certainly one of the old fashioned variety!) is usually for a predetermined period. Where this is so it will amount to a fixed-term contract. Consequently if the employment is not renewed at the end of the period of apprenticeship that will operate as a dismissal in law.[35] However, that does not mean that an individual who is not retained as a time served tradesman at the end of his apprenticeship will be entitled to a redundancy payment. This is clear from *North East Coast Shiprepairers Ltd,* in which the employment of an apprentice terminated when his apprenticeship came to an end. Under an agreement between the company and the unions setting out the procedure to apply at the end of an apprenticeship, the company would normally have taken the individual on as a journeyman fitter if such work had been available. But at the time the apprenticeship ended there was no work as a journeyman fitter available for him. He was therefore informed, some two weeks before his apprenticeship was due to end, that his contract of apprenticeship would expire on that date and that the company would not be able to offer him employment thereafter. He was given a redundancy payment. The employer then sought to recoup the redundancy payment from the Secretary of State which application was rejected. The employment tribunal and the EAT upheld the decision that the employer was not entitled to recoup the sum since there had been no redundancy. The EAT considered that the tribunal had correctly held that the respondents' failure to offer an apprentice re-engagement as a journeyman when his apprenticeship expired, did not amount to dismissal on grounds of redundancy. The EAT reasoned that the individual's dismissal was due to the fact that his contract of apprenticeship, which was a fixed term contract, had come to an end without being renewed (there being no need for it to be renewed) and he was not offered re-engagement under a different contract of employment as a journeyman fitter. The EAT also

---

[34] *Hay v. Greater Glasgow Health Board,* EAT/1301/97.
[35] *North East Coast Shiprepairers Ltd v. Secretary of State for Employment* [1978] I.R.L.R. 149; [1978] I.C.R. 755, EAT.

held that even if there was an implied term in his contract of employment that at the expiry of his apprenticeship the individual could normally expect to be employed as a journeyman, there was no certainty that he would be so employed and, in any event, such employment would be under a new, different contract of employment.

It will also be very difficult to successfully argue that a dismissal arising from the expiry of a fixed term contract of apprenticeship is unfair. The difficulties arising are evident in *R Small v. Lex Mead Southampton*[36] which, although only a tribunal decision, is illuminating. The applicant was on a four year apprenticeship which expired on May 30, 1976. During his apprenticeship he received a number of warnings. He was dismissed in June 1976 after he repaired a car so badly it went on fire. A tribunal held that he had been dismissed under the provisions equivalent to those found in section 95(1)(b) of the ERA 1996 since his apprenticeship was for a fixed term of four years and that term had expired "without being renewed under the same contract".

The reason for the applicant's dismissal was because his fixed term apprenticeship contract expired "without being renewed under the same contract". Although the applicant was not offered employment as a tradesman after his apprenticeship expired because of dissatisfaction with his capability, that was not the reason for his dismissal. Even if the applicant had been employed as a tradesman, he still would have been dismissed, so far as the relevant statutory provision was concerned, at the end of his apprenticeship because employment as a tradesman would not have amounted to a renewal of his fixed term "under the same contract". This reason—that his apprenticeship contract had expired—amounted to "some other substantial reason" for not renewing his term under the same contract.

In the circumstances it was held that the respondents acted reasonably in dismissing the applicant in this way since there was no reason to renew his apprenticeship for a further term. The tribunal considered that it may well be that Parliament intended that where an apprentice's contract expires, that is a dismissal and cannot give rise to a complaint of unfair dismissal, because the circumstances cannot be envisaged under which an apprentice would be taken on for another term as an apprentice.

> "Were the respondents reasonable to allow his term to expire without renewing it under the same contract? We find that they were. There was no reason to grant him further indentures of apprenticeship for a further term. It may well be that the legislature intended that where an apprentice's contract expires that is a dismissal and cannot give rise to a complaint of unfair dismissal, because one cannot envisage circumstances under which an apprentice would be taken on for another term as an apprentice. As we have found that the employers were acting reasonably, we find that the dismissal was not contrary to the statute and therefore not unfair".

[36] [1977] I.R.L.R. 48, IT.

Consistent with the foregoing is the fact that regulation 16 of the draft Fixed-Term Employees (Prevention of Unfavourable Treatment) Regulations 2001[37] explicitly excludes apprenticeship contracts from the ambit of the Regulations.

Like any other contract of employment, a contract for a fixed term can 7.18 be terminated by mutual consent in which case any non-renewal will not be classified as a dismissal.[38]

Redundancy and Waiver of Rights

Non-renewal of a fixed term contract may amount to a dismissal by 7.19 reason of redundancy.[39] Under section 197(3) of the ERA 1996 an employee engaged under a fixed term contract of two years or more can waive his right to a redundancy payment on the expiry of the contractual term if the waiver is made in writing before the expiry of the term.[40] The section has the practical effect of allowing employers to escape their obligation of making a redundancy payment by issuing successive two-year contracts containing waiver clauses.[41] It is important to note that the waiver will only be valid in relation to rights that would arise where the employee was claiming a redundancy payment in relation to dismissal arising on the ground of non-renewal of the contract. The right to claim a redundancy pay where there is a dismissal for redundancy before the end of the fixed term cannot be excluded.[42] Section 197(5) states that where a fixed term contract is renewed, the waiver in the original contract will not apply to the renewed contract. Any renewal must therefore contain its own waiver clause. As part of its consultation on the implementation of the Fixed Term Workers Directive[43] the Government has indicated that it is considering abolishing the right to use redundancy payment waivers in fixed term contracts.

Additional limitations on the rights of fixed term contract employees

Employees on short duration fixed term contracts are excluded from 7.20 certain other legal rights. For example, an employee employed under a fixed term contract of three months or less is excluded from the right to

---

[37] See later in this chapter.

[38] *Manson and Johnston v. (1) University of Strathclyde and (2) Automated Microscopy Systems,* EAT/356/87. *Cf.* draft reg. 8 of the Fixed-Term Workers (Prevention etc.) Regulations 2001.

[39] s.136(1)(b).

[40] It is almost certain that those subsections of s.197 which are still in force will be repealed in the near future: see the draft of the Fixed-Term Employees (Prevention of Less Favourable Treatment) Regulations 2001, para. (4) of the Schedule thereto. Previously it was also possible to waive one's right to claim unfair dismissal on the expiry of a fixed term contract. However, the ability to exclude unfair dismissal rights in circumstances in which the employee had entered into a fixed term contract was removed by s.18, ERA 1999 in all cases with effect from October 25, 1999, subject to transitional provisions.

[41] See, *e.g. Kingston upon Hull City Council v. Mountain* [1999] I.C.R. 715, EAT where a worker who had been continuously employed from 1976 until 1991 was re-engaged on two successive contracts for a fixed term of two years. Both contracts contained a waiver clause. Despite the fact that there had been an employment relationship from 1976 until 199 there was still no right to a redundancy payment.

[42] *Wallace v. CA Roofing Services Ltd* [1996] I.R.L.R. 435.

[43] See later in this chapter.

a guarantee payment unless s/he has completed a period of three months' continuous employment ending with the day before that for which s/he seeks his guarantee payment.[44] The same group of employees is excluded from the right to payment when medically suspended on certain grounds.[45] While it will therefore be sensible to check, when one is advising on the rights of employees engaged on short duration fixed term contracts that they qualify for any particular right which is sought, it may be that there will be a review of legislative provisions concerning the rights of fixed term contract employees given the developments noted below.

Fixed Term Work Directive

7.21   A Directive bringing into effect a Framework Agreement on fixed term work was adopted in June 1999.[46] Member States were required to implement its provisions in domestic law by July 10, 2001. At the time of writing the United Kingdom has not yet done so. However, the Government has pointed out[47] that the Directive gives Member States which have "special difficulties" up to an extra year to implement. It considers that public consultation on the Directive revealed particular problems with implementation in the United Kingdom. Notwithstanding these difficulties the DTI has issued, in draft, the Fixed-Term Employees (Prevention of Less Favourable Treatment) Regulations 2001.[48] It should be noted that the discussion which follows is based on the draft Regulations. Obviously, the final content of the Regulations may differ from that found in the draft.

The purpose of the Framework Agreement is to (a) improve the quality of fixed term work by ensuring the application of the principle of non-discrimination; and (b) establish a framework to prevent abuse arising from the use of successive fixed term employment contracts or relationships.[49]

Throughout the Framework Agreement reference is made to "workers". Clause 2 of the Agreement specifies that it applies to "fixed-term workers who have an employment contract or employment relationship as defined in law, collective agreements or practice in each Member State. This is the same definition as is used in the Framework Agreement on Part-time Work. Clause 3 of the Agreement defines a fixed term worker as "a person having an employment contract or relationship entered into directly between an employer and a worker where the end of the employment contract or relationship is determined by objective conditions such as reaching a specific date, completing a specific task, or the occurrence of a specific event". This definition is considerably wider than the orthodox position in the United Kingdom where, as noted previously, a distinction is made between fixed term

---

[44] ERA 1996, s.29(2)(a).

[45] ERA 1996, s.65(2)(a).

[46] Directive 99/70/EC.

[47] See DTI consultation paper on fixed term contracts, available from the DTI website noted below.

[48] Hereinafter, the Fixed Term Regulations, available at http://www.dti.gov.uk/er/fixed/draftregs.pdf

[49] Cl. 1 of Framework Agreement.

contracts and those for a specific purpose which are of uncertain duration.[50] The draft Fixed Term Regulations appear to adopt the approach of the Directive in that they merge these concepts, defining a "fixed-term contract" for the purpose of the Regulations as one which is "made for a specific term which is fixed in advance", or which "terminates on the completion of a particular task or upon the occurrence or non-occurrence of any other specified event".[51]

It is notable that the draft Regulations limit the scope of the protection to "employees" rather than to workers with "employee" being narrowly defined as an individual who works or worked under a contract of employment which, in turn, is defined as a contract of service or apprenticeship.[52] This is in contrast to the Part-Time Workers (Prevention etc.) Regulations 2000, the scope of which, as noted above, was extended from employees to the wider group "workers" after consultation on the draft Regulations. It should also be noted, despite the terms of the definition in the draft Fixed Term Employees Regulations, that those employed under a contract of apprenticeship are specifically excluded from the scope of the draft Regulations.[53] Agency workers are also excluded as are those on government training schemes and work experience connected to higher education.[54] Such exclusions are specifically allowed under the terms of the Framework Agreement.[55] However, it remains to be seen if the restriction to "employees" as narrowly defined in the draft Regulations will be found to be in accordance with the requirements of the Framework Agreement (and, accordingly, the Directive). It is also proposed, in terms of special classes of person, that the armed services are excluded from the scope of the Regulations while police officers and those in Crown employment are included.[56]

Leaving aside the issue of scope of coverage, the draft Regulations have a good deal in common with the Part-time Workers (Prevention etc.) Regulations 2000.

The Directive and the draft Regulations confer on a fixed-term employee the right not to be treated in a less favourable manner, in relation to the terms of her/his contract or by being subjected to a detriment, than a comparable employee who is not employed on a fixed term contract solely because s/he is a fixed term employee unless such treatment is objectively justified.[57] However, this provision does not extend to the amount of pay due under the contract or occupational pension scheme rights. While at first sight the exclusion of pay may seem startling this is explained by the fact that the United Kingdom Government considers that the parent Directive, due to its legal basis, does not apply to pay. Any inclusion of a provision in the Regulations which extended to pay would therefore be *ultra vires*. The Government is consulting on whether it needs to introduce primary legislation to fill this gap.

---

[50] See *Wiltshire CC v. NATHFE* above.
[51] Draft reg. 1(2).
[52] Draft reg. 1(2).
[53] Draft reg. 16.
[54] Draft regs 17 and 18.
[55] Framework Agreement Cl. 2(2).
[56] Draft regs 11—15.
[57] Cl. 4 of the Directive and draft reg. 2.

Under draft regulation 3, an employee who considers that s/he may have been less favourably treated on the ground of fixed term contract status is entitled to receive, on request, a written statement of reasons for the treatment in question. Such a statement can be used in evidence in tribunal proceedings under the Regulations.

Draft regulation 4 gives a fixed term contract employee the right to be informed of suitable available vacancies while draft regulation 5 makes it automatically unfair[58] to dismiss an employee or subject her/him to a detriment for any of the following reasons:

The employee has—

- Brought proceedings against the employee under the Regulations;
- Requested from his employer a written statement of reasons under regulation 3;
- Given evidence or information in connection with such proceedings brought by any employee;
- Otherwise done anything under the Regulations in relation to the employer or anyone else;
- Alleged that the employer had infringed the Regulations;
- Refused (or proposed to refuse) to forgo a right under the Regulations; or
- That the employer believes or suspects that the employee has done or intends to do any of the things mentioned in sub-paragraph (a).

Clause 5 of the Framework Agreement requires the introduction of measures to prevent the abuse by employers of fixed term contracts. Its terms are reflected in draft regulation 7 which states that where an employee has been continuously employed for four years or more on fixed term contract(s) and is then employed on another fixed term contract without a break in continuity this last contract is to regarded for all purposes as a contract for an indefinite duration.[59]

Draft regulation 6 confers jurisdiction on employment tribunals to hear complaints for breach of draft regulations 2 (less favourable treatment), 4(1) (provision of information on vacancies) or 5(3) (right not to be subjected to detriment). The procedural conditions applying are set out in the draft regulation 6. These are in fairly standard terms, specifying:

- A three month time-limit for lodging claims, with a just and equitable extension—detailed provisions are set out in respect of the date from which the three month period will run
- That if a complaint is successful a tribunal can make a declaration of rights, order the employer to pay compensation to the complainant and/or recommend that the

---

[58] Dismissal includes the failure to renew a fixed term contract for any of the reasons specified in sub-clause (4) of draft reg. 5.

[59] No period of continuous employment before the date on which the regulations come into force will count for the purposes of computing the four year period—draft reg. 7(2).

employer take, within a specified period, action appearing to the tribunal to be reasonable for the purpose of obviating or reducing the adverse effect on the complainant of any matter to which the complaint relates. It should be noted that compensation for less favourable treatment under draft regulation 2 is not to include an award of solatium.[60] The draft Regulations reflect the terms of the Part Time Workers (Prevention etc.) Regulations etc. in relation to duty to mitigate and contributory conduct. There are also identical provisions in relation to the liability of employers and principals.[61]

The implementation of the Regulations will affect a sizeable number of employees given that estimates based on the Labour Force Survey suggest that the number of people working on fixed term contracts in the United Kingdom is between 1.1 and 1.3 million with the number rising by approximately seven per cent between 1994 and 2000. The Government estimates that:

- 25,000–53,000 employees will benefit from proposals to end discrimination in (non-pay) benefits by £19–40 million. Legislation to cover pay and pensions would benefit employees by a further £51–124 million.
- Improved access to training would benefit fixed term employees by £33–76 million and could have benefits to business of £26–180 million per year from increased productivity.
- Measures to prevent abuses of fixed term contracts would benefit 2,000–17,000 fixed term employees by £3–16 million, depending on the policy option chosen (if the duration of successive fixed term contracts was limited to 3, 4 or 5 years).
- Removing the redundancy waiver for fixed term contracts would benefit 52,000–117,000 employees by £28–70 million, depending on the option chosen to prevent abuses.

In addition, it is acknowledged that there may be other benefits, such as greater job security or greater willingness to work on a fixed term contract, that are difficult to quantify.[62]

---

[60] Draft reg. 6(10).
[61] Draft reg. 10.
[62] Government Regulatory Impact Assessment on the draft regulations, available on the DTI website.

CHAPTER 8

CONSTITUTION AND JURISDICTION OF EMPLOYMENT TRIBUNALS

CONSTITUTION

8.01 Employment tribunals, which were first established in 1964, are creatures of statute. The Employment Tribunals Act 1996[1] is the first separate primary legislation devoted to the constitution, powers and procedures of employment tribunals. Section 1 of that Act restates the power of the Secretary of State to make provision for the establishment of employment tribunals.

Detailed provisions governing the constitution and the broad outline of the procedures to be adopted by employment tribunals are set out in the Employment Tribunals (Constitution and Rules of Procedure) (Scotland) Regulations 2001.[2] The principal Rules of Procedure governing Employment Tribunals in Scotland are to be found in Schedule 1 to the Regulations. In cases designated as raising issues of national security the rules set out in Schedule 2 amend the provisions of Schedule 1. Similarly, in equal value cases under the Equal Pay Act, Schedule 1 is amended by the provisions in Schedule 3. Special rules apply to Levy Appeals (set out in Sched. 4), appeals against notices issued under the Health and Safety at Work Act 1974 (set out in Sched. 5), and appeals against non-discrimination notices (set out in Sched. 6). Tribunal procedure in England and Wales is governed by the Employment Tribunals (Constitution and Rules of Procedure) Regulations 2001, which are in similar but not identical terms to the regulations applicable in Scotland.[3] Presiding over the system is the President of the Employment Tribunals (Scotland) who is appointed by the Lord President and who must be a solicitor or advocate of at least seven years standing.[4] There are also Regional Chairmen who are responsible for the administration of justice by tribunals in an area specified by the President.[5]

The Central Office of Employment Tribunals is located in Glasgow and there are also full-time tribunal offices in Edinburgh, Dundee and Aberdeen. Cases are also heard regularly in Inverness and, where

---

[1] Hereinafter ETA. The Employment Tribunals Act 1996 received royal assent as the Industrial Tribunals Act 1996. The title of the Act was changed, and industrial tribunals were generally renamed "employment tribunals" by the Employment Rights (Dispute Resolution) Act 1998 (c. 8), s.1.

[2] S.I. 2001 No. 1170, hereinafter "2001 Regulations".

[3] S.I. 2001 No. 1171.

[4] 2001 Regulations, reg. 3.

[5] 2001 Regulations, reg. 8.

necessary, suitable accommodation will be hired elsewhere so that cases may be heard locally.

Most cases are heard by a full tribunal made up of a legally qualified 8.02 chairman, who must be an advocate or solicitor of at least seven years standing,[6] and two lay members, one from a panel nominated by trade unions/organisations representative of employees and one from a panel nominated by organisations representative of employers (such as the CBI).[7] Proceedings which are normally to be determined by a three member tribunal can, with the consent of both parties, be heard and determined in the absence of any one member other than the chairman.[8]

Tribunals are often referred to as "Industrial Juries"[9] and the lay members are encouraged to make use of their industrial knowledge and experience in the decision-making process. Although it is the role of the chairman to set out the detailed reasoning supporting the decision of the tribunal, each member has a vote of equal weight and there can occasionally be circumstances where the lay members outvote the chairman. Where a decision is made by a majority there is normally a dissenting opinion contained in the written decision. The vast majority of decisions are, however, unanimous.

The Trade Union Reform and Employment Rights Act 1993 intro- 8.03 duced changes which enabled certain types of case to be heard by a chairman sitting alone. The type of proceedings which can be heard by a chairman sitting alone are now listed in section 4(3) of the ETA and include claims in respect of unlawful deduction from wages, breach of contract cases, certain proceedings under the National Minimum Wage Act 1998, proceedings where the respondent does not, or has ceased, to contest the case and cases where both parties have given their written consent to the case being heard by a chairman sitting alone. However, such cases may still be heard by a full tribunal if the chairman considers this appropriate, bearing in mind certain criteria.[10] The EAT in Scotland has, on a number of occasions, been critical of decisions made by chairmen sitting alone and has pointed to the role which lay members can play in ensuring that a decision is in accordance with the practicalities of industrial life. For example, in *Hussman Manufacturing Limited v. William Weir*[11] Lord Johnston observed: "this is another example of a case of a Chairman sitting alone, without the benefit of input from lay members which might have been quite critical on the question of good industrial relations in the context of the practicalities in operating a plant agreement. We once again have, therefore, to observe that we find this situation unsatisfactory, and inappropriate".

Aside from the right to hear certain specified types of cases alone, a chairman also has a general power, subject to limited exceptions, to do any act required or authorised by the 2001 Rules. This includes striking out of proceedings, giving directions, conjoining cases and determining

---

[6] 2001 Regulations, reg. 5. Note the term "chairman" is a legal term which is applied whether the incumbent is male or female.
[7] 2001 Regulations, reg. 5(1)(b) and (c).
[8] 2001 Regulations, reg. 9(3).
[9] *Williams v. Compair Maxam Ltd* [1982] I.C.R. 156, EAT.
[10] See ETA, s.4(5).
[11] [1998] I.R.L.R. 288, EAT.

issues of entitlement to bring or contest proceedings.[12] Where a chairman has jurisdiction to make a decision on his own he can exercise the same powers as the full tribunal. In particular, he is entitled to hear oral evidence and submissions, to decide contested issues of fact and to consider documentary evidence.[13]

JURISDICTION

8.04 Employment tribunals can only exercise the jurisdiction conferred upon them by statute[14] although it should be noted that they are under a duty to give effect to European Community law.[15] An employment tribunal must always be satisfied that it has jurisdiction to hear a particular complaint, even if no jurisdictional point is raised by the parties to the proceedings. Furthermore, even if a jurisdictional point has not been raised before an employment tribunal it can be raised on review or appeal.[16] In considering whether it has jurisdiction to hear a particular complaint an employment tribunal must be satisfied that:

1. It has territorial jurisdiction;
2. It has jurisdiction under a particular statute to hear a claim of the type being made; and
3. All the jurisdictional rules set out in the relevant statutory provisions have been met.

For example, the tribunal must be satisfied that the claim has been made in time or that an extension of time has been granted (where appropriate), the applicant has the required status to make a claim (for example it may be necessary for the applicant to have been employed under a "contract of employment" as defined in a particular statute), and that the employer is actually required to comply with the provisions of the legislation under which the claim is made (for example, employers employing fewer than 15 people are not obliged to comply with the employment provisions of the Disability Discrimination Act 1995).[17]

TERRITORIAL JURISDICTION

8.05 Employment tribunals in Scotland have jurisdiction to hear a claim where:

---

[12] r.15, set out in Sched. 1.

[13] *Tsangacos v. Amalgamated Chemicals Ltd* [1997] I.R.L.R. 4, EAT disapproving of *Mobbs v. Nuclear Electric Plc* [1996] I.R.L.R. 536, EAT.

[14] ETA, s.2.

[15] *Secretary of State for Scotland v. Wright and Hannah* [1991] I.R.L.R. 187, EAT. See also *Biggs v Somerset County Council* [1996] I.R.L.R. 203, CA in relation to the extent of that duty.

[16] *Russell v. Elmdon Freight Terminal Ltd* [1989] I.C.R. 629, EAT. *See Crees v. Royal London Insurance* [1997] I.R.L.R. 85, EAT for an unsuccessful attempt to raise various new points before the EAT by arguing that they were jurisdictional issues.

[17] This is likely to change in the future as a result of the E.C. Framework Directive (2000/78/EC).

(a) the respondent or one of the respondents resides or carries on business in Scotland; or

(b) the proceedings relate to a contract of employment the place of execution or performance of which is in Scotland; or

(c) the proceedings are to determine a question which has been referred to the tribunal by a sheriff in Scotland.[18]

Rule 21 allows the President or a Regional Chairman, with the consent of the President of the Employment Tribunals (England and Wales), to direct that proceedings be transferred to the Office of Employment Tribunals (England and Wales) although parties must have the opportunity to show cause why such a direction should not be made. A similar provision exists in relation to the transfer of proceedings from England or Wales to Scotland.[19]

TRIBUNAL JURISDICTION AND COMMUNITY LAW

Having stated that the jurisdiction of employment tribunals is derived 8.06 entirely from a range of statutory provisions it is important to note that for a number of years it was considered that tribunals also had jurisdiction to hear "free-standing" claims under European Community law.[20] More recently, the Court of Appeal has decided that this is not the case and that tribunals only have jurisdiction to consider the provisions of Community law in claims which are made under domestic statute.[21] However, if the provisions of Community law are in conflict with domestic law, an employment tribunal, like any other domestic court, must disapply the provisions of domestic law to the extent that they are incompatible with Community law.[22]

Following upon the decision in *Francovich v. Italian Republic*,[23] in which it was held that individuals who suffered loss as a result of the failure of a Member State to implement the provisions of Community law could sue the state for damages, there was speculation about whether employment tribunals could hear such claims. However, in *Potter v. Secretary of State for Employment*[24] the Court of Appeal held, bearing in mind that employment tribunals are creatures of statute with purely statutory jurisdiction, that a *Francovich* claim must be pursued in the same way as any other claim for damages in the ordinary courts.

---

[18] 2001 Regulations, reg. 11(5).

[19] See Employment Tribunals (Constitution and Rules of Procedure) Regulations 2001 (S.I. 2001 No. 1171).

[20] See *Secretary of State for Scotland v. Wright and Hannah* [1991] I.R.L.R. 187, EAT; *Rankin v. British Coal* [1993] I.R.L.R. 69, EAT.

[21] *Biggs v. Somerset County Council* [1996] I.R.L.R. 203, CA; *Barber v. Staffordshire County Council* [1996] I.R.L.R. 209, CA.

[22] *Biggs*, above.

[23] [1992] I.R.L.R. 84, ECJ.

[24] [1997] I.R.L.R. 21, CA (*sub nom. Secretary of State for Employment v. Mann*).

STATUTORY CLAIMS WHICH CAN BE MADE BEFORE AN EMPLOYMENT
TRIBUNAL

8.07 The rules governing the range of individuals, in terms of employment status and the like, entitled to bring particular claims are outlined in the chapters dealing with the substantive law governing statutory rights. The following sets out the statutory provisions which endow employment tribunals with jurisdiction to hear claims. The time-limits which apply to such claims are also specified:

Equal Pay Act 1970

8.08 Section 2: Claims in respect of breach of an equality clause. Such claims must be made within six months of the termination of employment.[25]

Employment Agencies Act 1973

8.09 Section 3A: Application by Secretary of State for an order prohibiting a person carrying on an employment agency or business. No time-limit.

Section 3C: Application by a person to whom a prohibition order applies for variation or revocation of the order. No time-limit applies.

Health and Safety at Work, etc. Act 1974

8.10 Section 24: Appeal against improvement or prohibition notice. Appeal should be made within 21 days of the date of service of the notice against which appeal is made.*[26] (See paragraph 8.28 as to the use of "*" in this text.)

Sex Discrimination Act 1975

8.11 Section 63: Complaints of discrimination on the ground of sex or marital status in the employment field. Complaints should be made within three months of the date when the act complained of was done.**[27]

Section 68: Appeal against non-discrimination notice in respect of acts within the jurisdiction of the employment tribunal. Appeals should be made within six weeks of service of the notice.[28]

Section 72: Application by the EOC in respect of discriminatory advertisements, instructions and/or pressure to discriminate relating to a case based upon the provisions of Part II of the Act. Case to be brought within six months of when the act complained of was done.**[29]

Section 73: Complaints by the EOC taking the form of "preliminary action" to establish that a person has done an act within the jurisdiction of the employment tribunal prior to action being taken under section

---

[25] EqPA, s.2(4), *Preston v. Wolverhampton Healthcare NHS Trust (No. 2)* [2001] I.R.L.R. 237; *National Power plc v. Young* [2001] I.R.L.R. 32.

[26] 2001 Regulations, Sched. 5, r.2.

[27] SDA, s.76(1).

[28] SDA, s.68(1).

[29] SDA, s.76(3).

71(1)[30] or section 72(4).[31] Proceedings under section 73 must be commenced within six months of when the act complained of was done.**[32]

Section 77: Complaint that a term of (a) an employment contract (b) a collective agreement or (c) a rule applied by: (1) an employer to an employee; (2) organisations of workers, employers and professional bodies to members or potential members; or[33] (3) bodies conferring trade or professional qualifications, is void. No applicable time-limit.[34]

Race Relations Act 1976

Section 54: Complaint of racial discrimination in the employment 8.12 field. Complaint should be made within three months of when the act complained of was done.**[35]

Section 59: Appeal against non-discrimination notice where the requirement imposed relates to acts which are within the jurisdiction of an employment tribunal. Appeals should be made not later than six weeks after the discrimination notice is served.[36]

Section 63: Proceedings by the CRE in respect of discriminatory advertisements, instructions or pressure to discriminate arising in a case based on any provision of Part II of the RRA (discrimination in the employment field). Proceedings should be commenced within six months of when the act to which the application relates was done.**[37]

Section 64: Complaints by the CRE taking the form of "preliminary action" to establish that an act has been done within the jurisdiction of an employment tribunal prior to a sheriff court application for interdict under section 62(1) or section 63(4) of the RRA. Complaint should be made within six months of the act in respect of which complaint is made.**[38]

Safety Representatives and Safety Committee Regulations 1977[39]

Regulation 11: Complaint by a safety representative that his employer has failed to give him time off with pay to perform his functions under the Regulations and the Health and Safety at Work Act 1974. Such a complaint should normally be made within three months of the failure in respect of which complaint is made.*[40]

---

[30] Application for an interdict to prevent persistent discrimination.
[31] Application for an interdict to prevent further breach of ss.38, 39 or 40 by an individual.
[32] SDA, s.76(4).
[33] Also, SDA 1986, s.6.
[34] SDA 1986, s.6(4A).
[35] RRA, s.68(1).
[36] RRA, s.59(1).
[37] RRA, s.68(4).
[38] RRA, s.68(5).
[39] S.I. 1977 No. 500.
[40] reg. 11(2).

Transfer of Undertakings (Protection of Employment) Regulations 1981[41]

8.13 Regulation 11(1): Complaint by a trade union, other employee representative or affected employees that an employer has failed to comply with regulation 10 (which imposes various duties in respect of consultation with employee representatives on the transfer of an undertaking). Complaint should be presented within three months of the completion of the relevant transfer.*[42]

Regulation 11(5): Complaint by an employee that the transferor or transferee has failed to pay compensation to an employee where such payment has been ordered as a result of a failure to consult. Complaints should be presented within three months of the date of the tribunal compensation order.*[43]

Industrial Training Act 1982

8.14 Section 12: Appeal against assessment of a training levy. Appeal to be made within timescale set out in the levy order.

Sex Discrimination Act 1986

8.15 Section 6(4A): Complaints relating to invalidity of discriminatory terms and rules—see SDA 1975, section 77.

Trade Union and Labour Relations (Consolidation) Act 1992

8.16 Section 66: Complaint by an individual who claims to have been unjustifiably disciplined by a trade union in breach of section 64 of the Act. Normally, a complaint should be presented within three months of the making of the determination claimed to amount to unjustifiable discipline.[44]

Section 67: Application for compensation following upon a declaration that a complaint under section 66 of the Act is well founded. Application to be made no sooner than four weeks after the declaration and no later than six months after the declaration.[45]

Section 68A(1): Complaint by a worker that his employer has made a deduction from his wages in breach of section 68 of the Act (which prevents an employer from making unauthorised or excessive union subscription deductions from wages). Complaint should normally be made within three months of date of payment of wages from which deduction (or last deduction in a series of deductions) was made.*[46]

Section 137(2): Complaint of refusal of employment as a result of membership/non-membership of a trade union or on related grounds in breach of section 137(1) of the Act. Complaint should normally be made within three months of the conduct to which the complaint relates.*[47]

---

[41] S.I. 1981 No. 1794.
[42] reg. 11(8)(a).
[43] reg. 11(8)(b).
[44] Trade Union and Labour Relations (Consolidation) Act 1992, hereinafter TULCRA, s.66(2).
[45] s.67(3).
[46] s.68A(1).
[47] s.139(1).

Section 138(2): Complaint by persons refused any service of an employment agency because of membership/non-membership of a trade union or on related grounds. Complaint should normally be made within three months of the date of the conduct to which the complaint relates.*[48]

Section 146(5): Complaint by an employee that he has been subjected to a detriment by his employer on the grounds that he is a member of a union, is seeking to be so, has or wishes to take part in union activities or because the employer is seeking to compel the employee to become a member of a union. Complaints should normally be made within three months of the action (or last in a series of actions) to which the complaint relates.*[49]

Section 161(1): Application for interim relief in cases where it is alleged that a dismissal is in breach of section 152 of the Act, which makes it unfair to dismiss on grounds related to union membership or activities. The application should be made within seven days of the effective date of termination.[50]

Section 168(4): Complaint that an employer has failed to permit an employee who is an official of a trade union recognised by the employer to take time off for union duties. Complaint should normally be made within three months of the date of the failure.*[51]

Section 169(5): Complaint that an employer has failed to pay an employee given time off under the provisions of section 168. Complaint should normally be made within three months of the date of the failure to pay.*[52]

Section 170(4): Complaint that an employer has failed, contrary to section 170(1), to permit an employee who is a member of an independent trade union recognised by the employer to take a reasonable amount of time off during working hours to take part in union activities. Complaints should normally be made within three months of the failure.*[53]

Section 174(5): Complaint that an individual has been excluded or expelled from a trade union in breach of section 174. Complaints should normally be made within six months of the exclusion or expulsion.*[54]

Section 176(2): Application for compensation by an individual declared to have been expelled or excluded from a union in breach of section 174. Application should be made no sooner than four weeks after the declaration and no later than six months from the date of the declaration.[55]

Section 189(1): Complaint that an employer has breached section 188 or section 188A by failing to consult and inform employee representatives/union/employees when multiple redundancies proposed, or by failing to perform any of the duties imposed in relation to the

---

[48] *ibid.*
[49] s.147.
[50] s.161(2).
[51] s.171.
[52] *ibid.*
[53] *ibid.*
[54] s.175.
[55] s.176(3).

election, by affected employees, of employee representatives. If upheld, such a complaint may lead to a "protective award". Complaints should normally be made before the date of the last dismissal or within three months of that date.*[56]

Section 192(1): Complaint by an employee that an employer has failed to pay remuneration due under a protective award. Complaint should normally be made within three months of the day (or last of the days) in respect of which there was a failure to pay remuneration.*[57]

Pension Schemes Act 1993

Section 126(1): Complaints that the Secretary of State has failed, contrary to section 124, to pay unpaid contributions to pension schemes in the event of an employer's insolvency. Such a complaint should normally be made within three months of the communication of the decision of the Secretary of State.*[58]

Disability Discrimination Act 1995

8.17   Section 8: Employment related complaints of unlawful discrimination on the ground of disability. Complaints should normally be made within three months of when the act complained of was done.**[59]

Employment Rights Act 1996

8.18   Section 11(1) and (2): Reference of questions concerning the provision and content of Statement of Employment Particulars (ss.1 and 4) and itemised pay statement (s.8). References should normally be made during the course of employment or within three months of termination of employment.*[60]

Section 23: Complaints of unlawful deductions from wages. Such complaints should normally be presented within three months of the payment of the wages from which the deduction was made (or the final deduction if there was a series of deductions).*[61]

Section 34: Complaint that an employer has failed to pay the whole or part of a guarantee payment. Such a complaint should normally be made within three months of the day in respect of which the guarantee payment was to be made.*[62]

Section 48: Complaint by an employee that he has been subjected to a detriment in breach of: (a) section 44—protects employees in a variety of circumstances concerned with health and safety matters, (b) section 45—protects employees who refuse to work on a Sunday in certain circumstances, (c) section 45A—working time cases (d) section 46—protects employees who perform the functions of an occupational pension trustee, (e) section 47—protects employees who perform functions or

---

[56] s.189(5).
[57] s.192(2).
[58] s.126(2).
[59] Sched. 3, para. 3.
[60] s.11(4).
[61] s.23(2).
[62] s.34(2).

activities as an employee representative or candidate for such a post. (f) section 47A—protects employee exercising the right to time off work for study or training (g) section 47B—protects an employee who has made a protected disclosure (h) section 47C—protects an employee from detriment in connection with pregnancy, childbirth or maternity, maternity or parental leave or time off for dependants. Normally complaints under this section should be made within three months of the act or failure to act (or last in a series of actions) to which the complaint relates.*[63]

Section 51(1): Complaint by an employee that his employer has breached section 50 in failing to allow time off for public duties. Complaint should normally be made within three months of the failure.*[64]

Section 54: Complaint by an employee under notice of dismissal by reason of redundancy that his employer has breached section 52 or section 53 by failing to allow him paid time off to look for work or arrange training. Complaint should normally be made within three months of the date on which it is alleged that time off should have been permitted.*[65]

Section 57: Complaint by an employee that her employer has breached section 55 by unreasonably refusing to allow her time off for ante-natal care and/or section 56 by refusing to pay her for such time. Complaints should normally be made within three months of the date of the ante-natal appointment concerned.*[66]

Section 57B: Complaint by employee that an employer has unreasonably refused to allow the employee to take time off under section 57A for a reason connected with the employee's dependants. Complaints should normally be made within three months of the date when the refusal occurred.*

Section 60: Complaint that an employer has failed, in breach of section 58 and section 59, to allow an employee who is a trustee of a relevant occupational pension scheme paid time off for performing trustee duties or undertaking related training. Such a complaint should normally be made within three months of said failure.*[67]

Section 63: Complaint that an employer has breached section 61 and/or section 62 by refusing an employee representative reasonable paid time off to perform the functions of the role. Complaints should normally be made within three months of the date from which the time off was taken or on which it is alleged that the time off should have been permitted.*[68]

Section 63C: Complaint that an employer (or principal in terms of s.63A(3)) has breached section 63A by unreasonably refusing to allow the employee to take time off for study or training, or has breached section 63(B) by failing to pay the employee in relation to such time. Such a complaint should normally be made within three months of the failure to allow time off or on which time off was taken.*[69]

---

[63] s.48(3).
[64] s.51(2).
[65] s.54(2).
[66] s.57(2).
[67] s.60(2).
[68] s.63(2).
[69] s.63C(2).

Section 70(1): Complaint that an employer has failed to pay whole or part of the remuneration due to an employee who is suspended on medical grounds (such failure being in breach of s.64) or on maternity grounds (such failure being in breach of s.68). Complaints should normally be presented within three months of the day in respect of which no or short payment has been made.*[70]

Section 70(4): Complaint that an employer has breached section 67 by failing to offer an employee suitable alternative work which is available rather than suspending her on maternity grounds. Complaints should normally be made within three months of the first day of the suspension.*[71]

Section 80: Complaint that an employer has prevented or attempted to prevent an employee from taking parental leave or unreasonably postponed a period of parental leave requested by an employee. Such a complaint should normally be made within three months of the event in respect of which complaint is made.*

Section 93: Complaint that an employer has breached section 92 by unreasonably failing to provide a written statement of reasons for dismissal or by providing reasons which are inadequate or untrue. Complaint should be made within three months of the effective date of termination.[72]

Section 111: Complaint by an employee of unfair dismissal (in breach of section 94). Complaint should normally be made within three months of the effective date of termination.*[73]

Section 128: Application for interim relief in certain types of dismissal cases. Such an application should be made within the seven days immediately following the effective date of termination.[74]

Section 163: Reference of questions concerning entitlement to or quantification of redundancy payments. Reference to be made within six months of the "relevant date" (see s.153 for definition).[75]

Section 170(1): Reference of questions concerning payments under section 166 (applications to Secretary of State for payment out of National Insurance Fund in the event of a failure by an employer to make redundancy/termination payments in certain circumstances). No time-limit but note a question will only be referred if an application has already been made to the Secretary of State.

Section 177(1): Reference of questions concerning the making of payments equivalent to redundancy payments in accordance with section 171 (which concerns the position of individuals employed other than under a contract of employment, such as Crown servants, etc.). No stated time-limit.

Section 188: Complaint by a person whose employer is insolvent and who has applied to the Secretary of State for a payment from the National Insurance Fund (under s.182) that the Secretary of State has failed to make the payment or has paid less than should have been paid.

---

[70] s.70(2).
[71] s.70(5).
[72] s.93(3).
[73] s.111(2).
[74] s.128(2).
[75] s.164(1).

Complaints should normally be made within three months of the date on which the decision of the Secretary of State was communicated to the applicant.*[76]

Employment Tribunals Act 1996

Section 3[77]: Complaints by employees (and counter-claims by 8.19 employers) for damages for breach of contract of employment where the claim arises on, or is outstanding at, termination of employment. Complaints should normally be made within three months of the effective date of termination or, if there was no effective date of termination, within three months of the last day on which the employee worked in the employment which has terminated.*[78]

Health and Safety (Consultation with Employees) Regulations 1996[79]

Schedule 2, paragraph 2: Complaints by employee safety representa- 8.20 tives or candidates standing for election to such a post that an employer has failed to allow them time off or to pay them for such time (in breach of regs 7(1)(b) or 7(2)). Complaint should normally be made within three months of the date when the failure occurred.*[80]

National Minimum Wage Act 1998

Section 11: Complaint by worker that an employer has failed to 8.21 produce relevant wage records in accordance with the procedure set out in regulation 10 or to allow inspection of them by the worker. Such a complaint must be made within three months of the expiry of the 14 day period allowed for the employer to respond to a production notice.*[81]

Section 19(5): Appeal by an employer against an enforcement notice issued by an officer appointed under the Act.

Section 22(2): Appeal by an employer against a penalty notice issued in response to failure to comply with an enforcement notice.

Section 24: Complaint by a worker that he has been subjected to a detriment, contrary to section 23 because he qualifies or may qualify for the national minimum wage or because of action taken or proposed by the worker or another to secure certain rights arising under the Act. Such a complaint should normally be made within three months of the act in respect of which complaint is made.*[82]

Working Time Regulations 1998

Regulation 30: Complaint by a worker that his employer has refused 8.22 to permit him to exercise rights under regulation 10(1) or (2) (daily rest), regulation 11(1)–(3) (weekly rest), regulation 12(1) or (4) (rest breaks)

---

[76] s.188(2).

[77] Read together with the Employment Tribunals (Extension of Jurisdiction) (Scotland) Order 1994 (S.I. 1994 No. 1624), as amended by the Employment Rights (Dispute Resolution) Act 1998.

[78] reg. 7.

[79] S.I. 1996 No. 1513.

[80] Sched. 2, para. 3.

[81] reg. 11(3).

[82] s.24(2), National Minimum Wage Act.

or regulation 13(1) (entitlement to annual leave) or refused to offer paid leave (regs 14(2) and 16(2)). Complaints in relation to compensatory rest periods are also included (regs 24, 25(3), 27(2)).

Tax Credits Act 1999

8.23   Section 7 and Schedule 3: Complaint by an employee that he has been subjected to a detriment because he is, will or may be entitled to a tax credit or as a result of action taken or proposed by the employee or another in connection with rights or benefits arising under regulations made under the Act or because a penalty was imposed on the employer or proceedings taken in relation thereto. A complaint should normally be made within three months of the act in respect of which complaint is made.*[83]

Disability Rights Commission Act 1999

8.24   Section 4 and Schedule 3, paragraph 10(2): Appeal against a non-discrimination notice issued in connection with a matter in respect of which the employment tribunal has jurisdiction. Appeal must be made within the period of six weeks beginning on the day after the notice is served.

Employment Relations Act 1999

8.25   Section 11: Complaint by a worker that his employer has failed or threatened to fail to comply with section 10(2) (worker to be allowed to accompanied at disciplinary or grievance hearing) or section 10(4) (hearing to be postponed if the chosen companion is unable to attend). Complaint should normally made within three months of the failure or threat.*[84]

Transnational Information and Consultation of Employees Regulations 1999

8.26   Regulation 27: Complaint by an employee that his employer has unreasonably refused to allow him paid time off in relation to duties associated with European Works Council (rights arising under regs 25 and 26). Such a complaint should normally be made within three months of the date when time off was taken or should have been permitted.*

Regulation 32: Complaint by an employee that he has been subjected to a detriment on the ground that he has performed functions as a member or representative of or candidate for a European Works Council or because he (or someone on his behalf) has sought paid time off for such activities. Complaint may also be made if detriment suffered on the ground that the employee took or proposed to take proceedings before an employment tribunal in order to enforce rights arising under the regulations or exercised or proposed to exercise various other rights similarly arising, in contravention of regulation 31.

---

[83] Sched. 3, para. 2(2).
[84] s.11(2), Employment Relations Act 1999.

Part-Time Employees (Prevention of Less Favourable Treatment) Regulations 2000.[85]

Regulation 8: Complaint that an employer has breached regulation 5 8.27 which gives a part-time worker the right not to be treated less favourably than a full-time worker in relation to the terms of his contract, or by being subjected to any other detriment or deliberate failure to act by his employer, unless such treatment can be objectively justified There is also the right to complain to an employment tribunal that the employer has subjected the employee to any detriment on any of the grounds in regulation 7(2) (which is essentially a provision dealing with victimisation arising from the fact that the employee has sought to enforce or retain rights arising under the regulations or helped another to do so). Such complaints must normally be presented within three months of the date of the less favourable treatment.**[86] In so far as the regulations apply to a member of the armed forces or the Reserve forces (reg. 13) the complaint must normally be presented within six months.**[87]

Extension of Time

In certain circumstances provisions do exist for the possible extension 8.28 of a time-limit. Those provisions marked with * allow for the possibility of an extension of time where it was not reasonably practicable to comply with the time-limit. Those provisions marked with ** allow a tribunal to hear a claim outwith the normal time-limit where it would be just and equitable to do so.

VOLUME OF CLAIMS BEFORE EMPLOYMENT TRIBUNALS IN SCOTLAND

As will be evident, employment tribunals have been given increasingly 8.29 wide jurisdiction over the course of their existence. They can now very properly be referred to as specialist employment courts with many legal and lay members who have developed an in-depth knowledge of employment law and practice. The number of applications registered by the Central Office of Employment Tribunals in Scotland has continued to rise year upon year. In 1989/90 the total number of applications registered was 3,341. In 1996/97 7,290 applications were registered with approximately half of the applications registered that year being unfair dismissal claims. In the year to March 31, 2001, 13,419 applications were registered in Scotland. Of these 3,821 were unfair dismissal claims and 2,527 were claims relating to unlawful deductions from wages. A surprisingly high number of claims (2,232) were lodged under the Part Time Workers Regulations but 2,228 of these were allocated to the Central Office of Employment Tribunals in Glasgow to be processed; this is suggestive of at least one, if not more, multiple claims. The next most numerically significant group of claims were those arising under the SDA 1975 (2,093).

---

[85] S.I. 2000 No. 1551.
[86] reg. 8(2).
[87] *ibid.*

CHAPTER 9

CONTINUITY OF EMPLOYMENT

THE STATUTORY FRAMEWORK

9.01 The calculation of the period of an employee's continuous employment is of considerable importance in relation to most statutory employment rights. Although it is now the case that some of the claims dealt with by employment tribunals do not depend upon any period of continuous employment at all, many important rights can only be pursued following employment for a specified period. For example, an employee pursuing a claim for unfair dismissal must establish one year of continuous employment with the employer and any period that breaks continuity can disqualify the employee from pursuing the matter.[1] Continuous employment is also of importance in calculating certain payments, such as a redundancy payment or the basic award in an unfair dismissal claim. In general terms, continuity is calculated in months and years. The period is calculated by working back from the relevant date, which, in a case of unfair dismissal, is the effective date of termination of employment. Weeks that count are accumulated to determine the total period of continuity. Weeks that do not count have the effect of breaking continuity.

Periods of continuous employment must be calculated in accordance with the statutory provisions, which are contained in Chapter I of Part XIV of the ERA 1996.[2] These cannot be negated by any agreement between employer and employee although such an agreement may provide for additional contractual entitlements in excess of the statutory minimum.[3]

An employee's service is presumed to be continuous unless the contrary is shown.[4] In practice this presumption is of considerable significance as it means that the onus lies on the employer to rebut it by proving that continuity has been broken at some stage during the employment relationship.

---

[1] ERA, s.108(1). The previous threshold of two years was amended following a challenge on the grounds that it was indirectly discriminatory in *R v. Secretary of State, ex parte Seymour-Smith and Perez* [1999] I.R.L.R. 253.

[2] The exception to this is the calculation of the qualifying period for annual leave under the Working Time Regulations 1998. Calculation of the qualifying period for statutory maternity pay is governed by Pt III of the Statutory Maternity Pay (General) Regulations 1986 (S.I. 1986 No. 1960) which incorporates ss.210–219, ERA.

[3] *Secretary of State for Employment v. Globe Elastic Thread Co. Ltd* [1979] I.R.L.R. 327, HL.

[4] ERA, s.210(5).

Although continuity is calculated with reference to months and years, 9.02 the period of continuous employment may be broken by any complete week that does not count towards continuity for the purposes of the calculation under the legislation. A period of continuous employment begins with the day on which an employee started work and ends with the day by reference to which the length of the period of continuous employment is to be calculated, being in most cases the effective date of termination of employment.[5] The date of commencement is normally not difficult to identify, assuming the necessary records are available. However, certain statutory exceptions apply—for example, for the purposes of calculating a redundancy payment, any service prior to the age of 18 does not count.[6]

Where a contract of employment is terminated by notice the effective date of termination is the date on which the notice expires.[7] If the contract is terminated without notice, then the effective date is the date on which the termination actually takes effect.[8] Where the contract terminates by reason of the expiry of a fixed term contract, the effective date is when it expires.[9] The relevant date in relation to redundancy payments is normally the same as the effective date of termination for unfair dismissal purposes except where the employee has accepted an offer of alternative employment but leaves during the trial period in which case the relevant date is the date of termination of the original contract.[10] Where the employee has given notice to leave earlier than the expiry of the employer's notice, the relevant date is the date on which the employee's notice expires.[11]

When the date of commencement and date of termination of the 9.03 period of employment have been identified, it is necessary to calculate the period of employment for continuity purposes. Depending on which right the employee is claiming, this is calculated in months (*i.e.* calendar months) or years (calculated as 12 calendar months).[12] As noted above, for the purposes of calculating any breaks in continuity, "weeks" are the periods to be applied. A week that does not count in computing the length of a period of continuous employment breaks continuity.[13] It is therefore necessary to examine the whole period of employment and then identify whether there is any gap of at least a complete week (from Sunday to Saturday)[14] which does not count for the purposes of the legislation and therefore does not preserve continuity. If there is such a break of a week or more, continuity is broken, subject to the exceptions set out below, and it is necessary to calculate any continuous employment from the end of the break.

---

[5] ERA, s.211(1).
[6] *ibid.*, s.211(2).
[7] *ibid.*, s.97(1)(a).
[8] *ibid.*, s.97(1)(b).
[9] *ibid.*, s.97(1)(c).
[10] *ibid.*, s.145.
[11] *ibid.*, s.145(3)
[12] *ibid.*, s.210(2).
[13] *ibid.*, s.210(4).
[14] *ibid.*, s.235.

WEEKS WHICH COUNT

9.04 It is no longer necessary for the employee to have worked for a minimum number of hours for the week to count. Section 212 of the ERA sets out in full the weeks that count as follows:

> "Weeks counting in computing period
> 212. (1) Any week during the whole or part of which an employee's relations with his employer are governed by a contract of employment counts in computing the employee's period of employment.
> (3) Subject to subsection (4), any week (not within subsection (1)) during the whole or part of which an employee is—
>> (a) incapable of work in consequence of sickness or injury,
>> (b) absent from work on account of a temporary cessation of work, or
>> (c) absent from work in circumstances such that, by arrangement or custom, he is regarded as continuing in the employment of his employer for any purpose.
> (4) Not more than 26 weeks count under subsection (3)(a) between any periods falling under subsection (1)."

It should be noted that subsection 3 above applies only where there is no contract in existence, for example where one contract has come to an end and there is a gap before the employee is re-employed under a new contract.

SICKNESS OR INJURY

9.05 For section 212(3)(a) above to apply, the employee must be incapable of carrying out the work which he was employed to do before the period of absence began rather than incapable of carrying out any work.[15] A maximum of 26 weeks may be counted during any one period of absence. In most cases the contract of employment continues during any period the applicant is simply absent from work.

TEMPORARY CESSATION OF WORK

9.06 Section 212(3)(b) covers situations where there is a cessation of work, where it is temporary, and where the reason for the employee's absence is the cessation of work. To determine whether it applies, it is necessary to examine the position of the individual employee and consider whether there was work available for that employee.[16] This provision may apply

---

[15] *Donnelly v. Kelvin International Services* [1992] I.R.L.R. 496, EAT. *Cf. G F Sharp & Co Ltd v. McMillan* [1998] I.R.L.R. 632, EAT for the effect of frustration of the employment contract through injury and the effect on continuity.

[16] *Fitzgerald v. Hall, Russell & Co. Ltd,* 1970 S.C. (HL) 1; [1970] A.C. 984, HL.

even where the cessation of work is regular and foreseeable.[17] Accordingly, it can happen that various periods of employment are "joined together" by virtue of cessations that qualify. In determining whether a cessation is temporary, it is necessary to look at all the circumstances in the light of the whole history of employment.[18]

ABSENCE BY ARRANGEMENT OR CUSTOM

Section 212(3)(c) ensures that continuity of employment is preserved 9.07 where there is no contract of employment in existence. Any absence specifically contemplated in the contract will preserve continuity anyway. Cases to which this provision has applied have tended to involve unpaid leave for extended holiday purposes, and absences due to a seasonal downturn in business.

UNFAIR DISMISSAL

If a dismissed employee is reinstated or re-engaged by his employer or 9.08 by a successor or associated employer then the employee's continuity of employment is preserved automatically.[19] This applies where the reinstatement or re-engagement is a consequence of: (1) an application being made to the employment tribunal for unfair dismissal; (2) a claim being made in accordance with a dismissal procedures agreement under section 110 of the ERA; (3) action taken by a conciliation officer under his relevant powers; or (4) the making of a relevant compromise contract—usually a compromise agreement under section 203 of the ERA.

WEEKS THAT DO NOT COUNT OR BREAK CONTINUITY

It should also be noted that the ERA makes provision for particular 9.09 breaks in employment that do not count towards continuous employment but do not break continuity either. Where an employee is absent because of his participation in a strike or lock-out[20] or because of military service[21] the absences do not form part of his continuous service but they do not cause continuity to be broken. Similarly, when determining a redundancy payment, any periods during which an employee has worked outside Great Britain will be discounted when calculating continuous service without continuity of employment being broken.[22]

From the above it will be seen that the calculation of a period of continuous employment is largely a question to be determined according

---

[17] *Ford v. Warwickshire County Council* [1983] I.R.L.R. 126, HL.
[18] *Fitzgerald*, above.
[19] Employment Protection (Continuity of Employment) Regulations 1996 (S.I. 1996 No. 3147).
[20] ERA, s.216.
[21] ERA, s.217.
[22] ERA, s.215.

to statutory provisions. In the majority of cases that come before employment tribunals it is relatively straightforward to identify the relevant period. In practice, the difficulties that arise are a result of a failure by the employer to retain sufficient records of periods worked by employees, an omission that can prove costly in view of the statutory presumption in favour of continuity.

CHAPTER 10

REDUNDANCY

BACKGROUND

A statutory redundancy scheme was introduced by the Redundancy 10.01 Payments Act 1965, the current provisions being found in Part XI of the ERA. Section 135 sets out the circumstances in which a redundancy payment is payable, that is when an employee is dismissed by reason of redundancy or is eligible by reason of lay off or short time working. The statutory scheme whereby employers were entitled to a rebate amounting to a percentage of any redundancy payment has ceased and accordingly the full liability for payment of the redundancy entitlement rests with the employer. The purpose of the redundancy payment is to compensate an employee for losing his employment, not to compensate for losses incurred as a result of being rendered unemployed. In effect, it is a reward for past services.[1]

Redundancy Defined

Section 139 of the ERA defines redundancy as follows: 10.02

"(1) For the purposes of this Act an employee who is dismissed shall be taken to be dismissed by reason of redundancy if the dismissal is wholly or mainly attributable to—

(a) the fact that his employer has ceased or intends to cease—
   (i) to carry on the business for the purposes of which the employee was employed by him, or
   (ii) to carry on that business in the place where the employee was so employed, or
(b) the fact that the requirements of that business—
   (i) for employees to carry out work of a particular kind, or
   (ii) for employees to carry out work of a particular kind in the place where the employee was employed by the employer, have ceased or diminished or are expected to cease or diminish."

---

[1] *Mairs (Inspector of Taxes) v. Haughey* [1993] I.R.L.R. 551. Payments in lieu of notice are taxable under Sched. E: *Thorn EMI Electronics Ltd v. Coldicott (Inspector of Taxes)* [2000] 1 W.L.R. 540, CA.

10.03   An employee does not have any entitlement to a redundancy payment
unless he can show that the circumstances come within the definitions
contained in the above section.[2] Accordingly, an entitlement arises when
the employer ceases business altogether, when the employer ceases
business in the place where the employee was employed, or when the
employer no longer needs as many employees to carry out work of a
particular kind. These definitions apply not only in determining whether
an employee has entitlement to a redundancy payment but also whether
the employer has been dismissed for the potentially valid reason of
redundancy under section 98.

A distinction must always be made between a cessation of a business
on the one hand and a transfer of a business or undertaking on the
other. Generally speaking, if the Transfer of Undertakings (Protection of
Employment) Regulations 1981[3] apply then contracts of employment
transfer to the acquirer of the business and there is no right to a
redundancy payment. However, if transfer-related dismissals are carried
out by the transferor or transferee the circumstances may coincide with
the above definition of redundancy, in which case there exists an
entitlement to a redundancy payment, albeit for the purpose of identifying whether the dismissal is potentially fair it is categorised as being for
"some other substantial reason justifying dismissal". Reference is made
to Chapter 12 on the transfer of undertakings.

Problems frequently arise in attempting to determine whether an
employee is entitled to a redundancy payment where the business ceases
"in the place where" the employee was employed. This is an important
question as the answer to it will dictate whether an employee, who
refuses to move to another site following the closure of a plant, is
entitled to a redundancy payment. If the employer offers a job at
another location this may constitute an offer of "suitable alternative
employment" in which case the employee's refusal may disqualify him
from entitlement to a redundancy payment. What is meant by the
"place" in which the employee is employed? Essentially, two tests have
been applied over the years. One has concentrated on the geographical
location itself (as apparently contemplated by the legislation), the other
on the terms of the employee's contract of employment.

10.04   The EAT addressed the question in *Bass Leisure Limited v. Thomas*,[4]
a case in which the employee was based at one of her employer's depots.
Her job involved visiting public houses and reporting back to base. The
depot at which she was employed was closed and she was moved to a
new depot on a trial basis. In the contract of employment her employers
had reserved a right to relocate her to a new geographical area. This
right was subject to certain conditions, which were not satisfied in this
case. The EAT considered the "contractual" and the "geographical"
tests. They held that the "place where the employee was employed" for
the purposes of section 81 of the Employment Protection (Consolidation) Act 1978[5] is to be established by factual inquiry. This should take
account of the employee's fixed or changing place of work as well as any

---

[2] ERA, s.135.
[3] Hereinafter TUPE.
[4] [1994] I.R.L.R. 104.
[5] Now ERA, s.139.

contractual terms which provide evidence of or define the place of employment and its extent but not terms which make provision for the employee to be transferred to another place.

The *Bass Leisure* decision was considered by the Court of Appeal in 10.05 *High Table Ltd v. Horst*[6] where the Court held that the place where an employee was employed for the purpose of determining the applicability of this statutory provision is to be determined by a consideration of the factual circumstances which obtained until the dismissal. In particular the Court held that the terms of the contract cannot be the sole determinant of the issue, regardless of where the employee actually worked. The Court also pointed out that if the question was to be answered solely with reference to the terms of the contract this could lead to the undesirable result that employers could defeat genuine redundancy claims simply by including mobility clauses in contracts of employment. The Court stated that: "The question what was the place of employment is one that can safely be left to the good sense of the employment tribunal". It is therefore open to the employment tribunal to take into account evidence of the terms of the contract of employment as well as evidence of where the employee worked in practice.

The third category of redundancy tends to give rise to most practical 10.06 and legal problems, *i.e.* the reduction in the requirement of the business for employees to do work of a particular kind. It is often said that when redundancy occurs it is the job that disappears, not the individual, and to some extent this is true. The starting point in any redundancy exercise should be for the employer to determine the requirements of the business in the abstract, *i.e.* irrespective of individuals. Many employers start to go wrong at this early stage in the process by earmarking people they perceive to be poor performers as targets for redundancy. Employment lawyers are familiar with inquiries along the following lines—"I think Mr X is fiddling his expenses—can I make him redundant?" or "Mrs Y has been off sick for six months—can I make her redundant now?" If a redundancy exercise is not carried out in accordance with the statutory test then there exists a strong possibility that the employer will fail to establish that a resultant dismissal was for a potentially valid reason. The House of Lords has held on appeal from Northern Ireland[7] that in deciding the issue of redundancy what is to be established is that the dismissal is "attributable" to the diminution of work. The causal connection is to be decided on the evidence and not as a matter of law.[8]

Jobs disappear for a variety of reasons, some outwith the control of the employer, some within. If sales have fallen as a result of recession, this will have a direct impact on a company's need to employ employees in work of a particular kind. On the other hand, the directors of a company may choose to create efficiencies by rationalising the way a particular job is carried out. An obvious example of this would be a reduction in requirements for employees because of computerisation. It is important to note that although many redundancies occur as a result

---

[6] [1997] I.R.L.R. 513, CA applied in *Shawkat v. Nottingham City Hospital NHS Trust (Remitting)* [1999] I.R.L.R. 340, EAT and *Church v. West Lancashire NHS Trust (No. 1)* [1998] I.R.L.R. 4.
[7] *Murray v. Foyle Meats Ltd* [1999] I.R.L.R. 562.
[8] *Arbuckle v. Scottish Power plc*, 2000 G.W.D. 10–358.

of financial difficulties experienced by the employer, it is not necessary for a business to be in such a position for a reduction in numbers to be justifiable.

In this type of case the real difficulty arises in attempting to identify what "the requirements of that business for employees to carry out work of a particular kind" actually means. In one early case,[9] the Court of Appeal held that it is necessary to concentrate on the skills involved and identify whether there has been some change in the requirements of the business for those particular skills. However, in a later case[10] the court concentrated on the type of employee, holding that the appointment of a different type of tradesman had the effect of diminishing the requirements of a business for people to carry out plumbing work and therefore that a plumber dismissed for this reason was dismissed by reason of redundancy.

QUALIFYING EMPLOYEES

10.07 Any employee who is dismissed on the ground of redundancy is usually entitled to a payment (see exceptions later). The qualifying period of employment is two years.[11] Both age and length of service are taken into account in calculating the amount of the payment. Part-time employees qualify on the same basis as full-time employees irrespective of the number of hours worked per week.[12] Payment of a statutory redundancy payment does break continuity of employment, but for redundancy payment purposes only.[13] For every year during the whole of which the employee was aged 41 or over, he is entitled to one and a half week's pay. For every year during the whole of which he was aged 22 or over he is entitled to one week's pay. For earlier years he is entitled to half a week's pay (weeks under the age of 18 do not count).[14] The maximum amount of a week's pay to be taken into account for the purposes of calculating a redundancy payment is £240[15] and the number of years used in the calculation may not exceed 20.[16]

Certain groups of employees are excluded from the legislation.[17]

Section 164 of the ERA provides that a claim for a redundancy payment may be made within a period of six months from the relevant date,[18] the employment tribunal having a power to extend the time-limit by a further period of six months if it considers it just and equitable to do so.

---

[9] *Chapman v. Goonvean and Rostowrack China Clay Company Ltd* [1973] I.C.R. 310, CA.

[10] *Murphy v. Epsom College* [1984] I.R.L.R. 271, CA.

[11] ERA, s.155.

[12] S.I. 1995 No. 31. These regulations were repealed by the ERA 1996, though the protection conferred on part-time employees is continued under the Act.

[13] ERA, s.214.

[14] ERA, s.162.

[15] ERA, s.227(1), modified by Employment Rights (Increase of Limits) Order 2001 (S.I. 2001 No. 21).

[16] ERA, s.162(3).

[17] Such as ERA, ss.199(2), 160, 161 and 191.

[18] As defined in ERA, s.145.

ALTERNATIVE EMPLOYMENT

A failure by the employer to consider alternative employment will almost 10.08
certainly render a dismissal unfair (see Chapter 11). If the employer is
able to offer further employment within four weeks of making the
employee redundant, then there is deemed to be no dismissal at all and
therefore no right to a redundancy payment.[19]

If the employer is able to offer terms and conditions of employment
that differ from those previously enjoyed, the employee is entitled to a
trial period of at least four weeks without prejudice to his right to claim
a redundancy payment. If the employee then leaves or is dismissed
during the trial period he is treated as having been dismissed for the
original reason and on the date on which his employment under the
previous contract ended.[20] The trial period may be extended by agreement between the parties for the purpose of retraining if the conditions
laid down in the legislation are met.[21]

If the employer is able to find other "suitable" employment and the
employee "unreasonably" refuses that offer of employment, there may
be no entitlement to a redundancy payment.[22] The "suitability" of the
offer and the reasonableness or otherwise of the refusal must be
determined in accordance with the facts of each case. Generally speaking, tribunals are prepared to interpret these provisions in a fairly
subjective way. If the employee has a reason that is genuine and is
important to him he will preserve his entitlement to a redundancy
payment.[23]

LAY OFF AND SHORT TIME WORKING

Lay off or short time working is covered in Chapter III of Part XI of the 10.09
ERA. In certain circumstances an employee is entitled to claim a
redundancy payment as a result of lay off or short time working. An
employee is taken to be laid off for a week if he is employed under a
contract on terms and conditions such that his remuneration under the
contract depends on his being provided by the employer with work of the
kind which he is employed to do but he is not entitled to any
remuneration under the contract in respect of the week because the
employer does not provide such work for him.[24]

For the purposes of the Act an employee is taken to be kept on short
time for a week if by reason of a diminution in work provided for the
employee by his employer (being work of a kind which under his
contract the employee is employed to do) the employee's remuneration
for the week is less than half a week's pay.

---

[19] ERA, s.138(1)(a).
[20] ERA, s.138(4).
[21] ERA, s.138(6).
[22] ERA, s.141.
[23] See, for example, *Cambridge and District Co-operative Society Ltd. v. Ruse* [1993]
I.R.L.R. 156, EAT.
[24] ERA, s.147(1).

To be eligible for a redundancy payment, the employee must have been laid off or kept on short-time working for four or more consecutive weeks ending with the date of service of a notice of intention to claim a redundancy payment, or within four weeks of the date of service or laid off or kept on short time working for a series of six more weeks (of which not more than three were consecutive within a period of 13 weeks, and the last week of the series must have ended on the date of the service of the notice or within four weeks of that date).[25]

10.10   The employee must give written notice of his intention to claim a redundancy payment no earlier than the last day of the last week of the period of lay-off or short-time working. It is also necessary for the employee to terminate the contract of employment by giving the notice specified in section 150(1) of the ERA. If an employee has served notice of intention to claim a payment, it is open to the employer to serve counter-notice (within seven days) that he will contest any liability to pay a redundancy payment. If the counter-notice creates a reasonable expectation that the employee will enter a period of employment of not less than 13 weeks within four weeks of that date, during which there would not be any lay-off or short-time working, the employee's claim for a redundancy payment is defeated.

It will be seen from the above that the statutory rules are complex and it is therefore not surprising that few claims for redundancy payments under these provisions are heard by employment tribunals. It should also be noted that the option of imposing lay-off or short-time working generally only rests with the employer who has had the foresight to include a contractual power to do so in the contract of employment. In the absence of such a power, the employee may be justified in resigning as a reaction to the breach (*i.e.* the imposition of lay off or short time working). In the event of an application to the employment tribunal on the ground of unfair dismissal being successful, the employee will be entitled at least to a basic award and possibly a compensatory award, the basic award being equal in amount to a statutory redundancy payment.

COLLECTIVE CONSULTATION

10.11   A failure to consult with employees or their representatives prior to the imposition of enforced redundancies will usually result in a dismissal being found to be unfair in terms of section 98(4).[26] This might be the case even when only one employee is affected. However, trade unions and employee representatives have a separate and distinct right to be consulted by an employer proposing larger numbers of redundancies.[27] Until relatively recently, employers were only obliged to consult formally with recognised trade unions. In *Commission of the European Communities v. United Kingdom*[28] the European Court of Justice held

---

[25] ERA, s.148(2).

[26] *Polkey v. A.E. Dayton Services Ltd* [1987] I.R.L.R. 503, HL.

[27] For consultation requirements in relation to redundancies at Community-scale undertakings see Transnational Information and Consultation of Employees Regulations 1999 (S.I. 3323 No. 99).

[28] Case C–383/92 [1994] I.R.L.R. 392.

that the United Kingdom was in breach of Community law because it had failed to implement in full the provisions of the Collective Redundancies Directive[29] and the Acquired Rights Directive[30] in particular in relation to consultation rights. Regulations were subsequently implemented within the United Kingdom to extend the existing consultation obligations.[31] One of the most significant aspects of these Regulations was the creation of "employee representatives" with whom the employer must consult in the absence of a recognised trade union.[32] The employee representatives are elected by the employees affected by redundancy (or a business transfer—they have a parallel function in relation to consultation about "relevant transfers" under TUPE). Employee representatives must be in the employment of the employer at the time when they are elected. They are elected for a specific purpose and do not require to continue as a permanent body. The Regulations give little guidance as to how the representatives should be elected, how they should perform their duties, how many there should be or how long they should serve.[33] Where employees are given the opportunity to elect representatives but this is not taken, then the employer has an obligation to consult with the employees individually.[34] This is not to be confused with the individual consultation requirements imposed by reason of dismissal under the ERA 1996.[35] Previously, the decision as to whether to recognise a union was at the whim of the employer. Importantly however the ERA 1999 introduced a scheme for compulsory recognition of trade unions where the majority of employees are in favour of this.[36] This should avoid situations where the workforce would prefer to be represented by a union during consultation and the employer, simply through the expedient of refusing to recognise a union, could consult instead with employee representatives elected for that purpose. These representatives often have no experience of negotiating with employers, nor do they have the network of support that is available to shop stewards through their union.[37] However it should be noted that where an employer voluntarily recognises a non-independent employee association in respect of a bargaining unit, then any application for recognition by an independent union in respect of that bargaining unit will not be admissible.[38]

The procedure for handling redundancies is to be found in Chapter 2 of Part 4 of the Trade Union and Labour Relations (Consolidation) Act 1992. Section 188 as amended by the above Regulations and the Trade

10.12

---

[29] Directive 75/129.

[30] Directive 77/187.

[31] Collective Redundancies and Transfer of Undertakings (Protection of Employment) (Amendment) Regulations 1995 (S.I. 1995 No. 2587) and the Collective Redundancies and Transfer of Undertakings (Protection of Employment) (Amendment) Regulations 1999 (S.I. 1999 No. 1925).

[32] s.188(1B), Trade Union and Labour Relations (Consolidation) Act 1992, hereinafter TULRCA; *cf. Northern Ireland Hotel and Catering College v. NATFHE* [1995] I.R.L.R. 83.

[33] See s.188A, TULRCA which sets the basic procedural requirements.

[34] s.188(7B), TULRCA.

[35] *King v. Eaton,* 1996 S.C. 74; [1996] I.R.L.R. 199.

[36] To be found in Sched. A1, TULRCA. The provisions apply only to employers who employ 21 "workers" on the day of receiving the formal request for recognition or an average of 21 workers in the 13 weeks ending with that day (para. 7). See generally Simpson (2000) 29 I.L.J. 193.

[37] The difference was particularly evident in the redundancies at the Motorola factory in West Lothian in Spring 2001, see *The Herald*, April 26, 2001.

[38] para. 35. See also Ewing (2000) 29 I.L.J. 267.

Union Reform and Employment Rights Act 1993 sets out the obligations that must be fulfilled by an employer proposing to carry out redundancies.[39] The employer must consult all persons who are appropriate representatives of any employees who *may be affected* by the proposed dismissals or *may be* affected by the measures taken in connection with those dismissals.[40] Employers will now have to consult over the consequential impact on "survivor" employees in such areas as organisation and workload. A numbers threshold applies and the employer is obliged to consult trade union representatives or employee representatives only when no fewer than 20 employees are to be made redundant within a 90 day period at one establishment.[41] The employer is obliged to consult in good time and in any event where the employer is proposing to dismiss 100 or more employees at least 90 days, and otherwise at least 30 days before the first of the dismissals takes effect. It should be noted that the obligation to consult is triggered where the employer imposes measures on a part of the workforce, on a group and not on an individual basis, involving the termination of their existing contracts of employment. This will amount to "dismissal as redundant" within the meaning of section 195(1) as amended to give effect to the Directive on Collective Redundancies.[42]

The legislation is quite specific about the process and states that it must include consultation about ways of avoiding the dismissals; reducing the numbers of employees to be dismissed; and mitigating the consequences of the dismissals. It must be undertaken by the employer "with a view to reaching agreement with the appropriate representatives".[43] In determining how many employees an employer is proposing to dismiss as redundant no account is to be taken of employees in respect of whose proposed dismissal consultation has already begun.[44]

The legislation requires the employer to disclose in writing to the appropriate representatives the following information:

1. the reasons for the proposals;
2. the numbers and descriptions of employees who it is proposed to dismiss as redundant;
3. the total number of employees of any such description employed by the employer at the establishment in question;
4. the proposed method of selecting the employees who may be dismissed;

---

[39] Where the employer has determined a plan of action which has two alternative scenarios, one of which included dismissals, then that constitutes a "proposal": *Scotch Premier Meat Ltd v. Burns* [2000] I.R.L.R. 639, EAT.
[40] s.188(1), TULRCA as amended by the 1999 regulations.
[41] For a discussion on "establishment" and redundancy consultation, see, "'Establishment' and Redundancy Consultation", Emp.L.B. 14–9.
[42] *GMB v. Man Truck & Bus UK Ltd* [2000] I.R.L.R. 636, EAT. Dismissal is to be construed in terms of s.95, ERA: see s.298, TULRCA 1992.
[43] TULRCA, s.188(2).
[44] TULRCA, s.188(3).

5. the proposed method of carrying out the dismissals, with due regard to any agreed procedure, including the period over which the dismissals are to take effect; and

6. the proposed method of calculating the amount of any redundancy payments to be made.

The employer has a defence available to him that there are special circumstances which render it "not reasonably practicable" to comply with the above requirements but in this event the employer is still required to take all such steps towards compliance as are reasonably practicable in those circumstances.[45] However the employer will have no relevant defence under the subsection if the reason for his inability to supply information is that it is being withheld by a parent company.[46]

In the event of a failure by the employer to comply with the 10.13 requirements of the section, a complaint may be made to the employment tribunal by the affected representative, the trade union, or any employees who have been or may be dismissed as redundant.[47] It is for the employer to show either that a representative with whom he consulted was in fact an "appropriate" representative or that any of the requirements of section 188A have been satisfied.[48] In the event that the application is successful, the employment tribunal is entitled to make a protective award in favour of the applicant. This comprises an order to pay remuneration for the protected period which begins with the date on which the first dismissals take effect, or the date of the award, whichever is earlier and is of such length as the tribunal considers just and equitable in all the circumstances. The maximum period for the protective award must not exceed 90 days. It may be for a period less than the maximum and the employment tribunal is obliged to consider all the circumstances with a view to making an award which is just and equitable "having regard to the seriousness of the employer's default in complying with the requirements of the legislation".

Any application to the employment tribunal must be lodged within three months of the date on which the last of the dismissals to which the complaint relates takes effect or during the period of three months beginning with that date. If the tribunal is satisfied that it was not reasonably practicable for the complaint to be presented during that period, it may allow the complaint to be presented within such further period as it considers "reasonable".[49]

At the time of writing, political agreement had been reached on 10.14 proposals for a European Directive on Informing and Consulting Employees. The preamble to the Directive criticises national legal systems as having failed to prevent serious decisions affecting employees being taken and made public without adequate procedures having been implemented to inform and consult the employees involved. The directive will give employees in undertakings with 50 or more employees the right *inter alia* to be informed about the undertaking's economic

---

[45] TULRCA, s.188(7).
[46] *ibid.*
[47] TULRCA, s.189(1).
[48] *ibid.*, ss.189(1A) and (1B).
[49] *ibid.*, s.192(2)(b).

situation and informed and consulted with a view to reaching agreement about decisions likely to lead to substantial changes in work organisation or contractual relations, including redundancies and transfers. The directive will set out a framework of obligations and it will be up to the Member States to devise measures for implementation according to domestic industrial practices. Final adoption of the Directive is expected in 2002 and the United Kingdom will then have three years to implement the provisions. Transitional provisions allow the directive to be applied in the first instance to undertakings with 150 or more employees. After two years it will apply to undertakings with 100 or more, and after a further two years, to those with 50 or more.

CHAPTER 11

UNFAIR DISMISSAL

INTRODUCTION

Until relatively recently, an employee who was aggrieved at the loss of 11.01
employment had little hope of obtaining a satisfactory remedy before the
courts. The first significant step forward took place in 1968 when the
Donovan Commission recommended that a statutory machinery be set
up whereunder employers would be required to establish a valid reason
to justify the dismissal of employees. This led to the creation of the
statutory right not to be unfairly dismissed, which was then introduced in
the Industrial Relations Act 1971. The basic structure of the right has
remained largely unchanged over the last 30 years but Parliament has
added a number of additional categories of dismissal that are unfair,
with a view to strengthening protection given to the individual employee.
Although employment law in general has become increasingly complex,
the law on unfair dismissal, at least, is largely based on the concept of
reasonableness. As one might expect, such a broad concept has invited
refinement from the courts but this has not been at the expense of the
principle that each case must ultimately be decided by applying the
statutory test to its own particular facts. The law as currently stated is to
be found in Part 10 of the Employment Rights Act 1996 (ERA).
Practitioners should always be mindful of the interaction between the
statutory regime and the common law, particularly in relation to the
implied term of mutual trust and confidence and the remedy of wrongful
dismissal.

JURISDICTION IN UNFAIR DISMISSAL CLAIMS

Every employee has the right not to be unfairly dismissed by his 11.02
employer.[1] Although no threshold of hours exists now,[2] an employee
must have one year's continuous service.[3] The one year qualifying period
was introduced in response to the rulings of the European Court of
Justice and the House of Lords in *R v. Secretary of State for Employment,*

---

[1] ERA, s.94(1).
[2] Removed by the Employment Protection (Part-time Employees) Regulations 1995
(S.I. 1995 No. 31) following the decision in *R v. Secretary of State for Employment, ex parte
Equal Opportunities Commission* [1995] 1 A.C. 1.
[3] ERA, s.108(1), as amended by the Unfair Dismissal and Statement of Reasons for
Dismissal (Variation of Qualifying Period) Order 1999 (S.I. 1999 No. 1436).

ex parte Seymour-Smith (No. 1)[4] which ruled that the then existing two year qualification period was indirectly discriminatory and in breach of the Equal Treatment Directive.[5] It is not possible for an employee to enter into an agreement which purports to amend the statutory tests for the computation of the qualifying period.[6]

Employees who are employed under contracts of employment are protected. Those employed in the police service are unable to bring unfair dismissal claims and specific provisions apply to those in Crown employment[7] and members of the armed forces.[8] Employees who have settled claims by means of a compromise agreement under section 203 of the ERA or by way of the COT3[9] procedure under the auspices of an ACAS conciliation officer are also prevented from making a complaint to an employment tribunal. An agreement covered by section 203 is void only "in so far as" it purports to exclude the employee's statutory rights. The agreement will therefore be valid and subsisting to the extent that it excludes liability for matters outwith section 203.[10] Other particular types of employment are dealt with in Part 13 of the ERA, as amended by the ERA 1999. One result of this amendment is to ensure that those who "ordinarily" work outside Great Britain can now bring a claim for unfair dismissal and the jurisdiction of the tribunal to hear such an application must be determined in accordance with ordinary conflict of laws principles.

Certain employment contracts may prove unenforceable on the ground that they are illegal. This may be because the contract is directly prohibited by statute,[11] because it is illegal at common law,[12] or because it is performed in an illegal way, even though it was lawful when entered into. The most common example of the latter category of illegality to come before employment tribunals is that relating to the evasion of tax. If the employee is aware that tax evasion is taking place in connection with his employment, he is unlikely to be able to enforce his contract of employment. The principle applies equally to the enforcement of statutory rights.[13] In *Hall v. Woolston Hall Leisure Ltd*[14] the Court of Appeal held that in instances where the contract of employment is not entered into for an illegal purpose nor prohibited by statute, illegal performance will only render it unenforceable where in addition to knowledge of the facts which make the performance illegal, the employee also actively participates in the illegal performance.[15]

---

[4] [1997] I.R.L.R. 315, HL; [1999] I.R.L.R. 253, ECJ; *No. 2* [2000] I.R.L.R. 263.

[5] Directive 76/207.

[6] *Collison v. BBC* [1998] I.R.L.R. 238, EAT.

[7] ERA, s.191 and s.200

[8] ERA, s.192.

[9] See Chap. 14.

[10] *Sutherland v. Network Appliance Ltd* [2001] I.R.L.R. 12, EAT. See also *Lunt v. Merseyside TEC Ltd* [1999] I.R.L.R. 458, EAT.

[11] *i.e.* statutory restrictions on the employment of children or young persons.

[12] *i.e.* involves criminality.

[13] *Hyland v. J.H. Barker (North West) Ltd* [1985] I.R.L.R. 403.

[14] [2000] I.R.L.R. 578. Although this case involved a claim of sex discrimination, the principles will apply equally to claims of unfair dismissal.

[15] See *Also Salvesen v. Simons* [1994] I.C.R. 409; *cf. Coral Leisure Group v. Barnett* [1981] I.R.L.R. 204, EAT.

WRONGFUL DISMISSAL

The concept of wrongful dismissal, which is based on breach of contract, 11.03 should be distinguished from that of unfair dismissal, which is derived from statute and is set out in Part 10 of the ERA. The remedy of wrongful dismissal derives from common law and depends upon the terms of the contract of employment, express or implied, rather than the statutory concept of reasonableness. An employer who is in material breach of contract will not be exculpated simply because the breach may have been reasonable and to introduce the statutory concept of reasonableness would be to confuse wrongful dismissal with unfair dismissal.[16] Most wrongful dismissal claims arise in cases where the employer dismisses the employee with no or insufficient notice. For example, a contract of employment may give the employer the right to dismiss summarily on the occurrence of certain defined acts of misconduct such as theft or violence. If the employee were then to be dismissed without notice, for example for poor performance, he would be able to argue that he was wrongfully (and probably unfairly) dismissed.

In the event of a claim for wrongful dismissal being successful, the employer will be liable to pay damages for the loss suffered following the dismissal. The award is calculated in accordance with common law principles and compensates the employee for losses incurred as a result of the breach of contract. As most employment contracts are terminable on appropriate notice being given, compensation normally covers the period that proper notice would have covered had it been given.[17] The amount of damages will take into account the losses the employee has suffered such as pay, bonus, commission, car benefits, and pension rights.[18] The employee is obliged to mitigate his losses.[19]

Claims for breach of contract may be heard by employment tribunals as well as by the civil courts.[20] However, the amount of damages which the tribunal can award is limited to £25,000 and for this jurisdiction to apply the claim must arise from or be outstanding on termination of employment.[21] To recover damages in excess of this amount an action would have to be raised in the appropriate civil court.[22] If the claim is to be brought before an employment tribunal then it must be presented within three months of the effective date of termination. An action in the civil courts can be raised within the normal limitation period applying to contractual claims.

---

[16] *W Wilson & Sons v. Thomas Johnstone,* EAT/953/00.

[17] Subject to the implied obligation of mutual trust and confidence. See Brodie, 1999 O.J.L.S. 83.

[18] On the extent of damages claimable, see *Malik v. BCCI* [1998] A.C. 20; *Johnson v. Unisys* [2001] I.R.L.R. 279.

[19] This principle means it is often more desirable for the employee to argue that the contract was kept alive despite the repudiation by his employer so that he can sue for his wages under the employment contract as a debt. There is no duty to mitigate a debt: see the powerful dissent of Sedley LJ. in *Cerberus Software Ltd v. Rowley* [2001] I.R.L.R. 160, CA.

[20] Employment Tribunals Extension of Jurisdiction (England and Wales) Order 1994 (S.I. 1994 No. 1623) and the Employment Tribunals Extension of Jurisdiction (Scotland) Order 1994 (S.I. 1994 No. 1624).

[21] 1994 Order, r.3.

[22] Subject to the decision of the House of Lords in *Johnson v. Unisys* [2001] I.R.L.R. 279.

ESTABLISHING A DISMISSAL

11.04 Before an unfair dismissal claim can proceed, the employee must establish that a dismissal has occurred. In certain very limited circumstances the contract of employment may be terminated by operation of law if it is incapable of performance in which case the doctrine of frustration may defeat any claim that depends upon a dismissal. The doctrine tends to apply most in cases where the employee has been sentenced to a lengthy period of imprisonment.[23] Occasionally it can apply in long-term ill health cases but here employment tribunals tend to be reluctant to hold that frustration has occurred, preferring generally to deal with termination on this ground as dismissal by reason of capability so, "it may well be that consideration has to be given as to the extent to which the doctrine of frustration of contract at common law sits properly with the statutory rights affording protection to employees on termination of employment".[24] In deciding whether a lengthy absence by reason of illness has caused the contract of employment to be frustrated, employment tribunals are likely to consider such factors as the terms of the contract, including provisions relating to sick pay; how long the employment was likely to last in the absence of illness; the nature of the employment; the nature of the illness or injury; and the period of past employment.[25]

Usually a dismissal occurs when the employer dismisses the employee. However, in certain circumstances a dismissal is deemed to have occurred if the employee resigns because of the actings of the employer. This is known as constructive dismissal and may give rise to a claim for unfair dismissal.[26] To succeed in such a claim it is not sufficient to establish that the employer has acted unreasonably. The employee must establish that by his actings the employer has repudiated the contract of employment. The onus of proof lies on the employee to establish this. As a result of the decision in the well known case of *Western Excavating (E.C.C.) Ltd v. Sharp*[27] it is necessary for the employee to establish the following: (1) that the employer breached the contract of employment; (2) that the breach was a fundamental breach, going to the root of the contract of employment; and (3) that the employee resigned as a response to the employer's breach and not for some other unconnected reason.[28]

11.05 There are many examples of conduct on the employer's part which will amount to a material and repudiatory breach of the contract. One of the most commonly argued reasons is that the employer has conducted

[23] *F.C. Shepherd & Company v. Jerrom* [1986] I.R.L.R. 358, CA.

[24] *per* Lord Johnston in *G F Sharp & Co Ltd v. McMillan* [1998] I.R.L.R. 632, EAT at para. 23. Where the parties have envisaged and insured against the risk of, *e.g.* illness or disability there is no place for the doctrine of frustration to operate: *Villella v. MFI Furniture Centres Ltd* [1999] I.R.L.R. 468, QBD.

[25] See Sir John Donaldson in *Marshall v. Harland and Wolff (No. 1)* [1972] I.C.R. 101 at 106.

[26] For the position where there is a dismissal because the employee is employed under a fixed term contract that has not been renewed under s.95(1)(b) see *BBC v. Kelly-Philips* [1998] I.R.L.R. 294.

[27] [1978] I.R.L.R. 27.

[28] For an example of an employee resigning while on sick leave six months after the employer's breach, see *Linda J Turbert v. Bruce Anchor (Scotland) Ltd* EAT/455/01.

himself in such a manner as to breach the implied term that he will not without reasonable and proper cause conduct himself in a manner that will destroy or seriously undermine the relationship of trust and confidence which exists between employer and employee.[29] This has been referred to as the duty not to act arbitrarily or capriciously in the exercise of a discretion or power open to an employer. It has been termed an obligation of fair dealing.[30] A breach of this term will often constitute a repudiation.[31] Following the recognition of the existence of the term by the House of Lords in *Malik v. BCCI*,[32] it has resulted in a strengthening of the position of the employee, for example protecting the right not to be suspended in the light of unfounded and spurious allegations.[33] The damages recoverable for a breach of the term may extend to damages for psychiatric injury.[34] Importantly however, the protection accorded to the employee by the implied obligation is potentially wider than that available under statute for unfair dismissal. In *Farront v. The Woodroffe School*[35] an employee was dismissed for gross misconduct for refusing to follow an instruction from his employers that they were not contractually entitled to demand of him. When the employee claimed unfair dismissal, he was unsuccessful, the following statement of the law being approved:

> "The jurisdiction based on [what is now ERA s.98 (4)] has not got much to do with contractual rights and duties. Many dismissals are unfair although the employer is contractually entitled to dismiss the employee. Contrariwise, some dismissals are not unfair although the employer was not contractually entitled to dismiss the employee".[36]

It is arguable that for an employer to unreasonably require an employee to do something which he has no contractual obligation to undertake is a breach of the implied term of mutual trust and confidence, even if such a request is not repudiatory *per se*. Of significance is the fact that a claim at common law does not discriminate between employees: there are no qualifying periods of service nor are there any categories of employee excluded from its protection.

The potentially wide-ranging nature of the protection offered by the implied term of mutual trust and confidence has, however, been curbed   11.06

---

[29] For other examples of the employer in material breach see *inter alia, British Broadcasting Corporation v. Beckett* [1983] I.R.L.R. 43 EAT; *W.A. Goold (Pearmark) Ltd v. McConnell* [1995] I.R.L.R. 516; *Millbrook Furnishing Industries v. McIntosh* [1981] I.R.L.R. 309, EAT.

[30] *per* Mr Recorder Langstaff Q.C. in *Shiner Ltd v. Hilton*, EAT/9/00 at para. 34.

[31] *Macari v. Celtic Football and Athletic Club Ltd*, 1999 S.C. 628; *J. V. Strong & Co Ltd v. Hamill*, EAT/1179/00. *Cf.* Lindsay J. (dissenting) in *Moores v. Bude-Stratton Town Council* [2000] I.R.L.R. 676, EAT.

[32] [1998] A.C. 20.

[33] *Gogay v. Hertfordshire County Council* [2000] I.R.L.R. 703, CA.

[34] *Gogay*, above; *Waters v. Commissioner of Police* [2000] I.R.L.R. 720, HL.

[35] [1998] I.R.L.R. 176, EAT.

[36] *London Borough of Redbridge v. Fishman* [1978] I.R.L.R. 69, EAT. See also Lord Browne-Wilkinson in *Halfpenny v. IGE Medical Systems Ltd* [2001] I.R.L.R. 96 at 101, para 32 (HL).

by the House of Lords in *Johnson v. Unisys*.[37] Here the plaintiff was psychologically vulnerable and was summarily dismissed by his employers for misconduct, without any allegations being put to him. He successfully claimed unfair dismissal. He subsequently raised an action for wrongful dismissal at common law seeking substantial damages, arguing that the way in which he had been treated by his employer was a breach of the implied term of mutual trust and confidence. Notwithstanding the hurdle of the rule in England preventing an award of damages for the *manner* of dismissal, the plaintiff was unsuccessful for the reason that their Lordships considered that to allow his claim would subvert the policy of the legislation on unfair dismissal. That legislation enacts a scheme that has no parallel at common law. The limits placed upon who is eligible for protection, and the damages that can be awarded to them,[38] would be completely pointless if these restrictions could be circumvented by the simple expedient of bringing a wrongful dismissal claim.

In many cases where the applicant establishes that a constructive dismissal has occurred, he will succeed in the unfair dismissal claim and that will be the end of the matter. However, it is open to the employer to argue that the reason for the constructive dismissal was still a potentially valid reason under the legislation and that he acted reasonably in all the circumstances. For example, this defence may be open to an employer seeking to bring about a business reorganisation that results in terms and conditions of employment being changed. The normal rules of fairness then apply. If the employer has consulted fully with employees, has attempted to reach agreement regarding the introduction of, for example, a new shift pattern, and has been left with no alternative but to impose it, it may be possible to demonstrate that a resigning employee was constructively dismissed but that the dismissal was fair.

11.07   The foregoing has assumed that the employee in fact claims constructive dismissal, *i.e.* that he accepts the employer's repudiation.[39] In principle where one party in a contract is faced with a repudiatory breach by the other, he has a choice: either he can accept the repudiation, thus bringing the contract to an end and the remedy is one of damages, or alternatively he can continue to perform his obligations under the contract. The contract in the latter situation is kept alive and the innocent party can then sue for debt. The distinction is more than academic; where damages are claimed there is a duty incumbent upon the pursuer to mitigate his loss. This principle has no application where the action is for payment of a debt. The question of whether the contract of employment is an exception to the rule that, generally speaking, a repudiation must be accepted to bring the contract to an end, remains

---

[37] [2001] I.R.L.R. 279.

[38] *e.g.* ERA 1996, ss.119, 124; Employment Rights (Increase of Limits) Order 1999 (S.I. 1999 No. 3375), ERA 1999, s.34(4).

[39] In cases where the conduct complained of amounts to a breach of the implied term of mutual trust and confidence, there may only be a material breach when a course of conduct is looked at cumulatively. The employee can therefore accept the repudiation after that course of conduct has ended without being held to have waived his rights: *Abbey National Plc v. Robinson*, EAT/743/99.

unresolved.[40] Perhaps the best practical guidance is set out in *Western Excavating* itself:

> "For the purpose of this judgement I do not find it either necessary or advisable to express any opinion as to what principles of law operate to bring a contract of employment to an end by reason of an employer's conduct. Sensible persons have no difficulty in recognising such conduct when they hear about it. Persistent and unwanted amorous advances by an employer to a female member of his staff would, for example, clearly be such conduct ... I appreciate that the principles of law applicable to the termination by an employee of a contract of employment because of his employer's conduct are difficult to put concisely in the language judges use in Court ... what is required for the application of this provision is a large measure of common-sense".[41]

WRITTEN STATEMENT OF REASONS FOR DISMISSAL

Every employee who has been continuously employed for a period of not less than one year is entitled to a written statement of reasons for dismissal.[42] The right is applicable if the employee is given notice of termination of his contract of employment, if the contract is terminated without notice, or on the non-renewal of a fixed term contract following its expiry. Although it is certainly good practice for the employer to issue written reasons for dismissal as a matter of course, he is not obliged to do so unless the employee has made the request. However, an employee is entitled to a written statement of reasons for dismissal without having to request it and irrespective of her period of continuous employment if she is dismissed at any time while she is pregnant, or after childbirth in circumstances in which her ordinary or additional maternity leave ends by reason of the dismissal.[43] 11.08

The legislation does not require the employee to make the request in writing but on receipt of the request, whether in writing or not, the employer is obliged to provide written reasons within 14 days. Any written statement is admissible in evidence in any proceedings.[44]

If the employer unreasonably fails to provide a written statement on request or if the particulars of reasons given in purported compliance are inadequate or untrue then the employee may make an application to the employment tribunal.[45] If the application is successful then the tribunal may make a declaration as to what it finds the employer's reasons were for dismissing the employee. The tribunal must also make an award

---

[40] The issues were brought into sharp focus before the Court of Appeal in *Cerberus Software Ltd v. Rowley* [2001] I.R.L.R. 160. See generally, McBryde, *The Law of Contract in Scotland* (1987), para 14–49 *et seq.*; *Chitty on Contracts* (28th ed., 1999) para 39–071 *et seq.*

[41] [1978] I.R.L.R. 27 at 27.

[42] ERA, s.92.

[43] *ibid.*, s.92(4).

[44] *ibid.*, s.92(5).

[45] *ibid.*, s.93(1).

requiring the employer to pay to the employee a sum equal to two weeks pay.[46] A complaint under these provisions must be presented within the same time-limit as an unfair dismissal claim arising out of the same circumstances.

NOTICE OF TERMINATION

11.09 At common law, either party giving the other notice can terminate a contract of employment for an indefinite period. The contract itself may state what notice is required to be given by the parties. If there is no provision in the contract setting out the length of notice required then the period may be determined on the basis of what is reasonable. This depends on the circumstances and factors such as the seniority of the position, the length of service, the nature of the employment and the frequency of pay days have been held to be relevant in determining this.[47]

In addition to the contractual or common law requirements there are also statutory notice periods which are set out in section 86 of the ERA. This provision sets out the minimum periods of notice, which are required to terminate the contract. However, these only apply to employees who have been continuously employed for at least a month.

If the statutory requirements apply then the employee is required to give a week's notice to the employer. An employer on the other hand must give notice based on a scale depending on the employee's length of service. The notice to be given is[48]: (a) one week's notice if the period of continuous employment is less than two years; (b) at least one week's notice for each year of continuous employment in excess of two years but less than 12 years; or (c) at least 12 weeks notice if the period of employment extends to 12 years or more. The requirements apply to most employees regardless of hours worked. The statutory notice periods override any shorter periods set out in the contract. However, if a longer notice period is set out in the contract or can be implied from the circumstances surrounding the relationship then that period will replace the statutory minimum period.

11.10 Unless agreed otherwise, the notice, whether under statute or contract, need not be given in writing although it is obviously preferable to do so. However, the notice must be clear in indicating the party's wish to terminate the contract and provide an ascertainable date of termination. This date is important when determining the effective date of termination in unfair or wrongful dismissal claims.[49] That an employer has

---

[46] ERA, s.93(2).

[47] *Hill v. C.A. Parsons & Co. Ltd* [1971] 3 All E.R. 1345

[48] ERA 1996, s.86.

[49] ERA, s.97 and the Employment Tribunals Extension of Jurisdiction (Scotland) Order 1994, reg. 7 or the relevant date in redundancy pay claims under ERA, s.145. An employment tribunal has no jurisdiction to hear a complaint of breach of contract brought before the effective date of termination or where there is no notice period before any act of dismissal: *Capek v. Lincolnshire County Council* [2000] I.R.L.R. 590, CA. See also *London Underground v. Noel* [2000] I.C.R. 109, CA.

issued an employee with his P45 is not necessarily determinative that the employer is dismissing the employee forthwith.[50] Once given, the notice may not usually be unilaterally withdrawn without the consent of the other party.[51] The contract terminates when the notice period expires regardless of whether the employee is required to work during it.[52]

The employer is entitled to dismiss the employee without notice if the employee commits a sufficiently serious breach of the contract. If, for example, the employee is guilty of gross misconduct then the employer will be entitled to dismiss the employee summarily, *i.e.* without notice. Likewise, if the employer commits a fundamental breach of the contract then the employee is entitled to terminate the contract without giving notice and claim constructive dismissal (see above).

If the employer fails to give the required notice, or gives insufficient notice, then an action claiming damages for breach of contract or wrongful dismissal is competent. The employer may usually dismiss the employee without notice and pay wages in lieu of notice, which sum represents the employee's entitlement to damages for breach of contract.[53]

The Reason for Dismissal

Although there is no longer an onus on the employer to establish the 11.11
reasonableness of the dismissal, he must still prove that there was a reason and that it was potentially fair under the legislation. A failure to establish either will inevitably result in a finding of unfair dismissal. As has been held by the House of Lords,[54] dealing with section 57 of the EP(C)A[55]:

> "The resolution of the question what is the reason or, if there is more than one, the principal reason for dismissal is important not only in relation to section 57(1) and section 57(2) but also in relation to section 57(3), for the question in section 57(3) is whether the employer acted reasonably in treating it as a sufficient reason for dismissing the employee and it must refer back to the reason or principal reason determined under section 57(1). As a matter of law, a reason cannot reasonably be treated as a sufficient reason for dismissal where it has not been established as true or that there were reasonable grounds upon which the employer could have concluded that it was true".

---

[50] *Villella v. MFI Furniture Centres Ltd* [1999] I.R.L.R. 468, EAT. *Cf. McLennan v. ICCS (Northern) Ltd & Ors*, September 29, 1998, Dundee Sheriff Court, unreported, Sheriff R A Davidson.

[51] *Riordan v. War Office* [1959] 3 All E.R. 552. Note that the parties can agree to their own effective date of termination: *Lambert v. Croydon College* [1999] I.R.L.R. 346, EAT.

[52] The date of dismissal can sometimes be taken to be the date on which temporary work undertaken after redundancy ends, rather than the date of redundancy itself, see *Stoddart International Plc v. Isabella Inglis Wilson*, EAT/337/00.

[53] But see *Malik*, above. *Cf. William Hill Organisation Ltd v. Tucker* [1998] I.R.L.R. 313, CA.

[54] *Smith v. City of Glasgow District Council* [1987] I.R.L.R. 326.

[55] See now ERA, s.98.

In the event that there is more than one reason for dismissal, the employer must establish the principal reason. A reason has been defined as a set of facts known to the employer or beliefs held by him, which cause him to dismiss the employee.[56] Generally, the employer is not permitted to rely upon information which was not known to him at the time when the decision was made[57] although evidence of such facts may be relevant in determining compensation in the event of a dismissal being found to be unfair.[58] The tribunal will be concerned to identify why the employer in fact decided to dismiss. An error by the tribunal in characterising the potentially fair reason, for example as capability as opposed to "some other substantial reason" is one with which the EAT may interfere, but they should be reluctant to substitute their own reason.[59]

Capability

11.12   Dismissal for a reason related to the capability or qualifications of the employee for performing work of the kind which he was employed by the employer to do is a potentially valid reason for dismissal. A definition is contained in section 98(3) of the ERA which states that "capability" means capability assessed by reference to:

(a) skill, aptitude, health or any other physical or mental quality; and

(b) "qualifications" means any degree, diploma or other academic, technical or professional qualification relevant to the position which the employee held.

In practical terms, the most common problems relate to the employee's ability to attend work or to perform work to the standard required by the employer. When dealing with dismissals related to the employee's health or any physical or mental quality, consideration should be given to the provisions contained in the Disability Discrimination Act. The DDA imposes certain duties on the employer which must be fulfilled when dealing with a disabled person. Particular attention should be paid to the duty to make "reasonable adjustments" thereby allowing the disabled person to remain in employment.[60]

It is also important to distinguish between lack of capability as opposed to deliberate misconduct because different considerations apply in determining the fairness or unfairness of the dismissal. In one case the EAT made the distinction between incapability due to an inherent incapacity to function and that which was the result of failure to realise the full potential of one's talents. Therefore, where the employee has not come up to the required standard through his own carelessness, negligence or idleness, the case is likely to be categorised as one of misconduct rather then capability.[61]

---

[56] *Abernethy v. Mott, Hay and Anderson* [1974] I.R.L.R. 213, CA.
[57] *W Devis & Sons Ltd v. Atkins* [1977] I.C.R. 662, HL.
[58] cf. *West Kent College v. Richardson* [1999] I.C.R. 511, EAT.
[59] *Wilson v. Post Office* [2000] I.R.L.R. 834, CA.
[60] DDA, s.6. For further information see Chap. 6.
[61] *Sutton and Gates (Luton) Ltd v. Boxall* [1978] I.R.L.R. 486, EAT.

Cases involving dismissal relating to the qualifications of the employee are rare. However, dismissal on this ground may be justified where, for example, it is a condition of employment that an employee hold a clean driving licence and the employee is then disqualified from driving.[62] Even although the employee may have ceased to have qualifications necessary for the job, the employer must still satisfy the employment tribunal that he has acted reasonably, for example, by seeking to employ the employee in a different capacity.

Conduct

Conduct is a potentially valid reason for dismissal although it is not 11.13 specifically defined in the legislation. While case law is a useful guide, it can be no more than that. Each case will turn on its own facts. Cases tend to be classified under one of three headings:

    (i) refusal to obey a lawful order[63];

    (ii) breach of disciplinary standards[64]; and

    (iii) criminal offences outside work[65].

In practice "conduct" covers a wide variety of situations and has been held to mean actions of such a nature, whether done in the course of employment or outwith it, that reflect in some way upon the employer-employee relationship.[66]

Redundancy

Redundancy is defined in section 139(1) of the ERA.[67] A dismissal for 11.14 a reason falling within the statutory definition is potentially fair. However, it should be noted that dismissals that follow a business reorganisation will not necessarily be by reason of redundancy if they do not arise as a result of work reducing or disappearing but may be potentially fair under the heading of "some other substantial reason justifying dismissal" (see below).[68]

---

[62] *Tayside Regional Council v. McIntosh* [1982] I.R.L.R. 272.

[63] See *Redbridge London Borough Council v. Fishman* [1978] I.C.R. 569 (refusal to work substantially increased teaching workload); *Farrant v. Woodroffe School* [1998] I.R.L.R. 176 (refusal to accept a change in duties).

[64] See *CA Parsons & Co Ltd v. McLoughlin* [1978] I.R.L.R. 65 (fighting); *British Leyland UK Ltd v. Swift* [1981] I.R.L.R. 91, CA (fraudulent use of company road fund licence); *Denco Ltd v. Joinson* [1991] I.R.L.R. 63, EAT (unauthorised use of employer's computer); *Adamson v. B and L Cleaning Services Ltd* [1995] I.R.L.R. 193, EAT (approaching customers with the intention of going into competition with the employer); *British Railways Board v. Jackson* [1994] I.R.L.R. 235, CA (employee intending to breach rules but not having actually breached them).

[65] See *P v. Nottinghamshire County Council* [1992] I.R.L.R. 362 (employee who was assistant groundsman at a girls school pleaded guilty to charge of indecent assault on his daughter); *Mathewson v. RB Wilson Dental Laboratory* [1989] I.R.L.R. 512, EAT (employee arrested and charged during lunch break for possession of cannabis); *Securicor Guarding Ltd v. R* [1994] I.R.L.R. 633, EAT (employee denied charges of sexual offences against children).

[66] *Thomson v. Alloa Motor Company* [1983] I.R.L.R. 403.

[67] See Chap. 9.

[68] This will be particularly relevant to cases where employees are "bumped": see, *e.g. Church v. West Lancashire NHS Trust (No. 1)* [1998] I.R.L.R. 4, EAT; *Shawkat v. Nottingham City Hospital NHS Trust* [1999] I.R.L.R. 340, EAT; [2001] I.R.L.R. 555, CA.

Contravention of a statutory enactment

11.15   Dismissal on this ground is rare.[69] It would be justifiable in circumstances where the continued employment of the employee would contravene a statutory provision. It might apply for example to a doctor disqualified from practising by the General Medical Council or a teacher disqualified by the General Teaching Council. Usually, dismissals that might be justified under this heading would also be justified under other potentially fair reasons. In order to fall under this heading the continued employment of the employee must actually contravene an enactment. Where the employer holds a genuine but incorrect belief that continued employment will contravene an enactment, this will instead fall under the heading of some other substantial reason justifying dismissal.[70]

Some other substantial reason justifying dismissal

11.16   This is a "catch all" category and in practice most potentially fair dismissals fall within one of the other categories specified in section 98. The "SOSR" defence is most commonly used by employers who seek to justify dismissals in the context of business reorganisations that do not come within the definition of redundancy. If the employer seeks to reorganise the business by terminating existing contracts of employment and offering new terms and conditions, the dismissal of an employee who refuses to accept the new terms and conditions is potentially fair under this heading.[71] This provision has been interpreted in a highly subjective way. It has been held by the EAT that:

> "Although an employer cannot claim that a reason for dismissal is substantial if it is a whimsical or capricious reason which no person of ordinary sense would entertain, if he can show that he had a fair reason in his mind at the time when he decided on dismissal and that he genuinely believed it to be fair, this would bring the case within the category of some other substantial reason. Where the belief is one which is genuinely held, and particularly is one which most employers would be expected to adopt, it may be a substantial reason even where modern sophisticated opinion can be adduced to show that it has no specific foundation".[72]

Certain reasons for dismissal are categorised under this heading by virtue of specific statutory provisions. Section 106 of the ERA provides

---

[69] For examples see *Sandhu v. Hillingdon London Borough* [1978] I.R.L.R. 208, EAT; *Taylor v. Alidair* [1978] I.R.L.R. 82.

[70] *Bouchaala v. Trust House Forte Hotels Ltd* [1980] I.R.L.R. 382.

[71] *Hollister v. National Farmers Union* [1979] I.R.L.R. 238. For other examples of SOSR dismissals see *RS Components Ltd v. Irwin* [1973] I.R.L.R. 239, NIRC (employer's pressing need to impose new restrictive covenant on employee to prevent future loss of business. Covenant rejected by employee); *Delabole Slate Ltd v. Berriman* [1985] I.R.L.R. 305 (changes must to be "workforce" not just terms and conditions); *Kingston v. British Railways Board* [1984] I.R.L.R. 146, CA (imprisonment even though not amounting to frustration may be SOSR); *Ely v. YKK Fasteners (UK) Ltd* [1993] I.R.L.R. 500, CA (employer insisting on teminating employment due to mistaken belief employee had resigned).

[72] *Harper v. National Coal Board* [1980] I.R.L.R. 260.

that the dismissal of a replacement for a permanent employee suspended on medical grounds and the dismissal of a replacement for a pregnant employee absent from work are to be treated as "some other substantial reason justifying dismissal". A dismissal for an "economic, technical or organisational" reason under TUPE also comes under this heading.[73]

General principles affecting reasonableness

As has frequently been pointed out by the EAT in particular, the 11.17 starting point in determining the reasonableness of a dismissal must be the words of the statute. Section 98(4) of ERA states:

"Where the employer has fulfilled the requirements of subsection (1), the determination of the question whether the dismissal is fair or unfair (having regard to the reason shown by the employer)—

> (a) depends on whether in the circumstances (including the size and administrative resources of the employer's undertaking) the employer acted reasonably or unreasonably in treating it as a sufficient reason for dismissing the employee, and
> (b) that question shall be determined in accordance with equity and the substantial merits of the case."

The EAT and higher courts have laid down a number of broad principles 11.18 and guidelines to be applied in unfair dismissal cases, but at the end of the day each case must be decided by applying its own particular facts to the statutory test. Although it is not essential for an employment tribunal to refer to the test in its decision, it should at least be implicit in the reasons that the statutory test has been followed.[74]

Procedural fairness

A failure to follow a fair procedure will invariably render a dismissal 11.19 unfair. For a number of years employment tribunals were able to find dismissals fair in circumstances where, although the employer had not followed a fair procedure, if he had done so he could reasonably have decided to dismiss.[75] In the leading case of *Polkey v. A.E. Dayton Services Limited*,[76] the House of Lords emphasised the distinction between matters that must be taken into account in determining the fairness of the dismissal and those that must be taken into account in determining the amount of compensation payable in the event of a finding of unfair dismissal. In particular, it was held that an employment tribunal is not bound to hold that any procedural failure by the employer renders the dismissal unfair. It is one of the factors to be weighed by the employment tribunal in deciding whether or not the dismissal was reasonable within section 98(4). It was held that the weight to be attached to such a procedural failure should depend upon the circumstances known to the

---

[73] See Chap. 11.
[74] *Conlin v. United Distillers* [1994] I.R.L.R. 169.
[75] As a result of the decision in *British Labour Pump Co. Ltd v. Byrne* [1979] I.R.L.R. 94.
[76] [1987] I.R.L.R. 503.

employer at the time of the dismissal, not on the actual consequence of any such failure. The House of Lords acknowledged that there are undoubtedly some cases where the offence is so serious and the factors sufficiently clear that whatever explanation the employee advanced it would make no difference. In such circumstances the dismissal may well be fair even although a proper procedure has not been followed. However, an employer who chooses to dismiss without following full and proper procedures is running a serious risk that the resultant dismissal will be unfair. Proper investigative, disciplinary and appeal procedures should not be seen merely as matters of form. Fair application of such procedures creates safeguards for employer and employee alike. An employer who observes an employee staggering at the work place may conclude that the employee is drunk and should be dismissed for breaching company rules. If the employee is drunk, perhaps no explanation will be acceptable to the employer. However, even a basic investigation may reveal that the behaviour is not the consequence of over indulgence but is a direct result of a medical condition.[77] In these circumstances, a failure to investigate the matter properly will inevitably lead to a finding that the dismissal is unfair.

11.20   An important procedural safeguard is an appeal procedure and although a decision on an internal appeal takes place after the original decision to dismiss, it is still very much an integral part of the dismissal process. If the employer refuses to allow the employee to pursue a right of appeal, this fact in itself may make the dismissal unfair. One of the leading authorities on this question is the case of *West Midlands Co-operative Society v. Tipton*[78] where the House of Lords held:

> "The Court of Appeal had erred in overturning the EAT's decision that the respondents' refusal to allow the appellant to exercise his contractual right of appeal against his summary dismissal rendered the dismissal unfair. The Appeal Court had wrongly taken the view that, in accordance with the decision of the House of Lords in *W Devis & Sons Ltd v. Atkins*, whether the employer acted reasonably or unreasonably within the meaning of s.57(3) of the Employment Protection (Consolidation) Act fell to be determined as at the date of the dismissal and nothing discovered after that date could be taken into account as relevant to that question, save in so far as it bore upon the employer's state of mind before the dismissal. A dismissal is unfair if the employer unreasonably treats his reason as a sufficient reason to dismiss the employee, either when he makes his original decision to dismiss or when he maintains that decision at the conclusion of an internal appeal. A dismissal may also be held to be unfair when the employer has refused to entertain an appeal to which the employee was contractually entitled and thereby denied to him the opportunity of showing that, in all the circumstances, the employer's reason for dismissing him could not reasonably be treated as sufficient . . . Whilst the apparent injustice

---

[77] *Hepworth Pipe Co Ltd v. Chahal*, EAT/611/80
[78] [1986] I.R.L.R. 112. Cf. *Alboni v. Ind Coope Retail Ltd* [1998] I.R.L.R. 131, CA *Parkinson v. March Consulting Ltd* [1997] I.R.L.R. 308.

to the employer in excluding from the question of reasonableness misconduct of the employee unrelated to the reason for dismissal is mitigated by the amended statutory provisions relating to compensation, there is nothing to mitigate the injustice to an employee which would result if he were unable to complain that his employer, though acting reasonably on the facts known to him when he dismissed the employee, acted quite unreasonably in maintaining his decision to dismiss in the face of mitigating circumstances established in the course of the domestic appeal procedure which a reasonable employer would have treated as sufficient to excuse the employee's offence on which the reason for dismissal depended".[79]

If an appeal process is conducted properly and if it amounts to a proper rehearing rather than just a review, then from the employer's point of view it can be a vehicle for curing defects that occurred at earlier stages in the process. It is essential that the appeal process is independent from the disciplinary process, and demonstrably so. As a general rule, employees seldom benefit from pursuing internal appeals and yet are often criticised for failing to do so. The position when advising an employer is clear—the employee should always be informed of any right of appeal and any appeal procedure should be applied in a fair and independent way. However, when advising an employee the position is less straightforward. Sometimes by appealing, the employee simply gives the employer an opportunity to cure any defect in the disciplinary process, thereby reducing the likelihood of success in an unfair dismissal claim. Furthermore, even if the employer is prepared to overturn the decision and voluntarily reinstate, the working relationship may be beyond repair. As to the effect of an internal appeal on the effective date of termination, a distinction is to be made between the situation where the employee is suspended with the possibility of his dismissal not being confirmed pending the internal appeal, and the instance where the employee is summarily dismissed with a possibility of reinstatement. In the former case the effective date of termination is the date of his appeal rather than the date he is informed that his employer intends to dismiss him, in the latter it is the date of the summary dismissal.[80]

Further guidance on procedures is to be found in the relevant provisions of codes of practice and employment tribunals are bound to take these into account.[81] Employers should always make themselves aware of the terms of the relevant codes, in particular the ACAS Code of Practice on Disciplinary and Grievance Procedures. This document is clear in its terms and generally speaking an employer who acts in accordance with it is likely to stand a reasonable prospect of success before an employment tribunal.

---

[79] At 112.

[80] *Drage v. Governing Body of Greenford High School* [2000] I.R.L.R. 314, CA; *cf. Hassan v. Odeon Cinemas Ltd* [1998] I.C.R. 127.

[81] A statutory provision to this effect is contained in s.207 of the Trade Union and Labour Relations (Consolidation) Act 1992.

Capability and fairness

11.21   Capability cases tend to fall into two categories—those dealing with ill health or absence and those dealing with poor performance. As cases vary so much on their facts, the principles that have emerged from the relevant case law are broadly stated. As a rule, in capability cases, employment tribunals are concerned to identify that the employer has provided adequate warning of the consequences of the failure to improve performance or attendance, adequate time within which to improve, and also that, where appropriate, alternatives to dismissal have been considered.

Absence cases are usually of two types—those involving persistent short-term absences and those involving one or more long-term absences brought about because of specific health reasons. In the former, warnings are appropriate. However, in dealing with the latter type of case, the application of disciplinary sanctions such as warnings is of less relevance. Proper consultation with the employee and, if appropriate, the obtaining of a doctor's report are more important considerations. The purpose is to ascertain the medical condition of the employee with a view to identifying when he is likely to be able to return to work. An employer seeking a medical report must always comply with the Access to Medical Reports Act 1988. As a general rule an employee who is absent as a result of ill health should not be dismissed while still in receipt of contractual sick pay and the provisions of the DDA should also be taken into account.

11.22   The Court of Session reviewed a number of authorities on the subject of ill health dismissal in *A. Links & Co. Ltd v. Rose*[82] and in particular quoted with approval the following passage from one of the leading decisions of the EAT on the steps that ought to be taken by an employer who is considering a dismissal on this ground[83]:

> "There have been several decisions of the Appeal Tribunal in which consideration has been given to what are the appropriate steps to be taken by an employer who is considering the dismissal of an employee on the ground of ill health. *Spencer v. Paragon Wallpapers Ltd* [1976] I.R.L.R. 373 and *David Sherratt Ltd v. Williams* are examples. It comes to this. Unless there are wholly exceptional circumstances, before an employee is dismissed on the ground of ill health it is necessary that he should be consulted and the matter discussed with him, and that in one way or another steps should be taken by the employer to discover the true medical position. We do not propose to lay down detailed principles to be applied in such cases, for what will be necessary in one case may not be appropriate in another. But if in every case employers take such steps as are sensible according to the circumstances to consult the employee and to discuss the matter with him, and to inform themselves upon the true medical position, it will be found in

---

[82] [1991] I.R.L.R. 353, CS. Compare the following recent examples: *British Gas Services Ltd v. McCaull* [2001] I.R.L.R. 60, EAT; *Villella v. MFI Furniture Centres Ltd* [1999] I.R.L.R. 468; *G F Sharp & Co Ltd v. McMillan* [1998] I.R.L.R. 632, EAT.

[83] *East Lindsey District Council v. Daubney* [1977] I.R.L.R. 181.

practice that all that is necessary has been done. Discussions and consultation will often bring to light facts and circumstances of which the employers were unaware, and which will throw new light on the problem".[84]

As is noted above, different principles apply in the case of persistent short-term absences where warnings, rather than consultation, may be the primary consideration in determining whether a dismissal is fair.[85]

Conduct and fairness

Any employer proposing to dismiss on the ground of conduct should have regard to the now famous guidelines laid down by the EAT in *British Home Stores Ltd v. Burchell.*[86] The following guidance has been followed by employment tribunals in many cases: 11.23

> "What the tribunal have to decide every time is, broadly expressed, whether the employer who discharged the employee on the ground of the misconduct in question (usually, though not necessarily, dishonest conduct) entertained a reasonable suspicion amounting to a belief in the guilt of the employee of that misconduct at that time. That is really stating shortly and compendiously what is in fact more than one element. First of all, there must be established by the employer the fact of that belief; that the employer did believe it. Secondly, that the employer had in his mind reasonable grounds upon which to sustain that belief. And thirdly, we think, that the employer, at the stage at which he formed that belief on those grounds, at any rate at the final stage at which he formed that belief on those grounds, had carried out as much investigation into the matter as was reasonable in all the circumstances of the case. It is the employer who manages to discharge the onus of demonstrating those three matters, we think, who must not be examined further".[87]

In *Boys and Girls Welfare Society v. McDonald,*[88] the EAT pointed out that the *BHS* test was formulated before the burden of proof, which previously the employer had to discharge, was neutralised. The EAT went on to consider how the test ought to be applied in practice, pointing out in the following passage that the test is of limited relevance in circumstances where there is little or no dispute on the facts: 11.24

> "Setting aside the question of onus of proof, it is apparent that the threefold Burchell test is appropriate where the employer has to decide a factual contest. The position may be otherwise where there is no real conflict on the facts. In *Royal Society for the Protection of Birds v. Croucher* [1984] I.R.L.R. 425, a decision of

---

[84] At 18.
[85] *Lynock v. Cereal Packaging* [1988] I.C.R. 670.
[86] [1978] I.R.L.R. 379, EAT.
[87] At para. 2.
[88] [1996] I.R.L.R. 129.

the Employment Appeal Tribunal presided over by Waite J, the employee was suspected of dishonesty in relation to reimbursement of private petrol use by way of false expenses claims. He admitted the offences but said by way of mitigation that on earlier occasions he had omitted to claim genuine expenses. The employment tribunal, applying the *Burchell* test, concluded that the employer had failed to carry out sufficient investigation and that the dismissal was unfair. On appeal the Employment Appeal Tribunal held that the employee having admitted the misconduct, there was little scope for further investigation and reversed the employment tribunal's finding of unfairness. At p.429, paragraphs 36–38, Waite J said:

'It is difficult to escape the impression that the source of error in the present case may have been their evident view that the test in *British Home Stores Ltd v. Burchell* [1980] ICR 303, 304 (Note), was one which fell to be applied automatically whenever reasonableness was in issue, at all events in cases of dishonesty, for the purposes of assessing whether a dismissal had been fair under s.57(3). The *Burchell* case, it will be remembered, was a case which concerned instances in which there has been a suspicion or belief of the employee's misconduct entertained by the employers.

Here there was no question of suspicion or of questioned belief: there the dishonest conduct was admitted. There was very little scope, therefore, for the kind of investigation to which this appeal tribunal was referring in *Burchell's* case; investigation, that is to say, designed to confirm suspicion or clear up doubt as to whether or not a particular act of misconduct has occurred. So we think that this may perhaps be another case where an employment tribunal has fallen into error by a misplaced and artificial emphasis upon the guidelines in the *Burchell* case, something to which this appeal tribunal had recent occasion to refer in *Lintafoam (Manchester) Ltd v. Fletcher*, The Times, 12 March 1984.

We repeat what we said then. The *Burchell* case remains, in circumstances akin to those that there were there under consideration, a most useful and helpful guideline; but it can never replace the soundness of an appraisal of all the circumstances of each particular case viewed in the round in the way that s.57(3) requires them to be viewed' ".[89]

That being so, in *Whitbread plc v. Hall*[90] the Court of Appeal has recently stated that the requirement of reasonableness in section 98(4) is as applicable to the investigation process as it is to the penalty imposed on the employee, even where he or she has admitted to the misconduct of which he is accused. Accordingly the tribunal should ask not only whether the dismissal was within the "band of reasonable responses" but should also apply that test to the procedure used in reaching the decision

---

[89] At para. 29.
[90] [2001] I.R.L.R. 275.

to dismiss. As was noted above, any decision to suspend an employee pending a disciplinary procedure will be subject to the implied obligation of mutual trust and confidence.[91]

Difficulties can arise where the employer has identified an act of misconduct but is unable to identify the perpetrator from a group. In certain limited circumstances the employer may be able to justify "group dismissals" but only if certain conditions are satisfied[92]: 11.25

- The misconduct in question must be such as would have justified dismissal had it been committed by an identified individual.
- The employer must satisfy the tribunal that the act in question was committed by one or more members of the group, each of whom would have been capable of committing it.
- The employer must have carried out sufficient investigation in an effort to identify the culprit.

One of the most important cases on the application of section 98(4) is *Iceland Frozen Foods Limited v. Jones*.[93] In its decision, the EAT summarised the principles that had emerged from previous case law. What is now known as the "*Iceland Frozen Foods* test" is still applied today in a substantial proportion of conduct (and indeed capability) cases. Its principles are used to determine whether dismissal has been too severe a penalty. The EAT summarised the legal position as follows: 11.26

- The starting point should always be the words of section 57(3) (now s.98(4)) themselves.
- In applying the section an employment tribunal must consider the reasonableness of the employer's conduct, not simply whether they (the members of the employment tribunal) consider the dismissal to be fair.
- In judging the reasonableness of the employer's conduct an employment tribunal must not substitute its decision as to what was the right course to adopt for that of the employer.
- In many (though not all) cases there is a band of reasonable responses to the employee's conduct within which one employer might reasonably take one view, another quite reasonably take another.
- The function of the employment tribunal, as an industrial jury, is to determine whether in the particular circumstances of each case the decision to dismiss the employee fell within the band of reasonable responses which a reasonable employer might have adopted. If the dismissal falls within the band the dismissal is fair. If the dismissal falls outside the band it is unfair.

---

[91] *Gogay v. Hertfordshire County Council* [2000] I.R.L.R. 703, CA. *Cf. Shiner Ltd v. Hilton*, EAT/9/00, Mr Recorder Langstaff Q.C.

[92] *Monie v. Coral Racing* [1980] I.R.L.R. 464, CA; *Parr v. Whitbread plc* [1990] I.R.L.R. 39, EAT.

[93] [1982] I.R.L.R. 439.

11.27 The test was considered with approval in *Boys and Girls Welfare Society v. McDonald*,[94] a case in which the EAT held that an employment tribunal had fallen into the trap of substituting its own view for that of the employer rather than asking itself whether in the true circumstances of the case dismissal fell within the range of reasonable responses. More recently however there have been attempts to re-visit the way in which the reasonableness test is interpreted by the Courts. In *Haddon v. Van Den Bergh Foods Ltd*,[95] Mr Justice Morison in the EAT doubted the utility of the band of reasonable responses test, finding that tribunals were effectively being asked to apply a test of perversity before they could find a dismissal to be unfair. He went on to hold that it was preferable for the tribunal to look at the facts and to consider how they would have acted in the circumstances. This reasoning was particularly unhelpful in that it unravelled prior decisions where tribunals had been careful *not* to substitute their own views in considering reasonableness.

The position has now been clarified by the decision in the joined cases of *Post Office v. Foley; HSBC Bank plc (formerly Midland Bank plc) v. Madden*.[96] Here the Court of Appeal effectively restored the "range of reasonable responses" test and confirmed that in applying the law of unfair dismissal enacted in sections 98(1), (2) and (4) of the Employment Rights Act 1996, employment tribunals should continue to apply the same interpretation as was placed on the equivalent provisions in the Employment Protection (Consolidation) Act 1978. Accordingly for all practical purposes the "band or range of reasonable responses" approach to reasonableness as set out in *Iceland Frozen Foods* remains binding. The Court pointed out that the test does not necessarily apply in every case and that there will be some where there is no band or range to consider since there is only one reasonable response. However, in cases where there is room for reasonable disagreement amongst reasonable employers as to whether dismissal for the particular misconduct is a reasonable or an unreasonable response, it is helpful for the tribunal to consider "the range of reasonable responses".

11.28 As noted above, it is an important principle of the law of unfair dismissal that each case must be determined on its own facts. Frequently, employees attempt to argue that their dismissals are unfair because others in similar circumstances have not been dismissed. A failure to apply disciplinary sanctions consistently may lead a tribunal to the conclusion that a particular dismissal lay outwith the range of reasonable responses open to the employer, but this is not automatically the case because it is seldom that the facts of different cases are identical. A balance has to be achieved between consistency and flexibility and the employer must be able to take into account features that distinguish one case from another, such as length of service or disciplinary record.[97]

Although, as the law currently stands, employees require one year of continuous employment to qualify for the right to make an unfair dismissal claim, it is recommended that fair disciplinary procedures should be applied to all employees, irrespective of length of service.

---

[94] [1996] I.R.L.R. 129.
[95] [1999] I.C.R. 1150.
[96] [2000] I.R.L.R. 827.
[97] See *Conlin v. United Distillers* [1994] I.R.L.R. 169, CS.

There are sound business, legal, and employment relations reasons for doing this. In cases where contractual disciplinary procedures apply, failure to follow these may well give rise to claims based on breach of contract. A failure may also infer discrimination. As direct evidence is seldom available to enable an applicant to establish an act of discrimination, employment tribunals are entitled to draw inferences from primary facts. For example, a female employee who has less than one year of service and is dismissed without any proper procedure may argue that a man in similar circumstances would have been subject to a formal procedure. Such a differential in treatment may assist a sex discrimination claim. Although the employer may claim that he treats all employees equally unfairly, irrespective of sex, this is not usually a popular argument!

Redundancy and fairness

Any employer seeking to enforce redundancies should ensure that 11.29 reasonable steps are taken to avoid job losses. It is not the function of the employment tribunal to judge the decision to reduce numbers, rather it is to ensure that in implementing the decision to make redundancies, the employer acts reasonably in terms of section 98(4).[98] However, the employer should be able to lead evidence that the matter has been fully and properly considered.[99] Useful guidance on handling redundancies is contained in the well-known case of *Williams v. Compair Maxam Ltd*,[1] where the EAT laid down the following guidelines, which outline the steps that ought to be taken by an employer contemplating redundancies:

1. The employer will seek to give as much warning as possible of impending redundancies so as to enable the union and employees who may be affected to take early steps to inform themselves of the relevant facts, consider possible alternative solutions and, if necessary, find alternative employment in the undertaking or elsewhere.
2. The employer will consult the union as to the best means by which the desired management result can be achieved fairly and with as little hardship to the employees as possible. In particular, the employer will seek to agree with the union the criteria to be applied in selecting the employees to be made redundant. When a selection has been made, the employer will consider with the union whether the selection has been made in accordance with those criteria.
3. Whether or not an agreement as to the criteria to be adopted has been agreed with the union, the employer will seek to establish criteria for selection which so far as possible do not depend solely upon the opinion of the person making the selection but can be objectively checked against such things as attendance record, efficiency at the job, experience, or length of service.

---

[98] *Campbell v. Dunoon and Cowal Housing Association Ltd* [1993] I.R.L.R. 496.
[99] *Ladbroke Courage Holidays Ltd v. Asten* [1981] I.R.L.R. 59, EAT.
[1] [1982] I.R.L.R. 83, EAT.

4. The employer will seek to ensure that the selection is made fairly in accordance with these criteria and will consider any representations the union may make as to such selection.
5. The employer will seek to see whether instead of dismissing an employee he could offer him alternative employment.

11.30 Although the above guidelines were stated to be applicable in a unionised environment, they contain useful guidance even for smaller employers, or for those who do not recognise trade unions. Consultation with employees and their representatives is of critical importance, one of the main purposes being to seek ways of avoiding redundancies. During a properly conducted consultation process one would expect management and employee representatives to address issues such as seeking volunteers for redundancy prior to enforcing job losses; redeployment of those threatened with redundancy to other jobs; and addressing other ways of saving costs and selection procedures. Many employers have rejected selection of candidates for redundancy on the basis of "last in first out", preferring now to assess on merit. If criteria for selection are generally fair and capable of being applied objectively, the employer will not be criticised for using them. The majority of problems tend to arise in connection with the *application* of selection criteria. The employer should therefore always ensure not only that fair criteria are being used but also that members of management who are involved in the selection process are fully trained in their application. It is advisable for management to ensure that proper appeal procedures exist, enabling employees to challenge selection at a higher level within the organisation. Because of the obligation on the employer to consult with employees faced with redundancy, a failure to do this in itself is likely to result in a finding of unfair dismissal[2] although in the event that consultation would have made little or no difference, compensation may be limited.[3] If an employee is in a position to argue that he would not have been selected for redundancy if a proper consultative process had taken place he may succeed in obtaining a substantial award of compensation.

11.31   The Court of Session considered the question of redundancy consultation in *King v. Eaton Ltd*[4] where it was stated:

"In determining whether consultation with the trade union did take place, it is necessary to consider what is meant by consultation in this context. This matter was considered in *Rowell v. Hubbard Group Services Ltd* [1995] I.R.L.R. 195. In the course of giving the opinion of the Employment Appeal Tribunal in that case Judge Levy QC quoted from Glidewell LJ in *R. v. British Coal Corporation and Secretary of State for Trade and Industry ex parte Price (No. 3)* [1994] I.R.L.R. 72 at p.75:
'Fair consultation means:

(a) consultation when the proposals are still at a formative stage;

---

[2] *Polkey v. A.E. Dayton Services Ltd* [1987] I.R.L.R. 503, HL.
[3] *ibid.*
[4] [1996] I.R.L.R. 199.

(b) adequate information on which to respond;
(c) adequate time in which to respond;
(d) conscientious consideration by an authority of a response to consultation.

Another way of putting the point more shortly is that fair consultation involves giving the body consulted a fair and proper opportunity to understand fully the matters about which it is being consulted, and to express its views on those subjects, with the consultor thereafter considering those views properly and genuinely.'

Judge Levy went on to say:

'There are no invariable rules as to what is to be done in any given situation; everything will depend on its particular facts. However, when the need for consultation exists, it must be fair and genuine, and should, we suggest, be conducted so far as possible as the passage from Glidewell LJ's judgment suggests.'

We entirely accept the definition of fair consultation expressed by Glidewell LJ, and we agree with the observations in the last-mentioned case. That being so, we have to ask ourselves whether there was fair consultation in the present case".[5]

In determining whether there has been a diminution of work "of a particular kind" the court must take a balanced approach rather than looking only at the employee's individual duties or the work carried out by his department or the business as a whole.[6]

Once again, the point must be made that although redundancy is different in nature from other potentially fair reasons, the same statutory test of fairness applies and it is to the words of the statute that an employment tribunal should always turn.

Automatically unfair reasons

Certain categories of dismissal are identified in the legislation as automatically unfair. In these cases all that the employee has to establish is that the dismissal was for one of the prohibited reasons as the employer is not able to rely on the statutory defence of reasonableness. The one year qualifying period[7] and the upper age limit[8] are both disapplied in relation to such cases.

A dismissal is automatically unfair if it is by reason of the fact that an employee is a member of an independent trade union or proposes to become a member of one; or the employee has participated or proposes to participate in trade union activities; or is not a member of a trade union or proposes to refuse to become or remain a member.[9] Dismissal for participating in "protected" industrial action[10] also falls into the

11.32

---

[5] At para. 20. See also *Mugford v. Midland Bank Plc* [1997] I.R.L.R. 208.
[6] *Church v. West Lancashire NHS Trust* [1998] I.R.L.R. 4, EAT; *Murray v. Foyle Meats Ltd* [1999] I.R.L.R. 562, HL; *Arbuckle v. Scottish Power plc,* 2000 G.W.D. 10—358.
[7] ERA, s.108.
[8] ERA, s.109.
[9] TULCRA, s.152.
[10] TULCRA, s.238A.

category of automatically unfair dismissals as does performing certain functions in relation to trade union recognition.[11]

Any employee who is dismissed for certain defined reasons relating to leave for family reasons is deemed to have been unfairly dismissed by virtue of the provisions of section 99 of the ERA, which lists various circumstances that would give rise to a claim.[12]

If a dismissal arises for health and safety reasons, then it is deemed to be automatically unfair by virtue of ERA, section 100. Section 100(1) lists five reasons for dismissal which would give rise to findings of automatically unfair dismissal and it should be noted that selection for redundancy on any of the grounds specified is also automatically unfair.[13]

11.33   A dismissal of an employee following a "relevant transfer" under the Transfer of Undertakings (Protection of Employment) Regulations 1981[14] is automatically unfair unless the employer succeeds in establishing the statutory defence, *i.e.* that the dismissal was for an "economic, technical or organisational reason entailing changes in the workforce". (See Chap. 11.)

A dismissal made because the employee refused or proposed to refuse to forgo rights existing under the Working Time Regulations 1998,[15] is rendered automatically unfair by section 101A of the ERA.

The Public Interest Disclosure Act 1998 inserted section 103A into ERA 1996. If an employee is dismissed for making a protected disclosure then this will be automatically unfair.[16]

By virtue of section 104 of the ERA a dismissal is automatically unfair if the reason for it is that the employee has brought proceedings against the employer to enforce a "relevant statutory right" or has alleged that the employer has infringed such a right. Section 104 defines "statutory rights" and these are rights that may be referred to an employment tribunal under the ERA; the right to a minimum period of notice of termination of employment; certain rights conferred by the Trade Unions and Labour Relations (Consolidation) Act 1992[17] and any rights conferred by the Working Time Regulations 1998.

Section 104A dictates that a dismissal is automatically unfair if the reason for the dismissal is that the employee sought to benefit from or enforce any of the rights conferred by the National Minimum Wage Act 1998. The dismissal will also be automatically unfair if the employee was dismissed because he took action which resulted in the employer being convicted of an offence under section 31 of the 1998 Act or simply if it can be shown that the reason for the dismissal was the very fact that the employee qualified for the national minimum wage. Section 104B is in very similar terms to section 104A and deals with dismissals resulting from the exercise of rights under the Tax Credits Act 1999.

An employee who is dismissed for asserting or proposing to assert his rights under the Part-Time Workers (Prevention of Less Favourable

---

[11] TULCRA, Sched. A1, para. 161.

[12] "Family reasons" relates to pregnancy, childbirth or maternity; ordinary, compulsory or additional maternity leave; parental leave; or time off for dependants: ERA, s.99(3).

[13] ERA, s.105(3).

[14] S.I. 1981 No. 1794.

[15] S.I. 1998 No. 1833.

[16] For protected disclosures see Chap. 2 above.

[17] *i.e.* those relating to deductions from pay, union activities and time off.

Treatment) Regulations 2000 is regarded as automatically unfairly dismissed,[18] as is an individual who is dismissed for performing or proposing to perform functions related to the Transnational Information and Consultation of Employees Regulations 1999.

Section 105 renders certain redundancy dismissals automatically unfair. If redundancy applies equally to one or more employees in the same undertaking as the dismissed employee and the employee was selected for one of the specified reasons, then the dismissal is automatically unfair. The listed reasons include those connected with pregnancy, health and safety, and assertion of statutory rights.

Employee Representatives have specific protection against unfair 11.34 dismissal by virtue of ERA, section 103 which provides that a dismissal is automatically unfair if the reason is that they performed or proposed to perform certain functions in that capacity.

Certain shop and betting workers are protected under section 101 of the ERA[19] and provision is also made in section 102 in relation to trustees of occupational pension schemes.

Unfair Dismissal—Remedies

In the event that an applicant is found to have been unfairly dismissed, three remedies are available to the employment tribunal—reinstatement, re-engagement and compensation.

Reinstatement

If the employee is successful in obtaining an award of reinstatement 11.35 then the order treats him in all respects as if he had not been dismissed.[20] The intention of the legislation, therefore, is that the employee should be put back in the same job as he was doing for the employer prior to the dismissal, that his terms and conditions of employment remain the same, and that he should be compensated for earnings and benefits lost during the period of unemployment. Sums received by way of pay in lieu of notice and earnings received from other employers are deducted.[21]

Before deciding to make an order for reinstatement the employment tribunal is obliged to consider the wishes of the applicant, the practicality of the order and, where the applicant caused or contributed to some extent to the dismissal, whether it would be just to order reinstatement.[22] For one or more of these reasons. reinstatement is seldom granted. Frequently the applicant does not wish to be reinstated. The very fact that he believes that he has been unfairly dismissed is in itself

---

[18] reg. 7.
[19] Although it should be noted that these provisions do not apply in Scotland.
[20] ERA, s.114.
[21] *ibid.,* s.114(4).
[22] *ibid.,* s.116(1).

likely to be an obstacle to rebuilding a relationship built on trust.[23] Often, by the time the case reaches the tribunal, the employee has found alternative employment and for this reason is unlikely to wish to return to work with the original employer. Furthermore, although reinstatement cases (*i.e.* those where the applicant has indicated on the Form IT1 that he seeks reinstatement as a remedy) are given priority on date listings, the passage of time that takes place between the dismissal and the hearing inevitably dulls the desire to return to the same employer. It is a regrettable fact of life that reinstatement seldom works and many applicants tend to recognise this at a relatively early stage in the proceedings. Some, however, seek the remedy of reinstatement as a tactical device. It is usually felt, with some justification, that the applicant's bargaining position is likely to be enhanced if he seeks a more expensive remedy than a simple award of compensation.

11.36   In determining whether it is practicable for the employer to comply with an order for reinstatement it is incumbent on the tribunal to hear evidence about this before making an award. Employers in particular should ensure that where it is known that an applicant is seeking the remedy of reinstatement they lead evidence at the hearing. Because of the way the legislation is drafted, the determination of the issue of practicability at the original tribunal hearing is in effect a provisional one. If, for some reason, the employer fails to comply with the reinstatement order then a further hearing is necessary to determine compensation payable in respect of the failure.[24] In deciding whether reinstatement is practicable, the tribunal should consider this test in the light of the employer's business at the relevant time.[25]

Turning to the question of contributory conduct, it will, generally speaking, not be appropriate for a tribunal to make an award of reinstatement in circumstances where it has found that the employee has contributed to his dismissal, particularly if his honesty is in question.[26]

Although an order for reinstatement is an order requiring the employer to re-employ the applicant, it is not enforceable as such. Where the employer fails to establish that it was not reasonably practicable to comply with it, then the tribunal is empowered to make an additional award of compensation. The additional award consists of between 26 and 52 weeks pay.[27] The tribunal is entitled to exercise discretion in fixing an amount between these figures and would be entitled, for example, to take into account the employer's reasons for failing to comply with the order. One situation that frequently arises is a

---

[23] It is instructive that in *Anderson v. Pringle of Scotland Ltd* [1998] I.R.L.R. 64, interim interdict was granted effectively keeping the pursuer in his job because there was no suggestion that there had been a breakdown of mutual trust and confidence between the parties.

[24] ERA, s.117. See also *Timex Corporation v. Thomson* [1981] I.R.L.R. 522, EAT; and *Port of London Authority v. Payne* [1994] I.C.R. 555; [1994] I.R.L.R. 9.

[25] *Port of London Authority v. Payne*, above.

[26] *United Distillers v. Harrower*, EAT/1151/96.

[27] s.117(3) as amended by Employment Rights Act 1999. Maximum limit £240 per week, modified by the Employment Rights (Increase of Limits) Order 2001 (S.I. 2001 No. 21) with effect from February 1, 2001. Art. 4(f) of the regulations state that they have effect where the date with which the Order should have been complied with is after February 1, 2001.

failure to comply based on the proposition that the employer no longer has trust and confidence in the employee. This can be a very genuine concern. For example, an employee who was employed in a position of trust may have been dismissed in circumstances where the employer was found not to have reasonable grounds for the belief that the employee had been dishonest. The way in which the employee had conducted himself during the employment tribunal proceedings may well have served to exacerbate the employer's feelings. Where there exists a genuine lack of trust the employment tribunal is unlikely to apply the maximum financial penalty. Indeed, a genuine lack of trust will usually operate as a bar to an award of reinstatement in the first place. Whether the employee was afforded internal appeal procedures, and whether he took advantage of them may be relevant to the award he would otherwise have received for the employer's failure to comply with an order for re-instatement. If there was such a procedure and the employee failed to take advantage of it, then the tribunal may reduce the compensatory award included in the award for unfair dismissal by such amount, if any, as it considers necessary, not exceeding two weeks pay.[28] Similarly where the employer prevented the employee from utilising such an appeals procedure, the compensatory award for unfair dismissal *shall* include a supplementary award

Reinstatement or re-engagement is only awarded in approximately three per cent of successful claims.

Re-engagement

An order for re-engagement is an order, on such terms as the tribunal 11.37 may decide, that the applicant be engaged by the employer, or by a successor of the employer or by an associated employer, in employment comparable to that from which he was dismissed or other suitable employment.[29] Re-engagement is a remedy that is seldom sought by applicants. This is surprising as one would expect advisers to recognise that it constitutes a much more wide ranging and potentially workable remedy than reinstatement. The very fact that it may be enforceable against a successor or associated employer widens the field considerably. For example, it is self evident that where an applicant has been unfairly dismissed because he has been unfairly selected for redundancy, he is unlikely to be awarded reinstatement. Jobs will probably have disappeared and the colleague who ought to have been dismissed if selection criteria were applied properly would have to be moved or dismissed if an order was to be complied with. A re-engagement order might allow an applicant to be re-employed in another part of the company unaffected by redundancies. To use another example, in cases of misconduct when witnesses are asked whether they would be prepared to consider reinstatement of the applicant, the stock response tends to be that they feel they could no longer trust him. That feeling may be genuine but not necessarily justified. Under a re-engagement order the applicant could be re-employed in a different part of the company where he did not have to work alongside the people who were involved in the original decision to dismiss.

---

[28] See s.127A(1) and (4).
[29] ERA, s.115.

It is a regrettable feature of the way in which cases are presented that those acting for applicants seldom take the time to investigate opportunities for re-engagement with a view to arguing for such an order. Particularly if the employer is a large organisation, a little research and preparation is likely to advance the applicant's interests considerably. The procedure for dealing with remedy differs between Scotland and England. In Scotland, the merits and remedy are dealt with together in one hearing. This has the advantage of avoiding delay and expense. In England, a separate hearing on remedy takes place if the applicant has been successful. This creates an additional step in the procedure but perhaps it has the advantage that by then the result of the case is known and when the hearing takes place the parties and their representatives are focused on the issue of remedy.

Unless the employee has contributed to his dismissal, the employment tribunal is obliged to award re-engagement on terms which are, so far as is reasonably practicable, as favourable as an order for reinstatement.[30]

Similar considerations of practicability and contribution apply as are relevant to reinstatement orders.[31]

Compensation

11.38   This is by far the most common remedy. If the tribunal finds that the applicant was unfairly dismissed then, in the absence of a re-employment order, it is empowered to make an award of compensation split into two parts—a basic award and a compensatory award.[32]

Basic award

11.39   The basic award is calculated in exactly the same way as a redundancy payment.[33] In certain specified cases a minimum award is payable.[34] In certain statutorily defined circumstances the basic award may be reduced.[35] The most common reasons for a reduction in the basic award are that the employee has received a redundancy payment or that he contributed to his dismissal.[36]

Compensatory award

11.40   In addition to the basic award the tribunal is entitled to make a compensatory award which is such amount as the tribunal considers "just and equitable in all the circumstances having regard to the loss sustained

---

[30] ERA, s.116(2)—(4).

[31] For an example where re-engagement could not be awarded on the basis that trust and confidence could not be restored, see *Wood Group Heavy Industrial Turbines Ltd v. Crossan* [1998] I.R.L.R. 680, EAT.

[32] Special awards were abolished by the ERA.

[33] ERA, s.119. With effect from February 1, 2001, the limit on a week's pay for the purpose of calculating statutory redundancy payments (and therefore the basic award) is £240.

[34] ERA, s.120. Presently £3,300.

[35] ERA, s.122.

[36] It should be noted that any deduction made in a *Polkey*, above, situation should be made before any deduction on account of contributory behaviour, see *David MacFarlane v. John Baillie t/a John Baillie Carpets*, EAT 10/5/01.

by the complainant in consequence of the dismissal in so far as that loss is attributable to action taken by the employer".[37] The tribunal may take into account earnings and benefits lost by the applicant as well as any expenses reasonably incurred in consequence of the dismissal. The applicant is under a duty to mitigate his losses in accordance with the principles that apply in relation to the common law of damages.

The tribunal has a wide discretion in determining the amount of the compensatory award in that it must be just and equitable in all the circumstances of the case. The award may include loss of earnings and benefits to the date of the tribunal hearing and beyond. It is incumbent on those representing applicants to ensure that they lead sufficient evidence of losses to enable the tribunal to make an award. This is particularly important in cases where future losses are being claimed. It may be necessary to lead evidence from someone qualified to speak to the applicant's prospects of obtaining alternative employment taking into account his skills and experience and the local job market. It goes without saying that it is necessary for the applicant to produce evidence of previous earnings including benefits as well as evidence of income received since the dismissal.

In presenting an applicant's case, it can be of considerable assistance to produce not only the relevant documentary evidence of losses but also a spreadsheet showing a detailed calculation.

One particularly important head of loss is that which applies in 11.41 relation to pension rights. Although this is a potentially complex head of loss its calculation can be simplified. Alternatively, it may be appropriate to lead expert evidence in support of this aspect of the claim. The value of this head of loss can be high and not infrequently exceeds the value of other heads of claim, and therefore it is essential to ensure that this is calculated properly. Now that the compensatory limit has been raised, no doubt more attention will be paid to this head of loss. Useful guidelines are available to assist with the calculation.[38] Calculations differ according to whether the applicant participated in a money purchase or final salary scheme and care should be taken to obtain all relevant information about the scheme in question at the earliest possible point in the proceedings, not least because information about pension losses will be relevant to negotiations about settlement.

As far as money purchase schemes are concerned, the calculation will centre around the value of the employers contributions to the scheme, starting from the date of dismissal, with perhaps a sum to compensate for any loss incurred by way of penalty for leaving the scheme early. The sum may be subject to a multiplier depending on the facts of the case and it will be for the applicant to prove future losses in this regard.

Final salary schemes involve different considerations. The tribunal will seek to assess the loss of pension rights from the date of the dismissal to the date of the hearing; loss of future pension rights and loss of enhancement of accrued pension rights. The first two are relatively straightforward to calculate and tribunals often follow the recommendation in the aforementioned guidelines to apply (unless there is specific

---

[37] ERA, s.123.
[38] *Industrial Tribunals — Compensation for Loss of Pension Rights* (Sara, Pugsley and Crump) available from HMSO.

evidence to contradict this) notional rates for employers contributions, being 10 per cent for non-contributory schemes and 15 per cent for non-contributory schemes. The calculation of the loss of enhancement of accrued pension rights is a much more complicated process and it is strongly recommended that those representing applicants take specialist actuarial advice with a view to presenting specialist evidence on such losses. An actuarial table has been produced by the Government Actuary's Department and this allows for a fairly basic calculation based on age, length of service and retirement date. This usually requires considerable modification in dealing with individual cases and practitioners should bear in mind that the figure produced should be reduced by a percentage to take account of the possibility of dismissal before the anticipated retirement date.

11.42   The compensatory award is subject to a statutory ceiling, currently £51,700.[39] Despite recent increases in the compensation limits, the median award for unfair dismissal cases has remained low, the figure for 2000/01 being £2,744.

---

[39] With effect from February 1, 2001.

CHAPTER 12

TRANSFER OF UNDERTAKINGS

INTRODUCTION

With the possible exception of discrimination, no other subject has 12.01
illustrated more forcefully the cultural and jurisprudential impact of
European law on the United Kingdom than the law relating to the
transfer of undertakings. The current Regulations[1] illustrate in timing
and content the reluctance of successive governments to transpose the
provisions of the Acquired Rights Directive[2] into domestic law. Directives normally require to be implemented within two years but in this
case it took some four years before the basic requirements of the ARD
saw the light of day in this country. Following the initiation of
proceedings[3] by the European Commission in 1992, the Regulations
were amended by the Trade Union Reform and Employment Rights Act
1993,[4] one of the most significant changes being the removal of the
"commercial venture" requirement. By insisting that TUPE should not
apply to undertakings or parts of undertakings that were not in the
nature of commercial ventures, the United Kingdom Government was
deemed to have failed to implement fully the requirements of the ARD.[5]

Issues raised by this legislation came sharply into focus during the
Conservative Government's privatisation or "contracting out" programme and the sometimes difficult question of how to define an
undertaking has been the subject of a number of important referrals to
the ECJ. Individuals and unions potentially affected by transfers are
often faced with uncertainty about whether they have protection under
TUPE and unfortunately in Scotland there exists no mechanism by
which parties can determine in advance of a transfer whether protection
will exist. Only an employment tribunal or court can decide whether
TUPE has in fact applied to a transaction and therefore until a decision
has been reached on particular facts, the parties must proceed on the

---

[1] The Transfer of Undertakings (Protection of Employment) Regulations 1981 (S.I.
1981 No. 1794), hereinafter TUPE.

[2] Originally, Directive 77/187 on Employees' Rights on Transfer of Undertakings. At the
time of writing the Government has yet to implement revised Regulations to transpose the
revised Directive (98/50/EC) which was to have been transposed no later than July 17,
2001. A consolidated Directive (2001/23/EC) was adopted in early 2001. A consultation
process is underway, see end of chapter. References will be to the 2001 Directive,
hereinafter ARD.

[3] See *E.C. Commission v. UK* [1994] I.C.R. 664.

[4] Hereinafter TURERA.

[5] See *Sophie Redmond Stichting v. Bartol* [1992] I.R.L.R. 366.

basis of their beliefs. Insecurity can exist for many months after the change of employer has taken place, until such time as an employment tribunal reaches a decision on the particular circumstances. In view of the substantial liabilities that can attach to employees the transferor and transferee may adopt opposing views about whether the Regulations apply, thereby creating considerable commercial uncertainty. The law is developing so rapidly that there is also considerable scope for a change of legal opinion or authority between the time of the transfer and the tribunal hearing.

There are three main consequences of TUPE applying to a transaction. First, the employment contracts of the employees employed in the undertaking in question, along with all the rights, powers, duties and liabilities of the transferor under or in connection with those contracts pass to the transferee (rights and obligations under occupational pension schemes are excepted). Secondly, any dismissal which is connected with the transfer is rendered automatically unfair unless it is for an economic, technical, or organisational reason entailing changes in the workforce. Thirdly, a relevant transfer triggers specific obligations to inform and consult with employee representatives. TUPE, therefore, is not only of interest to practitioners working in the employment law field. Anyone who is involved in advising on any type of business transfer must acquire a reasonable understanding of how the Regulations work in practice.

The Acquired Rights Directive

12.02 The Council of the European Communities adopted the original ARD on February 14, 1977. The Directive was revised in 1998 and a consolidated Directive adopted in 2001. The primary objective remains the approximation of the laws of the Member States relating to the safeguarding of employees' rights in the event of transfers of undertakings, businesses or parts of businesses.
Article 1 provides:

> "there is a transfer within the meaning of this Directive where there is a transfer of an economic entity which retains its identity, meaning an organised grouping of resources which has the objective of pursuing an economic activity, whether or not that activity is central or ancillary".

It is important to note that this definition is arguably more precise than the definition in the original ARD and has been developed in response to the considerable number of applications to the ECJ for clarification as to the circumstances in which the ARD will apply. The decisions prior to the adoption of this definition therefore must now be treated with caution but it is to be hoped that more clarity will emerge from the early decisions on this definition. Article 3(1) provides that the transferor's rights and obligations arising from a contract of employment or from an employment relationship existing on the date of a transfer within the meaning of Article 1(1) shall, by reason of such transfer, be transferred to the transferee. Article 3 also allows Member States to provide that the transferor shall continue to be liable in respect of obligations that arose from a contract of employment or an employment relationship. The latter provision has not been adopted in the United Kingdom. In a public consultation document[6] the Department of Trade and Industry has made it clear that it opposes any move to make it mandatory for Member States to introduce joint and several liability between transferor and transferee. Article 3(3) requires the transferee to continue to observe terms and conditions agreed in any collective agreement and allows Member States to limit the period for observing such terms and conditions for a period of not less than one year. The latter provision does not form part of United Kingdom legislation.

Article 3(4) provides that this protection does not extend to 12.03 employees' rights to old age, invalidity or survivors' benefits under "supplementary company or inter company pension schemes outside the statutory social security schemes in Member States". However, it also requires Member States to adopt the measures necessary to protect the interests of employees and of persons no longer employed in the transferor's business at the time of the transfer in respect of rights conferring on them immediate or prospective entitlement to old age benefits, including survivors' benefits, under supplementary schemes. This particular provision has been the subject of litigation in the United Kingdom.

Article 4 provides that the transfer of an undertaking, business, or part 12.04 of a business, shall not in itself constitute grounds for dismissal by the transferor or the transferee. However, it is expressly provided that this will not stand in the way of dismissals for economic, technical, or organisational reasons entailing changes in the work force. Furthermore, if a contract of employment or employment relationship is terminated because a transfer involves a substantial change in working conditions to the detriment of the employee, the employer is to be regarded as having been responsible for termination of the contract of employment or of the employment relationship, thus giving rise to a potential claim by the employee. Thus, in the United Kingdom, the employee may have recourse to a constructive dismissal claim.

Article 7 deals with information and consultation. In particular, the 12.05 transferor and transferee are required to inform "the representatives of their respective employees" affected by a transfer of the date or proposed date of the transfer, the reasons for the transfer, the legal, economic and social implications of the transfer for the employees, and any measures envisaged in relation to the employees. The transferor is required to give such information to the representatives of his employees in good time, and in any event before his employees are directly affected by the transfer as regards their conditions of work and employment. If either transferor or transferee envisages measures in relation to his employees, he is required to consult representatives of the employees in good time on such measures with a view to seeking agreement. United Kingdom courts and tribunals must interpret domestic legislation in the light of the Directive and therefore practitioners should be aware of these foundations. The extent to which the more important provisions have in fact been directly implemented in United Kingdom law are highlighted later in the chapter

---

[6] URN 98/513 (December 1997).

APPLICABILITY OF TUPE—A GENERAL SUMMARY

12.06 Regulation 3 defines a relevant transfer for the purposes of the regulations and provides that:

> "(1) . . . these Regulations apply to a transfer from one person to another of an undertaking situated immediately before the transfer in the United Kingdom or part of one which is so situated.
>
> (2) . . . these Regulations so apply whether the transfer is effected by sale or by some other disposition or by operation of law.
>
> (4) It is hereby declared that a transfer of an undertaking or part of one:
>
> > (a) May be effected by a series of two or more transactions;
> > (b) May take place whether or not any property is transferred to the transferee by the transferor."

12.07 Regulation 2(1) defines an undertaking as including any trade or business. The definition includes the transfer of part of an undertaking provided that it is transferred as a business. It is necessary to consider each transaction on its own facts in determining what constitutes an undertaking or part of an undertaking.[7] It should be noted that until TUPE is amended to transpose the provisions of the new ARD that this definition applies in the United Kingdom (notwithstanding arguments open to parties to seek to rely directly on the ARD or to challenge the U.K. provisions).

The ECJ has formulated the basic test to be applied in a series of judgments issued over the last decade. Factors have been identified that might point towards or against the existence of a transfer. The Court has frequently been criticised for failing to provide clear guidance on this central question but would defend itself by pointing out that its function is not to lay down rigid criteria to be applied by national courts, nor indeed to reach decisions on the facts of particular cases referred, but to answer the specific questions referred by national courts on interpretation of the relevant Directive. It is important to understand this when considering the meaning and scope of decisions of the ECJ. An understanding of the ECJ approach to date and the United Kingdom response is necessary to interpret the existing United Kingdom provisions and the new ARD definition.

12.08 The seminal decision was that issued in *Spijkers*,[8] the first in a line of judgments in which the ECJ clarified that the ARD applies where the undertaking retains its identity after the transfer. The case involved a slaughterhouse company whose activities had ceased by the time it was sold. Goodwill had disappeared and the sale consisted only of the slaughterhouse buildings and other goods. The Court stressed that all

---

[7] This makes it difficult to overturn tribunal decisions on appeal to the EAT. It is not uncommon for the EAT to conclude that a case could have been decided either way on its facts—see comments of Morison J. in *ECM (Vehicle Delivery Service) Ltd v. Cox* [1998] I.R.L.R. 416, EAT.

[8] *Spijkers v. Gebroeders Benedik Abbattoir CV* [1986] E.C.R. 1119.

the circumstances had to be considered, but that a mere sale of assets would not be sufficient to constitute a transfer. On the other hand, it stated that the fact that goodwill or existing contracts were not transferred, or that a period of time elapsed before activities were resumed, were not conclusive factors against a transfer having taken place. It would not be possible for the court to lay down rigid guidelines to identify transfers and one must therefore proceed on the basis of a "factors" approach when examining the circumstances surrounding a purported transfer. The factors include the type of undertaking or business in question; whether or not the tangible assets of the business (*e.g.* buildings and moveable property) have been transferred; the value of the intangible assets of the business at the time of transfer; whether the majority of employees are taken over by the new employer; whether the customers of the former business are transferred; the degree of similarity between the activities carried on before and after the transfer, and the length of any period during which those activities were suspended.

Advisers must therefore consider all the circumstances and then address a two-part test in order to determine whether TUPE applies. First, is there in existence an entity that is capable of being transferred and, secondly, following the "transfer" has that entity retained its identity?

It is clear that "transfer" is wider than "sale". In the *"Daddy's Dance Hall"* case[9] the ECJ held that the Directive would apply: "as soon as there is a change, resulting from a conventional sale, or from a merger of the natural or legal person responsible for operating the undertaking who, consequently, enters into obligations as an employer towards the employees working in the undertaking, and it is of no importance to know whether the ownership of the undertaking has been transferred". 12.09

Following the decision in *Rask*[10] it was clear that the ARD could apply to outsourcing. The case involved the contracting out of canteen services on Philips' premises. The contractor, ISS, entered into an agreement with Philips whereby they would be responsible for managing their canteens. The Court stated: 12.10

"Thus where the owner of an undertaking entrusts, by means of an agreement, the responsibility for providing a service to his undertaking, such as a canteen, to the owner of another undertaking who assumes, by reason of it, the obligations of an employer vis a vis the employees who are engaged in the provision of that service, the resulting transaction is capable of falling within the scope of the Directive as defined in Article 1(1). The fact that, in such a case, the activity transferred is only an ancillary activity of the transferor undertaking not necessarily related to its objects cannot have the effect of excluding that transaction from the scope of the Directive. Similarly, the fact that the agreement between the transferor and the transferee relates to the provision of services provided exclusively for the benefit of the transferor in return for a fee, the

---

[9] *Foreningen af Arbejdsledere i Danmark v. Daddy's Dance Halls A/S* [1988] E.C.R. 739.
[10] *Rask and Christensen v. ISS Kantinservice A/S* [1993] I.R.L.R. 133.

form of which is fixed by agreement, does not prevent the Directive from applying either".[11]

12.11   The high watermark was the case of *Schmidt*.[12] The employee was employed by a German bank to clean the premises of a branch office. She was the only person employed in that capacity and was dismissed when the branch office was refurbished. The cleaning work was taken over by a company that was already carrying out cleaning functions for most of the banks other premises. Although the company offered the employee employment, she declined the offer because the net effect of the terms and conditions offered was that she would be in receipt of lower pay. She challenged her dismissal and her case was referred by the German Courts to the ECJ.

The first question considered by the ECJ was whether the cleaning operations, if transferred by contract to an outside firm, could be treated as part of a business within the meaning of Article 1(1) of the Directive. The ECJ, referring to the *Rask* case, concluded that the Directive does apply in principle when a business contracts-out responsibility for operating one of its services, such as cleaning, to another undertaking which thereby assumes the obligations of an employer towards the employees assigned to those duties. The Court then went on to consider whether the Directive could apply where the activity in question was performed by a single employee prior to the transfer. The Court concluded that the application of the Directive did not depend on the number of employees assigned to the part of the undertaking that was the subject of the transfer. Again, in this case, the Court emphasised that the decisive criterion in assessing whether or not the Directive applied was whether the operation in question retained its identity after the transfer. It was confirmed that this is a matter for the national court (*i.e.* an employment tribunal) to decide and in doing so the national court should take into account a wide range of factors.

The first indication that the ECJ was sympathetic to reducing the influence of the Directive was seen in the case of *Rygaard*[13] where it insisted that the Directive could only apply to the transfer of a stable economic entity whose activity was not limited to performing one specific works contract. The Directive was also held not to apply in the case of *Henke*[14] but again the circumstances were quite unusual involving the reorganisation or transfer of public administration functions; it also has to be seen in the context of the German system of public and constitutional law which prohibits certain tasks being carried out other than by public bodies.

12.12   Of much greater significance has been the decision of the ECJ in *Süzen*[15] (which to an extent was heralded by the decision of the EFTA court in *Eidesund*[16]). The issue in *Süzen* was the re-letting of a cleaning

---

[11] At para. 17.
[12] *Christel Schmidt v. Spar und Leihkasse der Fruheren Amter Bordesholm, Kiel und Cronshagen* [1994] I.R.L.R. 302 ECJ.
[13] *Rygaard v. Stro Molle Akustik* [1996] I.R.L.R. 51.
[14] *Henke v. Gemeinde Schierke* [1996] I.R.L.R. 701.
[15] *Süzen v. Zehnacker Gebaudereinigung Gmb H Krankenhausservice* [1997] I.R.L.R. 255.
[16] *Eidesund v. Stavanger Catering* [1996] I.R.L.R. 684.

contract and in that respect is identical to the circumstances which had occurred in *Dines*[17] in which, the Court of Appeal had held that where one contractor was replaced by another there had occurred the transfer of an undertaking. The ECJ in an apparent change of approach to the interpretation of the Directive concluded that where one contractor was replaced by another the Directive did not apply if there was no concomitant transfer of significant assets or the taking over by the new employer of a major part of the workforce. No longer was the ECJ prepared to leave the questions of the existence and transfer of an undertaking to the tribunal's consideration of the factors identified in *Spijkers*. Instead and for the first time the ECJ was seeking to set out parameters within which the tribunal would have to operate.

As part of its judgment the ECJ has also embraced the distinction between an entity and an activity by noting that an entity cannot be reduced to the activity entrusted to it and that the term entity refers to an organised grouping of assets and persons facilitating the exercise of an economic activity. The effect of this was to render application of the Directive and therefore TUPE less likely in the situation which arises typically where one contractor loses a contract to another bidder or even where the contract is taken back in-house for in those situations there is a considerable possibility that the new contractor will not require or be prepared to take over assets or staff associated with the performance of the contract.

In the subsequent case of *Betts*[18] the Court of Appeal emphasised the 12.13 importance of the decision in *Süzen*. The Court having had the advantage of considering the *Süzen* judgment acknowledged that it did represent a significant shift of emphasis and cautioned that some of the earlier decisions would require to be reconsidered.

It appeared after *Süzen* that where the incoming contractor chose not to employ any of the existing employees then that in itself would be a significant factor weighing against TUPE applying. The inevitable subsequent confusion triggered many cases where both companies denied responsibility for the employees.

The position was perhaps further complicated by the Court of Appeal decision in *ECM*[19] The case concerned drivers and yardsmen who operated a contract delivering cars to dealerships from Grimsby docks. ECM won the contract. The trade union had argued on their behalf that TUPE applied and had threatened unfair dismissal complaints if they were not taken on by ECM. The tribunal found that this was why they had not been taken on. The EAT noted that the reason why the men had not been taken on was to avoid the application of TUPE. In the event no employees or assets were transferred.

The EAT found that there was indeed a TUPE transfer and noted:

"The issue as to whether employees should have been taken on cannot be determined by asking whether they were taken on."

[17] *Dines v. Initial Healthcare Services Limited and Pall Mall Services Group Limited* [1994] I.R.L.R. 336.
[18] *Betts v. Brintel Helicopters & KLM* [1997] I.R.L.R. 361
[19] *ECM Vehicle Delivery Service) Ltd v. Cox* [1999] I.R.L.R. 559, CA.

The Court of Appeal upheld the decision but not, it appears on this ground. The conclusion was noted that it was still for national courts to make the "necessary factual appraisal" in determining whether or not there is a transfer using the criteria enunciated in *Spijkers*. The key question remains whether the undertaking has continued and retained its identity in different hands. While it is difficult to reconcile the decision with those in *Betts* and *Süzen*, Mummery L.J. stated "The importance of *Süzen* has, I think, been overstated".[20] It had been hoped that the decision in *ECM* would prove to have a stabilizing effect on the law in this area in the United Kingdom. However, a number of decisions seemed to retreat from the wider approach advocated in that case.[21] The difficulty with *Süzen* and the subsequent decisions which have adopted its reasoning, is that the circular reasoning is encouraged (as identified in *ECM)*, that the application of the transfer rules, designed to ensure the protection of employees, can be made dependent upon whether the transferor's employees are taken on by the transferee.

12.14   This difficulty was addressed directly by the EAT in three decisions in 2000—*RCO Support Services,*[22] *Argyll Training Ltd,*[23] and *Cheesman.*[24] In the first, there was a change in hospitals providing in-patient care within an NHS Trust area. There followed a change in contractors providing catering and cleaning. No staff were taken on by the new contractor. The EAT found that, despite this, the same business was being carried out by a different firm and as such, TUPE applied.

In *Argyll Training* the EAT sitting in Scotland found that TUPE applied where a training company lost a contract to another which did not take on the sole employee or any tangible assets. The EAT highlighted the intangible asset of the work placement portfolio which did transfer. The EAT found that TUPE could be found to apply even where there was no significant transfer of assets or the majority of relevant employees. The decisive criterion is still as set down in *Spijkers* and is whether the business in question retained its identity, indicated *inter alia* by the actual continuation or resumption of the same or similar activities.

In *Cheesman,* the contract to supply maintenance to local authority housing transferred to a new contractor. Neither assets nor employees transferred. The tribunal found that there was no transfer in the circumstances. The EAT summarised the recent authorities and found that the case should be remitted to a tribunal for further consideration.

These three recent decisions are arguably compatible with the ECJ decisions prior to *Süzen* but difficult if not impossible to reconcile with that decision. Nevertheless, at least in the United Kingdom the judgments could be seen to be developing a consistent approach. The controversy, however, was ignited again in early 2001 with the ECJ

---

[20] That reasoning on motive was followed by the CA in *ADI v. Firm Security Group Ltd* [2001] I.R.L.R. 542.

[21] *e.g. North East Lincolnshire Council v. Beck,* EAT/1362/97, unreported; *ADI(UK) Ltd v. Willer* [2001] I.R.L.R. 542; *Whitewater Leisure Management Ltd v. Barnes* [2000] I.R.L.R. 456.

[22] *RCO Support Services Ltd v. Unison* [2000] I.R.L.R. 624, EAT.

[23] *Argyll Training v. Sinclair* [2000] I.R.L.R. 630, EAT.

[24] *Cheesman v. R Brewer Contracts Ltd* [2001] I.R.L.R. 144.

decision in *Oy*.[25] The case was referred from Finland and concerned the operation of bus services in Helsinki. The incoming contractor operated the same or similar routes to the former operator and hired a majority of the drivers on inferior terms. It did not require the buses that had been used before as it was arranging a fleet of its own. The ECJ found that consideration must be given to the type of undertaking and that here an asset reliant contract had been transferred without the assets and therefore there was no transfer.

As Lindsay J. has remarked, "The English and European authorities in this area now convey a message which, for its breadth of possible interpretation, would be the envy of even the Delphic Oracle".[26] It is extremely difficult to see how the wide approach adopted by the EAT in 2000 and the Court of Appeal in *ECM* and *ADI* will be sustainable particularly in light of the new definition set out in the ARD if, as expected, it is adopted in the proposed new Regulations.

The directive is capable of applying to "contracting in" as well as to "contracting out".[27] It is also applicable to transfers between companies in the same corporate group.[28] Crucially however, the regulations do not apply where only the shares in a company are transferred, since there is no change in employer who continues to be the company which retains its legal personality.[29]

Having considered when TUPE applies, it is necessary to examine what terms and conditions of employment actually transfer.

TRANSFER OF TERMS AND CONDITIONS

The key provision is regulation 5 as amended by TURERA. Regulation 5(1) provides that:

> "Except where objection is made . . . a relevant transfer shall not operate so as to terminate the contract of employment of any person employed by the transferor in the undertaking or part transferred but any such contract which would otherwise have been terminated by the transfer shall have effect after the transfer as if originally made between the person so employed and the transferee."

Regulation 5(2) provides that:

> (a) "On the completion of a transfer, all the transferor's rights, powers, duties and liabilities under or in connection with any such contract shall be transferred by virtue of this Regulation to the transferee; and
> (b) anything done before the transfer is completed by or in relation to the transferor in respect of that contract or a person

12.15

---

[25] *Oy Liikenne AB v. Liskojarri and Juntunen* [2001] I.R.L.R. 171.

[26] *Argyle Training v. Sinclair* [2000] I.R.L.R. 630 at 634, EAT.

[27] *Council of the Isles of Scilly v. Brintel Helicopters Ltd and Ellis* [1995] I.R.L.R. 6.

[28] Case C–234/98 *Allen v. Amalgamated Construction Company Ltd* [2000] I.R.L.R. 119, ECJ.

[29] *Brookes v. Borough Care Services* [1998] I.R.L.R. 636, EAT.

employed in that undertaking or part shall be deemed to have been done by or in relation to the transferee."

In other words, in relation to contracts of employment, the transferee is substituted for the transferor and the transferee becomes liable for outstanding liabilities under the contract of employment. The regulations apply to persons employed immediately before the transfer as well as those dismissed before the transfer if they are dismissed for a reason connected with the transfer.[30]

12.16   Often it can be difficult to identify the terms of the contract of employment. Express and implied terms transfer but a written statement of main terms and conditions of employment will not necessarily reveal all of the terms of the contract. Frequently, statements are out of date and this can give rise to substantial practical difficulties. Many terms and conditions of employment are incorporated into individual contracts by virtue of collective agreements. Even if the collective agreement is terminated, terms that have been incorporated into the individual contracts will remain as liabilities for the transferee (collective agreements transfer by virtue of reg. 6).

In practice the most important right is the right to receive pay at the same rate as existed prior to the transfer. For commercial reasons, the transferee may seek to reduce the pay of transferring employees. Under normal circumstances domestic law would allow employer and employee to agree a variation in terms and conditions of employment. However, this would not appear to be possible if the operative reason for the change is the transfer.[31] The fact that the transferee cannot alter such terms and conditions even with consent of the employee can create significant pressures on the business. It would seem that, as the law stands at the moment, the transferee may be encouraged to reduce numbers rather than reduce pay, because at least he may be able to argue that such dismissals are fair, rather than face the prospect of claims for breach of contract or deductions from pay running for some time into the future. An employer's liability to pay damages to an employee based on delict rather than out of the contract of employment will still transfer to the transferee, as will any rights the transferor may have to be indemnified from a policy of employer's liability insurance.[32] However the transferee cannot be primarily liable for breaching the implied obligation of trust and confidence between the employees and the transferor simply by suggesting that there would be changes to the terms of employment after the transfer. The confusion inherent in such a claim was explained by Lord Johnston:

> "It cannot be again disputed as a matter of common law that a third party cannot be held responsible for a breach of contract between two other parties, unless by a wholly separate wrong whereby he or she has induced that breach. No such suggestion is made in this case. Accordingly, if there is to be any liability upon

---

[30] *Litster v. Forth Dry Dock & Engineering Co. Ltd*, 1989 S.C. (HL) 96; *Clark & Tokeley v. Oakes* [1998] I.R.L.R. 577, CA.

[31] *Wilson v. St Helens Borough Council*.[1998] I.R.L.R. 706, HL.

[32] *Bernadone v. Pall Mall Services Group* [2000] I.R.L.R. 48, CA.

the appellants, it must come to them under the transfer Regulations which itself assumes that there was a breach of contract by the transferor creating a liability which becomes transferred".[33]

The transferee may also be forced to recognise an external bargaining process over which he has no control. In one case[34] the employees moved from public to private sector following a transfer. While in the public sector their pay and conditions had been determined by a national bargaining process in that their contracts of employment incorporated National Joint Council awards. The EAT held that the employees were entitled to continue to benefit from these awards after the transfer, even although the new employer was not a party to the bargaining process.

WHICH EMPLOYEES ARE TRANSFERRED?

Regulation 5(3) provides that a person employed in an undertaking 12.17 transferred by a relevant transfer is a reference to a person so employed immediately before the transfer. In order to prevent abuse of this provision, it was determined in *Litster*, that this phrase should be construed as if there followed the words "or would have been so employed if he had not been unfairly dismissed in the circumstances described in regulation 8(1).

Matters are less straightforward when only part of a business is transferred as some of the employees may work partly for the transferred function and partly elsewhere. At what level of involvement in the transferred function do they acquire TUPE rights?

The answer to this question is not straightforward. The protection provided by TUPE and the ARD where the transfer relates only to part of an undertaking extends only to employees assigned to that part of the undertaking as clarified in *Botzen*.[35] This approach has been applied in *Duncan Web Offset*[36] and the decision underlines that the question of whether an employee is assigned to a part of an undertaking that is transferred is a matter of fact to be determined by the employment tribunal having regard to a variety of factors including time spent on the part transferred as opposed to other parts not transferred, value of the service given by the employee and any provisions of the employee's contract as well as the allocation of the costs of the employee.

THE "RIGHT" TO OBJECT

Regulation 5(4A) incorporates an amendment inserted by TURERA, 12.18 which became effective on August 30, 1993. It provides that where an employee informs the transferor or transferee that he objects to becoming employed by the transferee, his contract of employment is not

---

[33] *Sita (GB) Ltd v. Burton* [1997] I.R.L.R. 501, EAT.
[34] *BET Catering Services Ltd v. Ball*, EAT/637/96.
[35] *Botzen and Others v. Rotterdamsche Droogdok Maatschappij* [1985] E.C.R. 519.
[36] *Duncan Web Offset (Maidstone) Ltd v. Cooper* [1995] I.R.L.R. 633.

transferred in accordance with regulation 5(1) and (2). Unfortunately, the regulations do not specify how the objection should be intimated, nor do they lay down any specific time scale for the objection to be effective. A recent case has demonstrated the practical effect of the provision. In *University of Oxford v. Humphreys*[37] the plaintiff was a former employee of the appellants. They decided to transfer his duties to another undertaking. The terms offered by the new employer, it was conceded, involved a substantial change in the plaintiff's terms and conditions. He objected to the transfer of his contract of employment under regulation 5(4A) TUPE. Furthermore he purported to terminate his employment without notice under regulation 5(5) on the basis that the transfer proposed a substantial detrimental change to his working conditions. The question was whether his claim for wrongful dismissal should be struck out on the basis that it was barred by regulation 5(4B).

The Court of Appeal held that the employee was allowed to claim constructive dismissal against the transferor employer. However the liability therefore does not pass to the transferee. Where an employee is claiming constructive dismissal in terms of regulation 5(5) it appears the test to be applied is separate and distinct from that applicable to a contractual wrongful dismissal claim. The orthodox approach in the latter situation is that there must be a repudiatory breach of contract by the employer to justify the employee resigning.[38] Where however the claim is in the context of a transfer of an undertaking, the question depends solely on whether there has been a substantial change in the employee's working conditions to his or her detriment regardless of whether this involves a breach of contract.[39]

TERMS AND CONDITIONS THAT DO NOT TRANSFER

12.19   Regulation 5(4) specifies that no criminal liabilities are transferred and therefore the transferee does not inherit any liability for criminal acts committed prior to the transfer. In *Kerry Foods Ltd v. Creber*[40] it was held that the duty to consult, whether or not there is a recognised trade union is a right which arises from the individual contracts between each worker and his employer. The liability for the failure in *Kerry Foods* was held to pass to the transferee. The problem with this reasoning however is that as a matter of policy, it removes any incentive from the transferor to comply with his obligation to consult, as any liability he may incur will simply pass to the transferee. In *TGWU v. McKinnon*[41] therefore, Lord Johnston made the distinction between a liability arising under TUPE itself, *i.e.* the failure to comply with regulation 10 and, a general liability arising out of or under the contract of employment, which would embrace all employees' particular rights in that context including the right to claim damages for personal injuries. Only the latter liabilities will transfer.

---

[37] [2000] I.R.L.R. 183, CA.
[38] *Western Excavating v. Sharp* [1978] I.R.L.R. 27.
[39] *Rossiter v. Pendragon plc* [2001] I.R.L.R. 256, EAT.
[40] [2000] I.R.L.R. 10, EAT.
[41] [2001] I.R.L.R. 597.

Regulation 7 of TUPE provides:

> "1. Regulations 5 and 6 above shall not apply—
>
> (a) to so much of a contract of employment or collective agreement as relates to an occupational pension scheme within the meaning of the Social Security Pensions Act 1975 or the Social Security Pensions (Northern Ireland) Order 1975; or
>
> (b) to any rights, powers, duties or liabilities under or in connection with any such contract or subsisting by virtue of any such agreement and relating to such a scheme or otherwise arising in connection with that person's employment and relating to such a scheme.
>
> 2. For the purposes of paragraph (1) above any provisions of an occupational pension scheme which do not relate to benefits for old-age, invalidity or survivors shall be treated as not being part of the scheme".

It does seem, therefore, that pension rights do not transfer either under the Directive or the United Kingdom regulations. In two employment tribunal cases it was held that the transferee is required to provide a pension with benefits equivalent to those provided by the transferor.[42] One decision was appealed to the EAT, which held that Article 3 of the Directive does not protect future pension rights. It had been argued that regulation 7 of TUPE should be interpreted in such a way as to transfer these rights but the EAT was not prepared to add words that were inconsistent with the terms of the legislation. Article 3 of the ARD as amended allows member states to make provision for the transfer of obligations relating to occupational pension schemes, an issue covered in the Government's background paper dealing with proposals for reform of TUPE (see below). In practice many transferees currently attempt to provide schemes broadly comparable to those in existence at the time of a transfer.

CHANGING TERMS AND CONDITIONS OF EMPLOYMENT

As some transfer related changes in terms and conditions of employment 12.20 may be envisaged, attention should be paid to the joined cases of *Wilson and others v. St Helens Borough Council and Meade v. British Fuels Ltd.*[43] The issue involves the practice of the transferee agreeing new terms of employment with employees whose contracts are to be transferred under TUPE. Is it possible to avoid the operation of TUPE by such agreements? In both cases the transferor purported to terminate the contracts of employees who had been offered and had accepted employment with the transferee but on less favourable terms and the question faced by the courts was whether such dismissals were prevented by the TUPE.

---

[42] *Warrener v. Walden Engineering IT,* Case Reference 22672/2; and *Perry v. Intec Colleges Limited* [1993] I.R.L.R. 56.
[43] [1997] I.R.L.R. 505, CA; and [1998] I.R.L.R. 706, HL.

The effect of the decision of the House of Lords—which is not entirely easy to understand—is that dismissals which are transfer related will not be void and ineffective as found by the Court of Appeal. The remedy for a dismissed employee is a claim of unfair dismissal. Nevertheless, there is still doubt as to the extent to which terms and conditions can be varied. The House of Lords have found that a variation to terms and conditions which go across with the transfer which is due to the transfer and for no other reason is invalid but that there can be a valid variation if the reason for the variation is not due to the transfer.

Unfortunately, there is very little guidance as to how the reason for the variation is to be determined. This means that variations which take place around the time of the transfer may be challenged later. The more certain route, of giving notice to terminate contracts and offering varied terms and conditions, brings with it potential damage to industrial relations and the risk of unfair dismissal claims.

TRANSFER RELATED DISMISSALS

12.21   In general terms, regulation 8 renders any transfer-related dismissal automatically unfair, subject to the statutory defence referred to below. This applies whether the transferor or the transferee implements the dismissal. Liability for the dismissal passes to the transferee. The dismissal is unfair if the "transfer or a reason connected with it" is the reason or principal reason for it. Unless the statutory defence applies, a dismissal is treated as unfair for the purposes of Part 10 of the ERA and the normal rules for assessment of compensation apply.

The defence is set out in regulation 8(2), which provides that where an economic, technical or organisational (ETO) reason entailing changes in the work force of either the transferor or the transferee before or after a relevant transfer is the reason or principal reason for dismissing an employee, then the employee will not be treated as having been unfairly dismissed. Instead, the dismissal is for "some other substantial reason justifying dismissal" (SOSR), which is a potentially valid reason for dismissal in terms of section 98 of the ERA. The phrase "economic, technical or organisational", has its origins in the ARD. It covers situations that would come within the United Kingdom definition of "redundancy" but is certainly wider than that. Crucial to the success of the defence is the principle that the economic, technical or organisational reason must "entail changes in the work force". Attempts have been made to argue that the SOSR defence can be used to justify dismissals implemented with a view to enforcing changes in terms and conditions of employment following a transfer. However, as was emphasised in one leading case[44] the ETO reason must entail a change in the work force, not merely a change in conditions. The Court of Appeal held that there has to be a change in the number of employees or possibly a substantial change in the nature of the jobs of members of the work

---

[44] *Delabole Slate Ltd v. Berriman* [1985] I.R.L.R. 305.

force for the defence to apply and that it must be connected with the future conduct of the business as a going concern.[45]

Each case must be determined on its own facts but it is suggested that in some respects at least it is appropriate for employment tribunals to consider the ETO defence in the light of principles that would normally apply in dealing with dismissals on the ground of redundancy. For example, they will not be inclined to question the business decision to reduce numbers, concentrating rather on the implementation of the decision and questions relating to consultation, selection, and alternative employment. However, the fact that SOSR is the reason for dismissal does suggest that the employer is allowed a degree of flexibility, which is appropriate given the special circumstances that apply on a transfer of an undertaking. Employers will have to ensure that they act in accordance with normal standards of fairness.[46]

COLLECTIVE AGREEMENTS AND TRADE UNION RECOGNITION

Regulation 6 provides for the transfer of a collective agreement made by or on behalf of a transferor with a recognised trade union. However, a collective agreement is presumed not to have been intended by the parties to be a legally enforceable contract unless it is in writing and contains a specific provision stating that the parties intended it to be a legally enforceable contract.[47] The majority of collective agreements in this country are not legally enforceable. However, as noted above, certain terms of collective agreements are frequently incorporated into individual contracts of employment, whether or not the collective agreement itself is legally binding. 12.22

Regulation 9 provides for the transfer of recognition agreements. These transfer in circumstances where after the transfer the undertaking or part of the undertaking transferred maintains an identity distinct from the remainder of the transferee's undertaking.

INFORMATION AND CONSULTATION

Regulation 10 creates obligations on the part of the employer to inform and consult recognised trade unions or employee representatives in connection with certain specified aspects of a transfer. Originally this regulation only created rights for recognised trade unions but these were extended to include other employee representatives,[48] and further amended so as to require consultation to take place in respect of employees who "may be affected by the transfer or may be affected by measures taken in connection with the transfer", with references to "affected employees" in relation to a relevant transfer being references to "any employees".[49] The employer must provide the following information to the employee representatives: 12.23

---

[45] *Whitehouse v. Chas A Blatchford & Sons Ltd* [1999] I.R.L.R. 492, CA.

[46] See *Brown v. Castle View Services Ltd* (London North Tribunal Case No. 2646/96).

[47] TULRCA, s.179.

[48] Collective Redundancies and Transfer of Undertakings (Protection of Employment) (Amendment) Regulations 1995 (S.I. 1995 No. 2587).

[49] Collective Redundancies and Transfer of Undertakings (Protection of Employment) (Amendment) Regulations 1999 (S.I. 1999 No. 1925).

1. the fact that the relevant transfer is to take place, when, approximately, it is to take place and the reasons for it;
2. the legal, economic and social implications of the transfer for the affected employees;
3. the measures which the employer envisages he will, in connection with the transfer, take in relation to those employees or, if he envisages that no measures will be so taken, that fact; and
4. if the employer is the transferor, the measures which the transferee envisages he will, in connection with the transfer, take in relation to such of those employees as, by virtue of regulation 5, become employees of the transferee or, if he envisages that no measures will be so taken, that fact.

This information must be provided long enough before the transfer to enable the employer to consult with the employee representatives and must be delivered or posted to the union or the elected representatives. The employer must also allow the appropriate representatives access to the affected employees and afford those representatives such accommodation and other facilities as may be appropriate.

If there are "affected employees" who are members of a recognised trade union, there must be consultation with that trade union as the "appropriate representative". In any other case, whichever of the following employee representatives the employer chooses:

1. employee representatives appointed or elected by the affected employees otherwise than for the purposes of the TUPE Regulations, who have authority from those employees to receive information and to be consulted about the transfer on their behalf; or
2. employee representatives elected by them, for the purposes of the TUPE Regulations, in an election satisfying the requirements of regulation 10A(1).

If there is no recognised trade union in respect of the affected employees, and those employees also fail to elect employee representatives within a reasonable time, then the employer must give every affected employee the information outlined above.[50]

Prior to the transfer, the employer is the transferor and as such may not have sufficient information to consult with employee representatives or the trade union about the intentions of the transferee. Regulation 10(3) obliges the transferee to give the transferor such information at such a time as will enable him to discharge the duty to consult.

Where the employer envisages that he will, in connection with the transfer, be taking measures in relation to any employees affected by the transfer, he is obliged to consult the appropriate employee representatives with a view to seeking their agreement to the measures to be taken. Thereafter he must, in the course of resulting consultations consider any representations made by the representatives, reply to them, and if he is

---

[50] reg. 10(8A).

rejecting representations, state the reasons for doing so. The employer may be able to demonstrate that there are special circumstances rendering it not reasonably practical to comply with this obligation but is still obliged to take all such steps towards performing the duty as are reasonably practicable in the circumstances.

Should the employer fail to consult, then the union, employee 12.24 representatives, or affected employees may present an application to the employment tribunal. The complaint must be presented within three months of the transfer and, if well founded, may result in an award of compensation, being a sum not exceeding 13 weeks pay per employee, or such other sum as the tribunal deems equitable. If the complaint has been directed against the transferor, he may show that it was not reasonably practicable to comply with the consultation obligations if the transferee failed to provide relevant information to enable him to consult. However, it is only competent for the transferor to do this if he gives the transferee notice of his intention to do so in which case the giving of the notice makes the transferee a party to the proceedings. The Regulations give no guidance as to the form and timing of such notice.

THE FUTURE

In September 2001 the DTI published a Public Consultation Document 12.25 detailing the Government proposals for reform in response to the 1998 revision to the ARD and the subsequent consolidated Directive adopted in early 2001. The consultation period extends to December 2001. The paper sets out the Governments current thinking on TUPE and signals that the definition of a transfer in the revised Directive is likely to be adopted and that there may be changes in relation to transfers within public administration and service provision changes, *i.e.* outsourcing. The proposals include the following:

- As regards pensions, the Government has indicated that it is considering either preserving public sector provision perhaps by separate legislation or providing a general degree of protection to public and private sector employees alike.
- It appears likely that a positive duty on transferors to provide information on current rights and obligations with an obligation to keep this information updated in the event of change. This would assist the current sometimes haphazard process of transferees making detailed requests for information in the hope that the transferors will make a timely response backed up where possible with warranties and indemnities.
- The extent to which terms and conditions can be lawfully effected is to be clarified by providing that changes for ETO reasons will be permitted.
- Changes to the provisions on insolvency aimed at promoting the sale of insolvent businesses as going concerns
- The preservation post transfer of the effect of CAC declarations on trade union recognition.

The stated aim of the reform proposals is to clarify the scope and effect of TUPE for both employers and employees. Whatever shape the draft regulations finally take in 2002, they are likely to be welcomed if they end the present uncertainty that can exist in a transfer situation.

CHAPTER 13

WORKING TIME AND THE NATIONAL MINIMUM WAGE

WORKING TIME REGULATIONS

The Working Time Regulations[1] were introduced in order to implement 13.01
the E.C. Working Time Directive.[2] The Directive was adopted pursuant
to Article 138 (ex 118a) of the E.C. Treaty as a health and safety
measure and should have been implemented in domestic law by November 23, 1996. However the Conservative Government of the day was
instinctively opposed to its implementation in line with the traditional
non-interventionist economic approach. In *United Kingdom of Great
Britain and Northern Ireland v. Council of the European Union*[3] the
Government argued that the Directive had no legal basis being in fact a
social policy measure which, as such, should have been made under
Article 95 (ex 100a) of the E.C. Treaty. Measures adopted under the
latter Article required unanimity as opposed to the simple majority
required under Article 138. The Court of Justice however confirmed that
Article 138 was indeed a sound legal basis for the Directive with one
minor exception:

> "Even without dwelling at great length on the relevant scientific
> studies which have been produced during the proceedings—a
> matter to which I shall return in due course—it cannot be denied
> that the provision of rest periods and the limitation of the weekly
> working time in fact contribute towards protecting the 'health' and
> 'safety' of workers within the broad meaning of Article 118a.
> Without such guarantees workers are exposed to the risk of
> frequently being required to work excessively long hours beyond
> their physical or psychological capabilities, thereby jeopardising
> their health and safety."[4]

While the ruling obliged the Government to implement the Directive
forthwith, a general election intervened. The regulations finally came
into effect on October 1, 1998. The late implementation of the Directive
resulted in a small group of legal claims being lodged, the claimants

---

[1] S.I. 1998 No. 1833, hereinafter WTR.
[2] 93/104/EC.
[3] [1997] I.R.L.R. 30, ECJ.
[4] *per* Advocate-General at para. 103.

arguing that they had suffered loss as a result of the delay in implementation.[5]

13.02   The WTR also implement some of the provisions of the E.C. Young Workers Directive which applies to workers between the ages of 16 and 18.[6]

Scope of the regulations

13.03   "Worker" is defined in regulation 2(1)[7] as including anyone who has entered into or works under (or where employment has ceased, worked under):

(a)   a contract of employment; or

(b)   any other contract, whether express or implied and (if express) whether oral or in writing, whereby the individual undertakes to do or perform personally any work or services for another party to the contract whose status is not by virtue of the contract that of a client or customer of any profession or business undertaking carried on by the individual.

The exact scope of this definition, which is also found in other statutory provisions,[8] will be worked out over time by the development of case law but it is thought to be broad enough to encompass, for example, casual workers and freelancers. Indeed, in "A Short Guide to the Working Time Regulations"[9] the DTI suggests that the definition of "worker" is such that it will include the majority of agency and freelance workers.

Agency Workers and Non-employed trainees

13.04   Although most agency workers will fall within the definition of "worker" under regulation 2(1), the position is put beyond doubt by regulation 36 which includes amongst those entitled to invoke the provisions of the regulations someone who—

(a)   is supplied by a person ("the agent") to do work for another ("the principal") under a contract or other arrangements made between the agent and the principal; but

(b)   is not, as respects that work, a worker because of the absence of a worker's contract between the individual and the agent or the principal; and

---

[5] See, *e.g. R v. Attorney-General for Northern Ireland, ex parte Burns* [1999] I.R.L.R. 315 a claim which relied on *Francovich v. Italy* joined cases C–6 & 9/90 [1991] E.C.R. I–5357; see also Case C–46/93 *Brasserir du Pecher SA v. Germany* [1996] E.C.R. I–1029.

[6] 93/34/EC. Many of the provisions of this directive have been implemented by the Health and Safety (Young Persons) Regulations 1997 (S.I. 1997 No. 135) (though see now the Management of Health and Safety at Work Regulations 1999 (S.I. 1999 No. 3242)) and the Children (Protection at Work) Regulations 1998 (S.I. 1998 No. 276).

[7] *i.e.* in identical terms to s.230(3), ERA 1996.

[8] See for example, the Part-time Workers (Prevention etc.) Regulations 2000, reg. 1(2).

[9] Issued by DTI, March 2000, URN00/632, available at www.dti.gov.uk/er.

(c) is not a party to a contract under which he undertakes to do the work for another party to the contract whose status is, by virtue of the contract, that of a client or customer of any profession or business undertaking carried on by the individual.

Regulation 42 specifies that persons receiving "relevant training" other than under a contract of employment are to be regarded as workers for the purpose of the regulations. Relevant training means work experience provided under a training course or programme and/or training for employment but does not include work experience or training provided by a person or institution whose main business is the provision of such training.[10]

Generally speaking the provisions of the regulations apply to Crown employees,[11] members of the armed forces,[12] any relevant member of House of Lords[13] or House of Commons staff,[14] and the police.[15]

Working Time

Regulation 2(1) of the WTR defines working time as: 13.05

(a) any period during which a worker is working, at his employer's disposal and carrying out his activity or duties;

(b) any period during which he is receiving relevant training; and

(c) any additional period which is to be treated as working time for the purposes of the regulations under a relevant agreement.

There would clearly seem to be three elements required therefore before time will fall to be treated as "working time" under (a): that a worker is (i) working, and (ii) at his employer's disposal and (iii) carrying out his activity or duties. This was recently highlighted by the ECJ considering the identical definition in Article 2 of the Working Time Directive in *Sindicato de Medicos*.[16] The pursuer was a union representing primary care doctors. It argued that the time spent on call by a doctor amounted to "working time". Sometimes the doctors were called in when on call but at other times they were able to pursue their own activities while simply remaining available. The ECJ held that only the time that a doctor spent "on call" which involved him attending his place of work or administering medical care fell to be counted towards his number of weekly working hours. Time when the worker, whilst on call, was free to pursue leisure activities did not amount to working time for the purpose of the Directive.

---

[10] reg. 2(1).
[11] reg. 37.
[12] reg. 38.
[13] reg. 39.
[14] reg. 40.
[15] reg. 41.
[16] Case C–303/98 [2000] I.R.L.R. 845, ECJ.

Maximum Weekly Working Time

13.06   One of the most publicised aspects of the regulations is the imposition of an average maximum working week of 48 hours.[17] In fact this maximum is to be calculated over a "reference period". This period will normally consist of 17 weeks, unless special conditions are met.[18] Where an employee has not worked for his employer for at least 17 weeks then the reference period in his case is the period that has elapsed since he commenced work with his employer.[19] Where an employee has been excluded from the scope of some of the provisions of the regulations by regulation 21 (see below), then the standard reference period for such an employee is one of 26 weeks.[20] Furthermore any collective or relevant agreement which determines that the regulations are to apply may, for objective or technical reasons or reasons concerning the organisation of the work, substitute for the 17 week (or 26 week) reference period any period not exceeding 52 weeks.[21] Regulation 4(2) places an obligation on the employer to take "all reasonable steps" to ensure that the 48 hour limit is complied with in relation to each worker employed by him to whom the limit applies.

Opting-out

13.07   Under regulation 4(1) an employee may contract out of the statutory maximum number of hours. Such an agreement must be in writing and must be obtained before the statutory maximum is exceeded. Regulation 5(3) states that any such agreement, in the absence of any express provision to the contrary, should be terminable on seven days written notice. Even where there is a written agreement providing for a longer period of notice it cannot exceed three months.[22] The agreement may be designed to cover only a limited period or it may apply indefinitely. Where the opt-out is found in a workforce agreement, then each employee must provide consent individually. It is insufficient that union representatives purport to consent to an opt-out agreement on behalf of all the employees whom they represent.[23] The employer must keep a record of hours worked by individuals who have opted-out of the statutory regime.[24]

    In *Barber v. RJB Mining (UK) Ltd*[25] pit deputies in Yorkshire were contractually bound to work 42 hours a week but regularly worked overtime. It was common ground between the parties that in the 17

---

[17] reg. 4(1).

[18] reg. 4(3)(a) and (b) and reg. 23(b).

[19] reg. 4(3).

[20] reg. 4(5).

[21] reg. 23(b),

[22] reg. 5(3).

[23] *Watson v. Swallow Hotels Ltd*, Employment Tribunal, Carlisle, January 4, 2000, Case No. 6402399/99.

[24] reg. 4(2) as inserted by the Working Time Regulations 1999 (S.I. 1999 No. 3372). This does not apply to the armed forces: reg. 25. Previously employers were required to keep detailed records of the actual hours worked in each reference period by each employee who had signed an opt-out—this requirement was dropped in order to lessen the burden of the regulations on employers.

[25] [1999] I.R.L.R. 308, HC.

weeks after the regulations came into force the deputies worked in excess of an average 48 hour week. After this period the deputies objected to working hours in excess of the 48 hour average prescribed by the regulations. They were required by their employer to do so nevertheless, and they continued to work under protest. They commenced proceedings in the High Court seeking a declaration of their rights under regulation 4(1) and injunctions to enforce their rights. The defendant argued that regulation 4(1) had to be read in conjunction with subsection (2) and the only obligation this imposed on the employer was to take all reasonable steps to ensure the limit on maximum weekly working time was observed. The only sanction for breach of this regulation, it was argued, was criminal. Moreover it was contended that there was adequate redress available to disaffected employees under section 45A and section 101A of the ERA 1996 (protection against detriment and dismissal for asserting rights under the WTR) or alternatively that the only mechanism of complaint under the WTR was to the employment tribunal under regulation 30. This was rejected by the High Court. Gage J. held that regulation 4(1) did indeed give rise to a free-standing right not to be required to work in excess of an average of 48 hours a week. He held that the right was an implied term in every contract of employment. The High Court therefore had jurisdiction to issue a declarator and stated:

> "It seems to me clear that Parliament intended that all contracts of employment should be read so as to provide that an employee should work no more than an average of 48 hours in any week during the reference period. In my judgement, this is a mandatory requirement which must apply to all contracts of employment. The fact that para.(1) does not state that an employer is prohibited from requiring his employee from working longer hours does not in my view prevent the paragraph from having the effect of placing an obligation on an employer not to require an employee to work more than the permitted number of hours. Such an obligation is in keeping with the stated objective of the Directive of providing for health and safety of employees".[26]

Interestingly however, the High Court did not accept that an injunction should be granted to restrain the employer from requiring the employees to work beyond the limit. This would have had a disproportionately damaging effect on the production, profitability and safety of some of the mines compared with the benefit to employees. Instead, the employees could choose not to work if they so wished and would be able to complain to an employment tribunal if they were subjected to a detriment or dismissal as a result.

Case law in this area is still in its infancy. There are few higher level authoritative decisions. However, some tribunal decisions cast light on the approach which is being taken to the interpretation of the maximum weekly hour provisions. In *Butterfield v. Bison Concrete Products Ltd*[27]

---

[26] At 31, para. 35.
[27] Employment Tribunal, Leeds, May 2, 2000. Case No. 1800114/00.

the employee signed an agreement opting-out of the statutory maximum number of hours that can be worked in an average week. Later a dispute arose between the parties as to the employee's time keeping. The employee responded that if the employer was unhappy with his performance it should not require him to work the extra hours. The employer instead imposed a 39 hour week on the employee, preventing him from working overtime. The employee then gave notice of his withdrawal from the opt-out agreement. Thereafter he sought overtime hours that would take him up to the 48 hour limit to assist some colleagues who were covering for others. The employer refused to allow him to work any hours in excess of the 39 hour week which had been imposed upon him on the basis that if he was not prepared to work the same hours as everyone else under normal circumstances he could not have the advantage of overtime. The employee successfully complained to an employment tribunal that he had suffered a detriment in terms of section 45A of the ERA 1996. It should be noted however, that it has been held that where an employer decides as a matter of policy to limit all employees' working hours to the maximum 48, the employee cannot complain if the employer thereby refuses to grant him overtime, even where there was a contractual right to such. The effect of regulation 4(1) is to vary the contract of employment automatically, such that the employee cannot complain of suffering a detriment where the employer is seeking to enforce the terms of the regulations.[28] If an employer delegates the responsibility for arranging the number of hours to be worked by each employee at a particular establishment on the basis that the hours will be arranged in compliance with the terms of the regulations, it has been held that the employer will not be in breach where the person to whom the responsibility has been delegated works in excess of that maximum.[29] Consent on the part of the employee to opt-out of the maximum number of hours cannot be inferred from the mere fact that he does not complain at the time of the number of hours he or she works.[30]

Annual Leave

13.08   Since November 23, 1999, regulation 13 has entitled an employee to 4 weeks leave per year.[31] The regulations state that the entitlement to annual leave does not arise until an employee has been continuously employed for 13 weeks.[32] A worker will be deemed to have been "continuously employed" for this period where his or her relationship with the employer has been governed by a contract for the whole or part

---

[28] *Clark v. Pershore Group of Colleges*, Employment Tribunal, Birmingham, February 24, 2000, Case No. 5203317/99.

[29] *Blacker v. Nader Arghand t/a Liqor Store*, Employment Tribunal, Brighton, March 29, 2000, Case No. 3100759/99.

[30] *Compton v. St. Regis Paper Co Ltd*, Employment Tribunal, Bedford, February 23, 2000, Case Nos. 1201178 & 1202171/99.

[31] For discussion of how one calculates the number of days leave which have accrued see *Taylor v. East Midlands Offender Employment* [2000] I.R.L.R. 760, EAT. For further discussion of the issues that surround calculation of holiday pay see *Thames Water Utilities v. Reynolds* [1996] I.R.L.R. 186, EAT.

[32] reg. 13(7).

of each of those weeks. In *Voteforce Associates Ltd v. Quinn*[33] it was held that a casual waitress serving at banquets as and when required was not employed under a contract of service nor did an umbrella contract exist for services over the required 13 week qualifying period. Rather there was a series of single contracts of short duration, with continuity broken between them and she was therefore not entitled to paid annual leave. However, the effect of this decision is academic following the judgment of the ECJ in *R v. Secretary of State for Trade and Industry, ex parte BECTU*[34] in which it was held that the requirement that a worker be continuously employed for 13 weeks before the entitlement to annual leave arose was contrary to the terms of the Working Time Directive. The Government has recently announced changes to the regulations in light of *BECTU* which will remove the qualifying period necessary before a worker is entitled to paid annual leave. The amendments will introduce a new regulation 15A which will allow employers to use an accrual system to manage the taking of leave over the first year of employment. Under this new provision, a worker may only take, in his first year, accrued leave, the rate of accrual being one-twelfth of the annual entitlement at the beginning of each month.[35]

While the leave may be taken in instalments, it must be taken in the leave year[36] and unless employment has been terminated cannot be replaced by a payment in lieu. In *Witley & District Mens Club v. Mackay*[37] the appellants employed Mackay. His contract of employment provided that where his employment was terminated by reason of dishonesty he would have no entitlement to any payment in lieu of accrued holiday entitlement. Regulation 14(2) makes provision for the calculation of payments in lieu on termination. Regulation 14(3) states that such a payment includes "such sum as may be provided for in a relevant agreement". When Mr Mackay claimed payment in lieu the club argued that they were entitled to pay him nothing in terms of the relevant agreement between him and the club. Regulation 35 provides that any agreement that purports to exclude or limit the operation of any provision of the regulations is void, save in so far as the regulations provide for an agreement to have such effect. Here the employers argued that the provision in regulation 14(3) for payment of "such sum" as may be provided for in a relevant agreement included the payment of "no sum". The employment tribunal awarded the applicant a payment in lieu. The employers appealed. However the EAT agreed with the tribunal. Regulation 14(3) had to be taken in its statutory context. On that basis they too were of the opinion that the basic purpose was to provide for paid annual leave. Payment in lieu could only occur on termination. The regulations provided a mechanism for the calculation of that payment. This could be dispensed with only where a relevant

---

[33] IDS Brief 694, October 2001, p.8; EAT/1186/00, July 19, 2001.

[34] Case C–173/99 *R v. Secretary of State for Trade and Industry, ex parte Broadcasting, Entertainment, Cinematographic and Theatre Union* [2001] I.R.L.R. 559, ECJ.

[35] Working Time (Amendment) Regulations 2001 (S.I. 2001 No. 3256).

[36] See reg. 13(3). This is October 1, 1998 and each subsequent anniversary or, if the employment commenced after that date, the date of the commencement and each subsequent anniversary; or, as stipulated for in a relevant agreement.

[37] IDS Brief 690, August 2001, p.10; EAT/151/00, June 7, 2001.

agreement provided for an alternative mechanism for payment of "such sum". Having regard to the residual prohibition on contracting out of the regulations this could not be construed so as to include a payment of nil. The provision to the contrary in the contract was void.

Notice

13.09　　Although most workers will take their annual leave by mutually convenient arrangement with their employer, the regulations contain detailed provisions on notice that may be given by either party seeking to take or requiring leave to be taken at a specified time.[38] Essentially, the worker may give a notice to his employer stipulating the days on which he requires leave.[39] This notice must be given to the employer on a day which gives him at least double the amount of days notice as the leave period will cover. The notice period is counted back from the first day of the leave period sought. So if a worker wishes 10 days leave, notice to take such leave must be given to his employer at least 20 days before the first day of that leave. An employer may require the worker to take leave or not to take leave on particular days by giving notice to the worker as many days in advance (counted back from the earliest day specified) as the number of days to which the notice relates.[40] This allows an employer a mechanism to serve counter-notice on a worker who serves a notice on him, requiring the worker not to take the leave which was sought. The power may be used more generally however by employers to preclude their employees taking leave at certain important times of year for the business. These provisions may be varied or excluded by relevant agreement.[41] The worker is entitled to a week's pay for each week of his leave entitlement.[42]

In *Gibson v. East Riding of Yorkshire Council*[43] the applicant was a swimming instructor paid at an hourly rate. Although the regulations were not in force at the time that she brought her claim, she sought to rely on Article 7 of the Working Time Directive. Article 7 states that employees are entitled to four weeks paid leave a year. Since the Government was late in implementing the Directive she claimed that she was entitled to rely on the provisions of the Directive against her employer, a public authority. The Court of Appeal held however that the Directive was not directly effective because it was insufficiently clear and precise. It contained no guidelines as to how a worker's entitlement was to be determined when he was in the initial stages of his employment, nor did it deal with the situation where there was more than one employer or where he was employed on a part time or commission basis. In *Davies & Ors v. M J Wyatt (Decorators) Ltd*[44] the EAT allowed an appeal against the judgment of an employment tribunal that an employer was not in breach of the regulations where it had deducted £20 a week from the employee's wages to fund the statutory 4 week entitlement to

---

[38] reg. 15.
[39] reg. 15(1).
[40] reg. 15(2).
[41] reg. 15(5).
[42] reg. 16.
[43] [1999] I.R.L.R. 358, EAT; rev'd [2000] I.R.L.R. 598, CA.
[44] [2000] I.R.L.R. 759, EAT.

paid leave. The EAT held that the employer was not allowed to unilaterally alter the employee's remuneration to discharge his liability under regulation 13.

Where a worker's contract provides for an annual leave entitlement over and above the statutory minimum, regulation 17 provides that the worker may not exercise both rights independently but may exercise whichever right is more beneficial to him.

Rest Breaks and Rest Periods

A rest period is defined as a period which is not working time, other 13.10 than a rest break or leave to which the worker is entitled under the regulations. Regulation 10(1) provides that an adult worker is entitled to a daily rest period of not less than eleven consecutive hours in each 24 hour period during which he works for his employer. The 24 hour period can however straddle two calendar days. Under regulation 11, a worker is entitled to a weekly rest period of not less than 24 hours in each 7 day period in which he works for his employer. This can be substituted by the employer for two 24 hour periods in each 14 day period or one uninterrupted period of 48 hours in each 14 day period. There is no reason why the weekly rest period should include a Sunday in preference to any other day, as rest on a Sunday is no more beneficial to the health and safety of a worker then any other day.[45] It should be noted that while generally, the minimum weekly rest period should be in addition to, and not inclusive of, the daily rest period, the weekly period may include the daily rest period where this is justified by objective or technical reasons, or reasons concerning organisation of work.[46]

Regulation 12 provides that all adult workers are entitled to a rest break if their daily working time is more than six hours. The terms on which this break is granted, including its duration, may be determined by a collective agreement or workforce agreement. Where there is no such agreement in place, this is a period of not less than 20 uninterrupted minutes, and the worker is entitled to spend it away from his workstation if he has one. Whilst it may be provided for in the collective or workforce agreement, the regulations do not provide any right to payment during a rest break. Certain groups of workers are, of course, entitled to a rest break independently of the WTR, most importantly workers who use display screen equipment.[47] In a similar vein there is special provision in the WTR for workers whose work rate is pre-determined or monotonous, to be provided with adequate rest breaks for the purpose of reducing the risk to the health and safety of those employees.[48] These provisions arguably require "adequate" rest breaks for such employees in addition to the basic entitlement to a 20 minute rest break under regulation 12.

---

[45] *United Kingdom of Great Britain and Northern Ireland v. Council of the European Union* [1997] I.R.L.R. 30, ECJ where the U.K. successfully challenged Article 5 of the Working Time Directive which stated that the minimum weekly rest period should "in principle" include Sunday.

[46] reg. 11(7).

[47] reg. 4, Health and Safety (Display Screen Equipment) Regulations 1992 (S.I. 1992 No. 2792).

[48] reg. 8.

Night Work

13.11   Regulation 2(1) defines a "night worker" as someone who, "as a normal course" works at least three hours of his daily time during night time. "Night time" is defined as the period between 11 p.m. and 6 a.m. unless another seven hour period (which must include the period between midnight and 5 a.m.) has been agreed in a relevant agreement. "As a normal course" has been held to mean nothing more than "as a regular feature" rather than being confined to someone who works night shifts exclusively or even predominantly. It followed that where a worker was required to work one week in every three-week cycle for three hours a night, she was a night worker for the purposes of the regulations.[49] Regulation 6(1) states that a night worker's normal hours of work in any reference period applicable to him shall not exceed an average of eight hours in each 24 hour period. Where the night worker carries out work which involves special hazards or heavy physical or mental strain, the employer must ensure that the worker does not work more than eight hours in any 24 hour period.[50] Regulation 7(1)(a) requires an employer to give an adult worker the opportunity of a free health assessment before assigning him to work which is to be undertaken during periods such that the worker will become a night worker, unless the worker has already had a health assessment and the employer has no reason to believe that the assessment is no longer valid. The employer must also ensure that the night worker has the option of a free health assessment at regular intervals of whatever duration may be appropriate in his case. Where a worker suffers from a medical condition which is considered by a registered medical practitioner to be connected to the fact that he is a night worker, the employer, where possible, must transfer the worker to alternative work which is suitable for him and which is not undertaken at night.[51]

Exemptions

13.12   Regulation 18 states that the provisions of the regulations covering:

- the 48 hour week (reg. 4(1) and (2))
- the length of night work (reg. 6(1), (2) and (7))
- health assessments and transfer to day work (reg.7(1) and (6))
- monotonous work (reg. 8)
- daily rest (reg. 10(1))
- weekly rest (reg. 11(1) and (2))
- rest breaks (reg. 12(1))
- paid annual leave (regs 13 and 16)

do not apply to the following sectors of activity:

- air, rail, road, sea, inland waterway and lake transport,

---

[49] *R v. Attorney-General for Northern Ireland, ex parte Burns* [1999] I.R.L.R. 315.
[50] reg. 6(7).
[51] reg. 7(6).

- sea fishing,
- other work at sea, or
- to the activities of doctors in training,
- where characteristics peculiar to certain specific services such as the armed forces or the police, or to certain specific activities in the civil protection services, inevitably conflict with the provisions of the regulations.

Whether the blanket exclusion of employees in these sectors from the protection of the regulations is compatible with the requirements of the parent Directive has been considered by the ECJ in *Bowden v. Tuffnells Parcels Express Ltd.*[52] The case concerns clerical workers engaged in the road transport business and their entitlement to annual leave. The employment tribunal held that the workers in question could not benefit from the provisions relating to annual leave as they worked in an excluded sector. The question of whether the exclusion applies to all workers in a particular sector irrespective of the type of activities they actually undertake was referred to the European Court of Justice by the EAT. The ECJ has decided that non-mobile workers in the transport sector are excluded from the scope of the Directive.[53]

Implementing legislation bringing the majority of these excluded sectors within the scope of the Working Time Regulations is required by August 1, 2003 as a result of an amendment to the Directive.[54] Essentially non-mobile workers will benefit in full and most mobile workers will benefit from the provisions concerning the maximum working week and paid annual leave. Certain mobile workers will continue to be excluded from the scope of the minimum break, rest periods and restriction on night work provisions. Provisions covering junior doctors are required to be implemented by August 1, 2004 save for the entitlement to a maximum working week of 48 hours which is being phased in over a 12 year period.

Other Exclusions

Domestic Staff

The provisions in the regulations relating to the 48 hour week, the length of night work, health assessments and transfer to day work, do not apply to a worker employed as a domestic servant in a private household.[55]   13.13

Unmeasured working time

Those provisions of the regulations which do not apply to the excluded sectors in terms of regulation 18, also do not apply, with the exception of paid annual leave, to workers falling within the scope of regulation 20. This provision applies essentially to workers who by the nature of their activities, determine their own working time. The examples given are: 13.14

---

[52] [2000] I.R.L.R. 560, EAT.
[53] IDS Brief 696, November 2001, ECJ, October 4, 2001 (Case C–133/0).
[54] No. 2000/34.
[55] reg. 19.

managing executives or other persons with autonomous decision taking powers, family workers, or workers officiating at religious ceremonies in churches and religious communities.

Other special cases

13.15   Other special cases set out in regulation 21 are exempt from the provisions on night work, minimum rest periods and breaks. These include:

- where the worker's activities are such that his or her place of work and place of residence, or different places of work, are distant from one another,
- where the worker is engaged in security and surveillance activities requiring a permanent presence in order to protect property and persons,
- where the worker's activities involve the need for continuity of service or production,[56]
- where there is a foreseeable surge of activity as may be the case in agriculture, tourism or postal services,
- where the worker's activities are affected by wholly unforeseeable events or an accident or an imminent risk of an accident.

Shift workers

13.16   "Shift work" is defined as "any method of organising work in shifts whereby workers succeed each other at the same workstations according to a certain pattern, including a rotating pattern, and which may be continuous or discontinuous, entailing the need for workers to work at different times over a given period of days or weeks". A "shift worker" is any worker whose work schedule is part of shift work.[57] The provisions on daily rest do not apply to a shift worker where changes in his shifts mean that he cannot take a daily rest period between the end of one shift and the beginning of the next one. The provisions on weekly rest do not apply to a shift worker where the changes in his shifts mean that he cannot take his weekly rest in the period between the end of his last shift and the start of his next one. The provisions on daily and weekly rest also do not apply to workers who are engaged in activities involving periods of work split up over the day, *e.g.* cleaning staff.

Collective and workforce agreements

13.17   Although generally an agreement which seeks to limit or exclude the application of the regulations is void,[58] employers and workers may enter into arrangements which enable the structure of working time and related calculations to be modified. The opt-out from the restriction on weekly work time discussed above is clearly one example of such an agreement. Employers may also benefit from the flexibility built into the

---

[56] See the examples of services that would fall within this exclusion in reg. 21(c).
[57] reg. 22(2).
[58] reg. 35(1).

regulations by entering into either collective agreements or workforce agreements which have effect in relation to the full workforce or part of it. Employers may use these provisions to contract out of and modify the rules on night work, rest periods and rest breaks and to adjust the reference period for calculating the 48 hour week to their advantage.[59] There are detailed provisions on the requirements for such agreements found in Schedule 1 to the regulations. The scope of the power to contract out of the regulations is however limited by the provisions on compensatory rest.

Compensatory rest

Regulation 24 requires that workers excluded from the normal 13.18 provisions of the regulations, whether by regulation 21 or 22 or by a collective or workforce agreement, who, as a consequence, have to work during a period which would otherwise be a rest period or rest break shall be given, where possible, an equivalent period of compensatory rest. In the exceptional cases where this is not possible for objective reasons, the employer must afford a worker such protection as may be appropriate in order to ensure his health and safety.

<h2 style="text-align:center">YOUNG WORKERS[60]</h2>

A "young worker" is defined for the purposes of the regulations as a 13.19 worker who has attained the age of 15 but not 18 and is over school age in terms of section 31 of the Education (Scotland) Act 1980.

Rest entitlements

Under regulation 10(2) a young worker is entitled to a rest period of not 13.20 less than 12 consecutive hours in each 24 hour period during which he works for his employer. However, this minimum rest period may be interrupted in the case of activities involving periods of work that are split up over the day or of short duration. This seems to place a young worker in a less favourable position than an adult worker who is entitled to an uninterrupted period of rest, albeit for one hour less. Regulation 10(2) does not apply where the young worker is a member of the armed forces[61] or is a young worker whose employment is subject to regulation under section 55(2)(b) of the Merchant Shipping Act 1995.[62] A young worker is also entitled to a weekly rest period of not less than 48 hours in each 7 day period.[63] Unlike the position with regard to adult workers the employer cannot average out this entitlement over two weeks. As far as rest breaks are concerned, where a young worker's daily working time is more than four and a half hours, he is entitled to a rest break of 30

---

[59] reg. 23.
[60] See s.28 of the Children and Young Persons (Scotland) Act 1937 (as amended) for the limits on the working hours of a child who is still at school.
[61] reg. 25.
[62] reg.26. See also the Merchant Shipping and Fishing Vessels (Health and Safety at Work) (Employment of Young Persons) Regulations 1998 (S.I. 1998 No. 2411).
[63] reg. 11(3).

minutes.[64] While an adult worker's entitlement is only to 20 minutes he has a right to an "uninterrupted" break. The young worker, on the other hand, can only take his entitlement consecutively if it is possible for that to happen. Where he works for more than one employer, his daily working time will be calculated by aggregating the number of hours worked by him for each employer.[65] Before a young worker can commence night work he must be given the opportunity of a free health assessment.[66] Under the Management of Health and Safety at Work Regulations 1999, the assessment must take particular account of

- the inexperience, lack of awareness of risks and immaturity of young persons;
- the fitting out and layout of the workplace or workstation;
- the nature, degree and duration of exposure to physical, chemical or biological agents;
- the form, range and use of work equipment and the way in which it is handled
- the organisation of processes and activities;
- the extent of health and safety training provided or to be provided to young persons
- risks from agents, processes and work listed in the annex to Council Directive 94/33/EC.

NATIONAL MINIMUM WAGE ACT 1998

13.21 The National Minimum Wage Act 1998[67] contains the basic structure for the national minimum wage regime and the establishment of the Low Pay Commission. Much of the detail is contained in the National Minimum Wage Regulations 1999.[68] The DTI has issued guidance notes which are useful in clarifying the provisions of the Act and the regulations. However, these have no legal status and are not to be confused with statutory Codes of Practice.[69]

Section 1(1) of the Act states that "A person who qualifies for the national minimum wage shall be remunerated by his employer in respect of his work in any pay reference period at a rate which is not less than the national minimum wage". A person qualifies for the NMW if he is an individual who is a worker and who is working, or ordinarily works, in the United Kingdom under his contract. He must also be beyond compulsory school age.

"Worker"

13.22 "Worker" is widely defined in the same terms as set out in section 230(3) of the ERA 1996. As the DTI Guidance notes point out the wide definition found in the section is essentially an anti-avoidance provision

---

[64] reg. 12(4).
[65] reg. 12(5).
[66] reg. 7(2).
[67] Hereinafter NMW.
[68] S.I. 1999 No. 584, hereinafter NMW Regulations.
[69] The guidance notes are available from www.dti.gov.uk/ir/nmw.

designed to exclude from its ambit only the genuinely self-employed. This policy is accentuated by the fact that there are special provisions in the Act to include agency[70] and home workers who would not otherwise be workers.[71]

Excluded classes

The right conferred by section 1(1) does not extend to workers under the age of 18.[72] Where the worker is under 26 years of age and is employed in the first 12 months of an apprenticeship or is employed under such a scheme but is less than 19 years of age he will not qualify for the minimum wage for work done under that contract.[73] In *Edmunds v. Lawson QC*[74] it was held that a pupil barrister aged over 26 seeking the national minimum wage was not employed under a contract of apprenticeship. Similarly where the worker is employed on a work placement that is part of an undergraduate degree or teacher training programme[75] or on most types of training or work experience schemes designed to assist him/her in obtaining work[76] the right is excluded. Share fishermen (s.43), voluntary workers (s.44) and prisoners working under the prison rules (s.45) are also excluded from the protection of the Act. The ERA 1999 amended the 1998 Act so as to exclude individuals who are residential members of religious and other communities which are charities, where the purpose of the community is to practice or advance a religious belief and all or some of the members live together for that purpose.[77] Regulation 2(2) of the NMW Regulations excludes au pairs from the protection of the Act but in such terms that the individual must be genuinely treated as part of the family with whom s/he is living and must not be charged for living accommodation or meals. Regulation 2(3) and (4) excludes family members working in the family business. Agricultural workers are covered by the Act but this does not affect any entitlement to a higher rate that may be conferred by agricultural wages legislation.

13.23

Rate of the National Minimum Wage

Under section 2 of the NMW the national minimum wage shall be such rate as the Secretary of State may prescribe from time to time. Workers who are aged between 18 and 21 inclusive are currently entitled to be paid not less than £3.50 per hour.[78] This rate also applies to workers aged 22 and above who are receiving accredited training during the first six months of their employment with a new employer. Workers aged 22 and over are entitled to be paid no less than the standard

13.24

---

[70] s.34.

[71] s.35.

[72] NMW Regulations 1999, reg. 12(1).

[73] *ibid.,* reg. 12(2).

[74] [2000] I.R.L.R. 391, CA.

[75] reg. 12(8).

[76] reg. 12(5)—(7).

[77] s.44A, NMW (as inserted by s.22, ERA 1999).

[78] From October 1, 2001 onwards: the government has agreed in principle to a further increase to £3.60 on October 1, 2002 "subject to the continuation of favourable economic conditions".

national minimum wage which was increased from £3.70 to £4.10 with effect from October 1, 2001.[79]

Has the National Minimum Wage been paid?

13.25   (i) Records: The employer has an obligation to keep records which are sufficient for the purpose of establishing whether he is remunerating the worker at a rate at least equal to the minimum wage.[80] A worker has the right to require the employer to produce the relevant records if s/he reasonably believes that s/he is not being paid the minimum wage.[81] Should an employer fail to produce these records then the worker can complain to an employment tribunal which shall award a sum equal to 80 times the hourly amount of the minimum wage in force at the time if it finds the complaint to be well founded.[82] The complaint must be presented to the tribunal within three months of the employer's failure to produce the relevant records.[83]

13.26   (ii) Calculation: Regulation 14 of the NMW Regulations sets out the method for calculating whether an employer has in fact paid to the worker his entitlement to the NMW. The calculation involves determining the total remuneration (calculated in accordance with subsection (2)) paid to an employee in the pay reference period and dividing this by the total number of hours worked (calculated in accordance with subsection (3)). The "pay reference period" is a month, or, where the worker is paid wages by reference to a period shorter than a month, that period.[84]

Total remuneration

13.27   The total remuneration in the pay reference period is calculated by reference to regulation 30. The following are required to be added together:

- all money payments paid by the employer to the worker paid during the reference period;
- any money payments paid by the employer to the worker in the following pay reference period in respect of the pay reference period (whether in respect of work or not);
- any money payment paid by the employer to the worker later than the end of the following pay reference period in respect of work done in the pay reference period, being work in respect of which:

    the worker is under an obligation to complete a record of the amount of work done,
    the worker is not entitled to payment until the completed record has been submitted by him to the employer, and

---

[79] The National Minimum Wage Regulations 1999 (Amendment) (No. 2) Regulations 2001 (S.I. 2001 No. 2673)—with a proposed increase to £4.20 as from October 1, 2002.

[80] reg. 38.

[81] s.10, NMW.

[82] s.11, NMW.

[83] s.11(3), NMW.

[84] Reg.10(2) deals with the situation where the worker's contract is terminated during the pay reference period.

the worker has failed to submit a record before the fourth working day before the end of that following pay reference period,

provided that the payment is paid in either the pay reference period in which the record is submitted to the employer or the pay reference period after that;

- where the employer has provided the worker with living accommodation during the pay reference period, but in respect of that provision is neither entitled to make any deduction from the wages of the worker nor to receive any payment from him, the amount determined in accordance with regulation 36.

As is evident from the payments that may be taken into consideration, it may not be possible to calculate whether a worker has received the national minimum wage in the pay reference period until after the following pay reference period. There are two main points to note about the provisions in regulation 30. Firstly, with the exception of the last paragraph, it is only money payments that are to be taken into account. Benefits in kind are therefore not relevant in calculating the total remuneration in a pay reference period.[85] Secondly, "payments" mean payments paid by the employer to the worker in his capacity as a worker before any deductions are made, excluding:—any advance of wages or a loan, any pension, retirement allowance or grant, or compensation for loss of office; any payment made as a consequence of a court order or in settlement of litigation between the parties (other than a payment due under the worker's contract); any payment referable to the worker's redundancy; or any payment under a suggestions scheme.[86]

Reductions to be made from total remuneration

From the total determined in accordance with the provisions in the preceding paragraph there needs to be subtracted "reductions" and "deductions" which fall under regulations 31 to 37. The following sets out the main reductions falling under regulation 31(1) which are to be subtracted from the total remuneration in a given period (although this list does not set out the finer detail in regulation 31:   13.28

1. any payments made in a reference period which fall to be included in an earlier reference period by virtue of regulation 30(b) or (c)[87]
2. payments made in respect of periods for which the worker is absent from work or taking part in industrial action.[88]
3. any premium paid in respect of overtime.[89]

---

[85] These are specifically considered under reg.9.
[86] reg. 8.
[87] reg. 31(1)(a).
[88] reg. 31(1)(b)(i). Does not apply to salaried hours work which is dealt with at reg. 31(1)(b)(ii).
[89] reg. 31(1)(c).

4. any money payment paid by the employer to the worker representing amounts paid by customers by way of a service charge, tip, gratuity or cover charge that is not paid through the payroll.[90]

5. any money paid by the employer to the worker by way of an allowance other than an allowance attributable to the performance of the worker in carrying out his work.[91]

6. any deduction falling within regulation 32 or payment made falling under regulation 34.[92]

7. any permitted deduction under regulation 37 in respect of living accommodation.[93]

Once the total remuneration has been determined it is necessary to divide that by the number of hours worked. There are various provisions for determining the hours that a worker has worked depending upon the type of work upon which he is engaged.[94]

The total working time

13.29   Regulation 15 determines which time counts for the purposes of time work. In addition to normal working time, time work includes time when a worker is available at or near a place of work for the purpose of doing time work and is required to be available for such work except where the worker's home is at or near the place of work and he is entitled to spend that time there. Workers who by arrangement sleep at or near their place of work may only count the time during which they are awake for the purposes of working. Subsection (2) deals with travelling time. Time spent travelling for the purpose of carrying out duties will normally be counted as time work except where (a) the travelling is incidental to the duties (not being assignment work) at a time when the worker would not ordinarily be working or (b) the travelling is between the workers home or residence and his normal place of work or assignment. In this respect travelling will be "incidental" unless the duties are actually carried out whilst travelling (for example, a train driver) and "assignment work" involves carrying out duties at different places to which the worker is required to travel not being the employer's place of work.[95]

In *Wright v. Scot bridge Construction Ltd*[96] the worker was a night-watchman who was required to be on the employer's premises between 5 p.m. and 7 a.m. seven nights a week for which he received £210 a week. His duties however were limited to being on the premises and performing small menial tasks. His principal purpose in fact was to be available to respond to intruder alarms. When not performing the menial tasks, he was permitted to read, watch television or sleep (and a sleeping facility

---

[90] reg. 31(1)(e).

[91] reg. 31(1)(d). See *Laird v. A K Stobbart Ltd* [2001] I.R.L.R. 591, EAT.

[92] reg. 31(1)(f), (g), (h).

[93] reg. 31(1)(i).

[94] See reg. 3 (time work), reg. 4 (salaried hours work), reg. 5 (output work), reg. 6 (unmeasured work).

[95] reg. 15(3).

[96] [2001] I.R.L.R. 589, EAT.

was provided for him). The employment tribunal found that at most he was required, for the purpose of working, to be awake for four hours per night (and this was being generous to him) and that this ought to be the basis for considering proper remuneration under the NMW. The EAT allowed his appeal on the basis that an employer requiring an employee to be present on premises for a certain number of hours to perform duties must remunerate the employee at the appropriate rate for those hours. In their view, regulation 15(1) only allows sleep to be discounted for national minimum wage purposes where an employee is given a specific time allocation for sleep. In this case the applicant was required to be on the employers' premises for 14 hours every night of the week and during that time the basic duties of a night watchman were fulfilled even if he was asleep since he could still respond to an alarm as soon as he was woken up. He was therefore entitled to be paid the national minimum wage for 14 hours per night.

There are similar provisions for calculating which hours can be counted for output work,[97] unmeasured work,[98] and training,[99] and for the calculation of the total number of hours worked for those types of work.[1]

Protection Against Dismissal and Victimisation

Workers have the right not to suffer unfair dismissal or other detriment on the ground of taking action, proposing to take action or of qualifying for the minimum wage or a particular rate of it.[2]   13.30

---

[97] regs 16 and 17.
[98] reg. 18.
[99] regs 16(5), 22(3) and 19(1).
[1] See reg. 21 (salaried hours work); reg. 24 (output work); reg. 27 (unmeasured work).
[2] ss.23—26, NMW.

CHAPTER 14

EMPLOYMENT LITIGATION

NEGOTIATING EMPLOYMENT CLAIMS

Conciliation and Compromise Agreements

14.01 British industrial relations, particularly in workplaces where trade unions are recognised by the employer, are characterised by negotiated bargains. Disputes, individual as well as collective, are resolved by agreements reached (in the main) voluntarily by the parties. In the event of a failure to reach agreement the protagonists have traditionally turned to third parties to assist—through conciliation, mediation or arbitration—in finding a solution to the impasse. Even since the flood of employment legislation in the 1980s giving encouragement to employers (in particular) to go to court in the event of trade disputes, there have been relatively few instances of employers or unions choosing litigation as a means of resolving their differences.

It is hardly surprising, therefore, that in 1968 when the Donovan Commission was considering the matter of individual dispute resolution through employment tribunals they envisaged a conciliation stage before a hearing, during which the parties would have an opportunity to reach a voluntary agreement to settle the matter.[1] The Donovan Report envisaged that such a process would not only be conducive to good industrial relations but would also be less costly for the parties.

14.02 The Conciliation Service of the Department of Employment and Productivity was given the task of providing conciliation in individual employment tribunal cases in 1972.[2] That Act introduced the right not to be unfairly dismissed and provided for conciliation to be offered to applicants and respondents on a voluntary basis in order to facilitate resolution of the matter and avoid the need for a hearing. Such a resolution might involve re-employment of the individual or the payment of a sum of compensation by the employer. There was no charge for this service to either party.

The Government of the day saw this stage as essential to the credibility of the system for resolving employment disputes. It mirrored the conciliation process in collective disputes and was seen primarily as contributing to good industrial relations with public confrontations between employers and ex-employees in tribunals being averted. Resolving disputes prior to a tribunal hearing also made economic sense in that

---

[1] Donovan Report, para. 584.
[2] See Industrial Relations Act 1971.

considerable expense to the Exchequer in funding industrial tribunal hearings was avoided.

Advisory, Conciliation and Arbitration Service[3]

The establishment of ACAS in 1974 as an organisation accountable to an appointed council and thus independent of government added to its credibility as the body chosen to inherit this conciliation role. Its status was codified in statute in the Employment Protection Act 1975 which also accorded settlements achieved through this process special signifi- cance in that such agreements drawn up by the conciliation officer were given exclusive power to void the right to pursue a tribunal complaint under the Act.[4] 14.03

Subsequent employment legislation has included parallel provision for ACAS conciliation and reference can be found to this in section 18 of the Employment Tribunals Act 1996,[5] which lists the statutory provisions in respect of which a conciliation officer may become involved.

ACAS conciliation

The principles

The duties of the ACAS conciliation officer are laid down in section 18 of the ETA. He is required, where a complaint has been made to the employment tribunal: 14.04

> "(a) if he is requested to do so by the person by whom and the person against whom the proceedings are brought, or
> (b) if, in the absence of any such request, the conciliation officer considers that he could act under this subsection with a reasonable prospect of success,
>
> to endeavour to promote a settlement of the proceedings without their being determined by an employment tribunal".[6]

Furthermore, according to section 18, the conciliation officer must "in particular" seek to promote the reinstatement or re-engagement of the employee by the employer (or an associated employer) on terms appearing to him to be "equitable". It has been suggested in one case that a conciliation officer must always take the initiative in suggesting re- employment as a possible avenue of settlement during the course of the conciliation process.[7] However, the court rejected this interpretation and supported the ACAS view that the statutory duty only requires the conciliation officer positively to promote re-employment "so far as [is] applicable in the circumstances of the particular case".[8] Failing re-

---

[3] Hereinafter ACAS.
[4] See now ERA, s.203 and paras 12–19 *et seq.*, below.
[5] Hereinafter ETA.
[6] ETA, s.18(2).
[7] *Moore v. Duport Furniture Products Ltd* [1982] I.R.L.R. 31, HL.
[8] ETA, s.18(4)(a).

employment, he is required to promote the settlement of the matter by the payment of a sum of compensation by the respondent.

14.05   The duty of the conciliation officer is also triggered when the employee has grounds for a claim to the tribunal but has yet to present an application.[9] Here, if either side asks him to attempt conciliation he must offer his services as if a complaint had actually been lodged. ACAS therefore has a role to play in avoiding tribunal claims as much as in attempting to settle them once they have been lodged.

The conciliation officer is, according to statute, obliged "where appropriate" to encourage the use of "other procedures" (usually interpreted as the employer's own internal discipline or grievance procedures) to resolve the matter. Specific provision is made in the ETA for matters communicated to the officer in the course of conciliation to be regarded as privileged and only admissible in evidence at the tribunal hearing with the parties' permission.[10] This has important practical implications that will be considered below. The organisational division between them reinforces this separation of the conciliation officer's function from the judgmental role of the tribunal.

14.06   In practice, it is essential for the conciliation officer to be seen to be independent—not just of the parties but of the employment tribunal itself—to enable him to discharge his role effectively. The internal guidelines of ACAS require the officer to act only with the consent of the parties and in a neutral and confidential manner. This means that the officer will not express an opinion on the merits of either party's case, or advise on the merits of any offers made by the other side or on whether or not they should pursue the case to a hearing. However, as explained in the leaflet[11] which is issued to all parties approached by the officer they will: "Convey information from one party to the other"; and "Help the parties to establish the facts at issue and discuss the possible options open to them. In this way, [they] aim to assist each of them to be able to reach an informed decision as to how they may proceed".

The underlying principle is that parties to the dispute are helped towards a solution but it is not imposed upon them; they decide themselves whether or not to settle and on what terms.

14.07   If settlement is achieved the officer will assist in drawing up the agreement. He may advise on how the terms can be recorded and on any statutory limitations that may exist on the wording proposed by the parties. The agreement can be recorded on a standard ACAS settlement form[12] a copy of which is sent to the office of the employment tribunals. In this way the settlement can be registered by the tribunal as having discharged the application and it may then be promulgated as a decision of the employment tribunal.

If the parties appoint representatives, the convention is that ACAS conciliation officers will not approach the parties themselves but will speak only to the representative unless instructed otherwise.

---

[9] ETA, s.18(3).
[10] ETA, s.18(7).
[11] Form COT 5.
[12] Form COT 3.

The practice

It has been suggested[13] that an agreement is not binding on an 14.08 applicant if the conciliation officer failed to advise him of the possibility of claiming compensation under specific heads. The EAT disagreed, finding that: "a conciliation officer is not under a statutory duty to advise or inform an employee of his right to claim for future loss of earnings or, more generally, to go through the framework of the relevant legislation with him and explain his rights to him". They went on to say that: "The nature of a conciliation officer's function must depend on the particular circumstances of each case". They found that, effectively, if the officer feels that a lengthy exposition of the applicant's rights would prejudice settlement then he is not obliged to raise such "obstacles" to the process of settlement. In practice, the officer is very likely to assist the parties in looking at possible heads of loss in the case in order to give them an indication of the parameters likely to be imposed by the tribunal and thus to assist in bringing the parties towards a compromise figure which is realistic in the circumstances.

It is not necessary for the parties to reduce the agreement to written form for it to be regarded as binding on them. So long as it complies with the ordinary law of contract in that there is a valid offer and acceptance and the parties intend to create legal relations it is potentially binding. This, of course, does not necessarily require a written contract. The courts have found[14] that offers and acceptances communicated between the parties via the conciliation officer are binding in law and there is no formal requirement for such agreement to be in writing. The ACAS officer will act on that basis unless he is informed by one or both parties that the offer or acceptance is only valid when conveyed in writing. This is, of course, particularly relevant when a representative indicates an offer or acceptance without firm instructions and care should obviously be taken not to commit the client to a particular position in conversation with the conciliation officer.[15] The offer and acceptance must be unconditional for the contract to be binding immediately and for it to be distinguished from an offer to negotiate.[16]

ACAS will not act when settlement has already been agreed between 14.09 the parties. They regard such agreement as precluding conciliation if it is firmly agreed and a fait accompli. By definition, conciliation requires some room for manoeuvre and a conciliation officer will not "rubber stamp" an agreement if the parties are already bound by it. This means that, if a sum of compensation is agreed between the parties but other matters—such as the terms of a reference or the details of the settlement agreement wording—remain to be resolved, the conciliation officer can be asked to assist with these matters and to commit the agreement to a Form COT 3.

This is a particular problem when asking a conciliation officer to assist in a case where an application has not yet been lodged with the tribunal. ACAS have decided that they need to be satisfied both that there is a

---

[13] See *Slack v. Greenham (Plant Hire) Ltd* [1983] I.R.L.R. 271.
[14] See *Gilbert v. Kembridge Fibres Ltd* [1984] I.R.L.R. 52, EAT.
[15] See *Freeman v. Sovereign Chicken Ltd* [1991] I.R.L.R. 408, EAT.
[16] See *G. R. Warrender & Son v. Clark*, EAT/86/89.

genuine possibility that the employee will indeed lodge an application
and that an agreement has yet to be finalised. Accordingly, they will ask
the employee personally to confirm that they have grounds for a tribunal
claim and that they intend to lodge it in the absence of an agreement. If
the parties claim that any agreement is conditional on the conciliation
officer acting, ACAS will require a commitment from the parties that it
is accepted that the terms of the agreement may be changed as a result
of the intervention of the officer before agreeing to become involved.
Obviously, if there is a potential unfair dismissal claim the employee
must have been dismissed, be under notice of dismissal or have resigned
before the conciliation officer will agree to act.

14.10   The wording of settlements provides further potential problems. The
conciliation officer performs a role in relation to statutory claims.
However, parties (particularly respondents) may wish to extend the
scope of the Form COT 3 wording to include claims in common law—
often contractual claims—or other matters. The policy of ACAS in these
circumstances is to advise the parties of the statutory authority and point
out that a Form COT 3 agreement might not automatically preclude
such claims but may simply be regarded as evidence of an intention to
settle such matters.[17] They will advise an applicant that, if there are any
outstanding claims, actual or potential, arising from their employment
apart from the employment tribunal matter, these may be voided by the
Form COT 3 settlement wording proposed by the respondent.

14.11   The extent to which advisers decide to discuss the merits of a case with
ACAS will depend on their own knowledge, the complexity of the case,
the availability of the evidence relied on by the other side and the
relevant legal authorities known to them. One important implication of
the steady increase in the workload of tribunals is that, as cases now take
longer to come to hearing there is more time available for negotiations
to take place. This is particularly noticeable in England and Wales. The
impact on time delays before hearings is less marked in Scotland, to
date.

The process

14.12   There is no particular rule that dictates the officer's decision as to who
to contact first in the conciliation process. It may depend on the
particular preference of the officer, the speed of receipt of Form ET3,
the issues raised in the application and the notice of appearance or,
simply, on who returns the officer's calls first. The officer will receive a
copy of Form ET1 from the central office of the employment tribunals
usually between two days and two weeks after the application has been
registered with a similar time-scale for Form ET3. It is the practice of
ACAS to send to the parties a standard letter informing them of the
identity of the officer dealing with the case and enclosing Form COT 5
describing the service.

The letter explains that the officer generally awaits the return of Form
ET3 before approaching the parties but that it is always open to either
party to take the initiative to call them. This sometimes creates problems
for the officer in that, on receipt of the ACAS letter, the respondent may

---

[17] See *Livingstone v. Hepworth Refractories* [1992] I.R.L.R. 63, EAT.

call the officer and seek advise on the terms of the notice of appearance. Such action would breach the ACAS impartiality guidelines and the officer will decline to advise the employer on matters such as this. However, if the employer is seeking to make an early (perhaps "nuisance value") offer to resolve the claim they may well wish to avoid the expense of obtaining legal or other skilled advice on the wording of Form ET3. In these circumstances it is not unusual for the officer to simply convey the offer to the applicant before Form ET3 is lodged. They may even point out to the applicant that should the employer incur the expense of lodging Form ET3, the offer may be withdrawn on economic grounds.

The unrepresented applicant may find that the officer offers to meet 14.13 with him to outline his role in more detail, to explain the employment tribunal process and to explore the merits of the matter from both sides. Occasionally, such an offer will be made to unrepresented employers if they have no experience of dealing with employment tribunals or the conciliation process. It is open to either party or their representative to request a meeting with the officer assigned to the case.

Occasionally, when a settlement seems imminent, a joint meeting may be chaired by the officer with a view to reaching agreement on the precise terms. The conciliation officer will be reluctant to suggest or agree to a joint meeting unless there is good evidence that settlement is possible in principle. This is in marked contrast to the approach of ACAS in collective conciliation where such meetings are normally the starting points for exploring settlement. The individual conciliation officer will be particularly reluctant to initiate a joint meeting where the parties merely use the opportunity to rehearse their arguments for the hearing (possibly with some acrimony)—rather than concentrate on seeking a compromise to settle the case.

Needless to say, if either party is not willing to participate in negotiations through the ACAS officer, ACAS will not act other than to give general information to either party on industrial tribunal procedures, if requested.

Assuming that the parties wish to use the service, the officer will 14.14 attempt to clarify the issues for both sides and convey offers and counter offers between the parties. Advisers must bear in mind that ACAS may not have been given copies of all accompanying documentation sent with Form ETIs and ET3s and certainly will rarely have seen further and better particulars sent informally (*i.e.* not as a result of an order from the tribunal) between the parties. Naturally, whether these should be copied by the parties to the conciliation officer will depend on tactical questions and the practical benefits of so doing. If the officer is asked or volunteers to copy case reports or details of relevant authorities to one party he will inevitably offer the same facility to the other side. He may advise on the procedures for obtaining witness or document recovery orders or for requesting answers to written questions but not on the merits or otherwise of so doing in the specific case. In cases involving discrimination he will advise generally on the rules covering service of statutory questionnaires but will refer the parties to the CRE or EOC for further assistance.

If the applicant wishes to withdraw the application following discussions with the officer or after reaching a private settlement with the employer the conciliation officer may offer to send a withdrawal form[18] for transmission to the respondent and the office of the employment tribunals.

14.15 The ACAS officer will inform the office of the employment tribunals when a conciliated settlement has been reached in order to ensure that the hearing is postponed. The Secretary of the Employment Tribunals will then confirm with the parties—especially the applicant—that a settlement has been achieved and adjourn the hearing pending receipt of the completed Form COT 3 settlement form. Naturally, if settlement is reached at such a late stage before the hearing that the members cannot reasonably be informed of the adjournment, the tribunal may require the attendance of one or more parties at the hearing to request in person that the proceedings be adjourned in the light of the agreement.

Once the wording of Form COT 3 is agreed, the conciliation officer will send the completed form (which has three carbonised copies attached) to the applicant or his agent for signature and onward transmission to the respondent's agent. Once the form is signed by both parties each receives a copy and the remaining two are returned to ACAS who forward the principal to the office of the employment tribunals. The Secretary of the Employment Tribunals will in due course promulgate a decision incorporating the terms of Form COT 3 and recording the fact that the case is discharged on this basis.

Pressures on the parties

14.16 It is clear that in some ways the conciliation process is weighted against unrepresented applicants. Inevitably, employers are more likely than the individual worker to have some experience in dealing with industrial tribunals and the conciliation and negotiation process and will have more of a feel for tactical considerations. They certainly have greater resources (human and financial) to call upon and will generally know that the likelihood of expenses being awarded in a case is extremely slim. On the other hand; the applicant with almost certainly no prior knowledge or experience of the tribunal will feel under pressure to settle—possibly accepting the first offer made. Applicants will often feel under pressure, as they seem in no position to negotiate. They cannot rely on the advice of the conciliation officer who is under an obligation not to assist either party by advising on the terms of any offer but who may have mentioned to the applicant that expenses are sometimes awarded against applicants for frivolous or vexatious claims.

14.17 Nor is lack of experience the unrepresented applicant's only handicap in the negotiations. Applicants may feel under economic pressure to settle (particularly if they have been unemployed for a period). They may be intimidated by the thought of appearing at the hearing and conducting what is probably a complicated legal action with no assistance other than the goodwill and tolerance of the tribunal. They may be fearful of publicity that may attach itself to the case and of prejudicing their future employment prospects. This can happen either by reason of the public airing of their alleged shortcomings by the respondent or simply by appearing to potential employers to be litigious. Tribunal

---

[18] Form COT 4.

decisions are often difficult to predict and the uncertainty created by this will often exert pressure on applicants to take the "bird in the hand" offered by the employer. Even represented applicants may find that their agent is more inclined to recommend acceptance of an offer than to risk all in the tribunal. On the other hand, there are countervailing pressures on applicants to resist settlement (at least at a token level). They may feel such a sense of injustice that they are prepared to risk losing at a hearing rather than give up the chance to air their grievances publicly. In these circumstances, the possibility of press interest in the case will be a spur to continue to a hearing rather than acting as a deterrent. The possibility (albeit practically and statistically unlikely) of re-employment being ordered by the tribunal may deter settlement as may the feeling (real or imagined) that their case is a "test case" which may serve to open doors for others in similar circumstances. Finally, the applicant's agent may of course be advising him not to accept a particular offer.

The respondent is not immune from pressure in this process. The 14.18 pressures of cost and inconvenience, possible publicity, the stress of the hearing for witnesses and legal advice to settle are the same as the pressures on applicants in favour of reaching a compromise to settle. On the other hand, employers may find that there are stronger pressures on them in favour of resisting settlement. The merits of the case and the legal advice that they may receive to resist settlement on the terms proposed by the applicant are important in this respect. The employer may have insurance against the costs of such legal action or be eligible through membership of an employers' association for free expert representation.

The employer will have the additional burden of the possible employee relations implications of settlement of a particular case. At its crudest, if it becomes known to the workforce that any employee dismissed by the employer need only lodge an application to the employment tribunal to have the employer pay a token sum in settlement, the employer will naturally find that this encourages claims. The current workforce (and their representatives) may portray any payment to an ex-employee as an admission of liability even if the payment was made on a purely economic basis to avoid the cost of a hearing. One issue that may arise is the assertion of the "right to manage" in a particular case. This can be crucial to an employer's decision to pursue the matter to hearing. The credibility of management and the disciplinary procedures may be debased as a result of settlement—creating potentially damaging longer-term consequences for the organisation.

Compromise agreements

Apart from reaching agreement through the auspices of ACAS the 14.19 parties may resolve their dispute by the use of a compromise agreement. Compromise agreements were introduced under the TURERA 1993 and the provisions that regulate their use are now to be found within section 203 of the ERA. Assuming that it complies with the statutory requirements, a compromise agreement will have the effect of discharging the employee's statutory rights referred to therein. The conditions are as follows:

1. the agreement must be in writing;
2. the agreement must relate to the particular complaint;
3. the employee must have received independent legal advice from a qualified lawyer as to the terms and effect of the proposed agreement and, in particular, its effect on his ability to pursue his rights before an employment tribunal;
4. there must be in force, when the adviser gives the advice, a policy of insurance covering the risk of a claim by the employee or worker in respect of loss arising in consequence of the advice;
5. the agreement must identify the adviser; and
6. the agreement must state that the conditions regulating compromise agreements under the Act are satisfied.

The term "qualified lawyer" is defined as meaning, in Scotland, a solicitor who holds a practising certificate or an advocate (whether in practice or employed to give legal advice).[19]

14.20   Compromise agreements are now widely used by practitioners as a means to settle any claims that may remain outstanding on employment. They can be a particularly effective way of bringing about a swift conclusion to what otherwise might be a protracted claim. As a result, there can be a considerable saving of expense on each side. From the employee's point of view, the matter is dealt with quickly, discreetly, and hopefully painlessly without the worry of a public appearance in a tribunal. From the employer's point of view one of the main advantages is certainty. Perhaps one of the most useful aspects of the procedure is that it allows both parties to deal with the difficult and sensitive issues surrounding termination of employment in a dignified and even constructive way. The procedure is often used to cover matters that would not necessarily come before a tribunal but clearly in these cases it is up to advisers to ensure that their clients have a binding agreement. It will be noted that there is no requirement under section 203 for the employer to have advice, the main purpose of the section being to ensure that an employee is properly advised before signing away statutory rights. It goes without saying that practitioners should advise their clients fully and in writing of the implications of such an agreement.

FUNDING EMPLOYMENT CLAIMS

Legal Advice and Assistance

14.21   Legal advice and assistance is available under the current legal advice and assistance scheme in Scotland (and the equivalent scheme in England). This represents a basic form of legal aid and is no different from that which is generally available in respect of a broad range of legal issues to those who qualify financially. Generally speaking, an applicant is entitled to basic preliminary advice regarding his or her legal position.

---

[19] ERA, s.203(4)(b).

The threshold for qualification is low and usually a financial contribution is payable by the applicant. A solicitor may apply for an increase in authorised expenditure under this scheme to cover matters such as completion of a Form ET1, negotiations with ACAS, preparation of documentary productions, taking statements from the applicant and witnesses and other preparations in connection with the hearing. Generally speaking, if a settlement is achieved, or if the applicant is successful at an employment tribunal hearing, having been in receipt of legal advice and assistance, the solicitor's charges will be payable out of the sums recovered. However, an applicant may be able to demonstrate that this would cause hardship in which case an application can be made to the Legal Aid Board for payment of the solicitor's fees.

Assistance By Way of Representation (ABWOR)

From January 15, 2001, applicants who are eligible for advice and assistance can also receive representation at employment tribunals in Scotland.[20] Support is also available if the hearing is remitted to a tribunal in England as long as the issue remains one of Scots Law. This change in the regulations followed several challenges under the Human Rights Act at preliminary hearings where it was argued that the lack of financial assistance for representation at employment tribunals was a breach of Article 6 of the European Convention on Human Rights. Although these challenges were unsuccessful, the Scottish Executive took the decision to extend assistance, acting on legal advice that a continued refusal would undoubtedly breach Article 6 on the basis that "equality of arms" is an essential element of a fair hearing. Despite the ensuing furore from spurious actions, such fears have so far proves unfounded, which is largely due to the fact that the regulations require a number of tests to be satisfied before the provision of ABWOR can be authorised by the Board. Indeed, the figures for the half-year period from January to June 2001 show that the Board had received only 353 requests for authority to provide ABWOR, 184 of which were granted.[21] 14.22

A solicitor must apply for the authority of the Board before ABWOR can be given. This is done when an increase for advice and assistance is requested. At the time of writing the initial limit for authorised expenditure is £80 and the normal procedure for obtaining increases applies. The Board's guidelines suggest that an initial increase to £250 can be granted to allow the solicitor obtain further information on the claim, retrieve documents, lodge the claim and to apply for authority to give ABWOR. Requests can also be made for increases to instruct counsel. 14.23

If the case proceeds to a hearing, at the time of writing the advocacy rate for a solicitor conducting a hearing is £54.80. this charge applies to "chamber" work—the hourly rate is £42.20. the Board's guidelines suggest that further increases of up to £600 may be granted to assist with representation and that larger increases can be requested where the hearing overruns or where expert witnesses are involved. There is no upper limit here and the guidelines state that requests will be considered on a case-by-case basis.

---

[20] S.S.I. 2001 No. 2.
[21] SLAB October 2001.

14.24   Authority to provide Assistance By Way of Representation will only
be granted if the applicant meets three criteria:

> (a) the case arguable;
> (b) it is reasonable in the particular1circumstances of the case
> that ABWOR be made available; and
> (c) the case is too complex to allow the applicant to present it
> to a minimum standard of effectiveness in person.

The Board states in its guidelines that the first criterion will be met if the
solicitor can show a *prima facie* case with regard to jurisdiction and the
legal basis of the claim. In considering whether it is reasonable to
provide ABWOR, the Board will look at various issues including
whether other rights or facilities are available to the client, whether thee
has been an attempt to negotiate a settlement, how the proceedings have
been funded to date, whether the applicant has been asked to lodge a
deposit, the likely outcome of the case compared with the likely cost, and
whether someone of moderate means would use their money to fund the
claim.

14.25   The third criterion (c), is undoubtedly the hardest to satisfy. Here the
Board will consider:

> (i) whether the determination of the issue may involve any
> procedural difficulties, consideration of a substantial ques-
> tion of law, or evidence of a complex or difficult nature.
> and/or
> (ii) whether the applicant is unable to understand the proceed-
> ings or to state his own case because of his age, inadequate
> knowledge of English, mental illness, other mental or
> physical disabilities or otherwise.

Under the first heading the Board advises solicitors to ask themselves if
there is something about the legal issues and/or evidence that makes the
case complicated from a lay person's point of view, with regard to issues
such as:

> • The number and types of witnesses.
> • The number and types of documents.
> • The level at which the opponent has representation.
> • Whether the hearing takes place in Scotland or England.

With regard to the level of the applicant's understanding of proceedings,
the Board states that the fact that an applicant is a poor communicator
or of low intelligence will not suffice. Examples they give of applicants
who would qualify for ABWOR on these grounds are those with mental
or physical disabilities (including mental illness) or immigrants with a
poor command of English.

14.26   The Board state in their guidelines that the factors listed under (i) and
(ii) are not exhaustive and that they will take all issues into account in
order to form a "balanced view" of a case's complexity and/or the

applicant's understanding. It remains to be seen how far this third criterion will restrict the provision of ABWOR for employment tribunals, but it should be noted that the test is more stringent than that for civil legal aid where the complexity of an action does not require to be shown. These factors coupled with the new tribunal rules on expenses (see 14.55 below) are likely to curb any rash or frivolous claims feared by employers.

Trade Union Assistance

Members of trade unions are normally able to obtain assistance in a 14.27 wide variety of ways. For example, a shop steward or full-time official may be able to provide advice and representation during any internal grievance, disciplinary, or appeal proceedings. In addition, the union may be able to provide representation at an employment tribunal hearing. This may be in the form of representation by an official of the union. Alternatively, union funds may be used to provide legal representation. Legal representation is more likely to be funded by a union where the case involves an issue of principle or where a number of applicants are involved.

Citizens Advice Bureaux and Voluntary Organisations

Citizens advice bureaux are able to provide a considerable amount of 14.28 assistance in connection with employment claims. Branches are located throughout the country and generally speaking one or more of the advisers in a local bureau will have some knowledge and experience of employment matters. CABs frequently represent employees at employment tribunal hearings and, of course, there is no cost to the applicant for the advice and representation given. Advice is also available to applicants from other locally and centrally funded organisations and projects.

Legal Indemnity Insurance

Legal indemnity insurance is available to employers and employees 14.29 alike. Naturally, employers are more likely to have cover for a wide variety of claims, including those relating to employment. However, it is increasingly common for employees to have indemnity to enable them to pursue unfair dismissal and breach of contract claims against their employers. A number of insurance companies provide this type of indemnity. When cover applies, the insurance company will scrutinise the merits of the case and if satisfied that indemnity applies in terms of its own policy, will then proceed to instruct solicitors to deal with the claim. There is an increasing tendency for insurance companies to instruct members of specialist panels to deal with claims in view of the increasingly complex nature of employment law. From the point of view of employees this kind of cover can provide a relatively low cost alternative to legal aid. From an employer's point of view, it may provide some peace of mind because of the potential for increasingly wider varieties of claims and attendant legal costs.

Employers' Associations

14.30   Many employers are members of employers' associations or federations and these can provide considerable assistance in the event of employment problems arising. One characteristic of employment law is the fact that advice taken about a problem at a very early stage can pay enormous dividends. Employment law is difficult enough for professionally trained solicitors; it creates enormous difficulties for people who are running businesses. Many employers' associations provide an advice giving service to their members and may even be able to assist with legal representation at a later stage.

The Equal Opportunities Commission

14.31   The EOC was set up under the SDA. Its functions are to work towards elimination of discrimination on grounds of sex and marital status, to promote equality of opportunity between men and women and to review the operation of anti-discrimination legislation.

Discrimination cases tend to be complex. They involve important issues of principle and have a tendency to attract publicity. They can be, therefore, lengthy and expensive. In these circumstances the EOC is in a position to provide valuable assistance in connection with individual complaints. The EOC is also empowered to institute proceedings itself in relation to discriminatory advertisements, instructions or pressure to discriminate and discriminatory practices. The EOC may give advice before a case even proceeds to the employment tribunal. For example, assistance may be given in relation to the completion of questionnaires under the SDA. It may also assist in providing legal advice or assistance and legal or other representation. By virtue of section 75(1) of the SDA, the EOC commissioners have discretion in deciding whether or not to assist a particular case. They may do so on the ground that the case raises a question of principle, on the ground that it is unreasonable having regard to the complexity of the case, or the applicant's position in relation to the respondent or another person involved, or to any other matter, to expect the applicant to deal with the case unaided, or by reason of any other special consideration.

Cases may, of course, involve consideration of other issues, such as unfair dismissal. In these circumstances, the EOC may be in a position to assist in relation to the sex discrimination element of the claim, leaving it to the applicant to find alternate ways of funding the remainder of the claim.

The Commission for Racial Equality

14.32   The Commission for Racial Equality fulfils a similar function in relation to race cases. Its duties are to work toward the elimination of discrimination on racial grounds, to promote equality of opportunity between persons of different racial groups, and to review the operation anti-discrimination legislation. Its statutory framework is to be found in the RRA and it operates in a broadly similar way to the EOC.

Pro Bono Representation

14.33   For a variety of reasons employment law lends itself well to what is now known as *pro bono* representation. Employment tribunals hear cases of increasing importance and complexity. Applicants (and indeed respondents) are frequently unrepresented and unaware of the full range of arguments that might be deployed on their behalf. European law has extended significantly the employment rights of individuals many of whom are low paid workers and cannot be expected to afford the luxury of legal representation. Many landmark judgments in the employment law field have their origins in employment tribunal proceedings wherein an unpaid representative argued the applicant's case. At present the legal profession is in a unique position to provide assistance to parties who might otherwise feel unable to seek redress through the medium of the employment tribunal system. Naturally the main beneficiaries of lawyers' willingness to undertake *pro bono* work tend to be applicants but it must not be forgotten that compensation and legal fees can place an enormous burden on small employers.

In these circumstances there are a number of steps which lawyers may take to assist clients who are unable to meet legal expenses, with benefits accruing to both parties to the relationship. The fact that parties to employment tribunal proceedings may be represented by whomsoever they choose means that, for example, trainee solicitors, for whom court appearances can seem to be a distant prospect, are able to gain extremely valuable advocacy experience at an early stage in their careers. Low risk cases such as low value claims to recover deductions from pay are ideal in this respect. Even for the experienced practitioner considerable satisfaction can be derived in creating access to justice for a client who might otherwise go unassisted. It is the view of the authors that there is a place for formal *pro bono* schemes within legal practices. Indeed, one such scheme has been instituted within chambers at the English Bar following an inquiry into the incidence of party litigants involved in cases in the Royal Courts of Justice.

Legal Aid for Employment Appeals

Both legal advice and assistance and legal aid are available for appeals 14.34 to the EAT. Application for full legal aid must be lodged at the earliest opportunity, preferably with an application for emergency legal aid as the appeal process will not be delayed pending the outcome of a legal aid application. An applicant for legal aid will require to satisfy the Legal Aid Board that the decision which is to be appealed against is wrong in law. Obviously, applicants also have to demonstrate financial eligibility. An applicant for legal aid who is a respondent in the appeal stands a reasonable prospect of obtaining legal aid subject to financial eligibility.

RULES OF PROCEDURE

Employment tribunals have dealt with employment claims since 1965, 14.35 having originally been established to hear appeals against employment training levies under the Industrial Training Act 1964. Procedure in employment tribunals in Scotland is governed by the Employment Tribunals (Constitution and Rules of Procedure) (Scotland) Regulations 2001,[22] the rules themselves being set out in Schedule 1. The 2001

---

[22] S.I. 2001 No. 1170. These repeal and replace the Industrial Tribunals (Constitution and Rules of Procedure) (Scotland) Regulations 1993.

regulations introduce a new "overriding objective" to deal with cases justly. In the rules themselves, of particular significance is rule 15(1), which allows a tribunal to regulate its own procedure, provided the rules do not require otherwise. It is for this reason that differences in practice have emerged between Scottish and English tribunals. Practitioners may also encounter regional variations in procedures, principally in relation to administrative matters. A number of the rules demonstrate a flexible approach to procedural, as opposed to substantive, matters. For example, by virtue of rule 15, a chairman may exercise a degree of latitude in relation to time-limits imposed by the rules. The paperwork is also relatively informal. For example, an application to extend a time-limit under rule 15, to allow more time to lodge a notice of appearance, only requires to be addressed in writing to the tribunal secretary. However, this relatively relaxed approach to the enforcement of the procedural rules governing case administration contrasts markedly with the approach taken with regard to application of statutory time-limits, for example those stipulating time-limits for initiating proceedings. Those in particular are applied very strictly indeed. As a general rule, therefore, practitioners will find that procedural issues are of less significance in employment tribunals than they might be in the civil courts. The absence of unnecessary procedural barriers is undoubtedly of considerable assistance in disposing of large numbers of increasingly complex cases within reasonable time-scales.

The Originating Application

14.36 Any application to an employment tribunal must be initiated by way of an originating application. Although it is not essential that this should be laid out in any set form, rule 1 requires that it should specify the names and addresses of the applicant and the respondent as well as the grounds, with particulars thereof, on which relief is sought. In practice, applications are submitted by way of a standard Form ET1, which is a pre-printed form available from the tribunal offices as well as job centres and unemployment benefit offices. The originating application should be sent to the central office of the employment tribunals in Glasgow. Representatives should always ensure that they use up to date forms and that any communications are sent to the correct address/fax number.

Problems frequently arise in relation to timeous presentation of complaints in view of the short and strictly applied time-limits. Often, applicants are unaware of the time-limits which apply to their claims and fail to seek professional advice until perilously close to (and often after) the expiry of the relevant period. This can mean that the adviser is ill-equipped to do justice to the grounds of the complaint. Such a problem should never be allowed to cause any delay in relation to submission of the claim and even if it appears that it is time barred, the representative should ensure that it is lodged immediately. The form ET1 should be completed using as much information as is available to set out the grounds of the complaint. It is always possible to add to the case by way of further particulars at a later stage. However, where possible, the relevant statutory cases should be specified at the earliest opportunity.

An originating application will normally specify one respondent but not infrequently it may be necessary for an applicant's representative to direct a claim against more than one party. For example, there may be doubt about the identity of the employer, or about which respondent would be liable in the event of the claim being successful. In these circumstances it may be necessary to add one or more additional respondents at some stage in the proceedings and rule 19 allows this. Assuming the originating application has been lodged within the relevant time-limit this provision may be used to add additional respondents even after that time-limit has expired. It has been held by the EAT sitting in Scotland that essentially the question is one relating to the discretion of the tribunal rather than time-bar.[23]

The Notice of Appearance

On receipt of an originating application, the respondent must take steps 14.37 to ensure that a notice of appearance[24] is lodged with the Secretary at the central office of the employment tribunals.[25] As with the originating application, there is minimal regulation regarding the form of the notice of appearance. It must confirm details of the respondent's full name and address, state whether he intends to resist the application and, if so, set out sufficient particulars to show on what grounds this will be done.

A respondent now has 21 days (previously it was 14) under rule 3 to lodge the notice of appearance. If the respondent fails to enter appearance then he is unable to take any part in the proceedings except for certain clearly defined purposes, although in practice an appearance is almost invariably entered. In any event, it is always open to him to apply for an extension of time to enable this to be done and in the event that the respondent lodges the Form ET3 outwith the 21-day period, this ought to be accompanied by an application, supported by reasons, to extend the statutory time-limit. It is no longer the case that a late application is deemed to include an application for an extension of time. Representatives who attempt to obtain an extension of time simply to obtain instructions or for other ill-defined reasons will usually find that such an application is refused on the basis that it is always possible to lodge the form containing brief grounds of resistance which can be supplemented later by way of further particulars. It is unlikely that a respondent will be penalised for amending the Form ET3 in the early stages of a case. However, different considerations apply after the hearing has started. In one case an employer was refused leave to introduce an amendment during the course of a hearing because it would have had the effect of substantially altering the case which was being argued.[26] In practice, problems of this nature tend to arise in constructive dismissal cases where the employer's initial defence amounts to a bare denial that there was a dismissal, but it thereafter occurs to him that there may be some advantage in arguing that even if the applicant establishes that he was constructively dismissed, the dismissal was fair. To use a straightforward example, the employee may have resigned following the imposition of a change in terms and

---

[23] *Gillick v. B.P. Chemicals Ltd* [1993] I.R.L.R. 437.
[24] Form ET3.
[25] r.3.
[26] *Blue Star Ship Management v. Williams* [1979] I.R.L.R. 16.

conditions of employment by the employer. In these circumstances, it would be perfectly proper, indeed advisable for the employer to resist the application on the basis that the circumstances did not amount to a constructive dismissal, but that should the tribunal decide otherwise, the dismissal was for a potentially valid reason, *e.g.* business reorganisation (some other substantial reason justifying dismissal) and was potentially fair under section 98(4) of the ERA.

Case Management

Further Particulars and Questions

14.38   Rule 4 of the new rules deals with case management and gives the tribunal, on the application of a party or on its own motion a number of powers to assist with the management of cases with regard to evidence, documents and witnesses. Failure to adhere to certain orders imposed by the tribunal under this rule can result in all or part of a claim being struck out or an award of expenses being made. The tribunal may now order the provision of witness statements, the new rule reflecting a procedure which has developed in England with a view to speeding up the process.

Where the tribunal itself or either of the parties feel that further particulars of one side's case are required then a further particulars order may be issued from the tribunal office.[27] Any such order will require the party to whom it is addressed to furnish in writing further particulars of the grounds on which that party relies and of any facts and contentions relevant thereto. The tribunal has power to set a time-limit for compliance with the order. Bearing in mind that originating applications and notices of appearance are often framed in brief terms, applying for a further particulars order can be an effective way of concentrating an opponent's mind. The granting of such an order usually assists in clarifying the issues to be adjudicated on by the tribunal but often has the additional advantage that it can assist in promoting a settlement. If the party to whom the further particulars order is addressed fails to comply with it then the tribunal, either before or at the hearing, may strike out the whole or part of the originating application or notice of appearance. Before doing so it must send notice to the offending party giving him an opportunity to show cause why the tribunal should not do so.

The tribunal is also empowered to put questions to a party with a requirement that written answers be furnished and it should be noted that a separate questionnaire procedure is available for persons who feel that they have been victims of acts of discrimination.[28]

Documents

14.39   Documentary evidence is increasingly important in employment tribunals, not least because of the need for employers to keep more detailed records relating to the employment relationship. There is no time-scale set down in the rules in relation to production of documents.

---

[27] r.4(3).
[28] SDA, s.74; RRA, s.65.

Nor does there exist any regulation of the form in which documents must be produced. In these circumstances, it is very much up to the parties to decide how best to present the documents on which they rely. This is one area where representatives frequently fail to present their cases to best advantage, and it is suggested that the following simple points should be borne in mind. Although there is no formal deadline for lodging documents it is self evident that to leave this step until the day of the hearing is to invite problems, unless there are very few documents to be relied upon. An opponent must be allowed reasonable time to study documents to be used at the hearing and will generally be allowed an adjournment for this purpose. It is preferable to lodge documents at least one week in advance of the hearing (or longer in more complex cases) and this in itself may bring about a settlement or a withdrawal. It must be remembered that one's opponent may not necessarily be in possession of the full facts until he has seen all documents in support of the other party's case. A very obvious example of this is the frequently encountered scenario involving an applicant who has conveniently forgotten about written warnings issued by the employer.

As a rule, tribunal secretaries in Scotland are happy to accept documentary productions at any time in advance of the hearing. In England the practice varies but even if the secretary is unwilling to accept bundles of exhibits in advance of the hearing, representatives will always be encouraged to communicate with each other with a view to preparing an agreed bundle. Whether in Scotland or England, preparation of an agreed inventory or bundle is always desirable. It has a number of advantages: it concentrates the minds of representatives in advance of the hearing; it reduces the scope for unnecessary duplication of documents; it narrows the scope of the evidence because it follows that if, for example, minutes of meetings can be agreed as being accurate it may be possible to restrict the evidence of witnesses to key points.

Thought should be given to the form in which productions are lodged. 14.40 All documents should be allocated "A" or "R" numbers for applicants and respondents respectively. It is the practice of the authors' firm to number each multi-paged document separately, *e.g.* R1(1), R1(2), R2, R3(1), R3 (2), etc. As a general rule documents should be produced in chronological order although practitioners may find it helpful to group certain documents together even if this takes them out of date sequence. Practitioners should be careful to ensure that only documents that are relevant to the determination of the issues before the tribunal are lodged. Those representing applicants should also ensure that these include documentary evidence in support of any claim for compensation, including loss of pension rights. It is surprising how often representatives fail to provide such basic documentary evidence in spite of the fact that in Scotland they are advised on the notice of hearing that they should do so. It should be noted that in England the question of remedy is dealt with at a separate hearing if the application is successful.

A tribunal has power by virtue of rule 4(5)(b) to require a person including a party to produce documents or to require one party to grant to another such recovery or inspection (including the taking of copies) of documents as might be ordered by a sheriff. Any application for a document recovery order should be made in writing and should be addressed to the tribunal secretary. It is suggested that a covering letter should explain why the documents are relevant to the issues to be decided in the case and that it should be accompanied by a schedule listing the documents in question with sufficient specification to enable them to be readily identified. It is always preferable to make an informal approach to the other party, requesting production of documents on a voluntary basis before seeking a formal order. If the opponent has refused, without good reason, to produce documents voluntarily, this fact will enhance the prospect of a formal order being granted by the chairman. Rule 4(5)(b) allows a tribunal to require any person to attend and produce any document relating to the matter to be determined and to appoint a time and place for this purpose. Persons who fail to comply with orders under rule 4(5) without reasonable excuse render themselves liable on summary conviction to a fine although this sanction is rarely invoked.

Witnesses

14.41　　If a witness is unwilling to attend, or requires an official document to safeguard his own position with his employer then a tribunal may, on its own motion or on the application of a party, issue a witness order. An application must be in writing and must state the reason why the order is required. Details should be given not only about why an order is necessary but also why the evidence of the witness is relevant to the proceedings. Usually witness orders will only be granted if the witness will be given more than 48 hours notice of his required attendance. A witness who fails to attend after a witness order has been served, unless he has been able to have it recalled, is liable on summary conviction to a fine.[29] Representatives do not have any power to cite witnesses. A tactic that is often deployed on behalf of applicants is to apply for witness orders for every conceivable witness in the respondent's organisation from the managing director down, with the obvious objective of forcing a settlement. This method is not to be recommended as it is seldom successful and does little to enhance the credibility of the representative.

When arranging the attendance of witnesses, representatives should bear in mind that leading too much evidence can be just as damaging as not leading enough. A great number of cases involve fairly standard unfair dismissal issues and these tend to follow a fairly well-trodden path. Usually the employer will arrange for two or three witnesses to be called to speak to investigation, discipline and if appropriate, any appeal. In such a case the applicant may call the person who accompanied him during the disciplinary process and perhaps even a witness to the event which led to the dismissal if there exists a factual dispute on this. It must be remembered that the tribunal will be concerned with the application of a specific statutory test and will not be persuaded to conduct the hearing as if it were a criminal trial.

It is always advisable, even if only as a matter of courtesy, to write to witnesses well in advance of the hearing not just to confirm arrangements for attendance but also to explain the procedure which will be followed at the hearing. It is also important to explain to them that

---

[29] r.4(5).

although employment tribunal hearings normally start promptly, it can be difficult to predict how long the evidence will take, and a certain amount of waiting will inevitably be involved.

Fixing the Hearing Date

One advantage of the employment tribunal system is that parties and 14.42 their representatives are generally given a fair degree of choice in selecting suitable dates for hearing. Time scales vary around the country but in Scotland parties receive, well in advance of the hearing, a list of proposed dates. This appears on a *pro forma* letter which also gives representatives an opportunity to state how many witnesses are likely to be called, how long the hearing is likely to last, and whether they consent to the case being heard by a chairman sitting alone. If a case is not concluded on the day or days allotted it will not continue on the following day, but will be allocated a further date some time in the future in which case some weeks or months may pass between hearings. For this reason, representatives ought to be careful to predict, as accurately as possible, the length of the hearing when responding to the date listing letter. Hearings usually take longer than representatives predict! The date listing letter should be responded to as promptly as possible and, once a hearing has been fixed, it will not be postponed unless there are good reasons for doing so.

Miscellaneous Powers of Tribunals

Rule 15 is the residual provision allowing a tribunal to regulate its own 14.43 procedure, however this is subject to the other rules. Under rule 19, the tribunal is entitled to join as a party any person against whom relief is sought. Rule 20 enables the tribunal to consolidate proceedings where common questions of law or fact arise from more than one originating application. Under rule 21 the tribunal resident may transfer to England an application which could be more conveniently determined there.

Conducting the Tribunal Hearing

Usually employment tribunal hearings commence at 10 a.m. In 14.44 Scotland each case will usually have a tribunal allocated to it by the hearing date in which case the hearing usually starts at the stated time. Witnesses should be forewarned that evidence is given under oath or on affirmation. It helps to put them at ease if they are told something of tribunal procedure beforehand. The room in which the hearing is held is not intimidating and is laid out in a manner consistent with the stated objective of informality in the proceedings. The only concession to formality is the slightly raised platform on which the tribunal chairman and members sit. Representatives, parties and witnesses remain seated throughout the proceedings although it is customary for all present to stand when the members of the tribunal enter and leave the room, and for witnesses to stand when taking the oath or affirming. A clerk from the office of the Secretary of the Tribunals is normally present at the commencement of proceedings and thereafter is summoned as required. It is not usual for the clerk to remain during the proceedings. No formal record of proceedings is kept apart from the chairman's notes. The chairman should always be addressed as "Mr Chairman" or "Madam Chairman" and the lay members as "sir" or "madam". The tribunal as a whole should be addressed as "Mr Chairman, members of the Tribunal". Expressions such as "Chair", "Members of the Panel" are definitely to be avoided.

Preliminary Determinations

14.45   By virtue of rule 6 of the 2001 Regulations, an employment tribunal may fix a preliminary hearing to determine any issue relating to the entitlement of any party to bring or contest the proceedings to which the originating application relates. The tribunal may fix such a hearing on the application of either party or on its own motion. In practice this rule can be used to determine a wide variety of preliminary issues including, for example, the question of whether an application is time-barred, whether the employee was employed by the respondent, etc. The rules do not give any specific guidance regarding how such a hearing should be conducted. If the facts material to the preliminary issue are not in dispute, it may not be necessary for any evidence to be led, the hearing being conducted solely on the basis of submissions by the parties or their representatives. On the other hand, it may be necessary to lead evidence from one or both parties. In these circumstances the evidence will be subject to the normal rules.

Pre-Hearing Reviews

14.46   The tribunal has available to it a procedure designed to identify and weed out weak cases. Rule 7 of the 2001 Regulations enables the tribunal at any time before the hearing, on the application of a party or of its own motion, to conduct a pre-hearing review. This consists of consideration of the contents of the originating application and notice of appearance, any written representations, and any oral argument advanced by or on behalf of a party. Although in theory either party's case may be scrutinised at a pre-hearing review, in practice, it is the applicant's case that is examined. If the tribunal's view is that the claim has no reasonable prospect of success, then an order may be made against a party to pay a deposit of an amount not exceeding £500 as a condition of being permitted to continue to take part in the proceedings. However, the tribunal is not empowered to make such an order unless it has taken reasonable steps to ascertain the ability of the party to comply with the order and has taken account of any information so ascertained in determining the amount of the deposit. The chairman is required to record the order and the tribunal's reasons in summary form. This document is then sent to the parties. It is accompanied by a note explaining that if the party against whom the order is made persists in participating in the proceedings, he may have an award of expenses made against him and could lose his deposit. If the party against whom the order has been made fails to remit the amount specified within 21 days of the order being sent to him or within any further period (not exceeding 14 days) allowed by the tribunal, then the originating application or notice of appearance will be struck out.

The deposit paid by a party is refunded in full except where the 14.47
tribunal has found against that party in a decision on the matter in
respect of which the party was ordered to pay the deposit. Furthermore,
the deposit is not refunded in circumstances where an award of expenses
has been made against the relevant party.

Rule 7(9) requires that no member of a tribunal which has conducted
a pre-hearing review should be a member of the tribunal at the hearing
of the originating application. Not surprisingly, tribunals are reluctant to
make deposit orders except in the clearest of cases. In the majority of
applications under this rule, the tribunal will simply express no opinion.
This is the appropriate course of action if the facts are in any way
contentious. Any respondent party seeking a pre-hearing review should
ensure that all relevant documentation is lodged with the tribunal
secretary prior to the hearing taking place.

Evidence

Rule 11 of the 2001 Regulations states as follows: 14.48

> "(1) The tribunal shall, so far as it appears to it appropriate, seek
> to avoid formality in its proceedings and shall not be bound by any
> enactment or rule of law relating to the admissibility of evidence in
> proceedings before the courts of law. The tribunal shall make such
> enquiries of persons appearing before it and witnesses as it
> considers appropriate and shall otherwise conduct the hearing in
> such manner as it considers most appropriate for the clarification
> of the issues before it and generally to the just handling of the
> proceedings.
> (2) Subject to paragraph (1), at the hearing of the originating
> application a party shall be entitled to give evidence, to call
> witnesses, to question any witnesses and to address the tribunal".

This rule is central to the *modus operandi* of employment tribunals,
which are not unduly restricted by detailed rules of procedure. Instead,
they are allowed to operate in a flexible way to enable them to adjust to
the circumstances of each individual case. They are in the unique
position of being faced with representatives from a wide variety of
backgrounds. Clearly, anyone with a legal training should possess the
skills necessary to lead evidence in a clear and concise way. However,
parties are often unrepresented or represented by people with no formal
legal training. In the latter circumstances, the employment tribunal
chairman will play more of an inquisitorial role. Where both parties are
represented, he or she will tend to allow the adversarial approach to
apply.

It will, generally speaking, be for the party upon whom the onus in law 14.49
lies to lead evidence first. The most obvious examples of this are unfair
dismissal claims. If the employment tribunal is dealing with a constructive dismissal claim, the applicant's case will be led first because the
applicant must establish that he or she has been dismissed before the
tribunal can determine whether the dismissal was fair. On the other
hand, if the employer admits that the applicant was dismissed, the onus
of proof lies upon the employer to establish that there was a reason for

dismissal and that the reason was one of the potentially fair reason listed in the statute. However, the order in which evidence is led doe tend to reflect the procedure in the ordinary courts, being divided inte three parts—evidence in chief, cross-examination and re-examination.

14.50 Evidence in chief should be led in such a way as to ensure that a representative does not ask leading questions. A leading question is a question that tends to suggest its own answer. It may be, of course, tha certain aspects of witnesses' evidence are not in dispute. In these circumstances it is perfectly permissible for a representative to ask the permission of the tribunal to "lead" on certain aspects of the evidence Ideally, this suggestion should also be discussed with the other party's representative prior to the commencement of the hearing. Clearly leading questions should not be asked of a witness in relation to matters that are central to the case. Throughout the evidence in chief, the witness should be referred to any documentary productions that are relevant to his evidence. Evidence in chief is the representative's opportunity to "paint the picture" and the representative must ensure that all matters pertinent to the witness's involvement in the case are covered during evidence in chief. It must be remembered that it is only in exceptional circumstances that a new matter may be raised in re-examination, *i.e.* a matter that does arise out of cross-examination.

14.51 Cross-examination is crucial to the success or failure of many cases. More or less every case will contain some disputed facts. In particular, cases involving allegations of discrimination will require a tribunal to consider very carefully the credibility of witnesses. Again, lay representatives will tend to find cross-examination difficult. It is essential that all material aspects of a party's case be put to the opponent's witnesses in cross-examination. A failure to do this can be fatal to the outcome of a case. Although certain allowances will be made for lay representatives, this is one rule that tends not to be relaxed. There are many different ways to cross-examine. The central purpose of cross-examination is to test the other party's case. This does not mean to say that one has to be loud and abusive. Indeed, it is suggested that the most effective way to cross-examine is to "build" one's client's case in a clear and logical way. Overly elaborate courtroom tactics can sometimes have the effect of alienating one or more members of the tribunal. It will be remembered that rule 11 requires the tribunal to conduct the hearing in such manner as it considers most appropriate for the clarification of the issues before it and generally to the just handling of the proceedings.

14.52 Re-examination is the opportunity to repair damage done in cross-examination. The party's own representative is entitled to ask questions following re-examination. However, this is a process that can easily be overdone. It is suggested that if one's witness has given evidence in a credible way and if the opponent's representative has not succeeded in doing any significant damage to that evidence in cross-examination, there is little or no need to re-examine. Repeating points in re-examination is not a process which endears one to the members of the tribunal and one should always ask oneself whether there is any need to re-examine at all.

Submissions

There is no set format for dealing with submissions. Indeed, there is 14.53 no formal requirement to make submissions at all. There is usually no need to rehearse the evidence except after a lengthy or complex hearing. Usually it is sufficient to refer the tribunal to the salient points in the evidence and thereafter make submissions on the applicability of the relevant law to the facts. It is usually not necessary to refer the members of the tribunal in detail to the well known cases. If a case is to be referred to in detail, it is helpful to arrange for photocopies to be made available to the chairman and members. In cases involving allegations of unfair dismissal or discrimination, the tribunal should be addressed not only on the merits of the case but also on matters relating to quantum, *e.g.* contribution, solatium, etc. Those involved in presenting complex cases may wish to consider preparing a written submission. This can be of considerable assistance in presenting an argument involving complex legal issues. It will generally still be necessary to supplement this with oral submissions but the members of the tribunal usually appreciate the trouble taken to prepare a written submission, not least because it saves a great deal of note taking time.

Regional Variations in Procedure

Scotland and England have their own distinctive legal systems. Most 14.54 employment legislation applies equally to Scotland, England and Wales. Scotland on the one hand and England and Wales on the other operate under different rules of procedure in employment tribunals. However, there are few differences apparent in these. If anything, the major differences arise in relations to the terminology used. Not infrequently English practitioners appear before Scottish tribunals and vice versa. Those who indulge in cross border forays will notice that in Scotland the process for retrieving documents is known as "document recovery" whereas in England it is known as "discovery". Awards of "expenses" as they are known in Scotland are referred to as awards of "costs" in England. In Scotland, additional respondents may be "sisted" whereas in England they are "joined". "Productions" in Scotland are referred to as "exhibits" before English tribunals. However, the starkest difference of all arises at the hearing itself. Witnesses who are due to appear before tribunals in Scotland are excluded from the proceedings until they give evidence. This follows the normal Scottish rule of procedure that applies in the civil courts. However, in England it is common place for all of the witnesses to be present throughout the hearing. It is difficult for Scots lawyers to come to terms with this procedure as the question of credibility of witnesses is one that arises to a great or lesser extent in more or less every case. For us it is difficult to understand how a tribunal can assess credibility properly if there is any likelihood that those giving evidence have been influenced by each other. Nevertheless, although this is the procedure that generally applies, it is always open for a representative to request that one or more witnesses be excluded during the giving of particular evidence.

The order in which submissions are made is also different in Scotland where the order of submissions follows the order of the evidence that has been led. In England and Wales the party on whom the onus of proof lies tends to have the last word.

Expenses

14.55   It is unusual for an employment tribunal to make an award of expenses. The normal court rule that expenses follow success does not apply. In terms of rule 14 of the 2001 Rules of Procedure, an award of expenses may only be made where, in the opinion of the tribunal, a party has, in bringing or conducting the proceedings, acted frivolously, vexatiously, abusively, disruptively or otherwise unreasonably. In practice, awards of expenses tend to be made against applicants, although they are competent against either party to the proceedings. This provision is also capable of applying to a respondent who has not entered appearance in relation to the proceedings. Previously the award of expenses could be a sum not exceeding £500, a sum agreed between the parties, or taxed expenses. The statutory maximum that a tribunal may now direct be awarded has now been raised considerably to £10,000. That an applicant may now be the subject of such an order is clearly a factor that he or she will have to give serious consideration when deciding whether to pursue a claim before a tribunal.[30] Expenses are normally taxed on the sheriff court scale.

Awards of expenses may be made in respect of postponements and there is a specific power to make such an order against a respondent where, on a complaint of unfair dismissal, the applicant has expressed a wish to be reinstated or re-engaged which has been communicated to the respondent at least seven days before the hearing of the complaint or the proceedings arise out of the respondent's failure to permit the applicant to return to work following pregnancy and the postponement has been caused by the respondent's failure without special reason, to adduce sufficient evidence regarding the practicability of re-employment.

Expenses may also be awarded following a pre-hearing review (see above).

The Decision

14.56   An employment tribunal is empowered to issue a decision orally at the end of a hearing but in Scotland this hardly ever happens. This contrasts with the practice in England, which invariably is to adjourn following evidence and submissions, and to reconvene shortly thereafter to issue an oral decision. In Scotland the practice which is usually followed is to issue a *pro forma* abbreviated decision within a day or two of the conclusion of the hearing. The advance notification letter, which is sent to both parties, states only that the applicant has been successful or unsuccessful and that a full written decision will follow in due course. In more difficult or complex cases the *pro forma* letter may be dispensed with, in which case it may be several weeks before the parties are aware of the outcome of the case. Decisions are by majority where the tribunal consists of three persons. If only two persons are sitting on the tribunal the chairman has a second or casting vote (r. 12(1)). Some time after the conclusion of the hearing (usually four to six weeks) the tribunal will issue reasons for its decision in extended form. The decision is signed by the chairman and, where the applicant has been successful, includes

---

[30] r.14(3)(a).

details of any award to be made in favour of the applicant, including any compensation payable. The decision is entered in the Tribunal Register.

If the respondent has failed to pay any sum awarded by the time the appeal period has elapsed, it is open to the applicant to obtain a certificate of the decision from the tribunal secretary. This is equivalent to a sheriff court decree and may be enforced by sheriff officers as such.

THE FUTURE OF EMPLOYMENT TRIBUNALS

Following the concern raised by the President of the EAT in *Smith v. Secretary of State for Trade and Industry*,[31] it has now been determined in *Scanfuture (UK) Ltd v. Secretary of State for Trade and Industry*[32] that, pre-1999, employment tribunals did not comply with Article 6(1) of the ECHR, which provides that "In the determination of his civil rights and obligations . . . everyone is entitled to a fair and public hearing within a reasonable time by an independent and impartial tribunal established by law". The fair-minded and informed observer would have harboured an objectively justified fear that the employment tribunal pre-1999 lacked both impartiality and independence, given that the DTI, a party to the proceedings in question, had a large role in the appointment of two out of the three members of the tribunal: they were responsible for fixing the lengths of their appointment, determining whether they should be re-appointed, and the level of their remuneration. While a deficiency of this nature would not, *per se*, necessarily amount to a breach of Article 6(1) of the ECHR, in this case the deficiencies were indeed determinative given the fact that an appeal lies to the EAT only on points of law. This was insufficient to bring the proceedings within the qualification to Article 6(1) which excepts those tribunals which are "subject to subsequent control by a judicial body that has full jurisdiction and does provide the guarantees of Article 6(1)". The tribunal's decision in the case was therefore set aside. However as a direct result of changes made to the powers and practices of the Secretary of State in relation to lay members, with effect from 1999, there are now sufficient safeguards in place to exclude any legitimate doubt as to an employment tribunal's independence and impartiality where the Secretary of State is a party to the proceedings.

Industrial tribunals became "employment tribunals" as a result of the 14.57 Employment Rights (Dispute Resolution) Act 1998, which received royal assent in April 1998. Of particular significance is the introduction of alternatives to tribunal claims. The Act introduces internal procedures and binding arbitration as methods of resolving employment disputes. These developments sit well with the approach of many unions and employers to employment disputes in an industrial (or should we say employee) relations environment that has changed significantly since tribunals first appeared. The current emphasis on "partnership" in the employment relationship means that it is generally preferable to have a third party assist in resolving a problem rather than adjudicating in such a way that one party is seen to win and the other to lose.

---

[31] [2000] I.R.L.R. 6.
[32] [2001] I.R.L.R. 416, EAT.

The Leggatt Review of Tribunals

14.58   Sir Andrew Leggatt was appointed by the Lord Chancellor to conduct a review of Tribunals. His report, "Tribunals for Users—One System, One Service", deals with tribunals generally although the majority of responses received to the consultation paper commented specifically on employment tribunals. The proposals focus upon a need for consistency and transparency across the tribunal system and for an increase in the flow of information to the "consumer" along with better frameworks for communication between the providers and the users of the service. A consistency of approach is called for in relation to different tribunals. Additionally, tribunals should take an "enabling approach" to cases thus ensuring parties do not feel intimidated or threatened and are able to fully and appropriately present their case. Parties having difficulties ought to be guided to find appropriate assistance.

14.59   In the first place, the report recommends that "there should be separation between the ministers and the authorities whose policies and decisions are tested by tribunals and the minister who appoints and supports them". With many tribunals there is clear confusion in the relationship between them and the policy makers, and it is proposed that these relationships be made clearer in order to avoid claims under the European Convention on Human Rights and the Human Rights Act 1998 to the effect that tribunals are not independent and operate contrary to the right to a fair trial. It is proposed that the tribunal system be presented as a single coherent structure resulting in easier access to all tribunals for the individual. However, within that structure individual tribunals ought to have the rules and procedures required to allow them to function comprehensibly.

14.60   Chapter 4 of the report is devoted to the idea of a more user-friendly system. Of great importance to the Review is the availability of information to the user, particularly information about initiating, preparing and presenting a case to the relevant tribunal. Procedures should remain such that individuals are able to represent themselves and information should be available in a number of formats to ensure it is accessible by all members of society. It was felt that these developments are required to ensure that the system meets ECHR requirements. Several recommendations were made regarding tribunal help-lines, interactive web sites and designated customer service points within tribunal offices. The aim of these improvements would be increased availability of information and communication between the service and the user. The Review also considered that financial eligibility testing ought to be available for public funding and that consistency in such testing is essential across the tribunal system. Additionally it was thought that *pro bono* advice is to be encouraged. The frequently raised issue of cost awards in tribunals was considered but the report concludes that there should be no general extension of the powers of tribunals to award costs.

14.61   A further recommendation is the creation of a Tribunals Service committed to ensuring best practice and high standards within the tribunal system. The Service would be an executive agency of the Lord Chancellor's Department. Improved training for all chairmen and members is specifically recommended with particular reference made to interpersonal skills and communication. Additionally a system of performance appraisal for all members and chairmen is recommended. The review also makes certain recommendations about active case management including the provision of suitable IT support to assist with this and with monitoring and tracking of cases and workflow. In line with the trend already witnessed in employment tribunals, the Review also concludes that more use ought to be made of preliminary procedures and hearings.

Not surprisingly, the area of employment tribunals attracted the most 14.62 comment and recommendations from those involved in the consultation exercise which was conducted in connection with the Review. While it appears there was much praise for the literature produced by employment tribunals and its availability, criticism was received regarding correspondence in individual cases. This lead to a positive recommendation that efforts be made to improve the clarity of this, specifically in relation to interlocutory orders and case management requirements. One subject which prompted a wealth of responses was that of employment advice and advisers. Much concern was expressed about individuals being vulnerable in this market with many requiring advice for the first and, probably only, time. This type of user is less likely to shop around for services and has no redress in the event that they feel they have not received adequate advice or guidance. Reference was made to the Blackwell Committee established in 1999 and its report which highlighted many of the same concerns regarding non-legally qualified employment advisers. The committee rejected the idea of statutory regulation but recommended, instead, a range of measures designed to improve the standard of service offered and to afford some protection to the tribunal user. None of these was implemented although the TUC is in discussion about a more pro-active role for unions and the drafting of a code of conduct for advisers. In view of the lack of progress following the Blackwell Committee's report, the Leggatt Review urges the Government to take more "stringent action" on this matter.

With regard to tribunal hearings, concern was expressed at the 14.63 attitude of some chairmen and their apparent inability to shake off legal formalities making it difficult for unrepresented parties to present their cases and raising the level of proceedings beyond the intended informality. It is clear that some employment cases are becoming increasingly complex to the extent that it is becoming more and more impracticable for users to represent themselves. The review considered that it would be appropriate for help to be available to individuals in such circumstances from the public purse but that the number of cases where such help would be necessary would be limited as long as the tribunal makes the effort recommended to ensure the informality and accessibility of the process. Concern was also raised about the independence of the employment tribunals in light of challenges already launched under the Human Rights Act 1998 (see above). Many thought that the service's links with the DTI were inappropriate due to its perceived involvement with employers and its direct involvement in a considerable number of cases each year. The Report recommends that the LCD take over administrative responsibility for Employment Tribunals and the EAT separating the administration from the policy making department.

14.64   Strong arguments were received by the Review committee both for and against the introduction of a general rule regarding costs. On one hand many respondents felt that the number of weak and vexatious cases is high and that the risk of an award of costs would be sufficient deterrent to reduce this. Alternatively, some feel that this would inevitably complicate matters and increase the need for legal representation. The conclusion reached was that more information is required and a study to be conducted by the DTI and LCD was recommended. In the meantime, it was felt that such a rule would be an undesirable disincentive to make a tribunal application. Finally, the report encourages further exploration of alternative dispute resolution along with a recommendation that ACAS receive further funding to expand its role, and advises that consideration should be given to widening the jurisdiction of tribunals and increasing their powers to create a more flexible and comprehensible system.

ALTERNATIVE DISPUTE RESOLUTION

14.65   In response to the increasing pressure on the tribunal system there has been a corresponding increase in interest in the alternatives. Alternative Dispute Resolution (ADR), particularly in the field of employment law, has consequently been the focus of much recent attention both within the profession and in the media. ADR can take a variety of forms. Notably, much use is now made of arbitration in construction cases and mediation in family cases. It is felt that employment disputes offer the potential for the development of ADR, ranging from ideas aimed at preventing disputes escalating and thereby preserving employment relationships to more formalised procedures, heralded by the introduction in England and Wales of the new ACAS Arbitration Scheme (due to be introduced in Scotland by the end of 2001). In July of this year the government published a consultation paper on this issue seeking views on a wide range of proposals focused on avoiding employment disputes and improving employer/employee relations. The government consultation paper "Routes to Resolution: Improving Dispute Resolution in Britain" was issued on July 20 by the Employment Relations Minister, Alan Johnson. As well as dealing with obvious ADR options it considers focusing on matters in the workplace to avoid disputes escalating in the first place.

14.66   The paper acknowledges that the number of tribunal applications appears to be spiraling and that, while the system should be able to support an increasing number of claims, there is merit in attempting to slow the increase and offer alternatives. It quotes the statistic that 64 per cent of tribunal applications come from employees who have made no attempt to resolve the problem complained of directly with the employer and that 60 per cent of small employers have no disciplinary or grievance procedures. It is thought that these are significant, and action to curb these numbers would reduce the number of applications which have trebled since 1990. The reason for the increase in applications is directly related to the increase in employment legislation and the trend within society generally to think of litigation as a solution. Unrealistic expectations attributed to media coverage of infrequent substantial awards is also thought to play a part. In light of the fact that only 25 per cent of applications proceed to a full hearing, there is an implication that compromise is possible in the majority of cases and, therefore, scope for a reasonable resolution at an early stage. Most practitioners would probably also agree that a significant number of cases involve a breakdown of communication and might not have reached the stage of an application to a tribunal had the communication been restored. The consultation paper concludes that written procedures increase the likelihood that matters will be addressed and resolved at an early stage of the dispute and that a generally higher standard of dispute management would prevent minor matters escalating beyond the internal procedures. Various suggestions have been made which might encourage better use of written procedures. Employees might be barred from making an application unless they can show that they have used the workplace procedures available to them. It has been suggested that an extension of the current time-limits would be required to complement this. Additionally, tribunals might be given the power to increase or reduce awards where either side has failed to take a reasonable minimum of procedural actions. To be a real incentive it is thought that the size of the potential change would require to be significant, possibly as much as 50 per cent.

A further proposal is to tighten up the requirement under section 1 of 14.67 the ERA 1996 to provide a statement of initial employment particulars. The rationale is that a lack of clarity in relation to the rights and responsibilities of each party in an employment relationship leads to disputes between them. Consequently, the existence of written terms and conditions reduces the likelihood of such disputes. The requirement to first define the relationship complicates other claims and is thought to be a good argument for giving the tribunal power to reflect a failure to comply with section 1 in any compensatory award made. Consideration is also being given to removing the 20 employee threshold applying to disciplinary and grievance procedures. It is also proposed that tribunals be given the power to disregard trivial errors in procedure and thereby mitigate the effect of *Polkey v. AE Dayton Services Ltd*.[33] The aim here is to reduce the number of cases being pursued to tribunal on the basis that although the applicant's case is weak they are confident of being awarded a basic award, some compensation and a perceived victory due to a procedural error on the part of the employer.

Having made these suggestions the paper also recommends that where 14.68 improved internal management has failed, ADR ought to be the next step. The success of ACAS in conciliation is cited as evidence that it has clear benefits and that any procedures which encourage early settlement talks as opposed to "door of the court" settlements are to be encouraged. It is, however, felt that ACAS involvement in some purely "technical" cases is a waste of resources. There are some cases, for example redundancy pay claims and breach of contract, where there is no scope for settlement and ACAS should not be obliged to offer their services unless the parties make a specific request. It is also suggested that a clearly defined period of conciliation might serve to focus parties' minds. To provide some relief to ACAS it has been mooted that the

---

[33] [1987] I.R.L.R. 503.

limits on compromise agreements which make them less attractive than COT3s be removed, thus encouraging other agents to become involved in this aspect or indeed mediation.

14.69   It remains to be seen which proposals will be adopted. However, there is little doubt about the proposition that the employment tribunal model will continue to exert its influence on the wider legal system, and that among its strengths are the ability to move with the times, to examine itself critically, and to use advancements in technology to assist with a more efficient delivery.

CHAPTER 15

CHALLENGING EMPLOYMENT TRIBUNAL DECISIONS

It would be very surprising if all those who appeared as parties before 15.01
employment tribunals were satisfied with the outcome of the hearing.
Just like any other legal forum the employment tribunal system is bound
to produce its share of individuals who are dismayed that it is they who
have lost the case rather than their adversary. However, mere dissatisfaction or displeasure at the outcome of a case will not be enough in itself
to mount a successful challenge to the decision. Leaving aside cases of
minor clerical error,[1] the only two methods whereby the decision of an
employment tribunal can be altered are by means of a review or appeal
and both of these options are only available in limited circumstances.

REVIEW

Schedule 1, rule 13 of the 2001 Regulations gives an employment 15.02
tribunal power, on the application of a party or of its own motion, to
review any decision[2] on the grounds that:

(a) the decision was wrongly made as a result of an error on the
part of the tribunal staff;

(b) a party did not receive notice of the proceedings leading to
the decision;

(c) the decision was made in the absence of a party;

(d) new evidence has become available since the conclusion of
the hearing to which the decision relates, provided that its
existence could not have been foreseen at the time of the
hearing; or

(e) the interests of justice require such a review.

---

[1] Sched. 1, r.12(8) Employment Tribunals (Constitution and Rules of Procedure)
(Scotland) Regulations 2001 (hereinafter "2001 Regulations") allows clerical or accidental
slips or omissions to be corrected at any time by a chairman.

[2] "Decision" is defined in reg. 2(2). It includes a declaration, striking out order,
recommendation or award of a tribunal and a determination in respect of entitlement to
bring or contest proceedings but excludes any other interlocutory order or decision
thereon.

An application for review may be made at the original hearing and, in any event, must be made no later than 14 days after the date on which the decision was sent to the parties.[3] Where the application for review is made after the hearing it must be made in writing, stating the grounds in full for the application.[4]

An application for review may be refused by the President, a regional chairman or the chairman of the tribunal which heard the case if it has, in that person's view, no reasonable prospects of success.[5] However, in *P.J. Drakard and Sons v. Wilton*[6] it was held that before refusing an application on this ground a chairman should give a party seeking the review a chance to elaborate on the grounds for the application if these are considered to be deficient in some way.

15.03   In the event that it is the tribunal itself which wishes to review the decision it must notify each party no more than 14 days after the date on which the decision was sent to the parties, explaining in summary form the grounds upon which and reasons why it is proposed to review the decision and give each party the opportunity to show cause why there should be no review.[7]

A review on the motion of the tribunal can only be conducted by the tribunal which made the decision now under review.[8] In the event of a review at the request of a party, such should normally be heard by the tribunal which decided the case but if that is not practicable or the decision was made by a chairman sitting alone it can be heard by a tribunal appointed by the President or by a regional chairman.[9]

On reviewing its decision a tribunal may confirm the decision or vary or revoke it. If it is revoked the tribunal must order a rehearing before the same or a differently constituted tribunal.[10] However, the power to review is wide enough to allow the tribunal to reverse its decision.[11]

15.04   The power to review of its own motion was only granted to tribunals in 1993.[12] It appears to be rarely used in Scotland but may be more widely used in England and Wales where it is more common for oral decisions to be issued on the day of a hearing, leaving more scope for relevant legal decisions or points of law to come to the attention of the tribunal after the decision has been announced orally but before it has been set out in writing.

The procedure at a review hearing, particularly in relation to whether oral evidence will be necessary, will depend upon the grounds for the application.

---

[3] 2001 Regulations, Sched. 1, r.13(4).
[4] *ibid.*
[5] 2001 Regulations, Sched. 1, r.13(5).
[6] [1977] I.C.R. 642, EAT.
[7] 2001 Regulations, Sched. 1, r.13(3).
[8] *ibid.*, Sched. 1, r.13(2).
[9] *ibid.*, Sched. 1, r.13(6).
[10] *ibid.*, Sched. 1, r.13(7).
[11] *Stonehill Furniture Ltd v. Phillipo* [1983] I.C.R. 556, EAT.
[12] Employment Tribunals (Constitution and Rules of Procedure) Regulations 1993, Sched. 1, r.11.

Review and Simultaneous Appeal

The fact that a decision is under appeal will not prevent a review hearing 15.05 taking place. However, the chairman should consult with the EAT Registrar if it is considered that it may be undesirable to make a decision on the review application pending the appeal hearing.[13]

Individual Grounds of Review

(1) In the event of it being suggested that a party did not receive notice 15.06 of the proceedings it will be for that party to surmount the presumption, established by the combined effect of rule 23, Schedule 1, 2001 Regulations and section 7 of the Interpretation Act 1978, once it is proved that the letter was properly addressed, stamped and posted, that the notice was duly served. To do so the party will have to prove that he did not actually receive it.[14]

(2) A party seeking a review on the basis that the decision was made in his absence must show a good and genuine reason for his failure to attend. It will normally be appropriate to allow the party who has applied for the review the opportunity to give oral evidence.[15]

(3) A party who seeks a review on the basis that new evidence has become available must be able to show that the evidence became available after the conclusion of the hearing and that its existence could not reasonably have been known or foreseen.[16]

(4) Rule 13(1)(e) allows a decision to be reviewed if the "interests of justice" require such a review. While this appears to give the tribunal a wide discretion it is not untrammelled and must be exercised bearing in mind the interests of both parties and the public interest which seeks, as far as possible, finality of litigation.[17] Cases under this head fall into two general categories: those arising as a result of some kind of procedural difficulty or mishap, such as a failure to allow a party a fair opportunity to argue a point of substance[18] and those where the decision of the tribunal is undermined by events shortly thereafter.[19]

Appeals to the Employment Appeal Tribunal (EAT)

Constitution and Jurisdiction of the EAT

The EAT was established under the provisions of the Employment 15.07 Protection Act 1975 and continues in existence by virtue of section 20(1)

---

[13] *Blackpole Furniture v. Sullivan* [1978] I.C.R. 558, EAT.

[14] *Migwain Ltd (In liquidation) v. Transport and General Workers' Union* [1979] I.C.R. 597, EAT.

[15] *Morris v. Griffiths* [1977] I.C.R. 153, EAT.

[16] See *Flint v. Eastern Electricity Board* [1975] I.R.L.R. 277, QBD for an example of an application on this ground which failed since the evidence sought to be adduced had been available at the original hearing. This case also examines the interrelationship between r.13(1)(d) and (e).

[17] *Flint*, above.

[18] See *Trimble v. Supertravel Ltd* [1982] I.R.L.R. 451 for an example.

[19] See *Yorkshire Engineering and Welding Co. Ltd v. Burnham* [1973] I.R.L.R. 316, NIRC; and *Ladup Ltd v. Barnes* [1982] I.R.L.R. 7, EAT.

of the Employment Tribunals Act 1996.[20] Its main function is to hear appeals arising from decisions of employment tribunals although it also has a limited original jurisdiction.[21] Under the provisions of section 21 of the ETA and regulation 11(10) of the Transfer of Undertakings (Protection of Employment) Regulations 1981 the EAT is given exclusive jurisdiction to hear appeals on any question of law arising from any decision of, or arising in any proceedings before, an employment tribunal concerning the provisions of the:

    (a) Equal Pay Act 1970
    (b) Sex Discrimination Act 1975
    (c) Race Relations Act 1976
    (d) Transfer of Undertakings (Protection of Employment) Regulations 1981
    (e) Trade Union and Labour Relations (Consolidation) Act 1992
    (f) Disability Discrimination Act 1995
    (g) Employment Rights Act 1996
    (h) National Minimum Wage Act 1998
    (i) Tax Credit Act 1999
    (j) Employment Tribunals Act 1996
    (k) Working Time Regulations 1998
    (l) Transnational Information and Consultation of Employees Regulations 1999
    (m) Part-time Workers (Prevention of Less Favourable Treatment) Regulations 2000

In addition, the EAT also has jurisdiction to hear appeals arising from various decisions of the certification officer.[22]

15.08   The members of the EAT consist of nominated judges, at least one of whom must be a Court of Session judge, nominated by the Lord President and one of whom is nominated to be the President of the Appeal Tribunal, and "appointed members" who have special knowledge or experience of industrial relations as representatives of employers or workers.[23] Temporary members may be nominated/appointed if required.[24]

The central office of the EAT is in London but the appeal tribunal is empowered to sit anywhere in Great Britain. In practice, it sits in London and Edinburgh, with cases arising from Scottish tribunals normally being heard by the Court of Session judge and two lay members. However, given that the EAT is a court with jurisdiction throughout Great Britain, it is possible for judges from the English judicial system to sit in Edinburgh and for the Court of Session judge to sit in London. This does happen from time to time.[25]

---

[20] Hereinafter ETA.
[21] See Trade Union and Labour Relations (Consolidation) Act 1992, ss.67(2) and 176(2) which deal with applications by union members for compensation from the union in certain circumstances.
[22] See TULCRA 1992, ss.9, 95, 104, 126.
[23] ETA, s.22.
[24] ETA, ss.23 and 24.
[25] A tradition has arisen of the Scottish EAT judge sitting in London and the EAT President sitting in Edinburgh for a week in June each year.

Normally, the EAT sits with a judge and two appointed members but it can sit with a judge and four appointed members.[26] In every case the appointed members must be evenly balanced between those with experience as representatives of workers and of employers.[27]

The officer in charge of administrative matters in the appeal system is the EAT Registrar. However, some of his functions are quasi judicial in nature (see below).

Procedure

The EAT in Scotland has the same powers, rights, privileges and 15.09 authority as the Court of Session in relation to: (a) attendance and examination of witnesses; (b) production and inspection of documents; and (c) all other matters incidental to its jurisdiction.[28]

Parties can appear on their own behalf or allow anyone else to represent them. In other words, it is not necessary for a representative to be legally qualified.[29]

The detailed rules governing the procedure of the EAT are set out in the Employment Appeal Tribunal Rules 1993[30] as amended by the Employment Appeal Tribunal (Amendment) Rules 2001[31] and supplemented by practice directions which are issued from time to time. The 2001 EAT Amendment Rules primarily introduce a procedure for appeals from decisions or orders of the Central Arbitration Committee (CAC) under the Transnational Information and Consultation of Employees Regulations 1999[32] and for first instance complaints under the 1999 regulations. The 2001 EAT Amendment Rules also amend the provisions of the 1993 EAT rules which deal with appeals from employment tribunals in cases involving issues of national security. The amendments inserted by the 2001 EAT Amendment Rules took effect from April 18, 2001 and apply to all proceedings after that date, irrespective of when they were commenced.

There is also a Practice Direction governing procedure in the EAT.[33] Certain of the provisions of the Practice Direction do not apply in Scotland. In particular, the directions relating to the production of the employment tribunal chairman's notes,[34] the provision and content of skeleton arguments[35] and to preliminary hearings by the EAT[36] do not apply. The provisions governing the listing of appeals in Scotland also differ from those which apply in England and Wales.[37]

---

[26] ETA, s.28.
[27] *ibid.,* s.28(2).
[28] *ibid.,* s.29.
[29] *ibid.,* s.29(1).
[30] S.I. 1993 No. 2854. Hereinafter EAT Rules.
[31] S.I. 2001 No. 1128, hereinafter 2001 EAT Rules.
[32] S.I. 1999 No. 3323.
[33] Practice Direction (Employment Appeal Tribunal Procedure) 1996 which came into force on April 15, 1996, the text of which can be found at [1996] I.R.L.R. 430; [1996] I.C.R. 422.
[34] Direction 7.
[35] Direction 8.
[36] Direction 14.
[37] Direction 12.

Institution of an Appeal

15.10		An appeal to the EAT must be submitted in a form substantially in accordance with that set out in the Schedule to the EAT Rules and must normally be accompanied by a copy of the extended written reasons for the decision or order of the tribunal.[38] The time-limit for instituting an appeal is 42 days from the date on which the extended written reasons were sent to the appellant or, in a national security case, 42 days from the date on which the document containing the decision or order of the tribunal (whether it contained reasons or not) was sent to the appellant. An appeal from the decision of the Certification Officer (in terms of s.254(2) TULRCA 1992), must be instituted within 42 days of the date on which the written record of that decision was sent to the appellant while an appeal from a declaration or order of the CAC must be commenced within 42 days of the date on which the written notification of that declaration or order was sent to the appellant. Time runs even if the question of remedy has been adjourned by the employment tribunal and even if an application for review has been made. It is possible to apply for an extension of time[39] but the circumstances in which such will be granted are limited.[40] Such an application will normally be treated as an interlocutory application to be determined by the Registrar from whose decision an appeal lies to the judge. The time-limit for such an appeal is five days from the Registrar's decision.[41]

			Particular note should be made of the need to enclose extended reasons with a note of appeal; if summary reasons are issued in the first instance by the employment tribunal extended reasons should be requested within 21 days of the summary reasons being sent to the parties.[42] If the employment tribunal refuses to issue extended reasons an appeal may be made to the EAT and an application may also be made that the EAT should exercise its discretion to hear the appeal on summary reasons.[43]

15.11		The notice of appeal must clearly identify the point of law which forms the ground of appeal.[44] If it appears to the Registrar that the grounds of appeal stated in the notice do not give the appeal tribunal jurisdiction to entertain the appeal he must notify the appellant of this and inform him of the reasons for the opinion.[45] No further action will be taken on the appeal unless the appellant then follows the procedure set out in the EAT Rules (as amended) at rule 3(8) to (10).[46]

			An appellant must ensure that full and sufficient particulars are given in support of a general ground of appeal such as "the decision was one which no reasonable tribunal could have reached and was perverse".[47]

---

[38] EAT Rules, r.3, but see provisions governing national security cases
[39] See EAT Rules, r.37(3) and Practice Direction 3.
[40] See *United Arab Emirates v. Abdelghafar* [1995] I.R.L.R. 243—referred to in direction 3(5); *Aziz v. Bethnal Green City Challenge Co Ltd* [2000] I.R.L.R. 111, CA.
[41] EAT Rules, r.21(2).
[42] Employment Tribunals (Constitution and Rules of Procedure) (Scotland) Regulations 2001, Sched. 1, r.12(4).
[43] Direction 2(2)
[44] Direction 2(3).
[45] EAT Rules, r.3 (3).
[46] The decision by the reviewing judge under r.3(10) may be subject to judicial review: *Mackenzie, Petr*, 2000 S.C. 1, OH.
[47] Direction 2(5).

Similarly, if there is a complaint about the conduct of the employment tribunal hearing (for example, relating to bias, improper conduct or procedural irregularity) the notice of appeal must include full and sufficient particulars of the complaint and a particular notification procedure must be followed.[48] The respondent to the appeal is the other party in the employment tribunal proceedings; he will be served with a copy of the notice of appeal[49] and is entitled to answer the appeal, relying on the reasons given by the employment tribunal or putting forward additional or other grounds, and to cross appeal, in accordance with the provisions of rule 6. It should be noted that special rules apply in relation to the respondent's answer and cross appeal in a national security case.[50]

Joinder of Parties

The EAT can, on the application of any person or of its own motion, 15.12 direct that any person be added or removed as a party to the proceedings.[51]

Interlocutory Applications

Interlocutory applications may be made to the EAT in writing, 15.13 specifying the direction or order sought.[52] Normally, these will be disposed of by the Registrar[53] although an application for a restricted reporting order will be decided by a judge or a full appeal tribunal.[54]

Where an interlocutory decision is made by the Registrar an appeal lies to the judge.[55]

A hearing for directions can also take place if necessary[56] and directions may be issued without a hearing.[57]

Fast Track Appeals

Appeals are normally heard in the order in which they are received 15.14 but in certain circumstances can be fast tracked.[58]

Miscellaneous Powers

The EAT also has specific powers in relation to: 15.15

(i) Making a "restriction of proceedings" order on the application of the Lord Advocate to debar vexatious litigants from instituting or continuing proceedings before the

---

[48] See direction 9.
[49] EAT Rules, r.4.
[50] *ibid.*, r.6(6)—(11) as amended by 2001 EAT Amendment Rules.
[51] *ibid.*, r.18.
[52] *ibid.*, r.19.
[53] *ibid.*, r.20.
[54] *ibid.*, r.20(3).
[55] *ibid.*, r.21.
[56] *ibid.*, r.24.
[57] *ibid.*, r.25.
[58] Direction 12(1).

employment tribunal or the EAT without leave of the EAT.[59]

(ii) Ordering an individual to attend as a witness or produce documents[60] although this is rarely used since it is extremely unusual for new evidence to be given at an appeal hearing.

(iii) In the interests of national security making any order that could be directed to be done by a Minister of the Crown under Rule 30A(1), including an order excluding an applicant or his representatives from the proceedings.[61]

(iv) Debarring parties from taking part in the proceedings in certain circumstances.[62]

(v) Reviewing its decision and correction of errors.[63]

(vi) Awarding expenses where proceedings were unnecessary, improper, vexatious or unreasonably conducted.[64]

(vii) Extending or abridging time prescribed by the Rules.[65]

(viii) Waiving the Rules in certain circumstances.[66]

There are also specific rules governing applications for compensation for exclusion or expulsion from a trade union or unjustifiable union discipline.[67]

Preparing for the Hearing

Documentary productions

15.16 Only those documents which are relevant to the point of law raised in the appeal and likely to be referred to at the hearing should be placed before the EAT.[68] It is possible to apply for a document which is not before the employment tribunal to be included in the documents before the EAT. The procedure for so doing is set out in direction 10.

Legal Authorities

15.17 Guidance on the use and citation of legal authorities is given in direction 15.

The Hearing and Hearing Restrictions

15.18 An oral hearing will usually be a public hearing[69] but can be private in limited circumstances.[70] Restricted reporting orders can also be made in

---

[59] ETA, s.33; EAT Rules, rr. 13—17. For an example of such an order being made see *A.G. v. Wheen*
[2001] I.R.L.R. 91, CA.
[60] EAT Rules, r.27, but see r.27(1A), inserted by the 2001 EAT Amendment Rules in relation to the special provisions applying in national security cases.
[61] *ibid.*, r.30A(2).
[62] *ibid.*, r.26.
[63] *ibid.*, r.33.
[64] *ibid.*, r.34.
[65] *ibid.*, r.37.
[66] *ibid.*, r.39.
[67] See EAT Rules, rr. 8–12 and 17.
[68] Direction 6(3).
[69] EAT Rules, r.29.
[70] EAT Rules, rr. 29(2) and 30A (inserted by 2001 EAT Amendment Rules).

appeals involving allegations of sexual misconduct.[71] Material can be deleted from judgments or other documents which could identify those affected by or making allegations of the commission of a sexual offence.[72] In *Chief Constable of West Yorks v. A*[73] the EAT held that an employment tribunal was not empowered under the provisions of the domestic regulations governing tribunal procedure to grant a restricted reporting order where the applicant was complaining of discrimination on the grounds that she was a transsexual. Such an order did not fall within the general provisions in rule 13 of the 1993 Constitution and Rules of Procedure Regulations (see now r.15 of the Constitution and Rules of Procedure (Scotland) Regulations 2001) nor did the tribunal have jurisdiction to grant a restricted reporting order under rule 14 (now r.16) as the treatment of A could not be said to amount to "sexual misconduct" just because she was a transsexual. Similarly, it was held that rule 23 of the 1993 EAT rules was so narrow in scope that *ex facie* it also prevented any order being made. However, the EAT held that the tribunal did have power to make a restricted reporting order (as did the EAT itself) which derived from Article 6 of the Equal Treatment Directive. Article 6 requires an effective remedy to be conferred upon those able to rely upon it, such as the applicant in this case who was making a claim against a police force which was an emanation of the State. There was unchallenged evidence that without a restricted reporting order, the applicant would be deterred from seeking a remedy. This would be contrary to the Community law principle of effectiveness which required that the applicant should not be subject to procedural rules which rendered virtually impossible or excessively difficult the exercise of rights conferred by Community law.

A Minister of the Crown under rule 30A(1), or the tribunal of its own motion, may direct that the proceedings be held in private for reasons of national security.[74] Restricted reporting orders can also be made in certain disability discrimination cases.[75]

It is not necessary at the hearing for the appellant's representative to read aloud the entire decision of the employment tribunal (unless requested to do so). Normally, the hearing begins with the appellant's representative referring to the grounds of appeal which have been lodged and making detailed submissions thereon. The respondent's representative then has the opportunity to make submissions. It is not unusual for the judge to ask questions and seek clarification during the course of the presentation of submissions. Lay members are also invited to ask questions normally at the end of a submission.

Normally an appeal hearing will be set down for two hours unless the Registrar is notified that the particular circumstances of the appeal are such that it may require a longer hearing to be set down.

---

[71] EAT Rules, r.23(3).
[72] EAT Rules, r.23(2).
[73] [2000] I.R.L.R. 465, EAT.
[74] r.23(6).
[75] r.23A.

Admissibility of new evidence

15.19   The EAT has a discretion to admit further evidence in limited circumstances, even where that relates to the subject matter of the original
tribunal application rather than to the conduct of that hearing or events
occurring thereafter. However, normally fresh evidence will only be
admitted in exceptional cases.[76] It should be noted that there is a limited
category of cases in which further evidence is allowed as a matter of
course. These involve appeals under TULCRA, s.9 and where state
immunity is an issue.[77]

Raising New Points of Law

15.20   The EAT will only allow a point of law which could have been but was
not raised at the employment tribunal hearing, and which forms no part
of the tribunal's reasoning, to be raised on appeal in limited circumstances. It is particularly unlikely to allow such a point to be made where
this would require the case to be remitted to the employment tribunal to
hear further evidence.[78] However, it may well allow a new point to be
argued if it arises from a decision of the House of Lords, Court of
Appeal or Court of Session issued after the original hearing.

Similar restrictions apply in relation to a respondent to an appeal who
seeks to rely on new points of law to support the tribunal's decision.[79]
However, a new point will usually always be allowed to be raised on
appeal where it relates to the jurisdiction of the employment tribunal to
hear the case.[80]

Appeal on Question of Law

15.21   The employment tribunal is master of the facts: "On all question of
fact the [Employment] Tribunal is the final and only judge and to that
extent it is like an [employment] jury".[81] Assuming that the employment
tribunal has directed itself properly on the facts and has not gone wrong
in law it is not open to the EAT to interfere with its decision or to
substitute its own decision even if the EAT would have come to a
different conclusion.[82]

Since an Appeal lies only on a question of law[83] the EAT can only
"interfere if it is satisfied the Tribunal has misdirected itself as to the
applicable law, or if there is no evidence to support a particular finding
of fact, since the absence of evidence to support a finding of fact has

---

[76] See *Wileman v. Minilec Engineering Ltd* [1988] I.R.L.R. 144; and *Borden (U.K.) Ltd v. Potter* [1986] I.C.R. 647.

[77] *Egypt v. Gamal-Eldin* [1996] I.C.R. 13, EAT.

[78] *Kumchyk v. Derby County Council* [1978] I.C.R. 1116, EAT; *Glennie v. Independent Magazines (UK) Ltd.* [1999] I.R.L.R. 719, CA.

[79] *McLeod v. Hellyer Brothers Ltd, Wilson v. Boston Deep Sea Fisheries Ltd* [1987] I.R.L.R. 232, CA.

[80] *Russell v. Elmdon Freight Terminal* [1989] ICR 629, EAT; *Barber v. Thames T.V. plc* [1991] I.R.L.R. 236, EAT.

[81] *British Telecommunications plc v. Sheridan* [1990] I.R.L.R. 27, CA, *per* Donaldson L.J.

[82] *Eclipse Blinds Ltd v. Wright* [1992] I.R.L.R. 133, CS.

[83] ETA, s.21(1).

always been regarded as a pure question of law. It can also interfere if the decision is perverse.[84]

In the early case of *Watling v. William Bird and Son (Contractors) Limited*[85] it was suggested that an error of law could occur where the tribunal "misunderstood or misapplied the facts". However, in *Sheridan* the Court of Appeal made it clear that this should not be treated as a "separate category" giving rise to an appeal. So far as the conclusions to be drawn from the facts are concerned, nothing less than perversity or a complete absence of evidence to justify a conclusion will amount to an error of law. Any claim that a tribunal "misunderstood or misapplied the facts" would have to fall within one or other of these categories.

15.22

Misdirection in Law

Misdirection or misapplication of the law can occur in a variety of ways including where the tribunal applies the wrong legal test, misinterprets a statutory provision or ignores some legal requirement. Cases under this head include those where there is procedural unfairness in breach of the rules of natural justice and where there is a failure to give adequate reasons to support a decision.

15.23

No Evidence

Cases will only fall into this category if there is no evidence to support a particular conclusion or finding of fact.[86] If it is submitted that there was insufficient evidence to justify a conclusion or finding of fact this will have to be argued (usually with difficulty) under the ground of perversity.

15.24

Perversity

For an employment tribunal decision to be considered perverse it must be shown that no reasonable tribunal properly directed in law could have reached the decision which this particular tribunal reached.[87]

15.25

It is very difficult to succeed in showing perversity; the decision of the tribunal must, in effect, offend reason. Various formulations of the test to be applied have been suggested, one of the most striking being May L.J.'s suggestion that a tribunal decision must not be disturbed on appeal "unless one can say in effect 'my goodness, that was certainly wrong' ".[88] This formulation has subsequently been criticised in *Piggot Brothers and Co. Limited v. Jackson*[89] in which it was suggested that a decision will only be perverse if it was "not a permissable option". *Stewart v. Cleveland Guest (Engineering) Limited*[90] provides a useful summary of the various formulations of the perversity test.

---

[84] *Sheridan*, above, *per* Donaldson L.J.
[85] [1976] 11 I.T.R. 70.
[86] See *Piggot Brothers and Co. Ltd v. Jackson* [1991] I.R.L.R. 309, CA; and *Sheridan*, above.
[87] *Melon v. Hector Powe Ltd* [1981] I.C.R. 43, HL.
[88] *Hereford and Worcester County Council v. Neale* [1986] I.R.L.R. 168, CA.
[89] [1991] I.R.L.R. 309, CA.
[90] [1994] I.R.L.R. 440, EAT.

Appeals on Interlocutory Orders

15.26   There is no distinction between appeals against final orders of tribunals (*i.e.* what would commonly be referred to as tribunal decisions) and interlocutory orders (for example, orders concerning recovery of documents). In each case the EAT can only intervene where there is an error of law.[91]

Binding Precedents

15.27   The EAT in Scotland is bound by decisions of the Inner House of the Court of Session and the House of Lords. The Scottish EAT has also stated that it would only depart from an opinion of the Court of Appeal on a matter which was purely related to a particular aspect of Scots law.[92] Strictly speaking, the EAT is not bound by its own decisions but "they will only be departed from in exceptional circumstances, or where there are previous inconsistent decisions".[93] If the EAT is faced with previous conflicting decisions it will try to resolve them and if necessary will direct employment tribunals which of the previous decisions they should follow.[94]

Disposal of an Appeal

15.28   After hearing an appeal the EAT may:

1. order that the appeal be dismissed;
2. order that the appeal be allowed and substitute its own decision for that of the employment tribunal; or,
3. order that the appeal be allowed and remit the case back to the same or to a differently constituted tribunal for re-hearing or for consideration of one or more particular points.

It is possible for an appeal to be allowed in part.

In Scotland it is unusual for the decision of the EAT to be given on the day of the hearing. Normally, the decision is given in written form some time after the hearing and is accompanied by a written judgment.

In the year to end of August 2001, 79 appeals were registered in Scotland. 105 appeals were rejected in terms of rule 3(3) of the Employment Appeal Tribunal Rules. Of those registered, 37 raised issues under Part X of the ERA 1996 (unfair dismissal) while the second most numerous category were appeals on jurisdictional issues of one sort or another (12 appeals).

Review of Decision of EAT

15.29   As previously noted, the EAT has the power to review its decision on its own motion or upon application.[95] This rarely occurs.

---

[91] *Medallion Holidays Ltd v. Birch* [1985] I.R.L.R. 406.

[92] *Brown v. Rentokil Ltd* [1992] I.R.L.R. 302, EAT.

[93] *Secretary of State for Trade and Industry v. Cook* [1997] I.R.L.R. 150, EAT.

[94] *Digital Equipment Co. Ltd v. Clements (No. 2)* [1997] I.R.L.R. 140, EAT; rev'd on other grounds [1998] I.R.L.R. 134, CA.

[95] See EAT Rules, r.33.

Further Appeal[96]

In Scotland, an appeal lies from the EAT to the Inner House of the   15.30
Court of Session and thence to the House of Lords. Leave to appeal
should normally be sought from the EAT.[97] If such is refused, an
application for leave can be made to the Court of Session. When hearing
appeals the primary concern of the Inner House should be not whether
the EAT's decision is correct but whether the decision of the employment tribunal is correct.[98]

---

[96] The detailed procedure and time-limits applying to appeal beyond the EAT are
outwith the scope of this work.
[97] *Mackay v. Highland Regional Council.* 1984 S.L.T. 146; P.D.17(4).
[98] *Hennessy v. Craigmyle and Co Ltd* [1986] I.R.L.R. 300.

CHAPTER 16

THE HUMAN RIGHTS ACT 1998

BY DAVID LECKIE[1]

"The Act will energise the whole of the United Kingdom's legal system. Its effects will be felt across the breadth of both civil and criminal justice. It will apply to both public and private law. It will be used to challenge existing procedures as well as substantive law ... The landscape of U.K. law will be transformed. For the first time our entire legal system, not having a written constitution, will be judged in our own courts against objective international standards"[2]

INTRODUCTION

16.01 Employment law is no stranger to Continental influence. Tribunals and practitioners are familiar with European jurisprudence and the origins of much of the current legislative framework are to be found in Europe. However, prior to the enactment of the Human Rights Act 1998 ("HRA") there was little reference in U.K. employment law and practice to the European Convention for the Protection of Human Rights and Fundamental Freedoms ("Convention") or to the substantial body of Convention case law. The HRA ensures that the Convention must be taken into consideration in all areas of law and practice. As far as the employment relationship is concerned, many of the rights and freedoms which are guaranteed by the Convention are of particular relevance and significance.

The HRA came into full effect across the U.K. on October 2, 2000,[3] and gives further effect to the Convention in domestic law. There are few pieces of legislation which have provoked more debate, controversy

---

[1] David Leckie is a partner in the London office of Maclay Murray and Spens: e-mail dl@Maclaymurrayspens.co.uk.

[2] Lord Woolf of Barnes, Preface to *Human Rights Law and Practice* (Lester and Pannick).

[3] The HRA had partial effect in Scotland from May 1999, as a result of the Scotland Act 1998, which made it unlawful for the Scottish Parliament and the Scottish Executive to act incompatibly with the HRA.

and media attention. This is because the HRA is a constitutional instrument which strikes at the very heart of the legal system and radically alters the way in which everything about the legal system is evaluated. Fears that the HRA would lead to a tidal wave of claims or provide "a field day for crackpots, a pain in the neck for judges and legislators and a goldmine for lawyers"[4] have largely proved to be unfounded. Although there have been a significant number of employment law challenges at all levels of the system, not many have been successful. However, as with other areas of law, the few successful challenges have had important consequences. In addition, it must always be borne in mind that once all domestic remedies have been exhausted, an appeal lies to the European Court of Human Rights in Strasbourg ("ECHR") whose decision is final and binding. Having regard to the significant number of cases in which the ECHR has ruled that the U.K. has infringed Convention rights,[5] it is likely that some of the forthcoming appeals will be successful.

The HRA ensures that full effect is given to the Convention across the U.K. in the legislative, executive and judicial processes, whilst preserving the principle of Parliamentary sovereignty. It adds an entirely new dimension to the U.K. legal systems and means that employers, lawyers and employment tribunals must give careful consideration to the Convention aspects of all employment issues.

THE MAIN PROVISIONS OF THE HRA

Despite the fact that the UK played a major role in drafting the 16.02 Convention and was the first State to ratify it in 1951, the Lord Chancellor at the time called it "a half baked scheme to be administered by some unknown court . . . so vague and woolly that it may mean almost anything". Although the first public call to incorporate the Convention into domestic law was in 1968, it was not until 1996, as part of the Government's programme of constitutional reform, that the consultation paper which led to the HRA was published.[6]

As the Convention is an international treaty, both Parliament and the judiciary have always been bound to observe and give effect to it. However, prior to the HRA, Convention rights did not, as such, form part of U.K. law and it was not generally possible for an aggrieved party to enforce Convention rights directly in the U.K. courts and tribunals. Although the acts of a public authority could be challenged by way of judicial review proceedings, this was a domestic remedy which was of limited application in respect of Convention rights and was of little assistance to employment lawyers. Where the remedy of judicial review was unavailable, the only recourse open to an aggrieved party was to petition the European Commission in Strasbourg directly. This was both expensive and slow. On average, it cost in the region of £30,000 and took five years to get a case before the ECHR.

---

[4] See *Hoekstra v. H.M. Advocate (No. 3)*, 2000 J.C. 391.
[5] Recent examples include *Hutton v. U.K.*, (Application No. 36022/97) ECHR, *The Times*, October 8, 2001; *PC and JH v. U.K.*, *The Times*, October 19, 2001, ECHR.
[6] *Bringing Rights Home*, Cm 3782.

As a result of the HRA, Convention rights can now be directly relied upon, argued and enforced in courts and tribunals at all levels across the U.K. The main provisions of the HRA are as follows:

Taking Convention Law into Account

16.03   Section 2 provides that when determining a question which has arisen in connection with a Convention right, courts and tribunals must take Convention law into account. Although the obligation is mandatory, this does not make Strasbourg jurisprudence binding. The Convention rights are set out in section 1 and Schedule 1 of the HRA (see para. 16.18 below). Convention law consists of judgements, decisions, declarations or advisory opinions of the ECHR, Commission and Committee.[7] In addition, when considering Convention jurisprudence, decisions of the national courts of the 41 Member States can be persuasive. Courts and tribunals have also given considerable weight to authorities from other jurisdictions whose constitutions include a Charter/Bill of Rights, such as Canada, USA, South Africa and New Zealand.[8]

Interpretation of Legislation

16.04   Section 3 provides that all U.K. legislation must, as far as it is possible to do so, be given effect to in a way which is compatible with Convention rights. This applies to all legislation whenever enacted and the obligation is widely framed so that it extends to cases which do not involve public authorities and places the obligation on all concerned with the interpretation of legislation, including the executive and the administration. This involves reading down legislation to reduce its effect and reading in meanings in an effort to construe the legislation so that it is compatible.[9]

Declaration of Incompatibily

16.05   Superior courts, such as the House of Lords, Privy Council, Court of Appeal, High Court, Court of Session and High Court of Justiciary have the power to make a "declaration of incompatibility" where they find that legislation is incompatible with the Convention (s.4).[10] Neither employment tribunals nor the EAT can make such a declaration.[11] Where such a declaration is made, it does not affect the validity, continuing operation or enforcement of the incompatible legislation. However, it may trigger a fast-track procedure in Parliament for the incompatibility to be rectified, where there are "compelling reasons" to do so.

---

[7] Since the Eleventh Protocol, which came into effect on November 1, 1998, the Commission ceased to exist and the Committee no longer refers cases to the ECHR—its function is limited to the execution of judgements.

[8] The Appendix to this Chapter sets out sources of Convention law and a list of useful websites which contain much of the information required.

[9] See *Secretary of State for Defence v. MacDonald* [2001] I.R.L.R. 431 for an example of the application of s.3.

[10] See *Wilson v. First County Trust* [2001] All E.R. (D.) 28, for an example of such a declaration being made in the U.K. courts.

[11] See *Younas v. Chief Constable of the Thames Valley Police*, EAT/795/00, March 28, 2001.

Unlawful Acts

Section 6 is one of the cornerstones of the HRA and makes it 16.06 unlawful for public authorities to act or to fail to act in a way which is incompatible with a Convention right.

"Public authority" was deliberately defined very widely to include courts and tribunals and any person whose functions are "functions of a public nature". It is clear from Parliamentary debates that there is a further category of "hybrid" public authority which performs part-public, part-private functions. Whilst some employers, such as Railtrack, fall into this category and are clearly public authorities when carrying out public functions, such as rail safety, the situation is far from straightforward and many employers are unsure of their status under the Act. Furthermore, the status of an employer may change depending on the nature of the function being carried out. For example, where a local authority has contracted out public functions to a private company in a public/private partnership, it is likely that the private company will, in that capacity, be a public authority—the ECHR has observed that "the State cannot absolve itself from responsibility by delegating its obligations to private bodies or individuals".[12]

It will ultimately be for the courts and tribunals to determine the question of what is a public authority under the HRA and this will often be a preliminary consideration in cases involving Convention rights. The Home Office has issued guidance which attempts to shed some light on how to resolve the public authority question. The factors to be considered are:

- whether the body performs or operates in the public domain as an integral part of a statutory system which performs public law duties
- whether the duty performed is of public significance
- whether the rights or obligations of individuals may be affected in the performance of the duty
- whether an individual may be deprived of some legitimate expectation in performance of the duty
- whether the body is non-statutory but is established under the authority of government or local government
- whether the body is supported by statutory powers and penalties
- whether the body performs functions that the government or local government would otherwise perform
- whether the body is under a duty to act judicially in exercising what amounts to public powers.

Action by Victims

Where a person claims to be a "victim" of an unlawful act by a public 16.07 authority, section 7 provides that such a person can either:

---

[12] *Costello-Roberts v. U.K.* (1993) 19 E.H.R.R. 112 at 132.

(a) bring proceedings against the public authority in the appropriate court or tribunal. Such proceedings cannot be brought in the employment tribunals or EAT and in Scotland the appropriate court is the Court of Session. Subject to any stricter rule imposed by the proceedings in question, this must be done within one year (or such longer period as the court/tribunal considers equitable) of when the act complained of took place. It also must relate to an act which took place after October 2, 2000; or

(b) rely on the Convention right concerned in any legal proceedings. This clearly includes proceedings before employment tribunals where one of the parties is a public authority. In this case, there is no time limit and where the legal proceedings are instigated by a public authority the HRA has a degree of retrospective effect, as Convention rights can be relied upon regardless of when the unlawful act in question took place.

"Victim" has the same meaning as in Article 34 of the Convention—a person, non-governmental organisation or a group of individuals actually and directly affected. This involves careful consideration of Convention jurisprudence; companies, trade unions and professional associations have all been held to fall within the definition of "victim" but only where the action complained of has had a direct effect on them.

Horizontal Effect

16.08   Although the HRA does not expressly apply to the actions of private parties, it nevertheless has an indirect effect on such parties. This is because courts and tribunals are themselves "public authorities" under the HRA and therefore must act compatibly with the HRA and give full effect to Convention rights in all disputes, including disputes where there is no public authority involved. Such a "horizontal effect" is of particular importance in the context of employment disputes, where it is often the case that neither of the parties are public authorities.

The practical consequences of the horizontal effect in employment tribunal proceedings is that either an applicant will include a human rights argument in the IT 1 to support a claim or the tribunal will itself raise Convention issues during the proceedings in order to ensure that it is acting compatibly with the HRA. However, where the employer is a public authority, an aggrieved employee can also bring proceedings against such an employer in the Court of Session, with an action under sections 6 and 7 of the HRA.

Remedies

16.09   A court or tribunal can grant such relief or remedy as it considers appropriate, taking into account the principles applied by the ECHR (s.8). Such awards for "just satisfaction" are usually between £1,000—£15,000 and often the ECHR will rule that the finding of a violation is itself sufficient recompense.

However, such relief or remedy must already be within the competence of the court or tribunal making the award. Accordingly, employment tribunals have no power to award any financial remedy under the HRA. They do, however, have the power to strike out a notice of appearance or to take any infringement of the HRA into account when making determination.

New Legislation

In respect of all Bills before Parliament, the Minister responsible for 16.10 such new legislation must, prior to its Second Reading, make a written statement confirming that the provisions of the Bill are compatible with Convention rights. Where such a statement cannot be made, the Minister must make a statement indicating that the government nevertheless wishes to proceed with the Bill. Parliamentary sovereignty is thus preserved. This also ensures that Parliamentary debate focuses on human rights issues.

THE CONVENTION

The Convention is a treaty of the Council of Europe which was adopted 16.11 on November 4, 1950, and which has been in force since 1953. There are currently 41 Member States which have signed and ratified the Convention. The Convention, as amended by the Eleventh Protocol, is in three sections and consists of 59 Articles, many of which are of a procedural nature.

The Nature of Convention Rights and Obligations

Convention obligations are not limited to the negative obligation of 16.12 refraining from interfering with a citizen's rights. There is also a positive obligation on public authorities to take steps to prevent violations occurring.[13] This clearly has important implications, not only for employers but also for employment tribunals. In the case of *Pearce v. Governing Body of Mayfield Secondary School*[14] the Court of Appeal emphasised that the respondents were a public authority and were under a positive obligation to ensure that the appellant's Article 8 rights were not violated.

Certain Convention rights are absolute and cannot be restricted in any way. However, most of the articles relevant to employment law, such as Articles 8, 9 and 10, are qualified rights and can be legitimately restricted in certain situations. The qualifications are contained in the text of the Articles themselves (see below). In addition, although Article 6 does not contain express words of qualification, it is not an absolute right.[15]

What qualified rights mean in practice is that it will, in some situations, be legitimate for an employer to restrict an employee's Convention rights. In assessing whether such a restriction is legitimate, a tribunal must seek to strike a fair balance between protecting an individual employee's rights and protecting the general interests of

---

[13] See *Lopez Ostra v. Spain* (1994) 20 E.H.R.R. 277.
[14] See below.
[15] See *Stott v. Brown*, PC [2001] 2 W.L.R. 81.

others, including other employees, the employer himself and the community as a whole. Limitations on Convention rights are interpreted strictly.

Proportionality

16.13   Any restriction placed on a Convention right must be "proportionate to the legitimate aim pursued"—this is known as the doctrine of proportionality and is the key test to be applied by courts and tribunals in assessing whether a restriction is justifiable. In order for a limitation of a Convention right to satisfy the proportionality test:

- the measure adopted must be "carefully designed to meet the objective in question" and must not be "arbitrary, unfair or irrational"
- the limitation must restrict the right in question as little as possible
- even if the above 2 tests are satisfied, the restriction may still be so severe as to be unjustifiable

In a human rights application, it is for the applicant to show there has been a violation. Where the right is qualified, it is for the respondent to show that the restriction imposed was justifiable and proportionate.

Interpretation of Convention Rights

16.14   The Convention is a "living instrument which must be interpreted in the light of present day conditions".[16] This means that the ECHR moves with the times to reflect changes in public attitudes and tolerances. The purpose of the Convention is to extend the rights and protections which it guarantees to as broad a class of person as possible. Accordingly, a dynamic, broad and purposive interpretation of the Convention is adopted by the ECHR to reflect this, and the same approach must be taken by UK courts and tribunals. In addition, the ECHR takes an autonomous approach to the interpretation of the Convention and can attribute meanings to words which go far beyond the interpretation given by UK courts and tribunals.

Margin of Appreciation

16.15   When considering the actions of Member States, the ECHR allows each State a margin of appreciation: "by reason of their direct and continuous contact with the vital forces of their countries the national authorities are in principle better placed than an international court to evaluate local needs and conditions".[17] This means that Member States are given a considerable degree of leeway to apply the Convention having regard to their prevailing political, economic and social climates.[18]

---

[16] *Tyrer v. U.K.* (1978) 2 E.H.R.R. 1.
[17] *Buckley v. U.K.* (1996) 23 E.H.R.R. 101 at 129.
[18] *e.g.* see *Petrovic v. Austria*, ECHR, March 27, 1998; 4 B.H.R.C. 232.

Precedent

There is no formal doctrine of precedent in Convention law, although 16.16 clearly the ECHR will carefully consider previous decisions and only depart from them if necessary in the circumstances. However, once a superior court in the U.K. has ruled on a point of Convention law it will not be open to an inferior court to depart from that precedent:

> "We are not permitted to re-examine decisions of the European Court to ascertain whether the conclusion of the House of Lords or the Court of Appeal may be inconsistent with those decisions, or susceptible to a continuing gloss."[19]

WAIVER OF RIGHTS

Certain Convention rights can be waived by agreement.[20] The doctrine 16.17 of waiver has particular importance in the employment law context, especially when considered against the background of a recent survey of 350 FTSE companies which has revealed that only 18 per cent of respondents have reviewed their employment procedures in light of the Act.[21] Contracts of employment, policies and procedures, confidentiality agreements, fixed term contracts and compromise agreements should all be carefully reviewed in light of the waiver doctrine. Where an employee contracts to work under certain conditions, such as email monitoring, it will be very difficult for such an employee to later argue a Convention breach.

However, in order for a waiver to be effective, "it must be established in an unequivocal manner". Even where there are express words of waiver the court will look at the whole circumstances and particularly the question of whether the applicant clearly understood the position.[22]

The ECHR has also held that rights can also be deemed to be have been tacitly waived by the failure by an applicant to rely upon the right in earlier proceedings. As a result, if a Convention right is to be relied upon, it should be pleaded at the first possible opportunity.

CONVENTION ARTICLES AND EMPLOYMENT LAW

The text of the Convention Articles relevant to employment law is set 16.18 out below, followed by examples of some of the many employment law issues which have arisen in respect of these rights. This is by no means an exhaustive overview of the issues involved, nor of the relevant case law.

---

[19] Court of Appeal Civil Division, *per* Judge L.J.
[20] See *Vereiging Rechtsinkels Utrecht v. Holland* No. 11308/84, 46 D.R.
[21] *The Times,* September 26, 2000.
[22] *Oberschlick v. Austria* (1991) 19 E.H.R.R. 389 and *Pfeifer* (1992) 14 E.H.R.R. 692; *Millar v. PF Elgin* Appeal Court, High Court of Justiciary, August 3, 2000.

Most human rights challenges are not restricted to consideration of a single Convention Article but include reference to a number of Articles. Accordingly, although Articles 2, 3 and 4 have very limited application to employment law, except in the most extreme cases, it is nevertheless important to consider these Articles, as they may be relied upon in addition to a claim under one of the other Articles.

Article 2—Right to life

"1. Everyone's right to life shall be protected by law. No one shall be deprived of his life intentionally save in the execution of a sentence of a court following his conviction of a crime for which this penalty is provided by law."

Although this Article may not immediately seem relevant to employment law, Article 2 has been interpreted to extend to the protection of "health and physical integrity". Public authorities have a positive duty to protect the public from risks to their health and safety and from harmful environmental exposure. Failure on the part of an employer to ensure a safe and healthy working environment could result in a challenge. The recent statistics published by the Health and Safety Executive[23] which show a 34 per cent rise in workplace fatalities is evidence of the potential employment law consequences of this Article.[24]

Article 3—Prohibition of torture

"No one shall be subjected to torture or to inhuman or degrading treatment or punishment."

Whilst torture should be a rare phenomenon in the U.K. workplace, the relevance of this Article is that "degrading" has been widely interpreted to include treatment which arouses feelings of fear or anguish which are capable of humiliating or debasing a victim or which drive a victim to act against his will or self conscience, or which constitutes an insult to a victim's human dignity. Various forms of discrimination may constitute "degrading" treatment.[25] Other challenges have included striking off a doctor from a medical register.[26]

Article 4—Prohibition of slavery and forced labour

"1. No one shall be held in slavery or servitude.

2. No one shall be required to perform forced or compulsory labour.

3. For the purpose of this Article the term "forced or compulsory labour" shall not include:

---

[23] Safety Statistics Bulletin 2000/2001, C65, HSE Books.
[24] See *LCB v. UK* (1999) 27 E.H.R.R. 212; *Guerra v. Italy* (1998) 26 E.H.R.R. 357.
[25] *East African Asian Cases* (1973) 3 E.H.R.R. 76.
[26] *Albert Le Compte v. Belgium* (1983) 5 E.H.R.R. 533.

> (a) any work required to be done in the ordinary course of detention imposed according to the provisions of Article 5 of this Convention or during conditional release from such detention;
>
> (b) any service of a military character or, in case of conscientious objectors in countries where they are recognised, service exacted instead of compulsory military service;
>
> (c) any service exacted in the case of an emergency or calamity threatening the life or well-being of the community;
>
> (d) any work or service which forms part of normal civic obligations."

This Article has resulted in a surprising number of ECHR employment related claims, such as the creative argument of a pupil advocate in Belgium who claimed his rights were violated when professional rules obliged him to represent a client pro bono,[27] a professional footballer's complaint about a transfer fee[28] and a dentist's complaint at having to provide fixed price dentistry.[29]

Article 6—Right to a fair trial

> "1. In the determination of his civil rights and obligations or of any criminal charge against him, everyone is entitled to a fair and public hearing within a reasonable time by an independent and impartial tribunal established by law. Judgment shall be pronounced publicly but the press and public may be excluded from all or part of the trial in the interests of morals, public order or national security in a democratic society, where the interests of juveniles or the protection of the private life of the parties so require, or to the extent strictly necessary in the opinion of the court in special circumstances where publicity would prejudice the interests of justice."

It was the successful challenge to the appointment of temporary sheriffs[30] which first made the headlines in Scotland and captured the imagination of lawyers across the U.K. This was followed enthusiastically by a number of other high profile challenges of all things judicial, including the fairness of the District Court system,[31] temporary judges in the Court of Session,[32] the system of planning appeals[33] and judges expressing views in newspapers.[34]

---

[27] *Van der Mussele v. Belgium* (1983) 6 E.H.R.R. 163.
[28] *X v. Netherlands* (1983) 6 E.H.R.R. 163.
[29] *Iversen v. Norway* (1963) 6 Y.B. 278.
[30] *Starrs v. Ruxton*, 2000 J.C. 208.
[31] *Clark v. Kelly*, 2001 J.C. 16.
[32] *Clancy v. Caird*, 2000 S.C. 441.
[33] *Bryan v. U.K.* and *R. v. Secretary of State for the Environment, Transport and the Regions, ex p. Alconbury* [2001] All E.R. (D.) 116.
[34] *Hoekstra v. H.M. Advocate (No. 3)*, 2000 J.C. 391.

Employment Tribunal Composition and Procedure

16.19   In *Secretary of State for Trade and Industry v. Smith*[35] the EAT
expressed "disquiet about the appearance of a lack of impartiality of the
employment tribunals when adjudicating upon claims against the Secretary of State". Although leave to appeal was granted by the EAT the
matter was subsequently settled. This decision was followed by the case
of *Scanfuture (U.K.) Ltd v. Secretary of State for Trade and Industry*[36]
where the fact that the lay members of the tribunal were appointed by
the Secretary of State was successfully challenged under Article 6 and
the case was remitted for a rehearing.

Even the language in which proceedings are conducted can be open to
challenge. In *Williams v. Cowell*[37] W was dismissed for communicating
with other Welsh speaking employees in Welsh. He claimed racial
discrimination. The employment tribunal sat in Wales and the proceedings were conducted in Welsh. W was successful but his employer
appealed to the EAT. W argued that the EAT proceedings should be in
Welsh and submitted that a failure to do so would contravene his Article
6 rights. The EAT refused to hear the case in Welsh and W appealed.
The Court of Appeal dismissed the appeal on the basis that there were
no grounds for overturning the EAT's exercise of discretion.

A vexatious litigant has also used Article 6 to unsuccessfully challenge
an order under the Employment Tribunals Act 1996, s.33, preventing
him from instituting or continuing proceedings before an employment
tribunal or the EAT without permission.[38] The Court of Appeal held
that Article 6 rights were not absolute and that a balance had to be
struck with the rights of others not to be burdened with unsubstantiated
claims.

Time limits, delay and other procedural matters can also be the
subject of Article 6 challenges. Indeed, most of the Scottish challenges
prior to October 2, 2000 concerned the question of procedural delay. In
M.P. v. Spain[39] a three-day time limit for lodging an appeal in civil
dispute was held by the ECHR to be unrealistic. However in
Goodchild v. Legal and General Assurance Society Ltd,[40] where a claim
was submitted out of time, the EAT held that the three-month time limit
and the "reasonably practicable" test contained in the Employment
Rights Act 1996, s.111(2) did not infringe Article 6. The EAT also
rejected the proposition that a litigant should not be held responsible for
the failings of his legal representatives.

As far as the conduct of tribunal proceedings is concerned, in
Villarnerva v. London Clubs Management Ltd[41] the EAT firmly stated
that Article 6 adds nothing to tribunal rules which enable tribunals to
deal with cases justly and cross-examine parties where appropriate.

---

[35] [2000] I.R.L.R. 6.
[36] [2001] I.R.L.R. 416, EAT.
[37] [2000] 1 W.L.R. 187.
[38] *Att.-Gen. v. Wheen* [2001] I.R.L.R. 91.
[39] 28090/95, October 21, 1997.
[40] unreported.
[41] Case 352/99.

As regards procedural delay, this is unlikely to be an issue within the tribunal system itself, due to the strict time limits imposed. However, it can be an issue where the case is subject to further appeal. In *Darnell v. U.K.*[42] a nine-year delay in bringing an NHS unfair dismissal claim to a conclusion was held to amount to a breach. The complexity of the case, the conduct of the applicant and the public authority are all factors to be taken into account in assessing any delay and each case must be decided on its own facts.[43]

Legal Aid

Although there is no right to free legal representation under the 16.20 Convention, where cases are complex, a failure to provide legal aid can amount to a breach of Article 6.[44] Failure to provide legal aid may also breach the equality of arms principle.[45] The availability of legal aid for tribunal proceedings was challenged in the case of *Gerrie v. Ministry of Defence.*[46] While this case awaited a hearing in the EAT, the Scottish Executive pre-empted any decision by enacting Regulations which extend legal advice and assistance to employment tribunal proceedings. This decision has not been followed in the rest of the U.K., which has led to an anomaly in the legal aid position across the U.K.

Pre-Employment Inquiries

Employers who carry out pre-employment inquiries in relation to job applicants must do so in a proportionate manner, as this can be open to challenge under Article 6 and other articles. In the recent case of *Devlin v. U.K.*[47] the ECHR ruled that a job applicant's Article 6 rights were infringed when the Secretary of State for Northern Ireland issue a national security certificate which certified that the refusal of employment was for the purpose of safeguarding national security and protecting public safety.

The facts of this case were that an Irish national applied for a position as an administrative assistant with the Northern Ireland Civil Service. He was informed that he was being recommended for appointment subject to satisfactory pre-employment inquiries. The Secretary of State then issued a certificate under section 42 of the Fair Employment (Northern Ireland) Act 1976. The applicant alleged that his appointment was blocked because he was a Catholic and a member of the Irish National Foresters. He invoked Articles 6, 8, 9, 10, 13 and 14. The ECHR ruled that Article 6 had been violated because there was no independent scrutiny by the fact finding bodies of the facts which led the Secretary of State to issue the certificate nor was any evidence as to why the applicant was a security risk presented to the fair employment tribunal. As the ECHR found that Article 6 had been breached it did not consider the other alleged breaches of other Articles.

---

[42] (1993) 18 E.H.R.R. 205.
[43] see also *Sussmann v. Germay* (1998) 25 E.H.R.R. 64.
[44] *Airey v. Ireland* (1979) 2 E.H.R.R. 305.
[45] See also *Buchanan v. McLean,* 2000 S.L.T. 928.
[46] Case 100842/99, ET.
[47] ECHR Application No. 29545/96. *The Times,* November 9, 2001.

Disciplinary Proceedings

16.21   Internal disciplinary proceedings are not covered by Article 6, as they are not decisive of civil rights and obligations—an aggrieved employee can instigate proceedings in the employment tribunals.

Professional disciplinary hearings or hearings which concern access to professions can be covered by Article 6.[48] However, where there is an ultimate right of appeal to a court, which itself complies with Article 6, any challenge to such disciplinary proceedings will fail. In *Tehrani v. U.K. Central Council for Nursing, Midwifery and Health Visiting*,[49] disciplinary proceedings were initiated against a qualified nurse in connection with allegations of misconduct. She lodged a petition for judicial review on the grounds that the proceedings by the Professional Conduct Committee, which had the power to remove her from the register, were not compatible with Article 6. The Court of Session held that there was no breach of Article 6, as the decisions of the PCC could be appealed to a court which has full jurisdiction and itself complies with the provisions of Article 6.

A similar decision was made in *Preiss v. General Dental Council*[50] which concerned the General Dental Council's disciplinary procedures following a decision to suspend the appellant's registration for 12 months. The Privy Council held that whilst the procedures of the GDC did not give the appearance of impartiality and independence necessary to comply with Article 6, nevertheless the fact that there was an ultimate right of appeal to the Privy Council which conducted a complete rehearing of the case, including a full reconsideration of the facts, saved the proceedings from being in breach of Article 6.

In *R (On the Application of Fleurose) v. Securities and Futures Authority*[51] a trader in securities applied for judicial review in respect of a decision by the Disciplinary Appeal Tribunal of the Securities and Futures Authority to uphold a finding that he was guilty of improper conduct. The Article 6 challenge was rejected on the basis that disciplinary proceedings did not entail the bringing of a "criminal charge" and therefore Article 6 did not apply.

Public Servants

16.22   The application of the Convention to public servants requires careful preliminary consideration. The matter has been considerably clarified by the case of *Pellegrin v. France*[52] where the ECHR ruled that:

> "the only disputes excluded from the scope of Article 6 of the Convention are those which are raised by public servants whose duties typify the specific activities of the public service in so far as the latter is acting as the depositary of public authority responsible

---

[48] *Le Compte v. Belgium* (1982) 4 E.H.R.R. 1; *Stefan v. UK* (1998) 25 E.H.R.R. C.D. 130.
[49] [2001] I.R.L.R. 208.
[50] [2001] I.R.L.R. 696.
[51] Administrative Court, April 26, 2001, Morison J.
[52] (2001) 31 E.H.R.R. 26. See also *Devlin v. U.K.* (Application No. 29545/96, ECHR).

for protecting the general interests of the State or other public authorities. A manifest example of such activities is provided by the armed forces and the police."

Further confirmation of the difficulties which public servants can find themselves in can be found in the case of *Younas v. Chief Constable of the Thames Valley Police*[53] where the appellant contended that the provisions of section 200 of the Employment Rights Act 1996, which prevents police officers from bringing unfair dismissal claims, are incompatible with Article 6. The EAT indicated that the case raised "difficult questions of law and fact" but concluded that, as it had no power to make a declaration of incompatibility, the matter should be raised in the Court of Appeal.

Other Challenges

There are many other examples of Article 6 challenges, such as the case of *R. v. Secretary of State for Health, ex p. C*[54] where a social worker was dismissed following allegations of abuse against a child. His subsequent complaint for unfair dismissal was dismissed, as was his appeal. His name was then entered on a register of individuals deemed unsuitable for work with children. He sought judicial review of the decision to place him on the register on the grounds that it infringed Article 6. The appeal was dismissed on the basis that the list was not determinative of his rights and obligations.

16.23

Article 8—Right to respect for private and family life

"1. Everyone has the right to respect for his private and family life, his home and his correspondence.

2. There shall be no interference by a public authority with the exercise of this right except such as is in accordance with the law and is necessary in a democratic society in the interests of national security, public safety or the economic well-being of the country, for the prevention of disorder or crime, for the protection of health or morals, or for the protection of the rights and freedoms of others."

Article 8 has far reaching implications for the employment relationship and there have been a number of important challenges both in the ECHR and in the domestic courts. Article 8 rights extend to the office environment.[55] However, as Article 8 rights are qualified, it is less likely that there will be a breach by employers where they have put in place appropriate employment policies which put employees on notice that the activity complained of will be carried out. It is also clear that each case will be decided on its own particular facts.

---

[53] EAT/795/00, March 28, 2001.
[54] (2000) 1 F.L.R. 627.
[55] *Niemitz v. Germany* (1993) 16 E.H.R.R. 97; *Halford v. UK* [1997] I.R.L.R. 471; *Malone v. U.K.*, 1984 ECHR 8691/79.

In *O'Flynn v. Airport Coach Co. Ltd*[56] a tribunal ruled that a random drug test which revealed cannabis in an employee's system did not infringe Article 8 because it was necessary for public safety. The nature of the applicant's duties were to help manoeuvre buses and serve hot drinks on buses. However in *Wilson v. David Lloyd Centre*[57] a dismissal was held to be unfair where an employee was dismissed after he was found with cannabis in a car park.

The use of private diaries in evidence have also been the subject of Article 8 analysis in *McDowell v. Serco Ltd*[58] where the tribunal itself raised the question of whether the use of the contents of a diary could infringe Article 8. The tribunal did not in this case have to rule on the question as agreement between the parties was reached.

In *Wilson v. De Keyser*[59] the EAT ruled that there was no breach of Article 8 where a letter written to the respondent's appointed medical expert included assertions concerning the applicant's private life. The employment tribunal had struck out the respondent's notice of appearance, having concluded that the letter was scandalous and in breach of Article 8. The EAT however held that there was no breach of Article 8 as no confidential information had been communicated and further held that the tribunal had failed to enquire in any event whether a fair trial was still possible, notwithstanding the letter.

Sexuality

16.24   Sexuality is an area where there have been successful ECHR challenges under Articles 8 and 14, most notably the cases of *Smith and Grady v. U.K.*[60] and *Lustig-Prean and Beckett v. U.K.*[61] which involved the sexuality of members of the armed forces. An example of the difficulties which are posed by the Convention and section 3 of the HRA can be found in the case of *Secretary of State for Defence v. MacDonald,*[62] where an RAF officer was forced to resign after admitting to being a homosexual. He brought an action under the Sex Discrimination Act 1975 and also claimed that his Article 8 and 14 rights had been breached. The employment tribunal dismissed the application. On appeal, the EAT ruled that, applying section 3 of the HRA, the word "sex" should be interpreted to included sexual orientation. However, in a landmark ruling the Court of Session overturned the decision of the EAT and held that sex meant gender and not sexual orientation and on that basis there was no discrimination.

Employee Surveillance

16.25   One of the main areas of concern is the issue of employee surveillance. Many employers monitor the use of telephone, email and the Internet, yet few have a policy in place to regulate such monitoring.

---

[56] Case No. 3300292/00.
[57] *The Times,* July 17, 2001.
[58] Unreported, Leeds ET.
[59] [2001] 1 I.R.L.R. 324.
[60] 33985/96.
[61] ECHR decision, September 9, 1999.
[62] [2001] I.R.L.R. 431.

Surveillance is less likely to breach Article 8 if the employees are made aware that it is taking place and agree to it. This should be done by way of some form of policy document which forms part of the contract of employment.

Employers must also have regard to the Regulation of Investigatory Powers Act 2000 which will make it a criminal offence, in certain situations, for an employer to intercept private communications without the consent of an employee. The Telecommunications (Lawful Business Practice) (Interception of Communications) Regulations 2000 came into effect on October 24, 2000. These Regulations set out the circumstances in which an employer can record or monitor employees' communications (such as Email or telephones) without the consent of either the employee or the other party to the communication.

These circumstances are very wide, and they include:

(a) for recording evidence of business transactions;
(b) ensuring compliance with regulatory or self-regulatory guidelines;
(c) maintaining the effective operation of the employer's systems (*e.g.* preventing viruses);
(d) monitoring standards of training and service;
(e) preventing or detecting criminal activity;
(f) preventing the unauthorised use of the computer/telephone system—*i.e.* ensuring the employee does not breach the company's E-mail or telephone policies.

It is necessary under the Regulations for employers to take reasonable steps to inform employees that their communications might be intercepted.

Covert filming has been considered in *Mohammed v. First Quench* 16.26 *Ltd.*[63] In this case a secret surveillance camera was set up as a result of a number of thefts. The same camera caught the applicant having sex with another employee. The applicant was dismissed and the dismissal was upheld by an employment tribunal. On appeal to the EAT, it was argued that the surveillance breached the applicant's human rights. The EAT rejected the appeal on the basis that the incident took place before the HRA came into effect and the respondent was not in any event a public authority. However, the EAT did indicate that where there was evidence of theft, then a limited covert surveillance operation may not breach Article 8. Such a view is fortified by the criminal case of *R. v. Wright*[64] where the Court of Appeal ruled that covert recordings of telephone conversations taken by Customs officers was both relevant and probative and that the admissibility of such evidence was fair. The court concluded that even where a violation of Article 8 is established this does not automatically lead to the exclusion of the evidence under Article 6. It is a question of balance between the gravity of the offence being investigated and the measures taken to investigate it. The use of covertly

---

[63] 2001, unreported.
[64] [2001] All E.R. (D.) 129.

obtained evidence at trial was further considered in the recent decision of *P.G. and J.H. v. U.K.*[65] In this case, the ECHR ruled that covert surveillance of a suspect's flat and further covert surveillance at a police station did infringe the applicant's Article 8 rights but the use of such evidence at trial did not infringe the applicant's Article 6 rights.

Accordingly, it would appear that an employment tribunal must not only consider whether there has been a breach of Article 8 in obtaining evidence against an applicant but it must go further and consider whether such a breach means that the applicant cannot have a fair hearing under Article 6.[66]

Article 9—Freedom of thought, conscience and religion

16.27

"1. Everyone has the right to freedom of thought, conscience and religion; this right includes freedom to change his religion or belief and freedom, either alone or in community with others and in public or private, to manifest his religion or belief, in worship, teaching, practice and observance.

2. Freedom to manifest one's religion or beliefs shall be subject only to such limitations as are prescribed by law and are necessary in a democratic society in the interests of public safety, for the protection of public order, health or morals, or for the protection of the rights and freedoms of others."

Article 9 should be read in conjunction with section 13 of the HRA and Article 14. Article 9 rights have been afforded considerable protection from interference. Where there is a conflict between competing rights, the ECHR has had strong regard for religious beliefs.[67] Religion and belief have been widely construed to include druidism,[68] veganism,[69] pacifism[70] and even non-belief. There have been a number of challenges in respect of expression and manifestation of belief[71] and time off work for religious beliefs. In *Ahmad v. U.K.*,[72] where a Muslim teacher was refused permission to attend weekly prayers, there was no breach of Article 9 as the teacher had willingly accepted his contract of employment in the knowledge that it may interfere with prayers. The same approach was adopted in *Steadman v. U.K.*[73] which involved a refusal to work on Sunday.

Although Article 9 rights may often be an issue in the employment relationship, it is a qualified right, as can be seen from the case of *R v. Taylor*[74] where the Court of Appeal ruled that the prohibition in the Misuse of Drugs Act 1971 in relation to the supply of cannabis did not

---

[65] *The Times*, October 19, 2001.
[66] See also *De Keyser, supra*.
[67] See *Otto-Preminger-Institut v. Austria* (1994) 19 E.H.R.R. 34.
[68] *Chappell v. U.K.* (1987) 53 D.R. 241.
[69] *X v. UK*, February 10, 1993, Commission.
[70] (1978) 19 D.R. 5.
[71] *Kokkinakis v. Greece* (1993) 17 E.H.R.R. 387.
[72] (1982) 4 E.H.R.R. 126.
[73] (1997) 23 E.H.R.R. C.D. 168.
[74] Court of Appeal October 23, 2001, *The Times*, November 15, 2001.

infringe a defendant's rights under Article 9, as the prohibition was necessary to combat the public health and safety dangers of drugs.

Article 10—Freedom of expression

16.28

"1. Everyone has the right to freedom of expression. This right shall include freedom to hold opinions and to receive and impart information and ideas without interference by public authority and regardless of frontiers. This article shall not prevent States from requiring the licensing of broadcasting, television or cinema enterprises.

2. The exercise of these freedoms, since it carries with it duties and responsibilities, may be subject to such formalities, conditions, restrictions or penalties as are prescribed by law and are necessary in a democratic society, in the interests of national security, territorial integrity or public safety, for the prevention of disorder or crime, for the protection of health or morals, for the protection of the reputation or rights of others, for preventing the disclosure of information received in confidence, or for maintaining the authority and impartiality of the judiciary."

Article 10 should be read with section 12 of the HRA and Article 14. This Article has led to a number of employment related challenges such as *Ahmed v. U.K.*[75] where restrictions on local government officers in "politically restricted" posts being involved in politics did not amount to a breach. By contrast, in *Defreitas v. Ministry of Agriculture*[76] a blanket restraint on civil servants' right to freedom of expressing political views was held to be excessive and disproportionate. Other examples have included soldiers distributing satirical material in barracks, the refusal to appoint a teacher who was a communist, dismissing a teacher of 10 years' service for being a communist and confiscating an artist's obscene paintings.

Dress codes will have to be re-examined in light of Article 10, although it would appear that provided there is a good reason for a particular dress code and this is made clear to employees by way of a policy, such a challenge is likely to be unsuccessful.[77]

Article 14—Prohibition of discrimination

16.29

"The enjoyment of the rights and freedoms set forth in this Convention shall be secured without discrimination on any ground such as sex, race, colour, language, religion, political or other opinion, national or social origin, association with a national minority, property, birth or other status."

---

[75] [1997] E.H.R.L.R. 670.
[76] [1998] 3 W.L.R. 675.
[77] *Smith v. Safeway* [1996] I.R.L.R. 456, CA; *Watson v. Waitrose, The Times,* March 13, 2001.

This Article does not provide for a free standing right not to be discriminated against. However, when a court or tribunal is considering any other Convention right, Article 14 can be relied upon as an additional argument in support of the application—some of the Articles which may trigger the application of Article 14 are Articles 3, 8,[78] 9, 10 or Protocol 1.[79]

In *Pearce v. Governing Body of Mayfield Secondary School*[80] the Court of Appeal held that a lesbian teacher who was subjected to gender specific homophobic abuse by pupils was not discriminated against on the grounds of sex, as she was not treated less favourably than a male teacher would have been if he had been subjected to similar abuse. As the HRA is not retrospective in its effect, it did not apply to this case. However, the Court observed that for a public authority to subject a person to such abuse would be a breach of Articles 8 and 14 and that now that the HRA is in effect, an applicant in a similar situation could instigate proceedings under sections 6 and 7 of the HRA.

Other Relevant Articles

16.30   Other Articles with employment law implications are Article 11 and Protocol 1, Article 1, the text of which is set out below.

Article 11—Freedom of assembly and association

> "1. Everyone has the right to freedom of peaceful assembly and to freedom of association with others, including the right to form and to join trade unions for the protection of his interests.
> 2. No restrictions shall be placed on the exercise of these rights other than such as are prescribed by law and are necessary in a democratic society in the interests of national security or public safety, for the prevention of disorder or crime, for the protection of health or morals or for the protection of the rights and freedoms of others. This Article shall not prevent the imposition of lawful restrictions on the exercise of these rights by members of the armed forces, of the police or of the administration of the State."

Protocol 1, Article 1—Protection of property

> "Every natural or legal person is entitled to the peaceful enjoyment of his possessions. No one shall be deprived of his possessions except in the public interest and subject to the conditions provided for by law and by the general principles of international law.
> The preceding provisions shall not, however, in any way impair the right of a State to enforce such laws as it deems necessary to control the use of property in accordance with the general interest or to secure the payment of taxes or other contributions or penalties."

---

[78] see *Abdulaziz, Cabales v. U.K.* (1985) 7 E.H.R.R. 471.
[79] see *Petrovic v. Austria* (1998) 4 B.H.R.C. 232.
[80] [2001] I.R.L.R. 669.

Useful Websites

The Act	www.hmso.gov.uk	16.31
Home Office	www.homeoffice.gov.uk/hract	
ECHR	www.echr.coe.int	
Commission	www.dhcommhr.coe.fr	
Committee	www.coe.fr.cm	
Council of Europe	www.coe.fr	
Council of Ministers	www.coe.fr/cm/	
European Court of Justice	www.europa.eu.int/cj	
European Union	www.europa.eu.int	
Cases alongside Convention articles	www.beagle.org.uk/hra	
Human rights Web	www.hrweb.org/resource.html	
Scottish Executive	www.scotland.gov.uk	
Scottish Human Rights Trust	www.scotrights.org/shrt.htm	
EAT	www.employmentappeals.gov.uk	
Scottish Courts	www.scotcourts.gov.uk	
Court Service	www.courtservice.gov.uk	
House of Lords	www.parliament-the-stationery-office.co.uk	
Liberty	www.liberty-human-rights.org.uk	
South African Constitutional Court	www.chem.wits.ac.za/law/contents.html	
Canadian Supreme Court	www.droit.umontreal.ca/doc/csccc/en/index.html	
USA Supreme & Federal Courts	www.findlaw.com/casecode/supreme.html	
Australian Courts	www.carrow.com/A/linkaust.html	
Indian Supreme Court	www.thesupremecourtofindia.com	
NZ Court of Appeal	www.austlii.edu.au/nz/cases/NZCA	
UN Human Rights Instruments	www.unhchr.ch/html/intlinst.htm	

Case Reports

European Human Rights Reports
Decisions and Reports
Commonwealth Cases
International Human Rights Reports
European Human Rights Review
Butterworths Human Rights Cases
Human Rights Alerter

Textbooks

Harris, O'Boyle and Warbrick, *Law of the European Convention on Human Rights*
Lester and Pannick, *Human Rights Law and Practice*
Grosz, Beaton and Duffy, Human Rights: *The 1998 Act and the European Convention*

CHAPTER 17

DATA PROTECTION

INTRODUCTION

The law of data protection, often seen as rather dry legal subject, is set 17.01
to play a pivotal role in the debate over employee privacy that has
emerged in recent years. Employee monitoring has become a critical
issue in modern workplace relations and, in particular, how an
employer's ability to monitor performance and behaviour of workers
interacts with their supposed right of privacy under the Human Rights
Act 1998. The key feature is that in monitoring staff, an employer is
almost certain to process data on those individuals, which in turn must
comply with the requirements of data protection law. This chapter seeks
to examine the new law on employee monitoring and the wider
implications of the Data Protection Act 1998.

MONITORING EMPLOYEE COMMUNICATIONS

The advent of modern technology has changed office culture such that 17.02
modern methods of communication such as electronic mail and use of
the Internet are features of daily life for many employees. We live in the
so-called information age where face-to-face contact has to compete with
video conferencing, mobile telephones and desktop faxing facilities.
Never before have employees generated so much information in both a
business and personal capacity and the employee dignity problem is that
employers have the technical ability to monitor all of it.

In the case of *Halford v. United Kingdom*[1] discussed in the human
rights chapter, the United Kingdom Government sought to argue that an
employer had the right to monitor employee communications at will
without any consent. This was rejected by the ECHR, which held that
the employee had a reasonable expectation of privacy under Article 8 of
the Convention. It has been suggested that the critical fact in *Halford* is
that the employee was not aware that her telephone calls on her private
line might be intercepted. Mindful of this decision, employers have
attempted a number of strategies with the purpose of seeking to ensure
that their workers are not given a "reasonable expectation of privacy".
Usually this attempt is by way of a communications policy which
expressly states that all communications may be monitored for lawful

---

[1] [1997] I.R.L.R. 471.

business purposes and that employees should not consider their correspondence to be private. Although such a policy may arguably be permitted by the new domestic legislation discussed below, one must remember that such legislation may be incompatible with, and in any event must be interpreted in light of, Convention rights and principles. Whether the courts will hold that an employer may legitimately destroy claims of privacy at work by way of a communications policy remains to be seen.

In the last few years the Government has sought to deal with this thorny issue in a number of ways. The introduction of the Regulation of Investigatory Powers Act 2000 (RIPA) provides that it is unlawful for a person, without lawful authority, to intentionally intercept a communication in the course of its transmission by way of a public or private telecommunications system.[2] This clearly includes employers monitoring and intercepting their employees' telephone calls, e-mails and Internet usage. Section 3 of the Act provides that such an interception will not be unlawful if both parties to the communication consent to the interception. However, the most important and controversial development has been the setting down of a range of "business purposes" for which employers may monitor communications of their employees without having to first obtain their consent. These business purposes were laid down in subordinate legislation, which the Secretary of State was empowered to enact under RIPA.[3] Any interception falling within the scope of these Regulations is therefore deemed to be lawful.

The Regulations are the legal basis upon which most employers now carry out their communications monitoring. The Regulations essentially state that communications may be intercepted for the following vague purposes, to:

- Establish the existence of facts relevant to the business (this may include keeping and checking transaction records, business negotiations and communications);
- Ascertain compliance with regulatory or self-regulatory practices or procedures relevant to the business (this may include ensuring communications comply with both external rules and internal employee communications or e-mail/internet policies);
- Ascertain or demonstrate standards which are or ought to be achieved by the person using the system (this may include monitoring for the purpose of quality control or staff training);
- Prevent or detect crime
- Investigate or detect the unauthorised use of systems (again this would legitimise monitoring to ensure that internal policies on e-mail/internet use or harassment are being complied with—it is also likely to allow further investigations where a complaint has been made); and

---

[2] s.1.
[3] s.4(2). The Telecommunications (Lawful Business Practice) (Interception of Communications) Regulations 2000 (S.I. 2000 No. 2699), hereinafter the Regulations.

- Ensure the effective operation of the system (this may include monitoring for viruses or other threats to the system).

Monitoring but not recording is permitted in the two following circumstances:

- For the purpose of determining whether or not the communications are relevant to the business (for example opening e-mail when an employee is off sick or on holiday); and
- For the purpose of monitoring communications to a confidential anonymous counselling or support helpline (only to protect or support helpline staff).

The above purposes are however subject to certain constraints. First, the interception must be solely for a purpose that is relevant to an employer's business. Only business communications or those that directly affect the business (for example downloading pornography or abuse of the system) are likely to be relevant. Communications that are clearly private and personal are unlikely to be relevant to a business and any monitoring of such may be unlawful.[4] In this respect, acceptable employee monitoring practice is likely to be heavily influenced by, and subject to, data protection law. Employers, where possible, should carry out "traffic monitoring" or implement nanny programs to detect abusive use of their systems rather than monitoring the content of communications.[5] The Information Commissioner[6] believes that all monitoring must be proportionate to the risks faced by the employer. Secondly, the employer must have made all reasonable efforts to inform every person who may use the system that interception may take place. Employees should be informed before they begin to use the system and external "senders" of information should be informed by way of, for example, an automated message at the start of a telephone call or a standard signature message attached to outgoing e-mails.

It is thought that the final Code of Practice issued by the Information Commissioner will impose restraints on the ability of employers to monitor employees generally (including their communications). The

---

[4] Although the definition of "relevant to a business" is extremely wide and includes any communication ". . . which otherwise takes place in the course of the carrying on of that business". It is thought that this part does not comply with the Human Rights Act since it allows disproportionate interception of clearly personal information.

[5] Intercepting a communication will nearly always be processing personal data under the Data Protection Act 1998. The draft Code of Practice (for which see below) states: "Only consider the monitoring of content if neither a record of traffic nor a record of both traffic and the subject of e-mails achieves the business purpose. In assessing whether monitoring of content is justified take account of the privacy of those sending e-mails as well as the privacy and autonomy of those receiving them . . . Do not open e-mails that are clearly personal". (p.30.) Note that the draft Code was drafted before the Regulations and as such does not take account of them. The final code is expected to elaborate on and provide guidelines for legitimate business monitoring.

[6] The Government supervisory authority responsible for implementing and enforcing the Act, known in previous incarnations as the Data Protection Registrar and latterly as the Data Protection Commissioner.

Commissioner takes a serious view of the scope that exists to conduct intrusive monitoring at a low cost, whether by software programs, surveillance cameras or location trackers such as active badges or smart cards. The importance of data protection law lies not just in the remedies that may be available under the Data Protection Act 1998 but also in the knock-on effect that the Code of Practice will have in establishing acceptable employer practice. An employer who gathers evidence against an employee in a way that fails to comply with the minimum standards may have difficulty in justifying the reasonableness of his investigation in an unfair dismissal context.

THE DATA PROTECTION ACT 1998

17.03 The Data Protection Act 1998 ("the Act") protects the personal data of individual employees. The law in this area has been driven by the E.C. and indeed the Data Protection Act 1984 was a direct consequence of a Convention on the processing of automated data.[7] Most employers were aware that the 1984 Act covered data held by computers. The Act goes beyond this and now covers manual data including most personnel files and other employee records. The new Act implements the E.C. Data Protection Directive.[8]

The tortuous definitions and complex structure of the Act means that it is not an easy piece of legislation to understand. It is fortunate therefore that the Government has produced clear guidance on the relevant provisions.[9] A key feature of the Act is that it is being phased in over a nine year period with two separate phases of transitional relief. This relief was intended to allow organisations (known under the Act as "data controllers"[10]) time to settle into the Act and get used to its provisions.

Key definitions

17.04   The Act is based around certain key definitions. Essentially the main requirement of the Act is that personal data must be processed in accordance with a set of "data protection principles" laid down in the Act.[11] Usually it will be clear when personal data is being processed but the Act carefully defines "data", "personal data" and "processing".[12] "Data" means information, which is processed automatically or recorded with the intention of being processed automatically, or forms part of an

---

[7] The Convention for the protection of individuals with regard to automatic processing of personal data (Council of Europe, Convention 108, 1981). The 1984 Act was repealed entirely by the Act.

[8] No. 95/46 adopted on October 24, 1995.

[9] See: http://www.dataprotection.gov.uk/.

[10] Employers may have to register through the notification procedure before they process any personal data: see ss.16—18 of the Act. For the purposes of this chapter reference will be made to "employer" instead of "data controller" and to "employee" rather than "data subject".

[11] s.4(4).

[12] All s.1(1).

accessible record,[13] or is recorded as part of a relevant filing system (or with the intention that it should form part of a relevant filing system). Manual employee data will only be covered by the Act if it forms part of (or will form part of) a relevant filing system. Information will form part of a relevant filing system only if it relates to individuals and is structured in such a way that by reference to individuals (*i.e.* individual personnel files) or to criteria relating to individuals (*i.e.* a table of employee absence information) "that specific information relating to a particular individual is readily accessible". In other words if the employee information is structured so as to enable quick access to information on particular individuals, it is likely to be "data" in terms of the Act. The effect of this is that most manual employee data will be covered by the Act. Only where an employer keeps his employee data in no order whatsoever or is not able to extract information about individuals readily will there be an argument that "data" does not exist under the Act.[14] Note that "personal data" means data which relates to a living individual who may be identified from that data or may be identified from that data and other data in the possession of the data controller. It includes any expression of opinion about the individual and any indication of intention in relation to that individual. Thus employee statistical information that does not allow for identification of individuals (whether directly or indirectly) would not be covered by the Act. Finally, "processing" is widely defined and includes nearly every imaginable action in relation to data including merely "holding".

Transitional relief

The first period of transitional relief under the Act ran from October 24, 1998 and is set to end on October 23, 2001. From this date onwards the data protection principles will apply to the processing carried out by every employer, and employees will have access to manual records containing their personal data (the typical example being their personnel file). Many employers were able to benefit during this period from being exempt from many of the provisions of the Act including the subject access rights. A second period of transitional relief will run from October 24, 2001 until October 23, 2007. This relief is much more limited. It will apply only to manual data held immediately before October 24, 1998. Such documents will be able to benefit from certain exemptions under the Act.[15]   17.05

The data protection principles

The main requirement under the Act is that personal data must be processed in accordance with the data protection principles. There are eight principles laid down in Part I of Schedule 1 to the Act, which are as follows: 17.06

---

[13] Accessible record is a term used by the Act to mean certain types of records including health records, educational records and other public records. Special rules apply to such data.

[14] Although it may seem ironic that employers with the worst manual data management avoid the provisions of the Act the assumption is that such employers are not using the data in any meaningful way.

[15] See Pt III, Sched. 8.

1. Personal data shall be processed lawfully and fairly and, in particular, shall not be processed unless (a) at least one of the conditions in Schedule 2 is met, and (b) in the case of sensitive personal data, at least one of the conditions in Schedule 3 is also met.

2. Personal data shall be obtained only for one or more specified and lawful purposes, and shall not be further processed in any manner incompatible with that purpose or those purposes.

3. Personal data shall be adequate, relevant and not excessive in relation to the purpose or purposes for which they are processed.

4. Personal data shall be kept accurate, and where necessary, kept up to date.

5. Personal data processed for any purpose or purposes shall not be kept for longer than is necessary for that purpose or those purposes.

6. Personal data shall be processed in accordance with the rights of data subjects under the Act.

7. Appropriate technical and organisational measures shall be taken against unauthorised or unlawful processing of personal data and against accidental loss or destruction of, or damage to, personal data.[16]

8. Personal data shall not be transferred to a country or territory outside the European Economic Area unless that country or territory ensures an adequate level of protection for the rights and freedoms of data subjects in relation to the processing of personal data.

The data protection principles must be interpreted in accordance with the provisions in Part II of Schedule 1 to the Act.[17] Most of them are self-explanatory but some elaboration is required in relation to the first data protection principle, which can be seen as the cornerstone of the Act.

The first principle: fair and lawful processing

17.07   The requirement of fair and lawful processing is perhaps the most important principle. First, a Schedule 2 condition must be satisfied before the data can be processed. Schedule 2 sets down a number of conditions, the most common one being that the individual concerned has given his or her consent to the processing. Consent is thought to require freely given specific and informed agreement, such that a positive act by the employee is required (for example the submission of a job application form or CV).[18] Employers therefore must ensure that employees consent to the processing of their personal data. The simplest

---

[16] One case highlighted in the Annual Report of the Information Commissioner 2000–01 involved a local authority refuse employee who found three black bin liners full of council employee personnel information at the local depot on its way to a public refuse tip.
[17] s.4(2).
[18] Art. 2(h) of the Directive, above.

way to achieve this is by way of a term in the contract of employment giving consent.[19] Alternatively, a number of other conditions may apply where the processing is *necessary* for certain purposes: for the performance of a contract to which the data subject is a party; for compliance with any legal obligation to which the data controller is subject (other than a contract); in order to protect the vital interests of the data subject; for the administration of justice or the exercising of functions of a public nature; for legitimate interests pursued by the employer except where such processing is unwarranted. The Information Commissioner narrowly interprets these alternative grounds with emphasis being placed on the word "necessary". Thus in a business acquisition situation the seller of a business will not normally have any authority to disclose employee information to a prospective purchaser unless that information is made anonymous so that individuals cannot be identified. Consent is unlikely given commercial sensitivity and although such processing may be in furtherance of a legitimate interest pursued by the employer it is not thought to be necessary to process employee names etc. in this way. The ground of complying with a legal obligation of course allows an employer to process PAYE information and keep any records that may be required under the Working Time Regulations 1998 or National Minimum Wage Act 1998. As for protecting the vital interests of an employee, the Information Commissioner has stated that this is likely only to apply in a life or death situation.

Secondly, data must be processed in accordance with the fair processing code set out at paragraphs 1 to 4 of Part II of Schedule 1. Essentially this requires that data should not be obtained in a misleading or deceptive way. It also states that data will not be processed fairly unless the employee is given certain information about the processing such as the identity of the employer and any representative of the employer who may be processing (such as an outsourced payroll administrator), the purpose or purposes for which the data will be processed and any other information in the circumstances that will enable fair processing (for example if the processing will be unusual or unexpected, details ought to be provided). This information may be given to employees in a variety of ways but the most useful way for an employer is to do this by issuing a data protection policy to employees. Such a policy will usually seek express consent for processing and will be drafted to meet all additional obligations under the Act. It allows an employer to put in place a data protection management system and at the same time informs employees of their rights under the Act.

Additional protection exists where the data in question is classified as "sensitive personal data". This refers to information concerning:

- racial or ethnic origin
- political opinion
- religious beliefs (or beliefs of a similar nature)
- trade union membership
- physical or mental health or condition

---

[19] But since consent must be informed the employer must indicate the purposes for which he will process data. This requirement overlaps with the second principle.

- sexual life
- the commission or alleged commission of any offence, or
- proceedings or sentence for any offence.

In addition to the above, this type of data must not be processed at all unless a condition in Schedule 3 is met. Again, explicit consent is one of the Schedule 3 conditions, which are generally narrower in their scope than the Schedule 2 conditions discussed above. The Information Commissioner has said that consent to process sensitive data must be absolutely clear and that in many cases "nothing less than clear written consent will suffice". The other conditions include being under a legal obligation to process (*i.e.* for SSP purposes) or where the processing is by health professionals and necessary for medical purposes. Processing information as to racial and ethnic origin is permitted for equal opportunities monitoring so long as the rights of employees are protected. The simplest solution for employers is to keep as little sensitive employee data as possible.

Right of access to personal data

17.08   The sixth data protection principle states that data shall be processed in accordance with the rights of data subjects under the Act. This extends the previous right of access that existed in relation to computer records to the manual records covered by the Act. Under section 7(1) of the Act an employee has a specific right to be told what personal data is held on him or her; be given a description of the data and the purposes for which it is processed (and to whom it may be disclosed); and, to have such information communicated to him or her in an intelligible form.[20] A copy of the information must be provided to the employee in a permanent form.[21] Seeking this information is known as making a "subject access request" in the language of the Act and should be in writing. An employer does not have to comply unless he is given sufficient information so as to enable him to locate the data in question and confirm the identity of the person seeking the data.[22] A fee may be charged for providing the information, which is currently no more than £10.[23] Employers must comply with the request promptly and at the latest within 40 days of receipt of the request or receipt of fee and required information whichever is the later.[24] Special provisions apply where the information sought would disclose data that identifies a third party (the employee not already being aware of such data). In these circumstances the employer should first seek the consent of the third party to disclosure, secondly, consider whether it is possible to disclose as much data as possible while protecting the identity of the third party by blanking out names etc., and thirdly, if this is not possible and consent is not given, to conduct a balancing exercise to determine whether it is

---

[20] s.7(1).
[21] s.8(2).
[22] s.7(3).
[23] s.7(2).
[24] s.7(8), (10)

reasonable in any event to disclose the data in question.[25] Employees are not entitled to access certain types of information. The main exclusions are personal data processed for the purposes of management forecasting or management planning where access would prejudice the conduct of the business and personal data containing intended negotiations with the employee.[26] An employee does not have a right of access to a reference concerning him in the hands of the person who gave the reference. There would not seem to be any difficulty however in seeking access to a reference in the hands of the recipient (subject to any modifications that may be required to protect the sender). A special right exists in relation to automatically processed data which evaluates an employee and thereby makes a significant decision concerning him or her.[27]

If an employer fails to comply with a subject access request, the employee may apply to the sheriff court or Court of Session for an order requiring the employer to comply.[28] The employee may also apply to the Information Commissioner for an assessment[29] and may be able to claim compensation where he or she can establish that damage has been suffered as a result of the employer's breach.[30]

Correction of inaccurate data

There are three methods under the Act by which an employee may 17.09 seek to have inaccurate data corrected. He or she may (a) write and ask the employer to amend the data; (b) ask the Information Commissioner for an assessment[31]; or (c) apply to the sheriff court or Court of Session for an order requiring the employer to correct the inaccuracy.[32] Employers do not have to amend inaccuracies as a matter of course but they must comply with the fourth data protection principle, which states that personal data shall be accurate and where possible kept up to date. Similarly, an employee may write to his or her employer and ask them to stop or not to begin processing personal data on the basis that such processing is likely to cause the employee substantial and unwarranted damage or distress.[33] If the employer will not amend the inaccuracy voluntarily or refuses to stop processing that causes damage or distress the employee will have to take formal action under (b) or (c) above.

Enforcement powers

An employee may apply to the Information Commissioner to make an 17.10 assessment as to whether processing has been carried out in compliance with the Act.[34] On receipt of such a request the Commissioner shall

---

[25] subs (4), (5) and (6). The factors to be taken into account are found in s.7(7). This is a subject that the Information Commissioner has published guidance on—see Appendix 1 to the draft Code of Practice and the Guidance note entitled: "Subject Access Rights and Third Party Information".

[26] Sched. 7.

[27] s.7(1)(d). See also s.12.

[28] s.7(9).

[29] s.42(1).

[30] s.13(1).

[31] s.42(1).

[32] s.14(1).

[33] s.10(1).

[34] s.42(1).

make an assessment in an appropriate manner having regard to the matters contained in section 42(3) of the Act. If further information is desirable the Commissioner has power to serve the employer with an information notice under section 43. If the Commissioner is satisfied that the data protection principles have been breached, an enforcement notice may be served under section 40 that requires the employer to take remedial action. An appeal lies from an information or enforcement notice to the Information Tribunal.[35] Note also that the Commissioner may exercise powers of entry and inspection under section 50.

Compensation

17.11   Where an employee suffers damage as a result of a breach of the Act, a claim for compensation may be made to the sheriff court or Court of Session. Compensation for distress may also be sought provided that the individual also suffers damage.[36] This may arise, for example, where an individual suffers damage as a result of an inaccurate reference being sent to a prospective employer.

Unlawful obtaining of personal data

17.12   Section 55 of the Act makes it an offence for a person to knowingly or recklessly, without the consent of the data controller obtain or disclose personal data or the information contained in that data or to procure the disclosure of that information to another person. Employees must be made aware of the serious consequences of interfering with the personal data of colleagues without authority. The Information Commissioner recommends making employees aware that this will be a disciplinary offence. Note that the Act does not prohibit an employer from disclosing employee data where consent has been given. The Commissioner considers that an employer must generally balance the benefits of disclosure with the reasonable expectation of employees that the employer will safeguard their privacy. Common disclosures may take place in the course of a business—for example details of key employees in an annual report. Where the disclosure is unusual or may be unexpected however, the Commissioner considers that the employer must give the employee advance warning.

The draft Code of Practice

17.13   In October 2000, the Information Commissioner issued a draft Code of Practice[37] for consultation on the use of personal data in the employer/employee relationship. This was issued to employers as being the best guidance that would be available until the consultation on the draft Code ended and the final Code was issued. The Commissioner received extensive replies to the consultation exercise and the final Code has been thereby delayed. It is finally about to be published in four parts in late 2001. It is for this reason that the guidance in the draft Code (extremely useful though some of it is) is not discussed in any detail in

---

[35] s.48. Formerly known as the Data Protection Tribunal.
[36] s.13.
[37] For her general powers in this area see s.51.

the present chapter. The draft Code does however give a good indication of the subject matter that the final Code is likely to deal with. The final Code is likely to set out in fairly prescriptive terms the minimum requirements that the Commissioner considers are necessary for employers to comply with the Act. It will also recommend standards of best practice in terms of data protection management. The entire employment relationship is likely to be covered in various sections including recruitment and advertising, keeping employee records, allowing access to and disclosing employee data, employee monitoring,[38] medical testing, discipline and dismissal and the retention of employee records. The final Code is set to coincide well with the ending of the main period of transitional relief and is likely to be welcomed by employers trying to come to terms with a whole new perspective on employee information.

---

[38] Including the controversial practice of CCTV monitoring, not discussed in this chapter. The draft Code suggests that such routine "known" monitoring is only likely to be justified where there are particular safety or security risks that cannot be addressed in another way. In her view, covert monitoring will rarely be justified and only in situations where specific criminal activity has been identified. Even then, private locations such as cloakrooms and offices should not be monitored without police involvement (p.26). Interested readers should note that the Commissioner has issued a Code of Practice for users of CCTV generally (July 2000). Employers using CCTV cameras must register this fact with the Information Commissioner by October 24, 2001.

INDEX